GIDEON'S SPIES

ALSO BY GORDON THOMAS

Nonfiction

DESCENT INTO DANGER

BED OF NAILS

PHYSICIAN EXTRAORDINARY

HEROES OF THE R.A.F.

THEY GOT BACK

MIRACLE OF SURGERY

THE NATIONAL HEALTH SERVICE AND YOU

THAMES NUMBER ONE

MIDNIGHT TRADERS

THE PARENT'S HOME DOCTOR *(with Ian D. Hudson, Vincent Pippet)*

TURN BY THE WINDOW *(with Ronald Hutchinson)*

ISSELS: THE BIOGRAPHY OF A DOCTOR

THE DAY THE WORLD ENDED *(with Max Morgan-Witts)*

EARTHQUAKE *(with Max Morgan-Witts)*

SHIPWRECK *(with Max Morgan-Witts)*

VOYAGE OF THE DAMNED *(with Max Morgan-Witts)*

THE DAY GUERNICA DIED *(with Max Morgan-Witts)*

ENOLA GAY/RUIN FROM THE AIR *(with Max Morgan-Witts)*

THE DAY THE BUBBLE BURST *(with Max Morgan-Witts)*

TRAUMA *(with Max Morgan-Witts)*

PONTIFF *(with Max Morgan-Witts)*

THE YEAR OF ARMAGEDDON *(with Max Morgan-Witts)*

THE OPERATION

DESIRE AND DENIAL

THE TRIAL: THE LIFE AND INEVITABLE CRUCIFIXION OF JESUS

JOURNEY INTO MADNESS

ENSLAVED

CHAOS UNDER HEAVEN

TRESPASS INTO TEMPTATION

MAGDALENE: THE WOMAN WHO LOVED JESUS

Fiction

THE CAMP ON BLOOD ISLAND

TORPEDO RUN

DEADLY PERFUME

GODLESS ICON

VOICES IN THE SILENCE

ORGAN HUNTERS

POISONED SKY

GIDEON'S SPIES

The Secret History of the Mossad

GORDON THOMAS

THOMAS DUNNE BOOKS
ST. MARTIN'S GRIFFIN
NEW YORK

THOMAS DUNNE BOOKS.
An imprint of St. Martin's Press.

Design by Maureen Troy

Library of Congress Cataloging-in-Publication Data

Gordon, Thomas.
    Gideon's spies : the secret history of the Mossad / Gordon Thomas.
       p.   cm.
    Includes bibliographical references (p. 367).
    ISBN 0-312-19982-1 (hc)
    ISBN 0-312-25284-6 (pbk)
    1. Israel. Mosal ie-modi' in ve-tafkidim meyuhadim—History.
2. Intelligence service—Israel—History. 3. Secret service—Israel—History. I. Title.
UB251.I78T49 1999
327'.125694—dc21   98-51810
                                                  CIP

10 9 8 7 6 5 4

ACKNOWLEDGMENTS

ISRAEL

Meir Amit	David Kimche
Barry Chamish	Ariel Merari
Yaakov Cohen	Reuven Merhav
Alex Doron	Danniy Nagier
Ran Edelist	Yoel Ben Porat
Raphael Eitan	Uri Saguy
Isser Harel	Zvi Spielman

and those who still cannot be named.

ELSEWHERE

Mohammed al-Fayed	Martin Lettmayer
Sean Carberry	John Magee
Sebastian Cody	John McNamara
Carolyn Dempsey	Laurie Meyer
Art Dworken	Madeleine Morel
Heather Florence	Samir Saddoui
Per-Erik Hawthorne	Susannh Tarbush
Diana Johnson	Michael Tauck
Amanda Harris	Richard Tomlinson
Emery Kabongo	Russell Warren-Howe
Otto Kormek	Stuart Winter
Zahir Kzeibati	Catherine Whittaker

each in their own way played their part.

AND LAST BUT NOT LEAST

William Buckley
William Casey   } among them they
Joachim Kraner   inspired the idea.

Edith—of course

and Tom Burke. Every author needs an editor who
is calm, far-sighted, patient, and incisive and cares
passionately for the book. Tom was all of these things.
I could not have asked for more—and never received
less. I owe him much.

CONTENTS

MOSSAD DIRECTORS GENERAL

1951–1952	REUVEN SHILOAH
1952–1963	ISSER HAREL
1963–1968	MEIR AMIT
1968–1974	ZVI ZAMIR
1974–1982	YITZHAK HOFI
1982–1990	NAHUM ADMONI
1990–1996	SHABTAI SHAVIT
1996–1998	DANNY YATOM
1998–	EFRAIM HALEVY

GLOSSARY

Active measures	Operations to influence or otherwise affect other nations' policies
ANC	African National Congress
ANO	Abu Nidal Organization
AFR	Automatic fingerprint recognition
AI	Artificial intelligence
AL	Specialist unit operating under deep cover in the United States
Aman	Israeli military intelligence
ASU	Active service terrorist unit
AWAC	Airborne warning and control aircraft
Babbler	Counterbugging device
Backstopping	Fake identification papers
Base	Permanent station in foreign country
Bat leveyha	Female assistant agent
Better world	Euphemism for killing enemy agent; similarly, to "send a person on vacation" means to injure him/her—the extent of the injury depends on whether the "vacation" is to be brief or long
Bioleverage	Euphemism for blackmail—literally, the use of derogatory information to coerce someone
Blind dating	Meeting place chosen by a contact to meet his controller
Blow-back	Fake stories fed to foreign news media
Bodel	A courier
BND	BundesNachrichtenDienst, German Federal Intelligence Service, concerned with both foreign and domestic intelligence
Bug	Electronic device for hearing and recording
Burn	An agent deliberately sacrificed in order to protect a more valuable spy
BW	Biological weapons
Case death	Operation that fails for no obvious reason
Case officer	In charge of field agents

CAT	Computer-aided tomography
Chamfering	Technique for opening sealed mail
CIA	Central Intelligence Agency
CIS	Commonwealth of Independent States
CIO	Central Imagery Office
Cold approach	Attempt to recruit a foreign national
Comint	Acronym for communications intelligence
Cover	Identity assumed by intelligence officer when abroad
Cultivation	Establishing rapport with a source of information
CW	Chemical weapons
Daylight	Highest form of alert
Dardasim	Agents operating in China
DEA	Drug Enforcement Administration
DI	Directorate of Intelligence
DCI	Director of Central Intelligence Agency
DIA	Defence Intelligence Agency
Diamond	Communications unit
DO	Directorate of Operations
Dry cleaning	Various techniques to avoid surveillance
ECM	Electronic countermeasure
EDP	Electronic data processing
Elint	Electronic intelligence intercepted from radar, satellites
Exfiltrate	Removing an agent from hostile country
Falach	Agent working in Lebanon
FACES	Facial Analysis Comparison and Elimination System
False flagging	Recruiting a person who believes he or she will be working for another country or interest
Fumigate	Sweeping an area for electronic bugs
Go-away	Prearranged signal not to make contact at previously arranged rendezvous
Grinder	Debriefing room, also used to interrogate suspects
Honey trap	Sexual entrapment for intelligence purposes
Humint	Intelligence gathered by agents in the field

IDA	Intelligence database
IED	Improvised explosive device
IFF	Identification, friend or foe
II	Image identification
Institute	Formal name of Mossad—Institute for Intelligence and Special Operations; originally called Institute for Coordination
IR	Infrared
ISA	Intelligence support activity
JIL	Joint Intelligence Center
Jumper	Agent working overseas on short-term assignment
Katsa	Case officer
Kidon	Operative specializing in assassination
LAKAM	Intelligence agency gathering scientific data
Legend	Bogus biography for katsa
LAP	Department of Psychological Warfare
Light cover	Katsa working under diplomatic cover
Loot	Intelligence gathered from operations
Mabuah	A non-Jewish informer
Measles	Assassination that appears to stem from natural causes
Meluckha	Recruiting department
Memune	Title given to director general of Mossad
Miketel	Bug for intercepting/recording telephone calls
Mishlashim	Dead letter box; a secure place for an agent to receive or drop off information
Music box	Radio transmitter
Naka	Writing system
Nativ	Agent working in former Soviet Union
Neviot	Surveillance specialist
NHITC	National Human Intelligence Tasking Center
NIC	National Intelligence Center
NSA	National Security Agency
NSTL	National security threat list
OAU	Organization of African Unity
Oter	Arab recruited to work with other Arabs

PFLP	Popular Front for the Liberation of Palestine
PLF	Palestine Liberation Front
PLO	Palestine Liberation Organization
Photint	Photographic intelligence
PROD	Technique for retrieving photographs from optical disc
Radint	Radar intelligence
Reg-sig	Recognition signal for katsa to make contact with field agent in public place
RAF	Red Army Faction (Germany)
Safanim	Unit to target PLO
Safe house	Apartment or house used for secret meetings or as an operations base
Shicklut	Surveillance department
Sleeper	Katsa/agent to be called upon in only the most dire circumstances
Slick	Hiding place for documents
Target	Intelligence assignment
Teud	Forged document
Telint	Telemetry intelligence
Vacuamer	Agent who provides details of all aspects of a target
Walk-in	Person who volunteers to serve
Wash	Recycling of a valid passport obtained by theft or purchased
Yahalomin	Special communications unit

OTHER INTELLIGENCE SERVICES

ISRAEL

IDF   Responsible for coordinating all intelligence for the General Staff of the Israeli Defense Forces. From time to time gives Mossad specific tasks.

AMAN   Intelligence branch of the IDF with specific responsibility for gathering military, geographic, and economic intelligence. Its prime focus remains the activities of Israel's Arab neighbors in the new millenium.

AFI   Intelligence branch of Israel's air force. Specializes in gathering signals intelligence and aerial reconnaissance. By the year 2001, the latter will be largely replaced by satellite, leaving AFI's role to provide conventional air support intelligence.

BP   Paramilitary-style border police in Israeli-occupied territories. Limited intelligence-gathering role.

NI   Naval intelligence unit of all Israeli seaborne forces. Work includes monitoring Israel's coasts and updating foreign naval resources.

GSS   Also known as Shin Bet or SHABEK. Responsible for internal security and defense of Israeli installations abroad such as embassies, consulates, and important Israeli organizations.

RPPC   Research and Political Planning Center advises prime minister of the day and his policymakers on long-term strategy.

UNITED STATES OF AMERICA

CIA   Conducts covert operations, provides intelligence analysis for the incumbent president. Forbidden by Executive Order from conducting assassinations.

DIA	Coordinates all military intelligence for the Joint Chiefs of Staff.
INR	State Department's small intelligence and research department (1999 staff approximately 500). Reports only to incumbent secretary of state.
NIO	Based in Pentagon. The National Imagery Office controls all U.S. satellite intelligence gathering. Constantly "tasked" by the CIA and DIA.
NRO	Pentagon-based. Works closely with NIO and has specific responsibility for all satellite hardware and deployment.
NSA	Operates from Fort George G. Meade, Maryland. Over the years its "spy in the sky" image has given the National Security Agency a glamour once only the prerogative of the CIA. Specializes in signals intelligence, cryptography. Works closely with NIO on satellite intelligence gathering.

United Kingdom

GCHQ	Its 7,000 (approx. 1999) staff act as Britain's "invisible eye in outer space." Formally known as Government Communications Headquarters, it monitors and decodes radio, telex, fax, and e-mail traffic in and out of the United Kingdom. Regularly "tasked" by Britain's two main intelligence services.
MI6	Also known as the Secret Intelligence Service. Staff of under 2,000 (1999) plan, carry out, and analyze worldwide clandestine operations and intelligence gathering.
MI5	2,000 staff (1999). Britain's prime internal counterespionage service. Specializes in monitoring all designated subversives in the country and conducts surveillance on a large number of foreign diplomats and embassies, including those of Israel.

Russia

GRU	Glavnoye Razvedyvatelnoye Upravlenie provides Kremlin with military intelligence. Staffed with

	the best of the former Soviet Union's intelligence services. Equipped with satellite surveillance.
FCS	Renamed the Federal Counter-intelligence Service, it is really the old KGB updated. Staff of 142,000 (1999). Focuses on border movement control, internal counter-intelligence, surveillance of all foreign diplomats, many journalists, and business people. Has a powerful secret police division with units in every major city in Russia.
SVR	Sluzhba Vneshnie Razvedaki runs worldwide, multilayered intelligence-gathering operation. Specialist units gather political, industrial, and commercial intelligence. Conducts covert operations, including assassinations.

CHINA

ILD	Harmless-sounding International Liaison Department, the organization engages in a wide range of covert activities. Prime target is the United States.
MID	Military Intelligence Department reports to the General Staff of the People's Liberation Army. Brief includes: updating all foreign military capabilities (especially the United States) and conducting satellite reconnaissance. Staff are attached to every PRC embassy and consulate.
MSS	Founded in 1983, the Ministry of State Security is responsible for all counter-espionage within China. Has a fearsome reputation.
STD	Based in Ministry of Defense, the large Science and Technology Department has two prime functions: to collate all signals traffic from the Chinese navy and overseas embassies; to target primarily U.S. firms working at the cutting edge of military and civilian technology.
NCNA	Nominally a news agency reporting on Chinese affairs. Has long been a cover for all other Chinese intelligence agencies engaged in clandestine activities.

FRANCE

DAS Miniscule (staff of under 50 in 1999). Focuses on assessing long-term defense planning work by other nations.

DPSD Direction du Production et de la Securite de la Defense. Responsible for gathering military intelligence abroad.

DRM At the coal-face of French satellite intelligence program. Divided into five sub-directorates. Reports directly to prime minister of the day.

DST The Directorate for Surveillance of the Territory is the largest and most powerful of France's intelligence agencies. Has several thousand employees. Operates both internally and overseas. Wide-ranging responsibilities include surveillance of all foreign embassies in Paris and conducting a large number of clandestine operations. Reports directly to incumbent minister of the interior.

DGSE Direction Generale de la Securite Exterieure. Brief is to gather industrial and economic intelligence, penetrate terrorist organizations, and conduct old-fashioned spying.

SGDN Reports to the incumbent prime minister, the Secretariat General de la Defense Nationale provides an overview of military intelligence developments in countries of interest to France.

JAPAN

NAICHO Part of Cabinet Research Office. Has a large budget to analyse defense policies of all major nations of interest to Japan.

MITI Responsible for gathering commercial and economic data worldwide.

PSIA The Public Security Investigation Agency concentrates on counter-terrorism and counter-espionage. Primarily operates internally but increasingly by 1999 had developed a global approach.

CHAPTER 1

BEYOND THE
LOOKING GLASS

When the red light blinked on the bedside telephone, a sophisticated recording device was automatically activated in the Paris apartment near the Pompidou Center in the lively Fourth Arrondissement. The light had been wired in by an Israeli communications technician who had flown from Tel Aviv to install the recorder, intended to allay any suspicions neighbors would have about the phone ringing at ungodly hours. The technician was one of the *yahalomin*, a member of a Mossad unit that dealt with secure communications in the safe houses of Israel's secret intelligence agency.

The one in Paris was like all the others. It had a bombproof front door and window glass which, like the panes in the White House, could deflect scanners. There were scores of such apartments in all the major cities in the world, either purchased outright or rented on long leases. Many were left unoccupied for lengthy periods, ready for the time they would be needed for an operation.

One had been conducted from the Paris apartment since June 1997, when Monsieur Maurice had arrived. He spoke fluent French with a slight Central-European accent. Over the years his neighbors had encountered others like him: men, and occasionally women, who arrived without warning, spent weeks or months among them, then one day were gone. Like his predecessors, Maurice had politely discouraged interest in himself or his work.

Maurice was a *katsa*, a Mossad field agent.

Physically he was nondescript; it had been said that even on an empty street he would pass virtually unnoticed. He had been recruited in what was still a halcyon time for Mossad, when its legend remained largely intact. His potential was spotted during Israel's compulsory military service, when, after boot camp, he had been drafted into air force intelligence. An aptitude for languages (he knew French, English, and German) had been noted, along with other qualities: he was good at filling gaps in a case study and drawing fact out of speculation, and he knew the limits of informed conjecture. Above all, he was a natural manipulator of people: he could persuade, cajole, and, if all else failed, threaten.

Since graduating from the Mossad training school in 1982, he had worked in Europe, South Africa, and the Far East. At various times he had done so under the guise of a businessman, a travel writer, and a salesman. He had used a number of names and biographies drawn from the library of aliases maintained by Mossad. Now he was Maurice, once more a businessman.

During his various postings he had heard of the purges back in "the Institute," the name its staff used for Mossad: corrosive rumors of disgraced and ruined careers, of changes at the top, and each incoming Mossad director with his own priorities. None of them had stemmed the loss of morale within the service.

This had increased with the appointment of Benyamin Netanyahu as Israel's youngest prime minister. A man with a proven intelligence background, he was supposed to know how things worked on the inside; when to listen, how far to go. Instead, from the outset, Netanyahu had astonished seasoned intelligence officers by dabbling in operational details.

At first this was put down to unnecessary zeal, a new broom showing he was ready to look into every closet to make sure there were no secrets he should know. But matters had become alarming when not only the prime minister but his wife, Sara, wanted to peer behind the looking glass into Israel's intelligence world. She had invited senior Mossad officers to call on her at home and answer her questions, claiming she was following the example of Hillary Clinton's interest in the CIA.

The featureless corridors of Mossad's headquarters building in Tel Aviv had echoed with the scandalized whispers of how Sara Netanyahu had demanded to see psychological profiles of world leaders she and her husband would be entertaining or visiting. She had especially asked for details about President Bill Clinton's sexual activities. She had also asked to review dossiers on Israel's ambassadors whose embassies they would be staying in during overseas trips, expressing an interest in the cleanliness of their kitchens and how many times the bedding was changed in the guest suites.

Bemused by her requests, Mossad officers had explained to the prime minister's wife that obtaining such information was not in their intelligence-gathering remit.

Some of the veterans had been removed from the mainstream of intelligence and given responsibility for small operations that required little more than creating paperwork which went virtually unread. Realizing their careers were stagnating, they had resigned, and were now scattered across the length of Israel, keeping themselves occupied with reading, mostly history, trying to come to terms with the fact that they were also yesterday's people.

All this had made Maurice glad to be out of Tel Aviv and back in the field.

The operation that had brought him to Paris had provided another chance to show he was a methodical and careful agent, one able to deliver what was expected. In this case the task was relatively simple: there was no real physical danger, only the risk of embarrassment should the French authorities discover what he was doing and quietly deport him. The Israeli ambassador knew Maurice was in Paris but had not been told why. That was standard operational procedure: if things went wrong, the envoy could plead ignorance.

Maurice's task was to recruit an informer. This was known in the esoteric language of Mossad as a "cold approach," suborning a foreign national. After two months of patient work, Maurice believed he was now close to succeeding.

His target was Henri Paul, assistant chief of the city's Ritz Hotel, who also acted as chauffeur to its celebrity guests.

One had been Jonathan Aitken, a minister in Britain's last Conservative government. Aitken had held special responsibility for coordinating arms sales and had built up a raft of contacts with Middle Eastern weapons dealers. This had led to *World in Action*, a TV investigative program, and the *Guardian* newspaper publishing highly damaging reports about Aitken's ties to men not normally found in the company of government ministers. Aitken had sued for libel. The case had come to hinge on who had paid Aitken's hotel account when he had stayed at the Ritz to meet some of his Arab contacts. In court, Aitken had sworn on oath that his wife had settled the account.

Through a third-party source, Mossad had tipped off investigators acting for the defendants that Mrs. Aitken had not been in Paris. The case had collapsed. Mossad, who had long regarded Aitken's activities as a threat to Israel, had effectively destroyed him.

In 1999, after facing a lengthy criminal trial in London, Aitken was found guilty of perjury and given a prison sentence. By then his wife had left him, and a man who walked the corridors of power for many years faced a bleak future.

Understanding if not sympathy, came from an unlikely source, Ari Ben-Menashe. (see Chapter 8). He had once experienced the rigors of a New York prison after his own fall from grace as intelligence coordinator for Prime Minister Yitzhak Shamir. The position had given Ben-Menashe a rare insight into how Mossad and Israel's other intelligence services operated. He regarded Aitken as "a man consumed by his own belief that he could outwit anyone. He did for years. But his mistake was to underestimate Mossad. They don't take prisoners."

Unlike Jonathan Aitken, whose life after prison holds little prospects, Ben-Menashe has made a spectacular recovery. By 1999 he had a well-established intelligence-gathering company based in

Montreal, Canada. It numbers among clients several African countries as well as some in Europe. Multinationals also seek his services, having assured themselves their anonymity will be protected by Ben-Menashe.

His staff includes several former Canadian secret intelligence service officers and others who had worked for similar Israeli and European organizations. The company provides a wide range of economic, industrial, and protection services. The staff know their way around the arms dealers and well understand the rules of negotiating with kidnappers. There is not a city in the world where they are without contacts, many of them nurtured by Ben-Menashe from his days as a serious player in the Israeli intelligence world. He and his associates constantly update themselves on shifting political alliances and can often foresee which Third World government will fall—and who will replace it. Small and compact, Ben-Menashe's company is in many ways modeled on Mossad, "moving," Ben-Menashe cheerfully admits, "like thieves in the night. That's the way it has to be in our business." And it pays well.

Equipped with a new Canadian citizenship, he has found himself once more working with "the princes and kings of this world . . . the famous and those who use their fortunes to buy better protection. For them all knowledge is power and part of my job is to provide that essential information."

In London he is a favored guest at the Savoy. In Paris it is the Ritz that greets him with deference.

In no time Ben-Menashe discovered that the hotel remained a meeting place for Middle Eastern arms brokers and their European contacts. He checked with Mossad colleagues. From them he learned just how important the hotel had become in Mossad's overall strategy. Ben-Menashe, a natural-born acquirer of information—"long ago I learned that nothing I hear goes to waste"—decided he would watch how matters developed. It was a decision that would eventually directly involve him in the fate of Diana, Princess of Wales and her lover, Dodi al-Fayed, the playboy son of the Ritz's owner, the mega-wealthy Mohammed al-Fayed.

Mossad had decided to have an informer in the Ritz who would be able to report on activities. It had set about the task by first obtaining the hotel's staff list; this had been done by hacking into the Ritz computer system. No one at the hotel's senior management level appeared to be a likely prospect; junior staff did not have the overall accessibility to guests for the task required. But Henri Paul's responsibility for security meant every area of the Ritz was open to him. His passkey could access a guest's safe-deposit box. There would be no questions asked if he wanted a copy of a person's hotel bill, no raised eyebrows if he asked to see the hotel's telephone log to obtain details of calls made by arms dealers and their contacts. He could know which woman a dealer had discreetly hired for a contact. As chauffeur to VIPs, Paul would be in a good position to overhear their conversations, witness their behavior, see where they went, whom they met.

The next stage had been to create a psycho-profile of Paul. Over several weeks information on his background had been unearthed by one of the resident katsas in Paris. Using a number of covers including an insurance company employee and a telephone salesman, the katsa had learned that Paul was a bachelor in no permanent relationship, lived in a low-rent apartment, and drove a black Mini but liked fast cars and racing the motorcycle of which he was part owner. Hotel staff had spoken of his liking a drink. There had been hints that, from time to time, he had used the services of an expensive hooker who also serviced some of the hotel's guests.

The information had been evaluated by a Mossad psychologist. He had concluded that there was an inherent vulnerability about Henri Paul. The psychologist had recommended that steadily increasing pressure, linked with the promise of substantial monetary reward to finance Paul's social life, could be the best way to recruit him. The operation could be a lengthy one, requiring considerable patience and skill. Rather than make further use of the resident katsa, Maurice would be sent to Paris.

As in any such Mossad operation, Maurice had followed well-tried guidelines. First, over several visits, he had familiarized himself with the Ritz and its environs. He had quickly identified Henri Paul, a muscular man with a certain swagger in his walk, who made it apparent that he sought approval from no one.

Maurice had observed the curious relationship Paul had with the paparazzi who staked out the front of the Ritz, ready to snatch photographs of the more newsworthy rich and famous guests. From time to time Paul would order the photographers to leave, and usually they would do so, circling the block on their motorcycles before returning. During those short trips, Paul would sometimes emerge from the hotel's staff entrance and engage the paparazzi in friendly banter as they passed.

At night, Maurice had observed Paul drinking with several of the paparazzi in one of the bars around the Ritz he patronized with other staff after work.

In progress reports to Tel Aviv, Maurice had described Paul's ability to drink considerable amounts of alcohol yet appear stone-cold sober. Maurice also confirmed that Paul's suitability for the role of informer overrode his personal habits: he appeared to have the essential access and a position of high trust.

At some point in his discreet surveillance, Maurice discovered how Paul was betraying that trust. He was receiving money from the paparazzi for providing details of guest movements, enabling the photographers to be in a position to snatch pictures of the celebrities.

The exchange of information for cash took place either in one of the bars or in the narrow rue Cambon, where the Ritz staff entrance was situated.

By mid-August that exchange had focused on the expected arrival at the Ritz of Diana, Princess of Wales, and her new lover, Dodi Al-Fayed, the son of the hotel's owner. They would stay in the fabled Imperial Suite.

All the Ritz staff were under strict instructions to keep details about Diana's arrival secret under penalty of instant dismissal. Despite this, Paul had continued to risk his career by providing details of the forthcoming visit to several paparazzi. From each he had received further sums of money.

Maurice saw that Paul had also begun to drink more heavily and had overheard Ritz staff complain that the assistant security chief had become even more of a martinet: he had recently fired a floor maid he had caught stealing a bar of soap from a guest bedroom. Several of the hotel's employees said that Paul was also taking pills and wondered if they were to help control his mood swings. Everyone agreed Paul had become more unpredictable: one moment he would be good-humored; the next he would display barely controlled anger over some imagined slight. Maurice decided the time had come to make his move.

The first contact was in Harry's Bar in the rue Daunou. When Paul came in, Maurice was already sipping a cocktail. The Mossad katsa smoothly struck up a conversation, and the security man accepted a drink after Maurice mentioned that friends of his had stayed at the Ritz. Maurice added they had been surprised how many other guests had been wealthy Arabs.

If it had been a shot in the dark, it produced a staggering result. Paul replied that many of the Arabs were rude and arrogant and expected him to jump when they raised a finger. Worst were the the Saudis. Maurice mentioned he had heard that Jewish guests were just as difficult. Paul would have none of it. He insisted that Jews were excellent guests.

On that promising note, the evening ended with an arrangement to meet again in a few days, over dinner at a restaurant near the Ritz. During the meal Paul confirmed, under Maurice's well-timed questions, much of what the katsa knew. The hotel security chief spoke of his passion for fast cars and his liking for piloting a small aircraft. But it was difficult to enjoy those habits on his salary.

That may well have been the moment Maurice began to exert pressure. Finding money was always a problem for such hobbies, but not an insoluble one. Almost certainly that perked Paul's interest.

What followed then developed a rhythm of its own: Maurice laying down the bait and Paul all too eager to take it. The hook in place, Maurice would then have begun to reel in the line with the skills he had acquired at the Mossad training school.

At some point Maurice would have planted the idea he might be able to help, perhaps mentioning he worked for a company that was forever looking for ways to update its database and would pay good money to those who could help do so. This was a favorite opening gambit for Mossad recruiters on a cold-approach operation. From there it would be a small step to tell Paul that many of the Ritz guests no doubt possessed the kind of information that would interest the company.

Paul, perhaps uneasy at the turn of the conversation, may have balked. Maurice would have then moved to the next stage, saying that of course while he understood Paul's reservations, they did come as a surprise to him. After all, it was common knowledge that

Paul already took payment for information from the paparazzi. So why turn away the chance to make some real money?

Looking back, Ari Ben-Menashe would judge the operation at this stage as developed along classic lines. "From my personal knowledge there is no one better than Maurice (his name for this one operation), at this. A cold-approach operation requires a real finesse. Move too quickly and the fish is off the hook. Take too long and suspicion is soon coupled with fear. Recruiting is an art all by itself and a European like Henri Paul is very different from hooking an Arab on the West Bank or Gaza Strip."

Maurice's undoubted skill at delivering his proposition and accompanying revelations of how much he knew of Paul's background would have been delivered with a combination of worldliness and persuasion, with the essential undertow of pressure. It would also have had an effect on Paul.

Even if he had not asked, he may well have realized that the man seated across from him at the dinner table was an intelligence officer or at least a recruiter for a service.

That may well be the reason for his response. According to an Israeli intelligence source who has a certain knowledge of the matter: "Henri Paul came straight out with it: Was he being asked to spy? If so, what was the deal? Just like that. No hedging or bullshit. Just what was the deal—and whom would he really be working for? That would have been the point when Maurice would have had to decide. Did he tell Paul he would be working for Mossad? There is no standard operational procedure for something like this. Every target is different. But Henri Paul was on the hook."

If so, Maurice may well have told Paul what would be required of him: obtaining information on guests, perhaps even bugging their suites, and noting whom they entertained. There would have been discussions about payment, accompanied by an offer to open an account in a Swiss bank or, if need be, to pay Paul in cash. Maurice would have given the impression that such matters were not a problem. At that point he may even have revealed that Paul would be working for Mossad. All this would be standard for the successful conclusion of a cold-approach operation.

Paul was very probably scared at what he was asked to do. It was not a question of his loyalty to the Ritz; like other members of the staff, he worked for the hotel because of the relatively high salary and the perks. Paul was understandably frightened he was getting in over his head and could well end up in prison if he was found spying on the hotel's guests.

Yet if he went to the police what would they do? Maybe they already knew that he was going to be propositioned. If he turned down the proposition, what then? If the hotel management learned he had already betrayed that most precious of all assets the Ritz offered—confidentiality—by informing the paparazzi, he could be fired, even prosecuted.

For Henri Paul in those last days of August 1997, there seemed no way out. He continued to drink, to take pills, to sleep restlessly, to bully junior staff. He was a man teetering close to the edge.

Maurice maintained the pressure. He often managed to be in a bar where Paul was drinking off-duty. The katsa's very presence could only have been a further reminder to the security chief of what he was being pressured to do. Maurice continued to visit the Ritz, sipping an aperitif in one of the hotel bars, lunching in its restaurant, taking afternoon coffee in a lounge. To Henri Paul it would have seemed as if Maurice had become a personal shadow. That would have only further increased the pressure on him, reminding him that there was no way out.

Compounding the pressure was the forthcoming visit of Princess Diana and Dodi Al-Fayed. Paul had been put in charge of their security while they were in the hotel, with particular responsibility for keeping away the paparazzi. At the same time the photographers were calling him on his cell phone seeking information about the visit; he was being offered large sums of money to provide details. The temptation to accept was another pressure. Everywhere he turned, there seemed to be pressure.

Though he managed to conceal it, Henri Paul was unraveling mentally. He was taking antidepressants, sleeping pills, and pep pills to get him through the day. This combination of drugs could only have furthered the strain on his ability to make reasoned judgments.

Later, Ben-Menashe felt if he had been running the operation, "that would have been when I would have pulled out. Henri Paul might well have been able to conceal from most people his mental state, but to an experienced operative like Maurice, trained to a high degree in making such observations, the evidence of deterioration would have been all too obvious. Almost certainly, Maurice would have told the man in charge in Tel Aviv, Danny Yatom, he should pull the plug . . . let it go. But for reasons only Yatom knows, he did not. Yatom was barely a year in the hot seat. He wanted to make a name for himself. Vanity, like arrogance, is one of the great dangers in intelligence work. Yatom has plenty of both and that's okay—except when it gets in the way of reality. And the reality was Mossad should have pulled out."

It did not. Yatom's consuming need to have his own man inside the Ritz drove him. But other events that no one could have foreseen were moving to their own climax.

The blinking light—signaling an incoming telephone call—which awoke Maurice was timed by the recorder at 1:58 A.M. on Sunday, August 31, 1997. The caller worked in the Paris gendarmerie accident unit and had been recruited by Mossad some years before; its computers classified him as a *mabuah*, a non-Jewish informer. On the totem pole of Maurice's Parisian contacts, his caller was somewhere near the bottom.

Nevertheless, the man's news about a traffic accident stunned Maurice. It had occurred less than an hour before, when a Mercedes sedan had struck a reinforced concrete pillar on the westbound roadway of the underpass beneath the place de l'Alma, a notorious accident spot in the city.

The dead were Diana, Princess of Wales, mother of the future king of England; Dodi Al-Fayed, son of Mohammed, the Egyptian-born owner of Harrods of Knightsbridge, the "Royal" store; and Henri Paul. The couple's bodyguard had been critically injured.

Hours after the accident Maurice flew back to Tel Aviv, leaving in his wake questions that would remain unanswered.

What part had his pressure played in the accident? Had Henri Paul lost control of the Mercedes, causing it to smash into the thirteenth concrete pillar of the underpass beneath the place de l'Alma, because he could see no way of extricating himself from the clutches of Mossad? Was that pressure linked to the high level of prescribed drugs found in his bloodstream? When he had left the Ritz with his three passengers, had his mind continued to vacillate

over what he should do about the pressure? Was he not only responsible for a terrible road accident but also the victim of a ruthless intelligence agency?

Questions would continue to fester in the mind of Mohammed
Al-Fayed. In February 1998, he publicly announced: "It was no
accident. I am convinced of that in my heart of hearts. The truth
cannot remain hidden forever."

Five months later, the British network ITV, screened a documentary that claimed Henri Paul had close links to French intelligence. He had none. The program also hinted that an unnamed
intelligence agency had been involved in the deaths; there were dark
hints that the agency had acted because the British establishment
feared Diana's love for Dodi could have "political repercussions"
because he was an Egyptian.

To this day Mossad's involvement with Henri Paul has remained
a well-kept secret—the way the service had always intended it
should remain. Mossad acted at the behest of no one outside Israel.
Indeed, few outside the service still have any idea of Mossad's part
in the death of the then most famous woman in the world.

Mohammed Al-Fayed, prompted by what he saw as a campaign
of villification in the English media, has continued to claim that
unnamed security services had been ranged against his son and Diana. In July 1998 two *Time* magazine journalists published a book
that included the suggestion that Henri Paul could have had some
connection with French intelligence. Neither Al-Fayed or the journalists offered any conclusive proof that Henri Paul was an intelligence agent or even an informer—and none of them came near
to identifying Mossad's involvement with him.

In July 1998, Mohammed Al-Fayed asked a number of questions
in a letter he sent to every one of Britain's members of Parliament,
urging them to raise the questions in the House of Commons. He
claimed that "there is a force at work to stifle the answers I want."
His behavior was seen as the reaction of a grieving father lashing
out in every direction. The questions deserve repeating, not because
they shed any light on the role Mossad played in the closing weeks
of Henri Paul's life, but because they show how the entire tragedy
has gained a momentum that only the true facts can stop.

Al-Fayed wrote of a "plot" to get rid of Diana and his son and
attempted to link all kinds of disparate events with his questions:

"Why did it take one hour and forty minutes to get the princess to hospital? Why have some of the photographers failed to give up some of the pictures they shot? Why was there a break-in that night at the London home of a photographer who handles paparazzi pictures? Why have all the closed-circuit television cameras in that part of Paris produced not one frame of videotape? Why were the speed cameras on the route out of film, and the traffic cameras not switched on? Why was the scene of the crash not preserved but reopened to traffic after a few hours? Who was the person in the press group outside the Ritz who was equipped like a news photographer? Who were the two unidentified men mingling in the crowd who later sat in the Ritz bar? They ordered in English, watching and listening in a marked way?"

Mossad had no interest in the relationship between Diana and Dodi. Their sole concern was to recruit Henri Paul as their informer in the Ritz. Regarding the mysterious news photographer: in the past Mossad has allowed its agents to pose as journalists. It may well have been Maurice keeping watch outside the hotel. The two unidentified men in the hotel bar may have had some connection to Mossad. It would no doubt comfort Mohammed Al-Fayed if that were true.

By 1999, Mohammed al-Fayed's belief in a "plot" had hardened to what he saw as "a full-blown criminal conspiracy." He insisted it had been manufactured by M15 and M16, and French intelligence with Mossad "manipulating in the background." To those who would listen, and they were steadily declining in number, he would name a London newspaper editor as well as a close friend of Diana as both having "direct links" to Britain's intelligence services.

The reasons why these services had become involved in the "conspiracy" was clear-cut in Mohammed's mind. "A decision had been made by the Establishment, and at the very top, that Diana must not be allowed to marry a Muslim. Then the future king of England, Prince William, would have an Arab as his stepfather and another as his grandfather. There was also a real fear that I would provide the money to allow Diana to become a rival to the Queen of England. The Establishment would do anything to end my son's relationship with the one woman he had ever truly loved."

Facts were never produced to support an allegation which, if proven, would surely accelerate the end of the Royal Family in Britain and perhaps pave the way to a crisis of confidence that could even sweep away a government.

Nevertheless, al-Fayed authorized his spokesman; Laurie Meyer, a former anchorman with one of Rupert Murdoch's television networks, to state to the media: "Mohammed firmly believes Di and Dodi were murdered by agents loyal to the British Crown and that other agencies were deeply involved in the crime. He further believes there is deep-seated racism within the Establishment."

To confirm that murder most foul had taken place, al-Fayed had employed the skills of a former senior Scotland Yard detective, John MacNamara. By early 1999 the soft-spoken investigator was scouring the world for evidence. Along the way, in Geneva, Switzerland, he met a former M16 officer, Richard Tomlinson, who claimed he had seen documents at M16 headquarters on the bank of the River Thames. Tomlinson insisted they described "a plan to murder the Serbian leader, Slobodan Milosevic—a plan that has unsettling parallels to the way Di and Dodi died. The M16 document stated that the 'accident' should happen in a tunnel where the chance of fatal injury is high. The weapon of choice the document recommended was a high-powered laser beam that could be used to temporarily blind the driver of the target vehicle."

Despite all his efforts, MacNamara has been unable to find any independent evidence to support Tomlinson's claims—and efforts to obtain the M16 document totally failed.

Then came news, reluctantly confirmed, that the United States National Security Agency, NSA, had some 1050 pages of documents on the couple. Al-Fayed launched an immediate court battle in Washington to obtain the documents.

"The more he is blocked, the greater is his determination," said the loyal Meyer. But, like others, he is not holding his breath. "It could take years to work its way through the system."

Part of the reason, I had discovered, was that Diana and Dodi had been under surveillance by ECHELON, one of NSA's most sensitive and ultra-secret surveillance systems. This global electronic network is of truly astounding proportions. It links satellites to a series of high-speed parallel computers. The system enables NSA and those it allows to share information—Britain is one—to intercept and decode virtually every electronic communication in the world—in real time. Searching for key words it had been fed, ECHELON can identify and segregate messages of interest to its users.

Following her divorce from Prince Charles, Diana had launched her campaign to abolish land mines. She was blunt, outspoken, and quickly gathered support that was not welcomed by the Clinton administration or in London and other European capitals. She was seen as a meddler, someone who did not understand what she was talking about.

"The reality was that the land mine manufacturing industry provided thousands of jobs. No one wanted to see the mines used—but no one wanted people put out of work because Diana had a bee in her bonnet," one Washington source told me; perhaps understandably he insisted on not being named in return for this insight.

The arrival of Dodi in Diana's life automatically meant he became part of ECHELON'S collection activities. Unknown to them, their every conversation, however intimate, was silently gathered up by ECHELON's satellites.

By 1997, Mohammed al-Fayed's name had also been added to the global computer search. ECHELON may well have been the first outside his family circle to know of his hope that his son would marry a princess of the line—and then later his claim that on the eve of their deaths he had planned to announce their engagement.

There is much in the NSA documents that may still cause further surprise—and provide proof, through Diana's own words, that she had indeed planned to marry her lover.

I only became aware of ECHELON's role shortly before publication of the original edition of this book in March 1999. It was then that I also became aware of just how far the deaths of his son and Diana had continued to consume Mohammed al-Fayed. It was a jolting experience to be exposed to such uncontrolled grief and his anger and belief in a conspiracy that fed it.

On a March afternoon I met Mohammed al-Fayed in the privacy of his private salon on the fifth floor of Harrods. Guarding its approaches were his personal bodyguards. Al-Fayed told me they "are all former SAS soldiers, totally loyal to me. I pay them well. They make sure I live. I have been threatened so many times. My car is bulletproof."

These revelations, delivered in a tense low voice, came as he entered the salon. I was not sure whether I should take his outburst as a warning or a reassurance I was safe to tell him anything he wanted to know.

He did not waste time in telling me what that was: access to all my Mossad contacts. "You give me the names. They give me the information I want. I give you one million pounds in whatever currency you want. No need to pay tax. I will take care of everything."

I had been warned that there is still an element of a souk trader in al-Fayed. For the next twenty minutes he launched into a diatribe that I was not quite prepared for. He attacked the Queen and Prince Philip and well-known figures he called "establishment whores and pimps." He reserved his greatest venom for the intelligence service, branding them "killers".

Picking up my book, which had been marked and annotated in the margin, he said again: "Mossad are the people who can tell me the truth. Bring them to me and I will make you a very happy man." Before I could respond, he launched an attack on Henri Paul: "I trusted him, *really* trusted him. I would have done anything for him because Dodi liked him. My son, like me, was too trusting. That was one of the reasons Diana loved him, wanted him to be her husband, a father to her children. But they didn't want it. The Queen and her husband, her lackeys, that awful brother of hers, Earl Spencer . . . none of them wanted it. None of them wanted a Wog in the family. You know what Wog is? A Wily Oriental Gentleman. Only they didn't see that Dodi *was* a gentleman. They smeared his character when he was alive. They continue to do so now he is dead. Yet all Diana needed was what she told me she needed: someone she could trust after all she had gone through . . ."

Those words do not convey the intensity of his delivery, the profanities he used, the wild hand gestures and, above all, the painful torment on his face. Mohammed al-Fayed was a man in pain. I could only listen as he continued to unburden himself.

"Did you know Diana was almost certainly pregnant . . . maybe eight weeks . . . and that Dodi, my son, was the father? Did you know that at the hospital in Paris, after her death, they removed many of her organs and that she came home to London as a mummy? Did you know that when we last met she told me how much she loved Dodi and how happy they were together?"

I said I did not know any of those things. For a long moment Mohammed al-Fayed sat there, tears close, his face working, lost in some inner world.

Then he said: "Tell me who can help me to find out all the truth about who arranged for my son and his beloved Diana to die?"

I told him I had in mind two people. One was Victor Ostrovsky (see Chapter 10). The other was Ari Ben-Menashe.

"Find them. Bring them to me," commanded Mohammed al-Fayed. At that moment there was more than a hint of an imperious pharaoh about him.

It took me a week to locate them. Ostrovsky was living in Arizona; he would only speak with me through an intermediary, a journalist who works for an Arab news magazine. In the end Ostrovsky had a short discussion with John MacNamara that led nowhere.

Ari Ben-Menashe had just returned from Africa when I spoke to him in Montreal. I told him about my meeting with al-Fayed. Ben-Menashe said "it is not altogether crazy what he says. That much I know already. There was a definite intelligence presence around Diana and Dodi in that last day in Paris."

He agreed to meet Mohammed al-Fayed in London the following week, early April.

Ben-Menashe's account of that meeting echoes what Mohammed al-Fayed had told me at our meeting. Ben-Menashe, a fastidious, unfailingly polite man, had been frankly shocked at the emotive language al-Fayed had used to attack members of the Royal Family. Nevertheless, he had agreed to make further enquiries in Tel Aviv to see how much more Mossad would be prepared to add to the material I had already published in the original edition of this book.

Ten days later he met with al-Fayed in his Harrods salon and told him that a number of intelligence services "might well have a case to answer." Ben-Menashe added he would be happy to put his own staff to work on building such a case and suggested a retainer fee of $750,000 a year plus expenses to be agreed mutually.

Meantime, independent of Ben-Menashe, I had continued to make my own enquiries to establish the role ECHELON had played in the last days of Diana and Dodi's lives.

I discovered through sources in Washington and elsewhere that the couple had continued to be under surveillance during the week they had spent cruising off the Emerald Coast of Sardinia on the *Jonikal*, the 60-meter yacht owned by Mohammed al-Fayed. ECHELON had also tracked the posse of paparazzi that had chased them in speedboats, on motorcycles, in cars. Time and again the *Jonikal* had evaded its pursuers. But ECHELON's computers picked up Diana's chagrin at being hunted. Conversations between her and Dodi, between the couple and their bodyguard, Trevor Rees-Jones, recorded by ECHELON, all reflect her tense mood. On that Friday night, August 28th 1997, she told Dodi she wanted to go to Paris "as soon as possible."

Within hours, arrangements had been finalized. A Gulfstream-IV was ordered to fly to Sardinia's private airport the following day. Tomas Muzzu, an elderly Sardinian with many years experience of driving celebrities around the island, was retained to drive the couple to the airport.

Muzzu's account of the conversation in the car is striking confirmation to what an ECHELON satellite had scooped up.

"They spoke in English, very loving words. From time to time Dodi, who spoke good Italian, spoke to me. Then he switched back to English. I do not speak that language very well, but my impression was of a couple very much in love and making plans for their future."

My sources insist that portion of the ECHELON tapes show the couple talking of marriage and the life they planned together. Dodi continuously reassured her that he would ensure their privacy by enlisting the services of the al-Fayed protection team.

The private jet left Sardinia after the pilot made an urgent call to European air traffic control center in Brussels to give him a priority take-off slot.

During the two-hour flight to Le Bourget airport ten miles north of Paris, the aircraft's occupants were monitored by ECHELON, the conversations of Di and Dodi once more uplifted to a satellite and then downloaded to computers at Fort Meade in Maryland.

While my source could offer no "smoking gun" proof, he was "in my own mind," convinced that "relevant parts" of the conversation were relayed to GCHQ, Britain's communications center. "From there they would find their way up through the Whitehall network. By then anything Diana said, any decision she made, would have been of prime interest to certain people in authority."

I put all this to Ari Ben-Menashe. His response was gratifying but frustrating. "You're very close to being on the button. How close I can't tell you." Ben-Menashe's position was simple. He was hoping to sign a lucrative contract with Mohammed al-Fayed. Any information would have to go to him first.

In the end, the contract would not materialize. Al-Fayed wanted first to see what "evidence" Ben-Menashe could show him before agreeing to pay.

Ben-Menashe, more used to dealing with governments than "a man with the manner of a souk trader," found himself handling "a number of somewhat hysterical telephone calls from MacNamara insisting I should show him documents. This was very surprising for a man who should have had some experience of how the security services work from his own days at Scotland Yard. I had to tell him that Mossad doesn't hand out documents willy-nilly. I had to explain to him, much as you do to a new copper on the beat, the facts of life in the intelligence community."

Thwarted, al-Fayed refused to retreat into silence. His spokesman, Laurie Meyer, found himself waging new battles with the media who, with increasing force, challenged al-Fayed's view of an "Establishment plot to murder my son and his future bride."

Watching from a distance, Ari Ben-Menashe felt that al-Fayed "was his own worst enemy. From all the enquiries I had made, at no expense to him, the sort of preliminary investigation I made before assigning my company to any such work, it was clear that the Royal Family as such has no case to answer. It may well be that privately they would not have wished Diana to marry Dodi. But that is a long way from saying they wanted the young couple murdered. That said, I did turn up some hard evidence that does point to the involvement of security services around the time of their deaths. There are serious questions to be asked and answered. But al-Fayed will not get answers the way he continues to behave. Fundamentally he does not understand the mentality of those he is trying to convince. And worse, he is surrounded by lackeys 'yes men' who tell him what he wants to hear."

Early in May 1999, John MacNamara flew to Geneva, Switzerland, to meet Richard Tomlinson, a former staff officer with MI6. For four years Tomlinson, who had once been tipped to be a high-flier in British intelligence, had run a relentless campaign against his former employers. Originally recruited at Cambridge University by an MI6 "talent spotter," Tomlinson had been abruptly sacked in the spring of 1995 after telling his MI6 personnel officer of his growing emotional difficulties.

In a telephone conversation he told me that "my honesty cost me my job. The 'powers-that-be' decided that despite my impressive results, I lacked a stiff upper lip."

Tomlinson described how he had tried to sue MI6 for unfair dismissal but the British government had successfully stopped his case coming before a court. Then its offer of a pay-off—"cash for my silence" was how Tomlinson put it—was withdrawn after an Australian publisher to whom Tomlinson had sent a synopsis of a book about his career with MI6, submitted the document to MI6 to see if publishing would lead to legal action. MI6 moved swiftly. Tomlinson was arrested as he was about to leave Britain and sentenced to two years in jail for breaching the Official Secrets Act.

Released from prison in April 1998, Tomlinson moved first to Paris and then to Switzerland. There he began to use Internet cafes to post highly embarrassing details of MI6 operations. This included revealing a high-level mole in Germany's Central Bank claiming the man—code-named Orcadia—had betrayed his country's economic secrets to Britain. He also disclosed details of a plot by MI6 to assassinate President Slobodan Milosevic of Serbia in 1992.

Then came the moment he moved from being just another disgruntled former spy into the world of Mohammed al-Fayed, already well-peopled with conspiratorial figures.

To the billionaire Tomlinson, by now almost penniless, was, al-Fayed told me, "like a sign from heaven." He encouraged Tomlinson to tell all he knew to the French judge investigating the deaths of Diana and Dodi.

In a sworn affidavit, Tomlinson claimed MI6 was implicated in the couple's deaths. Agents of the service had been in Paris for two weeks prior to their deaths and had held several meetings with Henri Paul, "who was a paid informer of MI6." Later in his affidavit, Tomlinson alleged "Paul had been blinded as he drove through the underpass by a high-powered flash, a technique which is consistent with MI6 methods in other assassinations."

Such allegations brought Tomlinson even deeper into al-Fayed's inner circle. The former agent was now more than "a sign from heaven." He had become, in al-Fayed's words to me, "the man who could unravel the terrible truth of an incident of such magnitude and historical importance."

It was to further encourage Tomlinson to continue with his campaign that MacNamara had flown to Geneva.

Ever since he had arrived in the city, Tomlinson had faced increasing insolvency. He could barely find the rent for his studio apartment. His efforts to raise money by writing travel articles had come to nothing. His efforts to be employed as a private detective had also failed because he feared to travel around Europe in case MI6 agents "snatched me." On the advice of MI6, he had been banned from being admitted to the United States, Australia, and France. Only Switzerland had offered him sanctuary on the grounds that any breaches of the Official Secrets Act was "a political crime" and therefore not a subject for extradition.

MI6 sources I have spoken to suggest that MacNamara had gone to see Tomlinson with a view to resolving the former spy's financial plight. More certain is that shortly afterwards Tomlinson had sufficient funds to launch what he called "my nuclear option." Using a sophisticated Microsoft program he had installed in his state-of-the-art computer, Tomlinson began to publish on his specially created and very expensive website the names of over one hundred serving MI6 officers—including twelve he said had been involved in a plot to kill Diana and Dodi.

There was no clear-cut, smoking-gun evidence offered against any of those agents. But within hours their names had been flashed around the world.

A stunned MI6 desperately tried to close down the website, but no sooner had they managed to close one than another opened. In London the Foreign Office admitted the breach of security was the most serious since the Cold War—"and the lives of some MI6 agents and their contacts have been put at risk." Certainly those named as working in Iran, Iraq, Lebanon, and other Middle East countries had to be urgently withdrawn.

But neither Tomlinson or Mohammed al-Fayed could have calculated one effect. So grave was the overall breach of security that the claim that a handful of MI6 agents had been involved in a plot against Diana went virtually unnoticed. It was dismissed as being part of al-Fayed's obsession.

In June 1999 matters took a more serious turn when al-Fayed's Harrods website published the name of a senior MI6 officer. The website alleged that the agent, who was then serving in the Balkans, had orchestrated "a vicious campaign" to smear al-Fayed and "destroy his reputation."

Britain's ministry of defense took the unusual step of publicly warning that publication had endangered the agent and his contacts in Kosovo and Serbia.

The agent's identity had been revealed alongside the site's online book where thousands of visitors have left messages commemorating the deaths of Diana and Dodi.

Laurie Meyer, the Harrods spokesman, promised to have the agent's name removed—"obviously it is an error."

Reports then surfaced in Germany's mass-circulation *Bild* that Richard Tomlinson had evidence that Henri Paul had installed a bugging device in the Imperial Suite at the Ritz Hotel and had obtained tapes of the "last intimate moments" of Diana and Dodi. Shortly before Paul drove them to their death, the couple had spent several hours alone in the suite.

The tapes, according to *Bild*, had become the subject of a hunt by MI6 to locate them.

Around this time Earl Spencer, Diana's brother, decided to intervene. He told American television audiences that at best "the romance my sister had with Dodi al-Fayed was no more than a summer fling. She had absolutely no intention to marry him."

Mohammed al-Fayed pointed out, with some justification, that the relationship between Spencer and Diana was hardly close at the time of her death.

None of this was any surprise to Ari Ben-Menashe. He had continued to follow the never-ending saga of al-Fayed's attempts "to prove his fixation that the Queen and Prince Philip organized a plot to kill Diana."

The highly experienced Israeli intelligence officer felt that, "in throwing in his lot with Richard Tomlinson, al-Fayed had lost the plot. He is now reduced to running to the tabloids. Yet I know for a fact that if he had gone about matters properly and organized a serious investigation he would have turned up some very surprising results. There *is* something very strange about the deaths of Diana and Dodi. No doubt about it. There was a case to investigate. But the trail has been muddied by al-Fayed himself. It may not even be his fault. He is surrounded by people who tell him to look here, not *there*. For some of them, keeping the whole thing going is a sort of pension for them. They know that every new, half-baked theory they come up with will encourage al-Fayed to spend more of his money in pursuing it. Along the way he tramples out of sight what evidence there may have been to uncover."

A hint of what that could be came in late June 1999 when it emerged that the mysterious white Fiat Uno seen zigzagging way from the scene of the death crash of Diana and Dodi was destroyed in a car crusher. In moments the Uno, from which traces of paint scrapes had been found in the tunnel, had been reduced to a block of scrap metal.

The claim was contained in a secret Mossad investigation that began within hours of the fatal crash. It had been launched by Mossad's then director general, Danny Yatom. He had been concerned that Mossad's determined attempts to recruit Henri Paul could lead to accusation that this had played a part in Diana's death.

The investigation focused on a period that covered the two weeks before the accident—or what al-Fayed still calls "the appearance of an accident to cover up murder"—and the days afterwards.

Mossad investigators discovered that as well as the agency's own presence in Paris prior to the death of the couple, there was a four-man MI6 team in the city. They were based at the British Embassy for the first week, but later moved into a rented apartment—"an MI6 safe house"—near the Ritz. One of the team checked into the hotel itself four days before the death of Dodi and Diana.

The Mossad report reveals that around August 14/15 1997, a CIA team also arrived in the city. The team had been tracking

Diana for some time, keeping tabs on her attacks on land mine manufacturers, many of which are US-based.

The CIA reports form part of the 1051 documents Mohammed al-Fayed has to battle through the American courts to obtain copies of. The U.S. Justice Department has claimed the documents contained material "sensitive to national security."

The Mossad report suggests that sensitivity could refer to why Britain had asked the United States to help in monitoring Diana.

"Britain saw her as a loose cannon," insisted al-Fayed. "In fact she was a woman of great courage who was ready to confront the land mines issue."

The Mossad investigation details how the various intelligence services hurriedly left Paris after the deaths of Diana and Dodi.

Mossad's report contains a detailed timetable of Dodi and Diana's last hours. It is partly based on firsthand observations by Maurice and his contacts. Other information came from Mossad's "back channel" contacts with agents in the French capital, from MI6, the CIA, and French Intelligence.

"I have been told by a former senior Israeli intelligence officer that all those services had a vested interest in Diana and Dodi," Mohammed al-Fayed has insisted.

Mossad's account of the final moments of the lives of Diana and Dodi begins at 11:45 P.M. Saturday, August 29, 1997, when Henri Paul was put in charge of the operation to whisk them away from the Ritz Hotel.

Mohammed al-Fayed still remembers vividly the instruction he had telephoned to Paul.

"I told him he must drive carefully, that he must never forget he had the life of the mother of the future king of England and my beloved son in his hands. I trusted him never to forget that. God knows, how I trusted him. God only knows now why I did."

The next Mossad entry is 11:50 P.M. In the Ritz bar Trevor Rees-Jones, who was there to body-guard Diana and Dodi, was in a huddle with other security men from the hotel staff and Henri Paul, discussing the route he would use.

Paul was very bullish. He said the hotel would provide two Range Rovers to act as decoys for the waiting paparazzi. That would give him enough time to get away. Rees-Jones is reported to have said the plan "sounds good to me."

00:15 A.M. Sunday, August 30. In the hotel lobby Henri Paul was using his cell phone to mobilize the two decoy vehicles.

00:19 A.M. The two decoy vehicles roared out of the Place Vendome that fronts the Ritz. Paparazzi give chase.

00:20 A.M. At the hotel's rear entrance Paul arrived with the Mercedes. He was seen by one of the eyewitnesses that Mossad subsequently interviewed as "drumming his fingers nervously on the steering wheel."

00:21 A.M. At the top of the Rue Cambon, a Mossad agent kept watch. He would later report that "a white Fiat Uno passed the top of the street."

The Mossad report states that in the car were two intelligence officers from the French security service, DST. The DST—more formally known as the Directorate for Surveillance of the Territory—is the largest and most powerful of France's intelligence agencies. With several thousand employees, it operates both internally and overseas. Its wide-ranging responsibilities include surveillance of all foreign embassies in Paris and conducting a number of clandestine operations. It reports to the incumbent minister of the interior.

00:22 A.M. The white Fiat Uno passed through traffic lights in the Place de la Concorde. Henri Paul's Mercedes is forced to temporarily stop at the lights.

00:23 A.M. The Mercedes approaches the Alma tunnel. Henri Paul would most certainly have seen the white Uno ahead of him.

00:24 A.M. The Mercedes, traveling at high speed, passed over the dip at the tunnel entrance. In the back seat Diana and Dodi would have experienced for a split second a sensation not unlike that of a plunging roller-coaster.

Seconds later there came a thunderous noise inside the tunnel. A roaring screeching of metal, a reverberating, crumping sound that seemed to go on and on.

Henri Paul and Dodi were dead. Diana was dying.

Moments later, according to the Mossad report, the white Uno had driven into a side street off the Avenue Montalgne. Waiting there was a pentachnicon, its ramp lowered. The Uno had driven up the ramp. The pentachnicon's doors had been closed.

Hours later the Uno had been gripped in the claws of the crusher. In moments it had become a piece of crushed metal, devoid of any identification.

There, at the time of writing, the matter rests. Can Tomlinson produce anything new? Could Ben-Menashe have found evidence that would finally satisfy al-Fayed's belief in a conspiracy? Was Diana really pregnant at the time of her death? Had Mohammed al-Fayed become so blinded by grief mingled with anger that he was ready to make this thesis fit the facts?

These questions will be revisited well into this new century. But they may never be answered fully enough to satisfy Mohammed al-Fayed or convince all those who believe him a dangerously misguided man who is using vast sums of money to nail down a truth that may, just may, be best kept under lock and key by all those directly involved.

Some of Maurice's colleagues have increasingly felt that the attempt to entrap Henri Paul was additional proof that Mossad has lurched a little further out of control, carrying out reckless international operations without taking into account the potential long-term consequences for itself, for Israel, for peace in the Middle East, and, ultimately, for the relationship with the Jewish state's oldest and closest ally, the United States of America. Several officers claimed that since Benyamin Netanyahu became prime minister in 1996, matters have worsened.

A veteran member of the Israeli intelligence community has said: "People are seeing those who work for Mossad are often thugs masquerading as patriots. That is bad for us [and] for morale, and, in the end, will have a bad effect on Mossad's relationship with other services."

Another experienced Israeli intelligence officer was equally blunt: "Netanyahu behaves as if Mossad is part of his own version of the Court of King Arthur; something new every day or the knights of his own Round Table get bored. That's why things have gone very wrong with Mossad. There's a need to ring the alarm bell before it's too late."

The first lesson I learned during a quarter of a century of writing about secret intelligence is that deception and disinformation are its stock-in-trade, along with subversion, corruption, blackmail, and, sometimes, assassination. Agents are trained to lie and to use and abuse friendships. They are the very opposite of the dictum that gentlemen do not read each other's mail.

I first encountered their behavior while investigating many of the great spy scandals of the Cold War: the betrayal of America's atomic bomb secrets by Klaus Fuchs, and the compromising of Britain's MI5 and MI6 by Guy Burgess, Donald Maclean, and Kim Philby. Each made treachery and duplicity his byword. I also was one of the first writers to gain access to the CIA's obsession with mind control, a preoccupation the Agency was forced to confirm ten years after my book on the subject, *Journey into Madness*, appeared. Denial is the black art all intelligence services long ago perfected.

Nevertheless, in getting to the truth, I was greatly helped by two professional intelligence officers: Joachim Kraner, my late father-in-law, who ran an MI6 network in Dresden in the post–World War II years, and Bill Buckley, who was station chief of the CIA in Beirut. Physically they were similar: tall, lean, and trim, with chins ready to confront trouble halfway. Their eyes revealed little— except to say if you weren't part of the answer, you had to be part of the problem. Intellectually formidable, their criticism of the agencies they served at times was astringent.

Both constantly reminded me that a great deal can be heard from what Bill called "murmurs in the mush": a deadly skirmish fought in an alley with no name; the collective hold-your-breath when an agent or network is blown; a covert operation that could have undone years of overt political bridge building; a snippet of mundane information that completed a particular intelligence jigsaw. Joachim added that "sometimes a few words, casually offered, could often throw a new light on something."

Proud of being members of what he called "the second oldest profession," both not only were my friends, but convinced me that secret intelligence is the key to fully understanding international relations, global politics, and diplomacy—and, of course, terrorism. Through them I made contacts in a number of military and civilian intelligence agencies: Germany's BND and France's DGSE; the CIA; Canadian and British services.

Joachim died in retirement; Bill was murdered by Islamic fundamentalists who kidnapped him in Beirut and triggered the Western hostage crisis in that city.

I also met members of Israel's intelligence community who first helped me by filling in the background of Mehmet Ali Agca, the Turkish fanatic who attempted to assassinate Pope John Paul in St. Peter's Square, Rome, in May 1981. Those contacts were arranged by Simon Wiesenthal, the renowned Nazi hunter and an invaluable Mossad "source" for over forty years. Because of his fame and reputation, Wiesenthal still finds doors readily open, especially in Washington.

It was in that city in March 1986 that I learned a little more of the tangled relationship between the intelligence communities of the United States and Israel. I was there to interview William Casey, then the director of the Central Intelligence Agency, as ongoing research for my book *Journey into Madness*, which deals in part with the death of Bill Buckley.

Despite his customized suit, Casey was a shambling figure. His jowled face was pale and the rims of his eyes were red as we sat in a Washington club; he looked like someone whose ectoplasm was running out after five years of directing the CIA.

Over a Perrier he confirmed the conditions for our meeting. No notes, no tape recordings; anything he said would be purely background. He then produced a sheet of plain paper on which were typed his biographical details. He had been born in New York on March 13, 1913, and graduated from St. John's University in 1937 with a law degree. Commissioned into the U.S. Naval Reserve in 1943, within months he had transferred to the Office of Strategic Services, the forerunner of the CIA. In 1944 he became chief of the OSS Special Intelligence Branch in Europe. Next came the chairmanship of the Securities and Exchange Commission (1971–73); then, in quick succession, he was undersecretary of state for economic affairs (1973–74); president and chairman of the Export-Import Bank of the United States (1974–76); and a member of the president's Foreign Intelligence Advisory Board (1976–77). In 1980 he became campaign manager for Ronald Reagan's successful bid for the presidency. A year later, on January 28, 1981, Reagan appointed him DCI, the thirteenth man to hold the single most powerful office in the U.S. intelligence community.

In response to my remark that he appeared to have been a pair of safe hands in a number of posts, Casey sipped more water and mumbled he "didn't want to get into the personal side of things."

He put the paper back into his pocket and sat, watchful and waiting for my first question: what could he tell me about Bill Buckley, who, almost two years earlier to the day—on Friday, March 16, 1984—had been kidnapped in Beirut and was now dead. I wanted to know what efforts the CIA had made to try to save Bill's life. I had spent time in the Middle East, including Israel, trying to piece together the background.

"You speak to Admoni or any of his people?" Casey interrupted.

In 1982, Nahum Admoni had become head of Mossad. On Tel Aviv's embassy cocktail circuit, he had a hard-nosed reputation. Casey characterized Admoni as "a Jew who'd want to win a pissing contest on a rainy night in Gdansk." More certain, Admoni had been born in Jerusalem in 1929, the son of middle-class Polish immigrants. Educated at the city's Rehavia Gymnasium, he developed linguistic skills that had earned him a lieutenant's stripes as an intelligence officer in the 1948 War of Independence.

"Admoni can listen in half a dozen languages," was Casey's judgment.

Later, Admoni had studied international relations at Berkeley and taught the subject at the Mossad training school on the outskirts of Tel Aviv. He'd also worked undercover in Ethiopia, in Paris, and in Washington, where Admoni had linked closely with Casey's predecessors, Richard Helms and William Colby. These postings had helped hone Admoni into a soft-spoken intelligence bureaucrat who, when he became Mossad's chief, in Casey's words, "ran a tight ship. Socially gregarious, he has as keen an eye for women as for what's best for Israel."

Casey's thumbnail sketch was of an operative who, he said, had "climbed through the ranks because of his skills at avoiding his superiors' 'corns.' "

His next words came in the same mumbling undertone.

"Nobody can surprise like someone you took to be friendly disposed. By the time we realized Admoni was going to do nothing, Bill Buckley was dead. Remember what it was like at the time over there? There had been the massacre of almost a thousand Palestinians in those two Beirut refugee camps. The Lebanese Christian forces did the killings; the Jews looked on in a kind of reversal of the Bible. Fact is, Admoni was in bed with that thug, Gemayel."

Bashir Gemayel was head of the Phalangists and later became president of Lebanon.

"We ran Gemayel as well, but I never trusted the bastard. And Admoni worked with Gemayel all the time Buckley was being tortured. We had no idea where exactly in Beirut Bill was held. We asked Admoni to find out. He said no problem. We waited and waited. Sent our best men to Tel Aviv to work with Mossad. We said money was not a problem. Admoni kept saying okay, understood."

Casey sipped more water, locked in his own time capsule. His next words came out flat, like a jury foreman handing down a verdict.

"Next thing Admoni was selling us a bill of goods that the PLO were behind the kidnapping. We knew the Israelis were always ready to blame Yasser Arafat for anything, and our people did not buy at first. But Admoni was very plausible. He made a good case. By the time we figured it wasn't Arafat, it was long over for Buckley. What we didn't know was that Mossad had also been playing real dirty pool—supplying the Hezbollah with arms to kill the Christians while at the same time giving the Christians more guns to kill the Palestinians."

Casey's less-than-full glimpse of what the CIA now believed had happened to Bill Buckley—that Mossad had deliberately done nothing to save him in the hope the PLO could be blamed, so frustrating Arafat's hopes of gaining sympathy in Washington—provided a chilling insight into the relationship between two intelligence services supposedly friendly with each other.

Casey had shown there was another side to the ties between the United States and Israel other than fund-raising and other manifestations of American-Jewish solidarity that has turned the Jewish state into a regional superpower out of a fear of the Arab enemy.

Before we parted, Casey had a final thought: "A nation creates the intelligence community it needs. America relies on technical expertise because we are concerned to discover, rather than secretly rule. The Israelis operate differently. Mossad, in particular, equates its actions with the country's survival."

This attitude has long made Mossad immune to close scrutiny. But, in two years of research for this book, a series of mistakes—scandals in some cases—has forced the service into Israel's public consciousness. Questions have been asked, and, if the answers are rarely volunteered, gaps have begun to appear in the protective body armor Mossad has worn against that outside world.

I spoke to more than a hundred persons either directly employed by, or working indirectly for, Israeli and other intelligence services. The interviews were spread over two and a half years. Many of the key people in Mossad agreed to be taped. Those recordings run to eighty hours and are transcribed to some 5,800 pages. There are also some fifteen foolscap notebooks filled with contemporaneous notes. This material will, as with previous books of mine, find their place in the research section of a university library. Several of those I spoke to urged I should focus on recent events; the past should only be used to illustrate events that are relevant to Mossad's role at the cutting edge of the current frontiers of espionage and intelligence gathering. Many interviews were with participants who had not been questioned before; often no amount of probing could produce a comfortingly simple explanation for the way they or others behaved. Many were surprisingly frank, though not all agreed to be fully identified. In the case of serving Mossad personnel, they are prevented by Israeli law from voluntarily allowing their names to be published. Some of the non-Israeli sources asked, and received, a guarantee of anonymity.

On the organization charts newspapers try to piece together and publish, many sources remain among the empty spaces. They still take their anonymity seriously and some wish to be known in these pages by an alias or only a first name: it does not make their testimony less valid. Their personal motives for breaking silence may be many: a need to secure their own place in history; a desire to justify their actions; the anecdotage of old men; even perhaps expiation. The same can be said for those who agreed to be identified.

Perhaps the best motive of all that drove them to break silence was a real and genuine fear that an organization they had served with pride was increasingly endangered from within—and that the only way to save it was to reveal what it had achieved in the past and what it is doing today. To understand both requires knowing how and why it was created.

BEFORE THE BEGINNING

Since dawn, the faithful had come to the most sacred wall in the world, the only remaining relic of Herod the Great's Second Temple in Jerusalem, the Wailing Wall. The young and the old, the lean and the fat, the bearded and the halding: all had made their way through the narrow streets or from outside the city walls.

Office clerks walked alongside shepherds from the hills beyond Jerusalem; newly bar mitzvahed youths proudly marched with men in the winter of their years. Teachers from the city's religious shuls were shoulder to shoulder with shopkeepers who had made the journey from a distance away, from Haifa, Tel Aviv, and the villages around the Sea of Galilee.

Uniformly dressed in black, each carried a prayer book and stood before the towering wall to recite portions of Scripture.

Down the centuries, Jews had done that. But this Friday Sabbath in September 1929 was different. Rabbis had urged as many men as possible to be united in public prayer and to show their determination to their right to do so. It was intended not only as an expression of their faith, but also as a visible symbol of their Zionism—and a reminder to the Arab population, who vastly outnumbered them, that they would not be cowed.

For months there had been persistent rumors that the Muslim population were once more becoming increasingly angry over what they saw as Zionist expansion. These fears had started with the 1917 Balfour Declaration and its commitment to a formal Jewish homeland in Palestine. To Arabs who lived there and could trace their ancestry back to the Prophet, this was an outrage. Land that they had farmed for many centuries would be threatened, perhaps even taken from them by the Zionists and their British protectors, who had arrived at the end of the Great War to place Palestine under a Mandate. The British had ruled as they did in other parts of the empire, trying to please both sides. It was a recipe for disaster. Tensions between Jews and Arabs had increased. There had been skirmishes and bloodletting, often over where the Jews wanted to build their synagogues and religious shuls. But the Jews were stubbornly determined to exercise their "prayer rights" at the Wailing Wall in Jerusalem. For them it was part of the core of their faith.

By noon, the hour of the shema prayer, there were close to a thousand reading aloud the ancient words of Scripture before the yellow sandstone wall. The rise and fall of their voices had its own soothing cadence.

Then, with stunning swiftness, missiles—stones, broken bottles, and tins filled with rubble—rained down on them. The assault had been launched by Arabs from vantage points around the Wailing Wall. The first crack of gunfire rattled, a ragged volley of musket shots from Muslim marksmen. Jews fell and were dragged away by their fleeing neighbors. Miraculously, no one was killed, though the injured numbered scores.

That night the leaders of the Yishuv, the Jewish community in

Palestine, met. They quickly realized that their carefully planned demonstration had lacked one essential: foreknowledge of an Arab onslaught.

One of those present at the meeting spoke for them all: "We need to remember Scripture. From King David onward, our people have depended on good intelligence."

Over cups of Turkish coffee and sweet pastries were sown the seeds for what would one day become the most formidable intelligence service in the modern world: Mossad. But its creation was still almost a quarter of a century away. All that the Yishuv leaders could suggest as a first practical step on that warm September night was to pool what money they could spare and call upon their neighbors to do the same. The cash would be used to bribe Arabs who were still tolerant toward Jews and who would provide advance warning of further attacks.

In the meantime Jews would continue to exert their right to pray at the Wailing Wall. They would not depend on the British for protection, but would be defended by the Haganah, the newly formed Jewish militia. In the months to come a combination of prior warning and the presence of the militia faced down Arab attacks. Relative calm between Arab and Jew was restored for the next five years.

In that period the Jews continued to secretly expand their intelligence gathering. It had no formal name or leadership. Arabs were recruited on an ad hoc basis: peddlers who worked in Jerusalem's Arab Quarter and shoeshine boys who burnished the boots of Mandate officers were put on the payroll, along with students from the city's prestigious Arab Rouda College, teachers, and businessmen. Any Jew could recruit an Arab spy; the only condition was the information was shared. Slowly but surely the Yishuv obtained important information not only about Arabs but about British intentions.

The coming to power of Hitler in 1933 marked the start of the exodus of German Jews to Palestine. By 1936 over three hundred thousand had made the long journey across Europe; many were destitute by the time they reached the Holy Land. Somehow food and accommodations were found for them by the Yishuv. Within months Jews made up over a third of the population. The Arabs reacted as they had before: from the minarets of a hundred mosques came the cries of the mullahs to drive the Zionists back into the sea.

In every Arab *mafafeth*, the meeting house where local Arab councilmen met, came the same raised voices of angry protests: We must stop the Jews from taking our land; we must stop the British giving them arms and training them.

In turn the Jews protested that the opposite was true, that the British were encouraging the Arabs to steal back land lawfully paid for.

The British continued to try to placate both sides—and failed. In 1936 sporadic fighting flared into full-scale Arab revolt against both the British and the Jews. The British ruthlessly suppressed the rebellion. But the Jews realized it would only be a matter of time before the Arabs struck with renewed fury.

Throughout the land young Jews rushed to join the Haganah. They became the core of a formidable secret army: physically hardened, crack shots, and as cunning as the desert foxes in the Negev.

The network of Arab informers was extended. A Haganah Political Department was set up to spread dissension through disinformation. Men who later became legends in the Israeli intelligence community learned their skills in that formative period before the start of World War II. The Haganah—the word means "defense" in Hebrew—became the best informed of all the forces in the Holy Land.

World War II brought a renewed uneasy peace to Palestine. Jews and Arabs sensed the grim future they would both face if the Nazis won. The first details of what was happening in the death camps of Europe had reached the Yishuv.

David Ben-Gurion and Yitzhak Rabin were among those who attended a meeting in Haifa in 1942. There was consensus that the survivors of the Holocaust must be brought to their spiritual home, Eretz Israel. No one could estimate how many there would be, but everyone agreed the arrival of the refugees would rekindle confrontation with the Arabs—and this time the British would openly side against the Jews. Britain had steadfastly said it would refuse to admit the survivors into Palestine after Hitler was defeated, on the grounds it would create a population imbalance.

Ben-Gurion's urging for an upgrade of the Haganah's intelligence capacity was fully endorsed by the meeting. More informers would be recruited. A counterintelligence unit would be formed to uncover Jews who were collaborating with the British and unearth "Jewish communists and dissenters in our midst." The new unit was known as Rigul Hegdi and was commanded by a former French foreign legionnaire working under cover as a traveling salesman.

Soon he was turning up Jewish women who consorted with officers of the Mandate; shopkeepers who traded with the British; café owners who entertained them. In the dead of night the culprits were brought before Haganah drumhead courts-martial; the guilty were either sentenced to be severely beaten or were executed in the Judaean hills by a single bullet in the back of the head. It was a precursor to the ruthlessness Mossad would later display.

By 1945 the Haganah included a unit responsible for procuring arms. Soon caches of Italian and German weapons captured in North Africa after the defeat of Rommel were being smuggled by Jewish soldiers serving with the Allies across the Egyptian Sinai Desert into Palestine. The arms came by ramshackle trucks and camel caravans and were stored in caves in the Wilderness where the Devil had tried to tempt Jesus. One hiding place was close to where the Dead Sea Scrolls were waiting to be discovered.

After the defeat of Japan in August 1945 ended the war, Jews who had served in Allied military intelligence units arrived to provide their expertise for the Haganah. The elements were in place to deal with what Ben-Gurion had forecast—"the war for our independence."

The trigger point he knew would be the *bricha*, the Hebrew name for the unprecedented operation to bring the Holocaust survivors from Europe. First they came in the hundreds, then thousands, then tens of thousands. Many still wore their concentration camp garb; each bore a tattoo with a Nazi identification number. They came by road and rail through the Balkans and then across the Mediterranean to the shores of Israel. Every available ship had been bought or rented by Jewish relief agencies in the United States—often at highly inflated prices: tramp steamers, coasters, landing craft from the beaches of Normandy, riverboats, anything that could float was pressed into service. There had not been an evacuation like it since Dunkirk in 1940.

Waiting for the survivors on the beaches between Haifa and Tel Aviv were some of the very British soldiers who had been ferried back to England from Dunkirk. They were there to carry out their government's order to keep out the Holocaust survivors. There were ugly clashes, but also times when the soldiers, perhaps remembering their own salvation, had looked the other way as a boatload of refugees struggled ashore.

Ben-Gurion decided that such acts of compassion were not enough. The time had come for the Mandate to end. That could only be done by force. By 1946, he had united the disparate Jewish underground movements. Fired by the unquenchable spirit of those who had first settled the land, the order was given to launch a guerrilla war against both the British and the Arabs.

Every Jewish commander knew it was a dangerous gamble: fighting on both fronts would stretch their resources to the very limit. The consequences of failure would be dire. Ben-Gurion ordered a no-holds-barred policy. Soon the catalog of atrocities was appalling on all sides. Jews were shot on suspicion of collaborating with the Haganah. British soldiers were gunned down and their barracks bombed. Arab villages were set to the torch. It was medieval in its ferocity.

For the Haganah, intelligence was critical, not least to spread disinformation to give the impression in British and Arab eyes that the Jews had far more men than they actually could muster. The British found themselves chasing a will-o'-the-wisp enemy. Among the mandate forces morale began to crumble.

Sensing an opening, the United States tried to broker a deal in the spring of 1946 urging Britain to admit into Palestine one hundred thousand Holocaust survivors. The plea was rejected and the bitter fighting continued. Finally, in February 1947, Britain agreed to leave Palestine by May 1948. From then on the United Nations would deal with the problems of what would become the State of Israel.

Realizing there must still be a decisive conflict with the Arabs to ensure the fledgling nation would not be stifled at birth, Ben-Gurion and his commanders knew they must continue to depend on superior intelligence. Vital data were obtained about Arab morale and military strength. Jewish spies positioned in Cairo and Amman stole the attack plans of the Egyptian and Jordanian armies. When what became known as the War of Independence started, the Israelis achieved spectacular military victories. But it also became clear to Ben-Gurion as the fighting continued that eventual victory must be predicated on a clear division between military and political aspirations. When victory did finally come in 1949, that division had not been properly settled—and that had led to feuding within the Israeli intelligence community over its responsibilities in peacetime.

Rather than dealing with the situation with his usual incisiveness, Ben-Gurion, as Israel's first prime minister, set up five intelligence services to operate both internally and abroad. The overseas service modeled itself on Britain's and France's security services. Both those services readily agreed to work with the Israelis. Contact was also established with the U.S. Office of Strategic Services (OSS) in Washington through the agency's head of counterintelligence in Italy, James Jesus Angleton. His bonding with Israel's fledgling spies would play a crucial role in the eventual bridge building between the two intelligence communities.

Yet, despite this promising start, Ben-Gurion's dream of an integrated intelligence organization working in harmony died in the birth pangs of a nation itself struggling for a cohesive identity. Muscle flexing remained the order of the day as his ministers and officials fought for power and positions. At every level there were clashes. Who would coordinate an overall intelligence strategy? Who would evaluate raw data? Who would recruit spies? Who should see their reports first? Who would interpret that information for the country's political leaders?

Nowhere was the jockeying more relentless than between the foreign ministry and the defense ministry, both of whom claimed the right to operate abroad. Isser Harel, then a young operative, felt his colleagues "saw intelligence work in a romantic and adventurous light. They pretended to be expert in the ways of the whole world . . . and sought to behave like fictional international spies enjoying their glory as they lived in the shadow of the fine line between law and licentiousness."

Meanwhile people continued to die, killed by Arab terrorists and their bombs and booby traps. The armies of Syria, Egypt, Jordan, and Lebanon still threatened. Behind them, millions more Arabs were ready to raise jihad, holy war. No nation on earth had been born into such a hostile environment as Israel.

For Ben-Gurion there was an almost messianic feeling about the way his people looked to him to protect them, in the way the great leaders of Israel had always done. But he knew he was no prophet, only a hard-bitten street fighter who had won the War of Independence against an Arab enemy with combined forces more than twenty times those at his disposal. There had not been a greater triumph since the boy shepherd David had killed Goliath and routed the Philistines.

Yet the enemy had not gone away. It had become cleverer and even more ruthless. It struck like a thief in the night, killing without compunction before vanishing.

For four long years the rivalry, squabbling, and sniping had gone on at all those meetings Ben-Gurion had chaired to try and resolve matters among the intelligence community. A promising foreign ministry plan to use a French diplomat as a spy in Cairo had been thwarted by the defense ministry. It wanted its own man for the job. The young officer, with no real experience of intelligence work, was caught in weeks by Egyptian security officers. Israeli agents in Europe were discovered to be working in the rampant black market to finance their work because there was an insufficient official budget to pay for their spying activities. Attempts to recruit the moderate Druze forces in Lebanon had ended when rival Israeli intelligence agencies disagreed on how they could be used. Often grandiose schemes were wrecked by mutual suspicion. Naked ambition was everywhere.

Powerful men of the day—Israel's foreign minister, the army chief of staff, and ambassadors—all fought to establish the supremacy of their favorite service over the others. One wanted the focus to be on the collection of economic and political information. Another thought intelligence should concentrate purely on the military strength of the enemy. The ambassador to France insisted intelligence should be run the way the French Resistance had operated in World War II, with every Jew in the land being mobilized. The ambassador to Washington wanted his spies protected by diplomatic cover and "integrated in the routine work of the embassy,

so as to place them above suspicion." The Israeli minister to Bu-
charest wanted his spies to work along the lines of the KGB—and
to be as ruthless. Israel's minister in Buenos Aires demanded that
agents concentrate on the role of the Catholic Church in helping
Nazis to settle in Argentina. Ben-Gurion had patiently listened to
every proposal.

Finally, on March 2, 1951, he summoned the heads of the five
intelligence agencies to his office. He told them that he intended
to place Israel's intelligence-gathering activities abroad in a new
agency called Ha Mossad le Teum, "the Institute for Coordina-
tion." It would have an initial budget of twenty thousand Israeli
pounds, of which five thousand pounds would be spent on "special
missions, but only with my prior approval." The new agency would
draw its personnel from the existing intelligence agencies. In every-
day usage the new agency would be called only Mossad.

Mossad "for all administrative and political purposes" would
come under the jurisdiction of the foreign ministry. However, it
would have on its staff senior officers representing the other organizations within the Israeli intelligence community: Shin Bet, internal security; Aman, military intelligence; air force intelligence;
and naval intelligence. The functions of the officers would be to
keep Mossad informed of the specific requirements of their "clients." In the event of disagreement over any request, the matter
would be referred to the prime minister's office.

In his usual blunt way Ben-Gurion spelled it out. "You will give
Mossad your shopping list. Mossad will then go and get the goods.
It is not your business to know where they shopped or what they
paid for the goods."

Ben-Gurion would act as a one-man oversight committee for the
new service. In a memo to its first chief, Reuven Shiloah, the prime
minister ordered "Mossad will work under me, will operate according to my instructions and will report to me constantly."

The ground rules had been set.

Twenty-eight eventful years after those Jews had sat through the
Jerusalem night in September 1929 discussing the vital importance
of intelligence to ward off further Arab attacks, their descendants
had an intelligence service that would become more formidable
than any other in the world.

The birth of Mossad, like that of Israel, was anything but smooth. The service had taken over a spy ring in Iraq that had been operating for some years under the control of the Israel Defense Forces' Political Department. The prime function of the ring was to penetrate the upper echelons of the Iraqi military and run a clandestine immigration network to bring Iraqi Jews out of the country to Israel.

In May 1951, just nine weeks after Ben-Gurion signed the order creating Mossad, Iraqi security agents in Baghdad swooped down on the ring. Two Israeli agents were arrested, along with dozens of Iraqi Jews and Arabs who had been bribed to run the escape network, which extended across the Middle East. Twenty-eight people were charged with espionage. Both agents were condemned to death, seventeen were given life sentences, and the others were freed "as an example of the fairness of Iraqi justice."

Both Mossad agents were subsequently released from an Iraqi jail, where they had been severely tortured, in exchange for a substantial sum of money paid into the Swiss bank account of the Iraqi minister of the interior.

Another debacle swiftly followed. The Political Department's longtime spy in Rome, Theodore Gross, now worked for Mossad under the new setup. In January 1952, Isser Harel, then head of Shin Bet, Israel's internal security service, received "incontrovertible proof" that Gross was a double agent, on the payroll of the Egyptian secret service. Harel decided to fly to Rome, where he persuaded Gross to return with him to Tel Aviv, convincing the traitor that he was about to be given a senior post in Shin Bet. Gross was tried in secret, convicted, and sentenced to fifteen years in jail. He would die in prison.

A crestfallen Reuven Shiloah resigned, a broken man. He was replaced by Harel, who would remain Mossad's chief for eleven years, a tenure never equaled.

Senior staff who welcomed him to Mossad headquarters on that September morning in 1952 could hardly have been impressed with Harel's physical appearance. He was barely four feet eight inches tall, with jug ears, and he spoke Hebrew with a heavy central European accent; his family had emigrated from Latvia in 1930. His clothes looked as if he had slept in them.

His first words to the assembled staff were: "The past is over. There will be no more mistakes. We will go forward together. We talk to no one except ourselves."

That same day he gave an example of what he meant. After lunch he summoned his driver. When the man asked where they were going, he was told the destination was a secret; dismissing the driver, Harel set off by himself at the wheel of the car. He returned with a box of bagels for the staff. But the point had been made. He would ask the questions.

That was the defining moment that endeared Harel to his demoralized staff. He set about energizing them with his own example. He traveled secretly to hostile Arab countries to personally organize Mossad networks. He interviewed every person who wanted to join the service. He looked for those who, like him, had a kibbutz background.

"People like that know our enemy," he told a senior aide who questioned the policy. "The kibbutzniks live close to the Arabs. They have learned not only to think like them—but think faster."

Harel's patience was as legendary as his bursts of anger; his loyalty to his staff became equally renowned. All those outside his closed circle were looked upon with suspicion as "unprincipled opportunists." He had no dealings with persons he saw as "bigots masquerading as nationalists, particularly in religion." Increasingly he showed an open dislike for Orthodox Jews.

There were a number of them in Ben-Gurion's government and they quickly came to resent Isser Harel, then tried to find a way to remove him. But the wily Mossad chief made sure he remained close to another kibbutznik, the prime minister.

It helped that Mossad's record now spoke for itself. Harel's agents had contributed to the success of the Sinai skirmishes against the Egyptians. He had spies in place in every Arab capital, providing a steady stream of priceless information. Another coup came when he traveled to Washington in 1954 to meet Allen Dulles, who had just taken over the CIA. Harel presented the veteran spymaster with a dagger bearing the engraved word of the psalmist: "the Guardian of Israel neither slumbers or sleeps."

Dulles replied: "You can count on me to stay awake with you."

Those words created a partnership between Mossad and the CIA. Dulles arranged for Mossad to have state-of-the-art equipment: listening and tracking devices, remote-operated cameras, and a range of gadgets that Harel admitted he never knew existed. The two men also formed the first intelligence "back channel" between their services, through which they could communicate by secure phone in the case of any emergency. The channel effectively bypassed the normal diplomatic route, to the chagrin of both the State Department and the Israeli foreign ministry. It did nothing to improve Harel's standing in diplomatic circles.

In 1961 Harel masterminded the operation to bring to Israel thousands of Moroccan Jews. A year later the tireless Mossad chief was in southern Sudan assisting pro-Israeli rebels against the regime. That same year he also helped King Haile Selassie of Ethiopia crush an attempted coup: the monarch had been a longtime ally of Israel.

But at home the Orthodox Jews in the cabinet were becoming more vociferous, complaining that Isser Harel had become insufferably autocratic and increasingly indifferent to their religious sensibilities, and that he was a man with his own agenda, perhaps even an aspiration to the highest political office in the land. Ben-Gurion's well-tuned political antenna was up, and relations between him and Harel cooled. Where before he had given Harel a virtual free hand, he now began to demand to be briefed on the smallest details of an operation. Harel resented the tight leash but said nothing. The whispering campaign against him intensified.

In February 1962, the innuendos coalesced over the fate of an eight-year-old boy, Joselle Schumacher. Two years before, the child had been kidnapped from his parents by an ultra-Orthodox sect.

The boy's maternal grandfather, Nahman Shtarkes, was a member of the sect Neturei Karta, the "Guardians of the Walls of Jerusalem." He was suspected of complicity in the kidnapping. Already there had been a huge police hunt for Joselle that had produced no clue as to his whereabouts. Nahman had been briefly imprisoned when he had refused to cooperate with the investigation. Orthodox Jews had turned the old man into a martyr; thousands had paraded with banners proclaiming Ben-Gurion to be no different from the Nazis, imprisoning an old man. Nahman had been released on "health grounds." The protests had continued.

Ben-Gurion's political advisers warned that the matter could lose him the next election. Worse, in the event of another war with the Arabs, some Orthodox groups could actually support them. The embattled prime minister had sent for Harel and ordered Mossad to find the boy. Harel argued it was not a task for the service. In his later words:

"The atmosphere turned to ice. He repeated he was giving me an order. I said I needed at least to read the police file. The prime minister said I had an hour."

The file was large but, as he read it, something stirred deep in Isser Harel—the right of parents to bring up their child without being pressured by extreme religious belief.

Joselle had been born in March 1953 to Arthur and Ida Schumacher. Due to family financial difficulties, Joselle had been sent to live with his grandfather in Jerusalem. The child found himself in a religious enclave, spiritually isolated from the rest of the city. Increasingly Nahman inducted his grandson into the sect's ways. When Joselle's parents visited, Nahman angrily criticized them for what he saw as their own wayward religious attitudes.

The old man belonged to a generation whose faith helped them survive the Holocaust. Nahman's daughter and son-in-law felt their prime role was to create a life for themselves in the young nation. All too often prayer had to take second place.

Tired of Nahman's constant criticism, Joselle's parents said they wanted him back. Nahman objected, arguing that to move him would disrupt Joselle's instruction into a prayer life that would serve him as an adult. There were more angry exchanges. Then, the next time they visited Jerusalem, Joselle had disappeared.

Both Orthodox and secular Jews had seized upon the incident to give full vent to an issue that continued to divide the nation, and was exemplified by Ben-Gurion's Labor Party only being able to survive in office by cobbling together various religious factions in the Knesset. In turn, those groups had obtained further concessions for the strict laws of Orthodoxy. But always they wanted more. Liberal Jews demanded that Joselle must be returned to his family.

Having read the file, Isser Harel told Ben-Gurion he would mobilize Mossad's resources. He put together a team, forty agents strong, to locate Joselle. Many of them were openly opposed to what they saw as a misuse of their skills.

He silenced their criticism with a short speech:

"Although we will be operating outside our normal type of target, this is still a very important case. It is important because of its social and religious background. It is important because the prestige and authority of our government are at stake. It is important because of the human issues which the case involves."

In the first weeks of the investigation the team soon discovered how formidable the investigation would be.

A future head of Shin Bet, then a Mossad agent, grew the curly sidelocks of the ultra-Orthodox and tried to penetrate their ranks. He failed. Another Mossad agent was ordered to maintain surveillance on a Jewish school. He was spotted within days. A third agent tried to infiltrate a group of Hasidic mourners traveling to Jerusalem to bury a relative within the walls of the city. He was quickly unmasked when he failed to utter the right prayers.

Those failures only made Harel more determined. He told his team he was certain the child was no longer in Israel but somewhere in Europe or even farther afield. Harel moved his operations headquarters to a Mossad safe house in Paris. From there he sent men into every Orthodox community in Italy, Austria, France, and Britain. When that produced nothing, he sent the agents to South America and the United States.

The investigation continued to be enlivened with bizarre episodes. Ten Mossad agents joined a Saturday-morning service at a synagogue in the London suburb of Hendon. The furious congregation called the police to arrest the "religious impostors" after their false beards came unstuck during scuffles. The agents were quietly released after the Israeli ambassador intervened with the Home Office. A venerated Orthodox rabbi was invited to Paris on the pretext that a member of a wealthy family wished him to officiate at a circumcision. He was met at the airport by two men dressed in the severe black coats and hats of Orthodox Jews. They were Mossad agents. Their report had an element of black comedy.

"He was taken to a Pigalle brothel, having no idea what it was. Two prostitutes who had been paid by us suddenly appeared and were all over the rabbi. We took Polaroid photographs and showed them to him and said we would send them to his congregation unless he revealed where the boy was. The rabbi finally convinced us he had no idea and we destroyed the photographs in front of him."

Another rabbi, Shai Freyer, surfaced in Isser Harel's ever-expanding search through the world of Orthodox Jewry. The rabbi was picked up by Mossad agents as he traveled between Paris and Geneva. When they became convinced, after rigorous questioning, that once more this was another dead end, Harel ordered Freyer to be held a prisoner in a Mossad safe house in Switzerland until the search ended. He feared the rabbi would alert the Orthodox community.

Another promising lead appeared. She was Madeleine Frei, the daughter of an aristocratic French family and a heroine of the French Resistance in World War II. Madeleine had saved a large number of Jewish children from deportation to the Nazi death camps. After the war she had converted to Judaism.

Checks revealed she was a regular visitor to Israel, spending her time with members of the Neturei Karta sect, and on several occasions she had met Joselle's grandfather. Her last visit to Israel had been around the time of the boy's abduction. Madeleine had not returned to Israel since then.

In August 1962, Mossad agents tracked her to the outskirts of Paris. When they introduced themselves, she physically attacked them. One of the agents summoned Isser Harel.

He explained to Madeleine "the great wrong" done to Joselle's parents. They had the moral right to bring up their son as they wished. No parents should be denied that right. Madeleine still insisted she knew nothing about Joselle. Harel saw his own men believed her.

He asked for Madeleine's passport. Beneath her photograph was one of her daughter. He asked an agent to bring him a photograph of Joselle. The facial structures of the children in both photographs were almost identical. Harel called Tel Aviv. Within a couple of hours:

"I had everything I needed to know, from details of her love life during her student days to her decision to join the Ortho-dox movement after renouncing her Catholic faith. I went back to Madeleine and told her, as if I knew everything, that she had dyed Joselle's hair to disguise him and smuggled the boy out of Israel. She flatly denied it. I said she must understand that the future of the country she loved was in grave danger, that in the streets of Jerusalem people she loved were throwing stones at each other. Still she refused to admit anything. I said the boy had a mother who loved him as much as she loved all those children she had helped in World War Two."

The reminder worked. Suddenly Madeleine began to explain how she had traveled by sea to Haifa, a tourist come to see Israel. On the boat she made friends with a family of new immigrants who had a child about the age of Joselle. She had led the little girl down the gangplank at Haifa, and the immigration officer had taken the child as Madeleine's own. He made a note of this in his records. A week later, under the very noses of Israeli police, she had boarded a flight to Zurich with her "daughter." Madeleine had even persuaded Joselle to dress in girl's clothing and have his hair dyed.

For a while Joselle had lived in an Orthodox school in Switzerland where Rabbi Shai Freyer was a teacher. Following his detention, Madeleine flew with Joselle to New York, placing him with a family who were members of the Neturei Karta sect. Harel only had one more question for her: "Will you give me the name and address of the family?"

For a long moment there was silence before Madeleine calmly said: "He is living at 126 Penn Street, Brooklyn, New York. He is known as Yankale Gertner."

For the first time since their encounter, Harel smiled. "Thank you, Madeleine. I would like to congratulate you by offering you a job with Mossad. Your kind of talent could serve Israel well."

Madeleine refused.

Mossad agents flew to New York. Waiting for them was a team of FBI agents, authorized to cooperate by U.S. Attorney General Robert Kennedy. He had received a personal request from Ben-Gurion to do so. The agents traveled to the apartment house at 126 Penn Street. Mrs. Gertner opened the door. The agents rushed past her. Inside, her husband was praying. Beside him was a pale-faced boy with a yarmulke on his head and dark side-curls framing his face.

"Hello Joselle. We have come to take you home," one of the Mossad men said gently.

Eight months had passed since Mossad had begun its search. Close to a million U.S. dollars had been spent on the operation.

The safe return of Joselle did nothing to bridge the religious divide within the country. Successive governments would continue to totter and fall at the whim of small ultra-Orthodox groups elected to the Knesset.

Successful though he had been in finding the boy, Isser Harel returned to Israel to face a powerful new critic, General Meir Amit, the newly appointed chief of Aman, military intelligence. Just as Harel had connived against his predecessor, he now found himself on the receiving end of Amit's barbed criticisms over the operation to rescue Joselle.

Amit, a formidable field commander, had become close to Ben-Gurion in the ever-shifting political sands of Israel. He told the prime minister that Harel had "wasted resources," that the whole rescue operation had been the sign of an intelligence chief who had been too long in the job. Forgetting that he had ordered Harel to mount the operation, Ben-Gurion agreed. On March 25, 1963, bruised by many weeks of intensive sniping, Isser Harel, at the age of fifty, resigned. Grown men were close to tears as he shook their hands and walked out of Mossad headquarters. Everyone knew it was the end of an era.

Hours later a tall, spare man with the hawkish good looks of the actor he could once have been strode briskly through its doors: Meir Amit had taken over. No one needed to be told that radical changes were about to happen.

Fifteen minutes after settling himself behind his desk, Mossad's new chief summoned his department heads. They stood in a group before him while he silently eyeballed them. Then, in the brisk voice that had launched countless battleground attacks, he spoke.

There would be no more operations to recover lost children. No undue political interference. He would protect each one of them from external criticism, but nothing could save their jobs if they failed him. He would fight for more money from the defense budget for the latest equipment and backup resources. But that was not a signal to forget the one asset he placed above all others: *humint,* the art of human intelligence gathering. He wanted that to be Mossad's greatest skill.

His staff found they were working for a man who saw their work as beyond day-to-day operations, but bearing results in years to come. The acquisition of military technology fell into that category.

Shortly after Meir Amit took command, a man who gave his name as "Salman" had walked into the Israeli embassy in Paris with an astounding proposition. For one million U.S. dollars in cash he could guarantee to provide what was then the world's most secret combat aircraft, the Russian MiG-21. Salman had concluded his astounding offer to an Israeli diplomat with a bizarre request. "Send someone to Baghdad, call this number, and ask for Joseph. And have our million dollars ready."

The diplomat sent his report to the resident katsa in the embassy. He had been one of those who had survived the purging that followed Meir Amit's appointment. The katsa sent the report to Tel Aviv, together with the phone number Salman had provided.

For days Meir Amit weighed and considered. Salman could be a confidence trickster or a fantasist, or even part of an Iraqi plot to try to entrap a Mossad agent. There was a very real risk that other katsas working under deep cover in Iraq would be compromised. But the prospect of getting hold of a MiG-21 was irresistible.

Its fuel capacity, altitude, speed, armaments, and turnaround servicing time had made it the Arab world's premier frontline fighter aircraft. Israel's air force chiefs would cheerfully have given many millions of dollars for just a glimpse of the MiG's blueprint, let alone for the actual plane. Meir Amit "went to bed thinking of it. I woke up thinking of it. I thought of it in the shower, over dinner. I thought about it every spare moment I had. Keeping up with an enemy's advanced weapons system is a priority with any intelligence service. Actually getting your hands on it almost never happens."

The first step was to send an agent to Baghdad. Meir Amit created an alias for him, as English as the name in his passport, George Bacon: "No one would think a Jew would have a name like that." Bacon would travel to Baghdad as the sales manager of a London-based company selling hospital X-ray equipment.

He arrived in Baghdad on an Iraqi Airways flight with several sample boxes of equipment and demonstrated how well he had absorbed his brief by selling several items to hospitals. At the beginning of his second week, Bacon made the call to the number Salman had provided. Bacon's reports to Mossad contained vivid descriptions.

"I used a pay phone in the hotel lobby. The risk the phone was tapped was smaller than making the call from my room. The number was answered at once. A voice asked in Farsi who was speaking. I replied in English, apologizing I must have the wrong number. The voice then asked, also in English, who was speaking. I said I was a friend of Joseph's. Was there someone there by that name? I was told to wait. I thought maybe they were tracing the call, that this was a trap after all. Then a very cultured voice was on the line saying he was Joseph and that he was glad I had called. He then asked if I knew Paris. I thought: Contact!"

Bacon found himself agreeing to a meeting in a Baghdad coffeehouse the following noon. At the appointed hour, a man smilingly introduced himself as Joseph. His face was deeply etched, his hair white. The agent's later report once more captured the surreal atmosphere of the moment:

"Joseph said how very pleased he was to see me, as if I was some long-awaited relative. He then started to talk about the weather and how the quality of service had dropped in cafés like this one. I thought, here I am in the middle of a hostile country whose security service would surely kill me if they had the chance, listening to an old man's ramblings. I decided whoever he was, whatever his connection was with Salman in Paris, Joseph was certainly not an Iraqi counterintelligence officer. That calmed me. I told him my friends were very interested in the merchandise his friend had mentioned. He replied, 'Salman is my nephew who lives in Paris. He is a waiter at a café. All the good waiters have left here.' Joseph then leaned across the table and said, 'You have come about the MiG? I can arrange it for you. But it will cost one million dollars.' Just like that."

Bacon sensed that perhaps, after all, Joseph was more than he appeared. There was a quiet certainty about him. But as he began to question him, the old man shook his head. "Not here. People could be listening."

They arranged to meet again the following day on a park bench along the Euphrates River, which flowed through the city. That night Bacon slept very little wondering if, after all, he was being slowly hooked, if not by Iraqi intelligence, then by some very clever con men who were using Joseph as a front.

The next day's meeting revealed a little more of Joseph's background and motives.

He came from a poor Iraqi Jewish family. As a boy he had been employed as a servant by a rich Marionite Christian family in Baghdad. Then, after thirty years of loyal service, he had been abruptly dismissed, wrongly accused of stealing food. He found himself, on his fiftieth birthday, cast out into the streets. Too old to find other work, he existed on a modest pension. He had also decided to seek out his Jewish roots. He discussed his quest with his widowed sister, Manu, whose son, Munir, was a pilot in the Iraqi air force. Manu admitted she too had a strong desire to go to Israel. But how could they possibly do that? Even to mention the idea was to risk imprisonment in Iraq. To leave anyone behind would guarantee the authorities would punish them severely, perhaps even kill them. And where would the money come from? She had sighed and said it was all an impossible dream.

But in Joseph's mind the idea took hold. Over dinner Munir had often told how his commander boasted that Israel would pay a fortune for one of the MiGs he flew, "perhaps even a million U.S. dollars, Uncle Joseph."

The sum had focused Joseph. He could bribe officials, organize an escape route. With that money he could somehow move the entire family out of Iraq. The more he thought about it, the more feasible it became. Munir loved his mother; he would do anything for her—even stealing his plane for a million dollars. And there would be no need for Joseph to have to organize the family's escape. He would let the Israelis do that. Everyone knew they were clever at such things. That was why he had sent Salman to the embassy.

"And now you are here, my friend!" Joseph beamed at Bacon.

"What about Munir? Does he know any of this?"

"Oh, yes. He has agreed to steal the MiG. But he wants half the money down now, then the balance delivered just before he does so."

Bacon was astounded. Everything he had heard sounded both genuine and feasible. But first he had to report to Meir Amit.

In Tel Aviv, the Mossad chief listened for an entire afternoon while Bacon reported every detail.

"Where does Joseph want to be paid?" Meir Amit finally asked.

"Into a Swiss bank. Joseph has a cousin who needs urgent medical treatment not available in Baghdad. The Iraqi authorities will give him permission to go to Switzerland. When he arrives, he expects to have the money already deposited by us."

"A resourceful man, your Joseph," Meir Amit commented wryly. "Once the money is in that account, we'll never get it back."

He put one more question to Bacon. "Why do you trust Joseph?"

Bacon replied. "I trust him because it is the only choice."

Meir Amit authorized half a million U.S. dollars should be deposited in the main branch of Credit Suisse in Geneva. He was gambling more than money. He knew he could not survive if Joseph turned out to be the brilliant fraud some Mossad officers still believed he was.

The time had come to brief Prime Minister Ben-Gurion and his chief of staff, Yitzhak Rabin. Both men green-lighted the operation. Meir Amit had not told them he had taken one more step—withdrawing the entire Mossad network from Iraq.

"If the mission failed, I didn't want anyone's head on the block except my own. I set up five teams. The first team was the communications link between Baghdad and me. They would break radio silence only if there was a crisis. Otherwise I didn't want to hear from them. The second team was to be in Baghdad without anyone knowing. Not Bacon, not the first team, no one. They were there to get Bacon out of the country if there was trouble, and Joseph, too, if possible. The third team was to keep an eye on the family. The fourth team was to liaise with the Kurds who would help in the last stages of getting the family out. Israel was supplying them with arms. The fifth team was to liaise with Washington and Turkey. For the MiG to be flown out of Iraq, it would have to fly over Turkish air space to reach us. Washington, who had bases in northern Turkey, would have to persuade the Turks to cooperate by saying the MiG was going to end up in the United States. I now knew that the Iraqis feared the possibility of a pilot defecting to the West, so they kept fuel tanks only half-full. That was something we could do nothing about."

There were still other problems. Joseph had decided that not only his immediate family but distant cousins should have the opportunity of escaping from the harsh Iraqi regime. In all he wanted forty-three persons to be airlifted to safety.

Meir Amit agreed—only to face a new worry. From Baghdad, Bacon sent a coded message that Munir was having second thoughts. The Mossad chief "sensed what was happening. Munir was first and foremost an Iraqi. Iraq had been good to him. Betraying his country to Israel did not sit well. We were the enemy. All his life he had been taught that. I decided the only way was to convince him the MiG would go straight to America. So I flew to Washington and saw Richard Helms, then DCI [director of the Central Intelligence Agency]. He listened and said no problem. He was always very good like that. He arranged for the U.S. military attaché in Baghdad to meet Munir. The attaché confirmed the plane would be handed over to the United States. He gave Munir a lot of talk about helping America catch up with the Russians. Munir bought it and agreed to go ahead."

The operation now took on a pace of its own. Joseph's relative received his Iraqi exit permit and flew to Geneva. From there he sent a postcard: "The hospital facilities are excellent. I am assured of a total recovery." The message was the signal that the second five hundred thousand dollars had been deposited.

Reassured, Joseph told Bacon the family were ready. On the night before Munir would make his flight, Joseph led them in a convoy of vehicles north, to the cool of the mountains. Iraqi checkpoints did not trouble them; residents moved every summer away from the stifling heat of Baghdad. In the foothills Kurds waited with the Israeli liaison team. They led the family deep into the mountains, where Turkish air force helicopters were waiting. Flying below radar, they crossed back into Turkey.

An Israeli agent made a call to Munir telling him his sister had safely delivered a baby girl. Another coded signal had been safely transmitted.

Next morning, August 15, 1966, at sunup, Munir took off for a practice mission. Clear of the airfield he kicked in the MiG's afterburners and was over the border with Turkey before other Iraqi pilots could be instructed to shoot him down. Escorted by U.S. Air

Force Phantoms, Munir landed at a Turkish air base, refueled, and took off again. Through his headphones he heard the message, in plain talk this time. "All your family are safe and on the way to join you."

An hour later the MiG touched down at a military air base in northern Israel.

Mossad had become a serious player on the world stage. Within the Israeli intelligence community the way matters were conducted in the future would be known as "BA"—before Amit—or "AM"—after Meir.

CHAPTER 3

ENGRAVINGS OF GLILOT

Exiting the highway north of Tel Aviv, Meir Amit continued to maintain his speed at a little above the speed limit. Discreetly bucking the system had continued to be part of his life since, almost forty years before, he had masterminded the theft of an Iraqi jet.

He put down blindly refusing to follow the rule book as stemming from his Galilean background: "We are a stubborn lot." He had been born in King Herod's favorite city, Tiberias, close to the shore of the Sea of Galilee, and spent most of his early life on a kibbutz. Long ago all traces of the region's flat accent had been smoothed away by his mother, an elocution teacher. She had also instilled her son's sense of independence, his refusal to tolerate fools, and a barely concealed contempt for city dwellers. Most important of all, she had encouraged his analytical skills and ability to think laterally.

In his long career he had used those qualities to discover an enemy's intention. Often action could not wait for certainty, and motive and deception had been at the center of his work. At times his critics in the Israeli intelligence community had been concerned at what they saw as his imaginative leaps. He had one answer for them all: Read the case file on the stolen MiG.

On this March morning in 1997, as he continued to drive out of Tel Aviv, Meir Amit was officially on the retired list. But no one in Israeli intelligence believed that was the case; his vast knowledge was too valuable to be put in cold storage.

The previous day Meir Amit had returned from Ho Chi Minh City, where he had visited former Vietcong intelligence officers. They had swapped experiences and had found common ground over besting superior opposition: the Vietnamese against the Americans, Israel fighting the Arabs. Meir Amit had made other trips to places where his secret maneuvers had once created havoc: Amman, Cairo, Moscow. No one dared to question the purpose of these visits, just as during his five momentous years as director general of Mossad—1963–68—no one had mounted a successful challenge over his sources or methods.

In that period he had turned humint, human intelligence gathering, into an art form. No other intelligence agency had been able to match his agents on the ground in collecting information. He had placed spies in ever greater numbers in every Arab country, across Europe, down into South America, throughout Africa, and in the United States. His katsas had penetrated the Jordanian *Mukabarat*, the best of the Arab intelligence services, and Syrian military intelligence, the most cruel. They were men of cool nerve and steel resolve that no novelist would have dared to invent.

Soon after he became director general, Meir Amit circulated within the service a memo stolen by an agent from Yasser Arafat's office:

"Mossad has a dossier on each of us. They know our names and addresses. We know there are two photographs with each of our files. One is a copy of how we look without a kaffiyeh and the other wearing one. So the Mossad have no difficulty tracking us down with or without our headdresses."

To create further fear, Meir Amit had recruited an unprecedented number of Arab informers. He worked on the principle that by the law of averages he would discover a sufficient number who would be useful. Bribed Arabs had betrayed PLO gunmen and revealed their arms caches, safe houses, and travel arrangements. For each terrorist killed by Mossad, Meir Amit paid an informer a bonus of one U.S. dollar.

In the run-up to the Six Day War in 1967, there was either a Mossad katsa or an informer inside every Egyptian air base and military headquarters. There were no fewer than three in the General High Command headquarters in Cairo, staff officers who had been persuaded by Meir Amit. How he had done so had remained his closely guarded secret: "There are some matters best left that way."

To each informer and agent in place he had given the same instruction: as well as "the big picture," he wanted "the small details. How far did a pilot have to walk from his barracks to the mess for his meals? How long was a staff officer held up in the notorious Cairo traffic jam? Did a key planner have a mistress?" Only he fully understood how such disparate matters would be used.

One katsa had managed to get himself a job as a waiter in the officers' mess in a frontline fighter base. Every week he provided details of aircraft readiness and the lifestyle of pilots and technicians. Their drinking habits and sexual pleasures were among the information secretly radioed to Tel Aviv.

Mossad's newly created Department of Psychological Warfare, Loh Amma Psichologit (LAP), worked around the clock preparing files on Egyptian fliers, ground crew, and staff officers: their flying skills, whether they had achieved their rank through ability or influence, who had a drink problem, frequented a brothel, had a predilection for boys.

Well into the night, Meir Amit pored over the files, looking for weaknesses, for men who could be blackmailed into working for him. "It was not a pleasant task but intelligence is often a dirty business."

Egyptian families of servicemen began to receive anonymous letters posted in Cairo giving explicit details of their loved one's behavior. Informers reported back to Tel Aviv details of family rows that led to aircrew going on sick leave. Staff officers had anonymous phone calls giving information about a colleague's private life. A teacher at school was called by a sympathetic-sounding woman to be told that the only reason a pupil was doing badly was because her father, a senior officer, had a secret male lover; the call led to the officer shooting himself. This relentless campaign caused considerable dissension within the Egyptian military and brought great satisfaction to Meir Amit.

By early 1967, it became clear from all the evidence his Egyptian network was producing that the country's leader, Gamal Abdel Nasser, was preparing for war against Israel. More informers were recruited by fair means or foul, helping Mossad to know as much about the Egyptian air force and its military command as did Cairo.

By early May 1967 he was able to give Israel's air force commanders the precise time of day they should launch a knockout strike against the Egyptian air bases. Mossad's analysts had produced a remarkable blueprint of life on all Egyptian air bases.

Between 7:30 A.M. and 7:45 A.M. airfield radar units were at their most vulnerable. In those fifteen minutes the outgoing night staff were tired after their long shift, while their incoming replacements were not yet fully alert, and were often late in taking over due to slow service in the mess halls. Pilots breakfasted between 7:15 A.M. and 7:45 A.M. Afterward they usually walked back to their barracks to collect their flying gear. The average journey took ten minutes. Most fliers spent a further few minutes in the toilets before going to the flight lines. They arrived there around 8:00 A.M., the official start to the day. By then ground crew had begun to roll out aircraft from their hangars to be fueled and armed. For the next fifteen minutes the flight lines were crammed with fuel trucks and ammunition trucks.

A similar detailed itinerary was prepared for the movements of staff officers in the Cairo High Command. The average officer took thirty minutes to drive to work from his house in one of the suburbs. Strategic planners were often not at their desks before 8:15 A.M. They usually spent a further ten minutes settling in, sipping coffee, and gossiping with colleagues. The average staff officer did not properly start studying overnight signals traffic from the fighter bases until close to 8:30 A.M.

Meir Amit told the Israeli air force commander that the time their aircraft must be over their targets should be between 8:00 A.M. and 8:30 A.M. In those thirty minutes they would be able to pulverize enemy bases, knowing that the Cairo High Command would be without many of its key personnel to direct the fight back.

On June 5, 1967, Israel's air force struck at precisely 8:01 A.M. with deadly effect, sweeping in low over the Sinai to bomb and strafe at will. In moments the sky turned reddish black with the flames from burning fuel trucks and exploding ammunition and aircraft.

In Tel Aviv, Meir Amit sat looking out of his office window toward the south, knowing his intelligence analysts had virtually settled the outcome of the war. It was one of the most stunning examples of his extraordinary skills—and even more remarkable given the numerical size of Mossad.

From the time he took over, Meir Amit had resisted attempts to turn Mossad into a version of the CIA or KGB. Those services between them employed hundreds of thousands of analysts, scientists, strategists, and planners to support their field agents. The Iraqis and Iranians had an estimated ten thousand field agents; even the Cuban DGI possessed close to a thousand spies in the field.

But Meir Amit had insisted that Mossad's permanent total staff would number little more than twelve hundred. Each would be handpicked and have multiple skills: a scientist must be able to work in the field should the need arise; a katsa must be able to use his specialist skills to train others.

To them all he would be the *memune*, which roughly translates from Hebrew as "first among equals." With the title came unfettered access to the prime minister of the day and the annual ritual of presenting his budget for the Israeli cabinet to rubber-stamp.

Long before the Six Day War he had established Mossad's ability to strike mortal terror into Israel's enemies, penetrating their ranks, vacuuming up their secrets, and killing them with chilling efficiency. He had soon made Mossad mythic in stature.

Much of that success came from the rules he laid down for selecting katsas, the field agents who, ultimately, were at the cutting edge of Mossad's success. He fully understood the deep and complex motives that allowed them, upon selection, to shake his hand, the gesture that acknowledged they were now his to command as he wished.

While much else had changed in Mossad, Meir Amit knew on that March morning in 1997 that his recruiting criteria had remained intact:

No katsa is accepted into Mossad who is primarily motivated by money. The overly zealous Zionist has no place in this work. It gets in the way of a clear understanding of what the job is all about. It is one that calls for calm, clear, farsighted judgment and a balanced outlook. People want to join Mossad for all kinds of reasons. There is the so-called glamour. Some like the idea of adventure. Some think joining will enhance their status, small people who want to be big. A few want the secret power they believe being in Mossad would give them. None of these are acceptable reasons for joining.

And always, always, you must ensure your man in the field knows he has your total support. That you will look out for his family, make sure his kids are happy. At the same time you must protect him. If his wife starts to wonder if he has another woman reassure her he has not. If he has, don't tell her. If she goes off the rails, bring her back on the straight and narrow. Don't tell her husband. You want nothing to distract him. The job of a good spymaster is to treat his people as family. Make them feel he is always there for them, day, night, no matter what the time. This is how you buy loyalty, make your katsa do what you want. And in the end what you want is important.

Each katsa underwent three years of intensive training, including being subjected to severe physical violence under interrogation. He, or she, became proficient in the use of Mossad's weapon of choice—the .22 caliber Beretta.

The first katsas stationed outside the Arab countries were in the United States, Britain, France, and Germany. In the United States there were permanent katsas in New York and Washington. The New York katsa had special responsibility for penetrating all UN diplomatic missions and the city's many ethnic groups. The Washington katsa had a similar job, with the additional responsibility of "monitoring" the White House.

Other katsas operated in areas of current tensions, returning home when a mission ended.

Meir Amit had also considerably expanded the organization to include a Collections Department responsible for intelligence-gathering operations abroad and a Political Action and Liaison Department, working with so-called friendly foreign intelligence services, mostly the CIA and Britain's M16. The Research Department had fifteen sections or "desks" targeting Arab states. The United States, Canada, Latin America, Britain, Europe, and the Soviet Union all had their separate desks. This infrastructure would, over the years, expand to include China, South Africa, and the Vatican. But essentially Mossad would remain the same small organization.

A day did not pass without the arrival of a fresh sheaf of news stories from overseas stations. These were circulated throughout the drab gray high-rise building on King Saul Boulevard. In Meir Amit's view, "If it made someone walk a little taller, that was no bad thing. And, of course, it made our enemies that more fearful."

Mossad's katsas were coldly efficient and cunning beyond belief—and prepared to fight fire with fire. Operatives incited disturbances designed to create mutual distrust among Arab states, planted black counterpropaganda, and recruited informers, implementing Meir Amit's philosophy: "Divided, we rule." In all they did, his men set new standards for cold-blooded professionalism, moving like thieves in the night leaving a trail of death and destruction. No one was safe from their retaliation.

A mission completed they returned to be debriefed in Meir Amit's corner-window office overlooking the broad thoroughfare named after Israel's Old Testament warlord. From his office he personally ran two spies whose bravery would remain without equal in the annals of Mossad. Recalling their contributions, his voice became tentative, the occasional smile one of apologetic self-protection, as he began by recounting biographical details.

Eli Cohen was born in Alexandria, Egypt, on December 16, 1924. Like his parents, he was a devout Orthodox Jew. In December 1956 he was among Jews expelled from Egypt after the Suez crisis. He arrived in Haifa and felt himself a stranger in his new land. In 1957 he was recruited into Israeli military counterintelligence, but his work as an analyst bored him. He began to inquire how he could join Mossad, but was rejected. Meir Amit recalled, "We heard that our rejection had deeply offended Eli Cohen. He resigned from the army and married an Iraqi woman named Nadia."

For two years Cohen led an uneventful life as a filing clerk in a Tel Aviv insurance office. Unknown to him, his background had surfaced in a trawl through Mossad's "reject files" by Meir Amit, who was looking for a "certain kind of agent for a very special job." Finding no one suitable in the "active" files, he had gone to the "rejects." Cohen seemed the only possibility. He was put under surveillance. The weekly reports by Mossad's recruiting office described his fastidious habits and devotion to his wife and young family. He was hardworking, quick on the uptake, and worked well under pressure. Finally he was told that Mossad had decided he was "suitable" after all.

Eli began an intensive six-month course at the Mossad training school. Sabotage experts taught him how to make explosives and time bombs from the simplest of ingredients. He learned unarmed combat and became a first-class marksman and an accomplished burglar. He discovered the mysteries of encoding and decoding, how to work a radio set, use invisible inks, and hide messages. He constantly impressed his instructors with his skills. His phenomenal memory came from memorizing tracts of the Torah as a young man. His graduate report stated he had every quality needed by a katsa. Still Meir Amit hesitated.

"I asked myself a hundred times: can Eli do what I want? I always showed him, of course, my confidence was always in place. I never wanted him for a moment to think he would always be one step from the trapdoor which would send him to kingdom come. Yet some of the very best brains in Mossad put everything they knew into him. Finally I decided to run with Eli."

Meir Amit spent weeks creating a cover story for his protégé. They would sit together, studying street maps and photographs of Buenos Aires so that Cohen's new background and name, Kamil Amin Taabes, became totally familiar. The Mossad chief saw how quickly

"Eli learned the language of an exporter-importer to Syria. He memorized the difference between waybills and freight certificates, contracts and guarantees, everything he would need to know. He was like a chameleon, absorbing everything. Before my very eye, Eli Cohen faded and Taabes took over, the Syrian who had never given up a longing to go home to Damascus. Every day Eli became more confident, more certain and keen to prove he could carry off the role. He was like a world champion marathon runner, trained to peak at the start of the race. But he could be running his for years. We had done all we could to show him how to pace his new life, to live the life. The rest was up to him. We all knew that. There was no big good-bye or send-off. He just slipped out of Israel, the way all my spies went."

In the Syrian capital, Cohen quickly established himself in the business community and developed a circle of high-level friends. These included Maazi Zahreddin, nephew of Syria's president.

Zahreddin was a boastful man, eager to show how invincible Syria was. Cohen played to that. In no time he was being given a guided tour of Syria's Golan Heights fortifications. He saw the deep concrete bunkers housing the long-range artillery sent by Russia. He was even permitted to take photographs. Within hours of two hundred T-54 Russian tanks arriving in Syria, Cohen had informed Tel Aviv. He even obtained a complete blueprint of Syria's strategy to cut off northern Israel. The information was priceless.

While Cohen continued to confirm Meir Amit's belief that one field agent was worth a division of soldiers, he eventually began to become reckless. Cohen had always been a soccer fan. The day after a visiting team beat Israel in Tel Aviv, he broke the strict "Business only" rule about transmissions. He radioed his operator: "It is about time we learned to be victorious on the soccer field."

Other unauthorized messages were translated: "Please send my wife an anniversary greeting," or "Happy Birthday to my daughter."

Meir Amit was privately furious. But he understood enough of the pressures on the agent to hope Cohen's behavior was "no more than a temporary aberration often found in the best of agents. I tried to get inside his head. Was he desperate and this his way of showing it by dropping his guard? I tried to think like him, knowing I'd rewritten his life. I had to try and weigh a hundred factors. But in the end the only important one was: could Eli still do his job?"

Meir Amit decided that Cohen could.

On a January night in 1965, Eli Cohen waited in his Damascus bedroom ready to transmit. As he tuned his receiver to go, Syrian intelligence officers burst into the apartment. Cohen had been caught by one of the most advanced mobile detection units in the world—supplied by the Russians.

Under interrogation he was forced to send a message to Mossad. The Syrians failed to notice the subtle change of speed and rhythm in the radio transmission. In Tel Aviv, Meir Amit received news Eli had been captured. Two days later, Syria confirmed his capture.

"It was like losing one of your family. You ask yourself the questions you always ask when an agent is lost: Could we have saved him? How was he betrayed? By his own carelessness? By someone close to him? Was he burned-out and we didn't realize it? Did he have some kind of death wish? That, too, happens. Or was it just bad luck? You ask, and go on asking. You never get the answer for certain. But asking can be a way to cope."

At no stage did the Syrians succeed in breaking Eli Cohen— despite the torture he endured before being sentenced to death.

Meir Amit devoted almost all his time trying to save Eli Cohen. While Nadia Cohen launched a worldwide publicity campaign for her husband's life—she approached the pope, the queen of England, prime ministers, and presidents—Amit worked more secretly. He traveled to Europe to see the heads of French and German intelligence. They could do nothing. He made informal approaches to the Soviet Union. He fought on right until, on May 18, 1965, shortly after 2:00 A.M., a convoy drove out of El Maza Prison in Damascus. In one of the trucks was Eli Cohen.

With him was the eighty-year-old chief rabbi of Syria, Nissim Andabo. Overcome by what was to happen, the rabbi wept openly. Eli Cohen calmed the old man. The convoy reached El Marga Square in the center of Damascus. There Eli recited the Vidui, the Hebrew prayer of a man about to face death: "Almighty God forgive me for all my sins and transgressions."

At 3:35 A.M., watched by thousands of Syrians and in the full glare of television lights, Eli stood on the gallows.

In Tel Aviv, Nadia Cohen watched her husband die and tried to kill herself. She was taken to a hospital and her life was saved.

Next day, in a small private ceremony in his office, Meir Amit paid tribute to Eli Cohen. Then he went back to the business of running his second prized agent.

Wolfgang Lotz, a German Jew, had arrived in Palestine shortly after Hitler came to power. In 1963 Meir Amit had selected him from a shortlist of candidates for a spying mission to Egypt. While Lotz underwent the same rigorous training as Cohen, once more, Meir Amit thought carefully about his agent's cover. Amit decided to make him a riding instructor, an East German refugee who had served in the Afrika Korps in World War II and had returned to Egypt to open an equestrian academy. The job would readily give him access to Cairo's high society, which was built around the city's riding fraternity.

Soon Lotz had developed a circle of clients that included the deputy head of Egyptian military intelligence and the chief of security for the Suez Canal zone. Emulating Cohen, Lotz persuaded his newfound friends to show off Egypt's formidable defenses: its rocket launchpads in Sinai and on the Negev frontier. Lotz also obtained a complete list of Nazi scientists living in Cairo who were working in Egypt's rocket and arms programs. Soon they were systematically executed by Mossad agents.

After two years under cover, Lotz was finally arrested and convicted. The Egyptians, sensing he was too valuable to kill, kept him alive in anticipation he could be traded for Egyptian soldiers captured in a future war with Israel. Once again, Meir Amit was deeply concerned over Lotz's capture.

Meir Amit wrote to Egypt's then president, Gamal Abdel Nasser, asking him to exchange Lotz and his wife in return for Egyptian POWs Israel had captured. Nasser refused. Amit applied psychological pressure.

"I let the Egyptian prisoners know they were all being held because Nasser refused to hand over two Israelis. We allowed them to write home. Their letters made their feelings very clear."

Meir Amit wrote to Nasser again saying Israel would publicly give him all the credit for recovering his POWs and would keep quiet about the return of Lotz and his wife. Nasser still did not agree. So Amit took the matter to the United Nations commander responsible for keeping the peace in the Sinai. The officer flew to Cairo and obtained the assurance that Lotz and his wife would be set free "at some future date."

Meir Amit "understood the coded language. A month later Lotz and his wife left Cairo in complete secrecy for Geneva. A few hours later they were back in my office."

Meir Amit recognized his katsas would need support in the field. He created the *sayanim*, volunteer Jewish helpers. Each sayan was an example of the historical cohesiveness of the world Jewish community. Regardless of allegiance to his or her country, in the final analysis a sayan would recognize a greater loyalty: the mystical one to Israel, and a need to help protect it from its enemies.

Sayanim fulfilled many functions. A car sayan, running a rental agency, provided a katsa with a vehicle without the usual documentation. A letting agency sayan offered accommodation. A bank sayan might unlock funds outside normal hours. A sayan physician would give medical assistance—treating a bullet wound for example—without informing the authorities. Sayanim only received expenses for their services.

Between them they collected technical data and all kinds of "overt" intelligence: a rumor at a cocktail party, an item on the radio, a paragraph in a newspaper, a half-finished story at a dinner party. They provided leads for katsas. Without its sayanim Mossad could not operate.

Again, Meir Amit's legacy would remain, though vastly expanded. In 1998 there were over four thousand sayanim in Britain, almost four times as many in the United States; while Meir Amit had operated on a tight budget, Mossad, to maintain its worldwide operations, now spent several hundred million dollars a month maintaining its "assets," paying the expenses of sayanim, running safe houses, providing logistics and covering operational costs. He had left them one other reminder of his time as their chief: a language of their own. Its report writing system was known as *Naka*; "daylight" was the highest form of alert; a *kidon* was a member of Mossad's assassination team; a *neviot* was a specialist in surveillance; *yahalomin* was the unit that handled communications to katsas; *sa-*

fanim was the one that targeted the PLO; a *balder* was a courier; a *slick* was a secure place for documents; *teuds* were forgeries.

On that March morning in 1997, as he drove to keep a rendezvous with the past, Meir Amit knew so much had changed in Mossad. Pressured by political demands, most notably from Prime Minister Benyamin Netanyahu, Mossad had become dangerously isolated from the foreign intelligence services Meir Amit had so carefully courted. It was one thing to live by the credo "Israel first, last, and always. Always." It was quite another, as he put it, to be caught "going through the pockets of your friends." The key word was "caught," he added with another bleak smile.

An example had been Mossad's increased penetration of the United States through economic, scientific, and technological espionage. A special unit, code-named Al, Hebrew for "above," prowled through California's Silicon Valley and Boston's Route 128 for high-tech secrets. In a report to the Senate Intelligence Committee, the CIA had identified Israel as one of six foreign countries with "a government-directed, orchestrated, clandestine effort to collect U.S. economic secrets."

The president of Germany's internal intelligence organization, the Bundesamt Fur Verfassungschatz (BFD), had recently warned his department heads that Mossad remained a prime threat to steal the republic's latest computer secrets. A similar caution was issued by France's Direction Générale de La Sécurité of the (DGS) after a Mossad agent had been spotted near the Satellite Imagery Interpretative Center at Creil. Israel had long tried to increase its capability in space to match its nuclear capability on earth. Britain's counterespionage service, MI5, included in its briefing to newly elected prime minister Tony Blair details of Mossad's efforts to obtain sensitive scientific and defense data in the United Kingdom.

Meir Amit did not object, as such, to these adventures, only that they often appeared to have been carried out with a lack of planning and disregard for long-term consequences.

The same applied to how LAP's psychologists conducted their campaigns. In his days the department had built up a global network of media contacts and used them with great skill. A terrorist incident in Europe would produce a call to a news organization contact with "background" that was of sufficient interest to be worked into the story, giving it the spin LAP wanted. The unit also created information for press attachés at Israeli embassies to pass on to a journalist over a drink or dinner, when a "secret" could be quietly shared and a reputation discreetly tarnished.

While the essence of that black propaganda still remained, there was a crucial difference: the choice of a target or victim. It appeared to Meir Amit that the decision was too often predicated on political requirements: a need to divert attention from some self-serving diplomatic maneuver Israel planned to make in the Middle East, or to regain its fluctuating popularity, especially in the United States.

When Trans World Airlines Flight 800 crashed off the southeastern coast of Long Island on July 17, 1996, killing all 230 people on board, LAP began a campaign to suggest the tragedy was masterminded by Iran or Iraq, both Israel's bêtes noires. Thousands of media stories quickly perpetuated the fiction. Almost a year later, after expending some five hundred thousand dollars and ten thousand work hours, the FBI's chief investigator, James K. Kallstrom, ruled out a terrorist bomb or any evidence of a forensic crime. Privately he told colleagues, "If there was a way to nail those bastards in Tel Aviv for time wasting, I sure would like to see it happen. We had to check every item they slipped into the media."

LAP struck again after the bombing of the Atlanta Olympic Games. The fiction was spread that the bomb had "all the signs" of being manufactured by somebody who had learned his skills from the bomb makers of Lebanon's Bekáa Valley. The story took off— and LAP brought the specter of terrorism home to an understandably fearful American public. The only suspect was a hapless security guard at the Games—a man who manifestly had no connection with international terrorism—and when he was cleared, the story died.

Again, Meir Amit understood the importance of reminding the world about terrorism. But the warning "needed to be copper-fastened, something I always insisted upon." The admission was followed by a shrug, as if some inner fire blanket had doused his spark of irritation. Long ago he had learned to hide his feelings and to be vague about details; for years his strength had been in concealment.

In his mind the downward spiral of Mossad had begun when

Prime Minister Yitzhak Rabin was assassinated at a peace rally in Tel Aviv in November 1995. Shortly before Rabin was gunned down by a Jewish extremist—a further sign of the deepening malaise Meir Amit saw in Israeli society—Mossad's then director general, Shabtai Shavit, had warned Rabin's staff that there might be an attempt on his life. According to one staffer the possibility was ignored as being too vague "to constitute a definite threat."

Under Meir Amit's command Mossad still had no mandate to operate within Israel, any more than the CIA could do so within the United States. Yet, despite his criticisms, Meir Amit liked to say that Mossad had shared the destiny of Israel. Under his tenure the impact of what it did had often reverberated around the world. Much of that he put down to loyalty, a quality that now seemed to have become passé. People still did their work—as dangerous and dirty as it had always been—but they wondered if they would be held accountable not only to some superior, but to some political figure in the background. That interference could account for the paranoia that regularly surfaced and challenged the concept that Israel is a true democracy.

Beside the highway between the resort of Herzliyya and Tel Aviv is a compound bristling with antennae. This is Mossad's training school. Among the first things a new political officer, a spy, at a foreign embassy in Tel Aviv learns is the location of the dun-colored building. Yet, for an Israeli publication to reveal its existence is still to run the risk of prosecution. In 1996 there was a furious debate within the country's intelligence community about what to do when a Tel Aviv newspaper published the name of Mossad's latest director general, the austere Danny Yatom. There was talk of arresting the offending reporter and his editor. In the end nothing happened when Mossad realized Yatom's name had by then been published worldwide.

Meir Amit was firmly against such exposure: "Naming a serving chief is serious. Spying is a secret business and not a pleasant one. No matter what someone has done, you have to protect him or her from outsiders. You can deal as harshly as you think fit with him or her inside the organization. But to the outside world he or she must remain untouchable and, better yet, unaccountable and unknown."

In his tenure as director general his code name had been Ram. The word had a satisfying Old Testament ring for a boy raised in the unquenchable spirit of the early pioneers at a time when the whole of Arab Palestine was in revolt against both the British Mandate and the Jews. From boyhood he had trained his body hard. Physically slight, Meir Amit became strong and fit, sustained by a belief that this was *his* land. Eretz Israel, the land of Israel. It did not matter that the rest of the world still called it Palestine until 1947, when the United Nations proposed its partition.

The birth of a nation, Israel, was followed by its near annihilation as Arab armies tried to reclaim the land. Six thousand Jews died; no one would ever be certain how many Arabs fell. The sight of so many bodies all but completed the maturing of Meir Amit. What deepened the process was the arrival of the survivors of the Nazi death camps, each bearing a hideous blue tattoo branded into his or her flesh. "The sight was a reminder of the depth of human depravity." From others the words would sound inadequately banal; Meir Amit gave them dignity.

His military career was the biography of a soldier destined for the top: a company commander in the 1948 War of Independence; two years later a brigade commander under Moshe Dayan; then, within five years, army chief of operations, the second-ranking officer of the Israel Defense Forces. An accident—the partial failure of his parachute to open—ended his military career. The Israeli government paid for him to go to Columbia University, where he took a master's degree in business administration. He returned to Israel without a job.

Moshe Dayan proposed Meir Amit should become chief of military intelligence. Despite initial opposition, mostly on the reasonable grounds that he had no intelligence experience, he was appointed: "The one advantage I had was that I had been a battlefield commander and knew the importance of good intelligence to the fighting soldiers." On March 25, 1963, he took over Mossad from Isser Harel. His achievements had become so many they needed a shorthand of their own: the man who introduced Mossad's policy of assassinating its enemies; who set up a secret working relationship with the KGB at the very time millions of Jews were being persecuted; who refined the role of women and the use of sexual entrapment in intelligence work; who approved the penetration of King Hussein's palace shortly before the Hashemite ruler became a CIA spy in the Arab world.

The techniques he created to achieve all that remain in use. But no outsider will ever learn how he first developed them. His jaw muscles tightening, all he would say was: "There are secrets and there are my secrets."

When the time had come when he felt Mossad could benefit from a new hand at the helm, he had departed with no fuss, called his staff together and reminded them that if ever they found being a Jew and working for Mossad created a problem between their personal ethics and the demands of the state, they should resign at once. Then, after a round of handshakes, he was gone.

But no incoming chief of Mossad failed to call upon him for coffee in his office on Jabotinsky Street, in Tel Aviv's pleasant suburb of Ramat Gan. On those occasions, Meir Amit's office door remained firmly closed and the phone switched off.

"My mother always said a trust broken is a friend lost," he explained in English, smiling an old man's wily smile.

Outside his immediate family—a small tribe of children, grandchildren, cousins, kith and kin stretching over generations—few really know Meir Amit. He would have it no other way.

On that March morning in 1997, behind his car wheel, Meir Amit looked surprisingly young, closer to sixty than his actual age of seventy-five. The physique that once enabled him to complete a stress test at an Olympian pace had softened; there was a hint of a belly beneath the well-cut blue blazer. Yet his eyes were still sharp enough to startle and impossible to fathom or penetrate as he drove toward an avenue of eucalyptus trees.

How many times he had made this journey even he could no longer count. But each visit reminded him of an old truth: "that to survive as a Jew still means defending yourself to the death."

The same reminder was on the faces of the soldiers waiting for rides under the trees outside the boot camp at Glilot, north of Tel Aviv. There was a swagger about them, even an insolence; they were doing their compulsory service in the Israel Defense Forces and imbued with the belief they served in the finest army on earth.

Few gave Meir Amit a second glance. To them he was another of the old men who came to remember at a war memorial close to where they waited. Israel is a land of such memorials—over 1,500 in all—raised to the paratroops, the pilots, the tank drivers, and the infantry. The monuments commemorate the dead of five full-scale conventional wars and close to fifty years of cross-border incursions and antiguerrilla operations. Yet, in a nation that venerates its fallen warriors in a manner not seen since the Romans occupied this land, there is no other monument in Israel, indeed the world, like the one Meir Amit helped to create.

It stands just within the perimeter of the boot camp and consists of several concrete-walled buildings and a mass of sandstone walls assembled in the shape of a human brain. Meir Amit chose that shape because "intelligence is all about the mind, not some bronzed figure striking a heroic pose."

The memorial commemorates so far 557 men and women of Israel's intelligence community, 71 of whom served in the Mossad.

They died in every corner of the world: in the deserts of Iraq, the mountains of Iran, the jungles of South and Central America, the bush of Africa, the streets of Europe. Each, in his or her own way, tried to live by Mossad's motto, "By way of deception, thou shalt do war."

Meir Amit knew many personally; some he had sent to their deaths on missions he conceded were beyond the "cutting edge of acceptable danger, but that is the regrettable unavoidability of this work. One person's death must always be weighed against our nation's security. It has always been so."

The smooth sandstone walls are engraved only with names and the date of death. There are no other clues to the circumstances in which someone died: a public hanging, the fate of all convicted Jewish spies in Arab countries; a murderer's knife thrust in an alley that had no name; the merciful release after months of prison torture. No one will ever know. Even Meir Amit could often only suspect, and he kept those dark thoughts for himself.

The brain-shaped memorial is only part of the memorial complex. Within the concrete buildings is the File Room, holding the personal biographies of the dead agents. Each person's early life and military service are carefully documented; the final secret mission is not. Each agent has his or her memorial day commemorated in a small synagogue.

Beyond the synagogue is an amphitheater where on Intelligence

Day families gather to remember their dead. Sometimes Meir Amit addresses them. Afterward they visit the memorial's museum, filled with artifacts: a transmitter in the base of a flatiron; a microphone in a coffeepot; invisible ink in a perfume bottle; the actual tape recorder that secretly recorded the critical conversation between King Hussein of Jordan and President Nasser of Egypt, the precursor to the Six Day War.

Meir Amit had burnished the stories of the men who used the equipment to the brightness of heroic myth. He would point out the disguise Ya'a Boqa'i wore when he slipped in and out of Jordan until he was captured and executed in Amman in 1949, and the crystal radio Max Binnet and Moshe Marzuk used to run Mossad's most successful network in Egypt before they died painful, lingering deaths in a Cairo prison.

To Meir Amit, they were all "my Gideonites." Gideon was the Old Testament hero who saved Israel against superior enemy forces because he had better intelligence.

Finally, it was time for him to go to the maze, accompanied by the museum's curator. They paused before each engraved name, gave imperceptible little head bows, then moved on. Abruptly it was over. No more dead to respectfully acknowledge—only ample space for more names on the sand-colored tombstone.

For a moment Meir Amit was again lost in reverie. In whispered Hebrew the old Mossad chief said to the curator: "Whatever happens, we must ensure this place lives on."

Apropos of nothing that had gone before, Meir Amit added that on his office wall in Damascus, President Hafiz al-Assad of Syria only has one picture, a large photograph of the site of Saladin's victory against the Crusaders in 1187. It had led to the Arab reconquest of Jerusalem.

For Meir Amit, Assad's fondness for the photograph "has a significance for Israel. He sees us the same way Saladin did—someone to be eventually vanquished. There are many who share that aspiration. Some even purport to be our friends. We have to be especially watchful of them. . . ."

He stopped, said his good-bye to the curator, and walked back to his car as if he had already said too much; as if what he had said would further energize the whispers beginning to circulate within the Israeli intelligence community. Another crisis in the nowadays uneasy alliance between Mossad and U.S. intelligence was about to surface—with potentially devastating effects for Israel.

Already caught up in the brewing scandal was one of the most colorful and ruthless operatives who had once served under Meir Amit, a man who had already secured his place in history as the capturer of Adolf Eichmann, yet still liked to play with fire.

CHAPTER 4

THE SPY IN THE IRON MASK

Wealthy residents in the exclusive suburb of Afeka in the north of Tel Aviv were used to seeing Rafael "Rafi" Eitan, a squat, barrel-chested elderly man, myopic and almost totally deaf in his right ear since fighting in Israel's War of Independence, return home with pieces of discarded lavatory piping, used bicycle chains, and other assorted metal junk. Wearing a pair of chain-store trousers and shirt, his face covered with a welder's guard, he fashioned the scrap into surreal sculptures with an acetylene torch.

Some neighbors wondered if it was a means of momentary escape from what he had done. They knew he had killed for his country, not in open battle, but in secret encounters that were part of the ceaseless undercover war Israel waged against the state's enemies. No neighbor knew exactly how many Rafi Eitan had killed, sometimes with his stubby, powerful hands. All he had told them was: "Whenever I killed I needed to see their eyes, the white of their eyes. Then I was very calm, very focused, thinking only of what I had to do. Then I did it. That was it." Accompanying the words was an endearing smile some strong men use when seeking the approval of the weak.

Rafi Eitan had for almost a quarter of a century been Mossad's hands-on deputy director of operations. Not for him a life behind a desk reading reports and sending others to do his bidding. At every opportunity he had gone into the field, traveling the world, jaw thrust forward, driven by a philosophy that he had reduced to one pithy sentence: "If you are not part of the answer, then you are part of the problem."

There had been no one like him for cold-blooded ruthlessness, cunning, an ability to improvise at ferocious speed, an inborn skill at outwitting even the best-laid plan and tirelessly tracking down a quarry. All those qualities had come together in the one operation that had given him lasting fame—the kidnapping of Adolf Eichmann, the Nazi bureaucrat who epitomized the full horror of Hitler's Final Solution.

To his neighbors on Shay Street, Rafi Eitan was a revered figure, the man who had avenged their dead relatives, the onetime guerrilla who had been given the opportunity to remind the world that no living Nazi was safe. They never tired of being invited into his house and listening again to him describe an operation that is still unrivaled in its daring. Surrounded by expensive objets d'art, Rafi Eitan would fold his muscular arms, tilt his square block of a head to one side, and for a moment remain silent, allowing his listeners to carry themselves back in their mind's eye to that time when, against all odds, Israel had been born. Then, in a powerful voice, an actor's voice playing all the parts, missing nothing, he began to tell his trusted friends how he had set about capturing Adolf Eichmann. First he set the scene for one of the most dramatic kidnapping stories of all time.

After World War II, tracking down Nazi war criminals was initially done by Holocaust survivors. They called themselves Nokmin, "Avengers." They didn't bother with legal trials. They just executed any Nazis they found. Rafi Eitan did not know of a single case where they killed the wrong person. Officially in Israel there was little interest in pursuing war criminals. It was a matter of priorities. As a nation Israel was clinging on by its fingertips, still surrounded by hostile Arab states. It was one day at a time. The country was almost broke. There was no spare cash for resolving the evil of the past.

In 1957, Mossad received the electrifying news that Eichmann had been seen in Argentina. Rafi Eitan, already a rising star in Mossad as a result of astute forays against the Arabs, was selected to capture Eichmann and bring him to Israel to stand trial.

He was told the outcome would have a number of significant benefits. It would be an act of divine justice for his people. It would remind the world of the death camps and the need to make sure they never happened again. It would place Mossad at the forefront of the global intelligence community. No other service had dared to attempt such an operation. The risks were equally great. He would be working thousands of miles from home, traveling on forged documentation, relying entirely on his own resources and working in a hostile environment. Argentina was a haven for Nazis. The Mossad team could end up in prison there or even be killed.

For two long years, Rafi Eitan patiently waited while the first tentative sighting was confirmed—that the man living in a middle-class suburb of Buenos Aires under the name of Ricardo Klement was Adolf Eichmann.

When the go order finally came, Rafi Eitan became "ice-cold." He had done all his thinking of what could go wrong. The political, diplomatic, and, for him, the professional repercussions would be enormous. He had also wondered what would happen when, having captured Eichmann, the Argentinian police intervened. "I decided I would strangle Eichmann with my own bare hands. If I was caught, I would argue to the court it had been the biblical eye for an eye."

El Al, the national airline, had specially purchased from the Mossad slush fund a Britannia aircraft for the long flight to Argentina. Rafi Eitan remarked:

"We just sent someone to England to buy one. He handed over the money and we had our plane. Officially the flight to Argentina was to carry an Israeli delegation to attend Argentina's one hundred fiftieth independence day celebrations. None of the delegates knew why we were going with them or that we had constructed a cell in the back of the aircraft to hold Eichmann."

Rafi Eitan and his team arrived in Buenos Aires on May Day 1960. They moved into one of seven safe houses a Mossad advance man had rented. One had been given the Hebrew code name Maoz, or "Stronghold." The apartment would act as the base for the operation. Another safe house was designated *Tira*, or "Palace," and was intended as a holding place for Eichmann after his capture. The other houses were in case Eichmann had to be moved under the pressure of an expected police hunt. A dozen cars had also been leased for the operation.

With everything in place, Rafi Eitan's manner became settled and determined. Any doubts of failure had lifted; the prospect of action had replaced the tension of waiting. For three days he and the team conducted a discreet surveillance on how Adolf Eichmann, who had once been chauffeured everywhere in a Mercedes limousine, now traveled by bus and alighted on the corner of Garibaldi Street in a suburb on the outskirts of the city, as punctual as he had once been in signing the consignment orders for the death camps.

On the night of May 10, 1960, Rafi Eitan chose for the snatch a driver and two others to subdue Eichmann once he was in the car. One of the men had been trained to overpower a target on the street. Rafi Eitan would sit beside the driver, "ready to help in any way I could."

The operation was set for the following evening. At 8:00 P.M. on May 11, the team's car drove into Garibaldi Street.

There was no tension. Everyone was long past that. No one spoke. There was nothing to say. Rafi Eitan looked at his watch: 8:03. They drove up and down the empty street. 8:04. Several buses came and went. At 8:05, another bus came. They saw Eichmann alight. To Rafi Eitan, "he looked a little tired, perhaps how he looked after another day of sending my people to the death camps.

"The street was still empty. Behind me I heard our specialist snatch-man open the car door. We drove up just behind Eichmann. He was walking quite quickly, as if he wanted to get home for his dinner. I could hear the specialist breathing steadily, the way he had been taught to do in training. He had got the snatch down to twelve seconds. Out of the door, grab him around the neck, drag him back into the car. Out, grab, back."

The car came alongside Eichmann. He half turned, gave a puzzled look at the sight of the specialist coming out of the car. Then the man tripped on a loose shoelace, almost stumbling to the ground. For a moment Rafi Eitan was too stunned to move. He had come halfway across the world to catch the man who had been instrumental in sending six million Jews to their deaths and they were just about to lose him because a shoelace had not been properly tied. Eichmann was starting to walk quickly away. Rafi Eitan leaped from the car.

"I grabbed him by the neck with such force I could see his eyes bulge. A little tighter and I would have choked him to death. The specialist was on his feet holding open the door. I tossed Eichmann onto the backseat. The specialist jumped in, sitting half on top of Eichmann. The whole thing didn't last more than five seconds."

From the front seat Rafi Eitan could smell Eichmann's sour breath as he struggled for air. The specialist worked his jaw up and down. Eichmann grew calmer. He even managed to ask what was the meaning of this outrage.

No one spoke to him. In silence they reached their safe house about three miles away. Rafi Eitan motioned Eichmann to strip naked. He then checked his physical measurements against those from an SS file he had obtained. He was not surprised to see that Eichmann had somehow removed his SS tattoo. But his other measurements all matched the file—the size of his head, the distance from elbow to wrist, from knee to ankle. He had Eichmann chained to a bed. For ten hours he was left in complete silence. Rafi Eitan "wanted to encourage a feeling of hopelessness. Just before dawn, Eichmann was at his lowest mental state. I asked him his name. He gave a Spanish one. I said, no, no, no, your German name. He gave his German alias—the one he had used to flee Germany. I said again, no, no, no, your real name, your SS name. He stretched on the bed as if he wanted to stand to attention and said, loud and clear, 'Adolf Eichmann.' I didn't ask him anything else. I had no need to."

For the next seven days Eichmann and his captors remained closeted in the house. Still no one spoke to Eichmann. He ate, bathed, and went to the lavatory in complete silence. For Rafi Eitan:

"Keeping silent was more than an operational necessity. We did not want to show Eichmann how nervous we all were. That would have given him hope. And hope makes a desperate person dangerous. I needed him to be as helpless as my own people were when he had sent them in trainloads to the death camps."

The decision on how to move him from the safe house to the El Al plane waiting to fly the delegation home was filled with its own black humor. First Eichmann was dressed in the spare El Al flight suit Rafi Eitan had brought from Israel. Then he was induced to drink a bottle of whiskey, leaving him in a drunken stupor.

Rafi Eitan and his team dressed in their own flight suits and liberally sprinkled themselves with whiskey. Thrusting a flight hat on Eichmann's head, and squashing him into the backseat of the car, Rafi Eitan drove to the military air base where the Britannia was waiting, engines running.

At the base gate Argentinian soldiers flagged down the car. In the back Eichmann was snoring. Rafi Eitan recalled:

"The car reeked like a distillery. That was the moment we all earned our Mossad Oscars! We played the drunken Jews who couldn't handle strong Argentinian liquor. The guards were amused and never gave Eichmann a second look."

At five minutes past midnight on May 21, 1960, the Britannia took off with Adolf Eichmann still snoring in his cell in the back of the plane.

After a lengthy trial, Eichmann was found guilty of crimes against humanity. On the day of his execution, May 31, 1962, Rafi Eitan was in the execution chamber at Ramla Prison: "Eichmann looked at me and said, 'Your time will come to follow me, Jew,' and I replied, 'But not today, Adolf, not today.' Next moment the trap opened. Eichmann gave a little choking sound. There was the smell of his bowel moving, then just the sound of the stretched rope. A very satisfying sound."

A special oven had been built to cremate the body. Within hours the ashes were scattered out at sea over a wide area. Ben-Gurion had ordered there must be no trace left to encourage sympathizers to turn Eichmann into a Nazi cult figure. Israel wanted him expunged from the face of the earth. Afterward the oven was dismantled and would never be used again. That evening Rafi Eitan stood on the shore and looked out to sea, feeling totally at peace, "knowing I had finished my assignment. That is always a good feeling."

As Mossad's deputy operations chief, Rafi Eitan's rolling gait continued to take him across Europe to find and execute Arab terrorists. To do so he used remote-controlled bombs; Mossad's handgun of choice, the Beretta; and where silence was essential, his own bare hands to either garrote a victim with steel wire or deliver a lethal rabbit punch. Always he killed without compunction.

When he returned home he stood for hours at his open-air furnace, wreathed in sparks, totally consumed with bending metal to his will. Then he would be off again, on journeys that often required several plane changes before he reached his final destination. For each journey he chose a different nationality and identity, built around the vast number of stolen or perfectly forged passports Mossad had patiently acquired.

In between killing, his other skill was recruiting more sayanim. He had a routine that played upon the Jewish love for their homeland.

"I would tell them that for two thousand years our people dreamed. That for two thousand years we Jews had prayed for deliverance. In song, in prose, in their hearts, we had kept alive the dream—and the dream kept us alive. Now it had happened. Then I add: to make sure it continues we need people like you."

In cafés along the Paris boulevards, in restaurants on the banks of the Rhine, in Madrid, Brussels, and London's Golders Green he would repeat the poignant words. More often than not, his vision of what it meant to be a Jew today would gain another sayan. To those who hesitated, he deftly mixed the personal and the political, retelling stories of his time in the Haganah with affectionate stories about Ben-Gurion and other leaders. The last resistance would melt away.

Soon he had over a hundred men and women across Europe to do his bidding: lawyers, dentists, schoolteachers, doctors, tailors, shopkeepers, housewives, secretaries. One group he particularly cherished: German Jews who had returned to the land of their Holocaust; Rafi Eitan called them his "survivor spies."

———

Toiling at the coal-face of Mossad operations, Rafi Eitan was careful to distance himself from the politicking that continued to bedevil the Israeli intelligence community. He knew what was going on, of course, the maneuvering by Aman, military intelligence, and Shin Bet to whittle away some of Mossad's supreme authority. He had heard about the cabals that formed and re-formed, and the "eyes only" reports they sent to the prime minister's office. But under Meir Amit, Mossad had remained rock steady, brushing aside any attempts to undo its prime position.

Then, one day Meir Amit was no longer in command; his brisk stride down the corridors was gone, along with his piercing gaze and the smile that never seemed to reach his lips. Following his departure, colleagues had urged Rafi Eitan to allow them to lobby for him to become Amit's replacement, pointing out that he had the qualifications and commanded loyalty and popularity within Mossad. But before Rafi Eitan could decide, the post went to a Labor Party nominee, the colorless and pedantic Zvi Zamir. Rafi Eitan resigned. He had no quarrel with the new Mossad chief; he simply felt that Mossad would no longer be a place where he would feel "comfortable." Under Meir Amit his brief had been to roam virtually unfettered; he felt that Zamir would do "things only by the book. That was not for me."

Rafi Eitan set himself up as a private consultant, offering his skills to companies who had to beef up their security or to a wealthy individual who needed to have his staff trained on how to protect him against a terrorist attack. But the work soon paled. After a year Rafi Eitan let it be known he was ready to step back into the fast lane of intelligence work.

When Yitzhak Rabin became prime minister in 1974, he appointed the aggressive, hands-on Yitzhak Hofi to run Mossad and made him answerable to the hawkish Ariel Sharon, who was Rabin's adviser on security affairs. Sharon promptly made Rafi Eitan his personal assistant. Hofi found himself working closely with a man who shared his own cutthroat attitude toward intelligence operations.

Three years later, in another reshuffle of government, a new prime minister, Menachem Begin, named Rafi Eitan as his personal adviser on terrorism. Eitan's first act was to organize the assassination of the Palestinian responsible for planning the 1972 Munich

Olympics massacre of eleven Israeli athletes. Their actual killers were already dead, each one executed by Mossad.

The first to die had been standing in the lobby of his Rome apartment building when he was shot eleven times at close range—a bullet for each murdered athlete. When the next terrorist to die answered a telephone call in his Paris apartment, his head was blown off by a small bomb planted in the receiver and triggered by remote control. Another terrorist was asleep in a hotel room in Nicosia when it was wrecked by a similar bomb. To create panic among the remaining members of the Black September group who had killed the athletes, Mossad Arab sayanim arranged for their obituaries to appear in local Arab newspapers. Their families received flowers and condolence cards shortly *before* each was killed.

Rafi Eitan set about finding and killing their leader, Ali Hassan Salameh, known throughout the Arab world as the "Red Prince." Since Munich he had flitted from one Arab capital to another, advising terror groups on strategy. Time and again when Rafi Eitan had been set to strike, the Red Prince had moved on. But finally he had settled among the bomb makers of Beirut. Rafi Eitan knew the city well. Nevertheless, he decided to refresh his memory. Posing as a Greek businessman he traveled there. In the next few days he had discovered Salameh's precise whereabouts and movements.

Rafi Eitan returned to Tel Aviv and made his plans. Three Mossad agents who could pass for Arabs crossed into Lebanon and entered the city. One rented a car. The second wired a series of bombs into its chassis, roof, and door panels. The third agent parked the car along the route the Red Prince traveled to his office every morning. Using precise timings Rafi Eitan had provided, the car was set to explode as Salameh passed. It did, blowing him to pieces.

Rafi Eitan had shown he was once more a player in the Israeli intelligence community. But Prime Minister Menachem Begin decided that Rafi Eitan was too valuable to risk on further such adventures. He told his adviser that from now on he must remain in the office and keep a low profile. Recently, John le Carré had used Eitan as a model for the central character who tracks down terrorists in his thriller *The Little Drummer Girl*.

But lending credibility to a novelist's imagination did little to settle Rafi Eitan's perpetual restlessness. He wanted to be where the action was, not stuck behind a desk or attending an endless round of planning meetings. He began to badger Prime Minister Begin to give him something else to do.

After some hesitation—for Rafi Eitan was an excellent adviser on counterterrorism—Begin appointed Rafi Eitan to one of the most sensitive posts in the intelligence community, one that would stretch him intellectually and satisfy his craving for a hands-on job. He was made director of the Bureau of Scientific Liaison, known by its Hebrew acronym, LAKAM.

Created in 1960, it had operated as the defense ministry's spy unit to obtain scientific data "by all means possible." In principle that had meant stealing or bribing people to provide material. From the beginning LAKAM had been hampered by the hostility of Mossad, who saw the unit as the proverbial "new kid on the block." Both Isser Harel and Meir Amit had tried to have LAKAM either closed down or absorbed into Mossad. But Shimon Peres, Israel's deputy defense minister, had stubbornly insisted that the defense ministry needed its own collecting agency. Slowly and laboriously, LAKAM had gone about its business, setting up offices in New York, Washington, Boston, and Los Angeles, all key centers for cutting-edge science. Every week LAKAM staff dutifully shipped boxes of technical journals back to Israel, knowing the FBI was keeping an eye on their activities.

This surveillance increased after 1968, when one of the engineers building the French Mirage IIIC fighter aircraft was discovered to have stolen over two hundred thousand blueprints. He received a four-and-a-half-year prison sentence—having given LAKAM the data to build its own Mirage replicas. Since then LAKAM had enjoyed little other success.

For Rafi Eitan, the memory of the Mirage coup was the deciding factor. What had been achieved before could be achieved again. He would take a now virtually moribund LAKAM and turn it into a force to be reckoned with.

Working out of cramped offices in a Tel Aviv backwater, he told his new staff, awed at now being commanded by such a legendary figure, that what he knew about science he could place in a test tube and still leave plenty of space. But, he added, he was a fast learner.

He immersed himself in the world of science, looking for potential areas to target. He left his home before dawn and often returned close to midnight with bundles of technical papers and read into the small hours; there was little time to relax by sculpting scrap metal. In between the huge amounts of data he absorbed, he reestablished contact with his old service. Mossad now had a new director, Nahum Admoni. Like Rafi Eitan, Admoni had a deep-seated suspicion of U.S. intentions in the Middle East. Outwardly, Washington continued to show an open commitment to Israel, and the CIA had kept open the back-channel contact Isser Harel and Allen Dulles had instigated. But Admoni complained that the information from that source was of little importance.

The Mossad chief was also concerned about reports from Mossad's own katsas and well-placed sayanim in Washington. They had discovered discreet meetings between high-ranking State Department officials and Arab leaders close to Yasser Arafat who had discussed ways to pressure Israel to be more accommodating over Palestinian demands. Admoni told Rafi Eitan he now felt he could no longer regard the United States as "a foul weather friend."

This attitude was reinforced in an incident that would shock American belief in its inviolability more than anything since the Vietnam War.

In August 1983, Mossad agents discovered an attack was being planned against the U.S. forces in Beirut, there as UN peacekeepers. The agents had identified a Mercedes truck that would contain half a ton of explosive. Under back-channel arrangements, Mossad should have passed on the information to the CIA. But at a meeting at Mossad headquarters overlooking King Saul Boulevard, staff were informed they were to "make sure our people watch the truck. As far as the Yanks go, we are not here to protect them. They can do their own watching. We start doing too much for the Yanks and we'll be shitting on our own doorstep."

On October 23, 1983, monitored closely by Mossad agents, the truck was driven at full speed into the headquarters of the U.S. Eighth Marine Battalion situated near Beirut Airport. Two hundred forty-one marines died.

The reaction in the upper echelons of Mossad, according to a former officer, Victor Ostrovsky, was, "They wanted to stick their nose into this Lebanon thing, let them pay the price."

That attitude had further encouraged Rafi Eitan to think seriously about targeting the United States. Its scientific community was the most advanced in the world, its military technology without equal. For LAKAM to get its hands on even some of that data would be a tremendous coup. The first hurdle to overcome would be the hardest: finding an informer sufficiently well placed to provide the material.

Using the list of U.S. sayanim he had helped compile during his time with Mossad, he put out the word that he was interested in hearing of anyone in the United States who had a scientific background and was known to be pro-Israeli. For months it produced nothing.

Then, in April 1984, Aviem Sella, a colonel in the Israeli air force who was on a sabbatical to study computer science at New York University, went to a party given by a wealthy Jewish gynecologist on the Upper East Side of Manhattan. Sella was a minor celebrity among the city's Jewish community as the pilot who had led an air attack three years before that had destroyed Iraq's nuclear reactor.

At the party was a diffident young man with a shy smile who seemed ill at ease among the small set of doctors, lawyers, and bankers. He told Sella his name was Jonathan Pollard and that the only reason he had come was to meet him. Embarrassed by such obvious adulation, Sella made polite small talk and was about to move on when Pollard revealed he was not only a committed Zionist, but worked for U.S. naval intelligence. In no time the astute Sella had learned that Pollard was stationed at the Anti-Terrorist Alert Center in one of the navy's most secret establishments at Suitland, Maryland. Pollard's duties included monitoring all classified material on global terrorist activities. So important was the work that he had the highest possible U.S. intelligence community security clearance.

Sella could not believe what he was hearing, especially when Pollard began to give specific details about incidents where the U.S. intelligence community was not cooperating with its Israeli counterpart. Sella began to wonder if Pollard was part of a sting operation by the FBI to try to recruit an Israeli.

Yet there was something about the intense Pollard that rang true. That night Sella called Tel Aviv and spoke to his air force intelligence commander. The officer switched the call to the Israeli air force chief of staff. Sella was ordered to develop his contact with Pollard.

They began to meet: at the skating rink at Rockefeller Plaza; in a coffee shop on Forty-eighth Street; in Central Park. Each time Pollard handed over secret documents to confirm the truth of what he said. Sella couriered the material to Tel Aviv, enjoying the frisson of being caught up in an important intelligence operation. He was therefore understandably stunned to be told that Mossad knew all about Pollard, who had actually offered to spy for them two years previously and had been rejected as "unstable." A Mossad katsa in New York had also described Pollard as "lonely . . . with an unrealistic view about Israel."

Unwilling to relinquish his role in an operation certainly more exciting than sitting before a classroom computer keyboard, Sella looked around for a way to keep matters alive. During his time in New York he had come to know the science attaché at the Israeli consulate in the city. His name was Yosef Yagur. He was Rafi Eitan's head of all LAKAM operations in the United States.

Sella invited Yagur to dinner with Pollard. Over the meal Pollard repeated that Israel was being denied information to defend itself against Arab terrorists because the United States did not wish to upset its relations with Arab oil producers.

That night, using a secure consulate phone, Yagur telephoned Rafi Eitan. It was in the early hours in Tel Aviv but Eitan was still at work in his study. It was almost dawn when he put down the phone. He was exultant: he had his informer.

For the next three months Yagur and Sella assiduously cultivated Pollard and his future wife, Anne Henderson. They took them to expensive restaurants, Broadway shows, first-night films. Pollard continued to hand over important documentation. Rafi Eitan could only marvel at how good the material was. He decided it was time to meet the source.

In November 1984, Sella and Yagur invited Pollard and Henderson to accompany them on an all-expenses-paid trip to Paris. Yagur told Pollard the vacation was "a small reward for all you are doing for Israel." They all flew first-class and were met by a chauffeured car and driven to the Bristol Hotel. Waiting for them was Rafi Eitan.

By the end of the night Rafi Eitan had finalized all the practical arrangements for Pollard to continue his treachery. No longer would matters continue in their free-and-easy way. Sella would fade from the picture, his role over. Yagur would become Pollard's official handler. A proper delivery system was worked out for documents to be handed over. Pollard would deliver them to the apartment of Irit Erb, a mousy-haired secretary at the Washington embassy. A high-speed Xerox had been installed in her kitchen to copy the material. Pollard's visits would be spaced between those to a number of designated car washes. While Pollard's car was being cleaned, he would hand over documents to Yagur, whose own car would be undergoing a similar process. Concealed beneath the dash was a battery-operated copier. Both Erb's apartment and the car-wash facilities were close to Washington's National Airport, making it easier for Yagur to fly back and forth to New York. From the consulate he transmitted the material by secure fax to Tel Aviv.

Rafi Eitan returned to Tel Aviv to await results. They exceeded his wildest expectations: details of Russian arms deliveries to Syria and other Arab states, including the precise location of SS-21 and SA-5 missiles; maps and satellite photographs of Iraqi, Syrian, and Iranian arsenals, including chemical and biological manufacturing plants.

Rafi Eitan quickly obtained a clear picture of U.S. intelligence-gathering methods, not only in the Middle East, but in South Africa. Pollard had provided reports from CIA operatives which provided a blueprint for the entire U.S. intelligence network within the country. One document contained a detailed account of how South Africa had managed to detonate a nuclear device on September 14, 1979, in the southern end of the Indian Ocean. The Pretoria government had steadfastly denied it had become a nuclear power. Rafi Eitan arranged for Mossad to pass over copies of all material relating to South Africa to Pretoria, virtually destroying the CIA network. Twelve operatives were forced to hurriedly leave the country.

During the next eleven months, Jonathan Pollard continued to asset-strip U.S. intelligence. Over one thousand highly classified documents, 360 cubic feet of paper, were transmitted to Israel. There Rafi Eitan devoured them before passing over the material to Mossad. The data enabled Nahum Admoni to brief Shimon Peres's coalition government on how to respond to Washington's Middle East policies in a manner previously impossible. One note taker at the Sunday cabinet meetings in Jerusalem claimed that "listening to Admoni was the next best thing to sitting in the Oval Office. We not only knew what was the very latest thinking in Washington on all matters of concern to us, but we had sufficient time to respond before making a decision."

Pollard had become a crucial factor in the mysteries of Israeli policymaking and the intricacies of choosing options. Rafi Eitan authorized an Israeli passport for Pollard in the name of Danny Cohen, as well as a generous monthly stipend. In return he asked Pollard to provide details about the electronic eavesdropping activities of the National Security Agency (NSA) in Israel and the bugging methods used against the Israeli embassy in Washington and its other diplomatic stations within the United States.

Before Pollard could supply the information he was arrested, on November 21, 1985, outside the Israeli embassy in Washington. Hours later Yagur, Sella, and the embassy secretary in Washington had all caught an El Al flight from New York to Tel Aviv before the FBI could stop them. In Israel they disappeared into the protective arms of a grateful intelligence community. Pollard was sentenced to life imprisonment and his wife to five years.

In 1999, Pollard could draw comfort from the tireless way powerful Jewish groups lobbied for his release. The Conference of Major American Jewish Organizations, a consortium of over fifty groups, had launched a sustained campaign to have him set free on the grounds that he had not committed high treason against the United States "because Israel was then and remains today a close ally." Equally influential Jewish religious groups such as the Reform Union of American Hebrew Congregations and the Orthodox Union, lent support. The Harvard Law School professor Alan M. Dershowitz, who had been Pollard's attorney, said there was nothing to show the spy had actually compromised "the nation's intelligence-gathering capabilities or betrayed worldwide intelligence data."

Alarmed at what they realized was a skilled public relations campaign orchestrated from Israel, the U.S. intelligence community took an unusual step. They moved out of the shadows into the public domain, setting out the facts of Pollard's treachery. It was both a bold and dangerous decision. It would not only cast a light on sensitive material but also mobilize the evermore powerful Jewish lobby to attack them. They had seen what it had done to others in the frenetic atmosphere of Washington. A reputation could be discreetly tarnished over a late drink at an embassy between acts at the Kennedy Center or over a quiet Georgetown dinner.

Those intelligence men feared that Clinton—"in one of his quixotic moments," a senior CIA officer told me—would free Pollard before he left office if that would ensure Israel entered into a peace settlement and give Clinton a last foreign policy success. The CIA's director at the time of writing, George Tenet, has warned the president "that Pollard's release will demoralize the intelligence community," Clinton was reported to have merely said: "We'll see, we'll see."

In Tel Aviv, Rafi Eitan has closely followed every move, telling friends that "should the day come when Jonathan makes it to Israel, I'd be happy to have a cup of coffee with him."

Meantime Eitan continued to rejoice at the success of another operation he had also mounted against the United States. It led to Israel's becoming the first nuclear power in the Middle East.

CHAPTER 5

GIDEON'S NUCLEAR SWORD

In the darkness of a Tel Aviv cinema in 1945, Rafi Eitan had watched the birth of the nuclear age over Hiroshima. While all around him young soldiers whistled and cheered at the newsreel footage of the devastated Japanese city, he had only two thoughts. Would Israel ever possess such a weapon? Suppose her Arab neighbors obtained one first?

From time to time down the years the questions had surfaced in his mind. If Egypt had had a nuclear bomb, it would have won the Suez War and there would have been no Six Day War or Yom

Kippur War. Israel would have been a nuclear desert. With a nuclear weapon, Israel would be invincible.

In those days, for an operative whose work was primarily concerned with killing terrorists, such strategic questions were only of academic interest and answering them was the province of others. However, when he took command of LAKAM, he began to seriously consider the matter. He now only had one question: Could he help to provide Israel with a nuclear shield?

Reading long into the night, fueled by the forty vitamin capsules he swallowed each day, he discovered how Israel's politicians and scientists had initially been divided over "going nuclear." In the files were details of angry exchanges within cabinet meetings, the bitter monologues of scientists, and always the overpowering voice of Prime Minister David Ben-Gurion cutting through the anguish, protests, and long-winded arguments.

Trouble had begun in 1956, when France had sent a twenty-four-megawatt reactor to Israel. Ben-Gurion announced its purpose was to provide a "pumping station" to turn the desert into an "agricultural paradise by desalinating a billion cubic gallons of seawater annually." The claim promptly led to the resignation of six of the seven members of the Israeli Atomic Energy Commission, protesting the reactor was actually intended to be the precursor of "political adventurism which will unite the world against us." Israel's leading military strategists supported them. Yigal Allon, a hero of the War of Independence, roundly condemned the "nuclear option"; Yitzhak Rabin, who would soon become the IDF chief of staff, was equally vocal in his protest. Even Ariel Sharon, then and still Israel's leading hawk, vehemently opposed a nuclear arsenal. "We have the best conventional forces in the region."

Ignoring all opposition, Ben-Gurion gave the order for the reactor to be sited in the Negev Desert, close to the bleak, sand-blown settlement at Dimona. Once a staging post on the camel caravan route between Cairo and Jerusalem, Dimona had long become a place time had passed by. Few maps marked its position in the desert south of Tel Aviv. But from now on no mapmaker would be allowed to pinpoint the location of Israel's first faltering steps into the nuclear age.

Dimona's silver dome—beneath which was the reactor—rose above the desert heat. Kirya le Mehekar Gariny, Dimona's Hebrew name, employed over 2,500 scientists and technicians. They worked within the most fortified plant on earth. The sand around the perimeter fences was continuously checked for signs of intruders. Pilots knew that any aircraft flying within a five-mile air exclusion zone could be shot down. Engineers had bulldozed an eighty-foot-deep chamber to house the reactor, part of an underground complex known as Machon Two. At its core was the separating/reprocessing plant that had been labeled "textile machinery" when shipped from France.

By itself the reactor could not provide Israel with a nuclear bomb. To produce one required fissionable material, uranium or plutonium. The handful of nuclear powers had agreed among themselves never to provide as much as a gram of either substance to all those outside their exclusive "club." Imposing though it was, the reactor at Dimona was little more than a showpiece until it received fissionable materials.

Three months after the reactor had been installed, a small nuclear material processing company opened for business in a converted World War II steel plant in the unappealing town of Apollo, Pennsylvania. The company was called the Nuclear Materials and Equipment Corporation, Numec. Its chief executive was Dr. Salman Shapiro.

On LAKAM's computer database of prominent American Jews with a scientific background, Shapiro was also listed as a prominent fund-raiser for Israel. Rafi Eitan knew he had found a potential answer to how to provide the Dimona reactor with fissionable material. He ordered a full check made into the background of Shapiro and every member of the plant staff. The investigation was entrusted to the katsa in Washington.

The inquiry launched, Rafi Eitan continued to immerse himself in a story that had switched from the desert heat of Dimona to the cool corridors of the White House.

Among the data the Washington katsa had sent was a copy of a memo written on February 20, 1962, by the U.S. Atomic Energy Commission to Shapiro, bluntly warning that the company's "failure to comply with security regulations may be punishable as provided by law, including the Atomic Energy Act of 1954 and by the espionage laws."

The threat increased Rafi Eitan's feeling he may have found a way into the U.S. nuclear industry. Numec appeared to be a company not only with poor security, but also lax bookkeeping and a management that left a great deal to be desired by America's nuclear watchdog. Those very deficiencies made the company an attractive target.

The son of an Orthodox rabbi, Salman Shapiro's brilliance had already carried him far. At Johns Hopkins University he had obtained his doctorate in chemistry by the age of twenty-eight. His capacity for hard work had seen him become an important member of the nuclear research and development laboratory at Westinghouse; the corporation was contracted to the United States Navy to develop submarine reactors. Checks on Shapiro's personal background revealed some of his relatives had been Holocaust victims and Shapiro, in "his typical discreet way," had provided several million dollars for the Technion Institute in Haifa that offered tuition in science and engineering.

In 1957 Shapiro had left Westinghouse and set up Numec. It had twenty-five stockholders, all openly sympathetic to Israel. Shapiro found himself head of a small company in an aggressive cutthroat industry. Nevertheless, Numec had won a number of contracts to recover enriched uranium, a process that usually led to the loss of a quantity of uranium during the salvage operation. There was no way of telling how great or when the loss had taken place. The revelation made Rafi Eitan pop his vitamins with even more satisfaction.

He continued to read how the already uneasy relationship between Israel and the United States over the desire of the Jewish state to become a nuclear power increased when Ben-Gurion traveled to Washington in 1960. At a series of meetings with State Department officials, he was bluntly told that for Israel to possess nuclear weapons would affect the balance of power in the Middle East. In February 1961, President John F. Kennedy wrote to Ben-Gurion suggesting that Dimona should be regularly inspected by the International Atomic Energy Agency.

Alarmed, Ben-Gurion flew to New York to meet with Kennedy at the Waldorf-Astoria Hotel. The Israeli leader was "very worried" about what he saw as "relentless American pressures." But Kennedy was firm: there had to be an inspection. Ben-Gurion gave in with what little grace he could muster. He returned home convinced "a Catholic in the White House is bad news for Israel." The prime minister turned to the one man in Washington he could trust, Abraham Feinberg, a Zionist supporter of Israel's nuclear aspirations.

At one level, the native New Yorker was the most important Jewish fund-raiser for the Democratic Party. Feinberg made no secret of why he had raised many millions: every dollar was to ensure the party backed Israel in Congress. He had also discreetly provided many more additional millions of dollars to create Dimona. The money came in cashier's checks to the Bank of Israel in Tel Aviv, thus avoiding the accountability of the Israeli foreign exchange controls. Ben-Gurion told Feinberg to "sort out the boy. Make the putz understand the reality of life."

Feinberg's method was straightforward political pressure—the kind that had already infuriated Kennedy when he was running for office. Then, Feinberg had bluntly told him: "We are willing to pay your bills if you will let us have control of your Middle East policy." Kennedy had promised to "give Israel every possible break." Feinberg had agreed to provide an initial campaign contribution of five hundred thousand dollars—"with more to come."

Now he used the same direct approach: if President Kennedy continued to insist on an inspection of Dimona, he should "not count on Jewish financial support in the next political election." Powerful support came from an unexpected source. Kennedy's secretary of state, Robert S. McNamara, told Kennedy he could "understand why Israel wants a nuclear bomb."

Nevertheless, Kennedy was resolute and Israel was forced to accept an inspection. The president did at the last minute grant two concessions. In return for access to Dimona, the United States would sell Israel Hawk surface-to-air missiles, then the most advanced defensive weapon in the world. And the inspection need not be carried out by the International Atomic Energy Agency, but by an American-only team—that would have to schedule its visit weeks in advance.

Rafi Eitan relished the detailed account of how the Israelis had duped the American inspectors.

A bogus control center was built over the real one at Dimona, complete with fake control panels and computer-lined gauges that gave a credible impression of measuring the output of a reactor engaged in an irrigation scheme to turn the Negev into lush pastureland. The area containing the "heavy" water smuggled from France and Norway was placed off-limits to the inspectors "for safety reasons." The sheer volume of heavy water would have been proof the reactor was being readied for a very different purpose.

When the Americans arrived, the Israelis were relieved to discover not one spoke Hebrew. It further lessened any possibility of the inspectors uncovering the true intention for Dimona.

The stage was set for Rafi Eitan.

Gaining access to the Numec plant was relatively easy. Israel's embassy in Washington requested permission from the U.S. Atomic Energy Commission "for a team of our scientists to visit the facility to better understand the concerns expressed by your inspectors on the reprocessing of nuclear waste." The request was granted, even though the FBI was now running a full-scale surveillance operation to discover whether Shapiro had been recruited as an Israeli spy.

He had not—and never would be. Rafi Eitan was satisfied that Shapiro was a genuine patriot, a Zionist who believed in the right of Israel to defend itself. Not only was Shapiro privately wealthy from family money and shrewd stock-market investments, his personal fortune had rapidly increased from the very large profits Numec had already made. Equally, unlike Jonathan Pollard, Shapiro was not a traitor; his love of America was manifest. Rafi Eitan knew that to even attempt to recruit him would be counterproductive. Shapiro would have to remain outside the operation beginning to crystallize in Rafi Eitan's mind.

Nevertheless, some risks were unavoidable. To learn more about Numec, Rafi Eitan had sent two LAKAM operatives to Apollo. They were Avraham Hermoni, whose diplomatic cover at the Israeli embassy in Washington was "scientific counselor," and Jeryham Kafkafi, a katsa operating in the United States as a freelance science writer.

Both agents toured the reprocessing plant but were not allowed to photograph it. Shapiro pointed out that would be a breach of Atomic Energy Commission regulations. They had found Shapiro welcoming but, in Hermoni's judgment, "a man run off his feet."

Rafi Eitan decided the time had come for him to go to Apollo. He put together a group of "inspectors." These included two scientists from Dimona with specialized knowledge of reprocessing nuclear waste. Another team member was listed as a director of the "Department of Electronics, University of Tel Aviv, Israel." There was no such post at the campus; the man was a LAKAM security officer whose task would be to try to discover a way of stealing fissionable waste from the plant. Hermoni was included: his job would be to point out the areas of poor security he had discovered during his previous visit. Rafi Eitan was traveling under his own name as a "scientific adviser to the office of the Prime Minister of Israel."

The delegates were approved by the U.S. embassy in Tel Aviv and visas were granted. Rafi Eitan had warned the team they could expect to be under FBI surveillance from the time they landed in New York. But, to his surprise, his experienced eyes saw no evidence of that.

The Israelis' arrival in Apollo coincided with Shapiro's return from another brainstorming tour of American university campuses, where he had been soliciting scientists who were "friendly" to Israel and would agree to go there and "solve its technical and scientific problems." He would underwrite all their expenses and make up any deficit in their salaries.

Rafi Eitan and his team's stay in Apollo was low-key. They took rooms in a motel and spent most of their time at the Numec plant learning the intricacies of converting highly enriched uranium from gaseous uranium hexafluoride. Shapiro explained that Atomic Energy Commission rules meant that Numec would have to pay penalties for any enriched material not accounted for, scaled at $10 a gram, $4,500 a pound.

Rafi Eitan and his spies left Apollo as quietly as they had come.

What followed can only be deduced from FBI reports, and even they leave tantalizing questions as to how much Salman Shapiro may have suspected was behind Rafi Eitan's visit. An FBI report stated that a month after the Israelis had returned home, Numec became a partner with the Israeli government in a business involving what was described as "the pasteurization of food and the sterilization of medical samples by irradiation."

Another FBI report complained that "with a warning notice posted on each container that it contained radioactive material, no one would open or examine them—and no one was prepared to let us do so."

The reason for the refusal was because the Israeli embassy in Washington had made it clear to the State Department that if any attempt was made to inspect the containers, they would place them under diplomatic immunity. The State Department called the Justice Department and warned of the serious diplomatic consequences that would follow any breach of that immunity. All the thwarted FBI agents could do was watch the containers being loaded on to El Al cargo planes at Idleward Airport.

Despite his best efforts, the CIA station chief in Tel Aviv, John Hadden, said he was unable to "firm up" that the containers were ending up in Dimona. The FBI logged nine shipments in the six months following Rafi Eitan's visit. They noted that the containers arrived at dusk and left before dawn: all were sheathed with lead, needed to transport enriched uranium, and each container was stamped with a pre-addressed stencil in Hebrew giving Haifa as the final destination. On several occasions, agents saw "stovepipes"—storage containers for enriched uranium—being placed in steel cabinets at the Numec loading dock. Each stovepipe bore a number showing it had come from the company's high-security vaults. But there was still nothing the FBI could do. An FBI memo spoke of "political pressure from State [Department] not to create a diplomatic incident."

After ten months the shipments abruptly stopped. The FBI could only assume that sufficient quantities of fissionable material had by then reached Dimona. During the agency's subsequent interviews, Shapiro denied he had supplied Israel with nuclear bomb-making material. The FBI said their check of company records showed there was a discrepancy in the amount of material reprocessed. Shapiro insisted the "most logical explanation" for any "lost" uranium was that it had seeped into the ground or had been "disposed of into the air." All told, the missing material amounted to one hundred pounds. Shapiro was never charged with any crime.

In the years that followed, Rafi Eitan could be forgiven for thinking how easy it had become to steal fissionable materials after the collapse of the Soviet Union. An incident that took place at Sheremeteyevo Airport in Moscow on August 10, 1994, proved exactly that.

At 12:45 P.M. on that day, Justiano Torres, somberly dressed in a gray business suit bought for this one journey, arrived deliberately late for Lufthansa Flight 3369 to Munich. Physically strong, he still sweated a little under the weight of the new black-leather Delsey suitcase. Torres produced his first-class ticket and smiled at the desk clerk. The smile was captured on a camera secretly installed behind the desk to record his every movement.

Other cameras had secretly filmed him over these past months.

Captured on film were his meetings with a disaffected Russian nuclear scientist, Igor Tashanka: their encounters out in the Stalin Hills; their trips on a pleasure steamer on the Moscow River; their dinners at Russian mafia-controlled restaurants; and finally, the meeting where Tashanka passed over the suitcase and in return received an envelope containing $5,000. In every sense, Torres could believe he had struck a wonderful bargain. The suitcase contained fissionable material.

Justiano Torres was a courier for a Colombian drug cartel who had expanded into trafficking in an even deadlier substance. The suitcase contained, in sealed containers, the two hundred grams of plutonium 239 that Tashanka had sold him. It had a street value of $50 million. The plutonium was so lethal that even coming in contact with a microscopic speck would be fatal. The contents of the suitcase were sufficient to make a small nuclear device.

For Uri Saguy, the former head of Israeli military intelligence, the prospect was "every thinking person's nightmare: a bunch of terrorists with their hands on enough fissionable material to devastate Tel Aviv or any other city. In day-to-day intelligence tasking, dealing with a nuclear threat ranks right at the very top."

The Israeli intelligence community had long known that terrorists could manufacture a crude nuclear bomb. An American physics graduate student in the 1970s had carried out and described each one of the processes required. His published work caused huge consternation with Mossad.

Doomsday scenarios were postulated. A bomb could arrive in pieces on board a ship, or be smuggled across a land border and assembled in Israel. The weapon would be detonated by remote control unless impossible demands were met. Would the government stand firm? Mossad's analysts decided that there would be no surrender. This expectation was based on a deep understanding of the terrorist mind at the time: in the 1970s even extreme groups would hesitate to detonate a nuclear bomb because of the political price they would pay. They would become outcasts to even those nations that covertly supported them.

The collapse of Soviet Communism had renewed Mossad's fears. An arena of new uncertainties had been created; no one could say for certain how the new political dimensions within Russia would develop. Already Mossad had discovered Soviet Scud missiles had been exported for hard currency to several Middle East countries.

Soviet technicians had helped Algeria build a nuclear reactor. Russia had a large stockpile of biological weapons, including a super-plague germ that could kill millions of people. Supposing even a small portion of it fell into the hands of terrorists? Even a small jar filled with the bug could decimate Tel Aviv. But above all it was the fear Russia would sell off its nuclear arsenal that was the pressing concern. For Uri Saguy that was a threat "no one could ignore."

Mossad psychologists drew up psycho-profiles of Russian scientists likely to provide materials and their motives: there were those who would do it purely for cash, others for complex ideological reasons. The list of Soviet facilities from which materials could be stolen was dauntingly large. Mossad's director general, Shabtai Shavit, sent two katsas to Moscow with special orders to infiltrate the scientific community.

One of them was Lila. Born of Jewish parents in Beirut, she had a degree in physics from the Hebrew University in Jerusalem and worked in Mossad's scientific intelligence section. She had witnessed the tentative meetings Torres had with Tashanka and how the deal making progressed.

Lila and her colleague had worked closely with Mossad agents in Germany and elsewhere. The trail had led her to Colombia and back into the Middle East. Other Mossad operatives had observed meetings in Cairo, Damascus, and Baghdad. New leads had opened up: Bosnia appeared to be a possible route for smuggling the plutonium 239 to its final destination—Iraq. But, not for the first time, knowing and proving the complicity of the Saddam regime were difficult.

That was why Torres was being allowed to fly on an unsuspecting commercial airliner with a lethal cargo. The decision to do so had been carefully weighed by the heads of Russian and German intelligence. They had concluded that the risk of the plutonium detonating was "infinitesimal." Permission for Torres to travel had been given by both their respective governments to see if Torres would lead them to the end user for the material. Israel had not been consulted on the matter. The operation was officially only a German-Russian one. In the past, Mossad, on more than one occasion, had been a silent partner where other agencies had claimed the credit.

From her vantage point overlooking the airport departure gates on that August morning, Lila knew her role in this case was over. A

Mossad agent—code-named Adler—was already positioned in the lobby of the Excelsior Hotel in midtown Munich, where Torres was to make his handover. Another agent—Mort—was at the Munich airport awaiting the arrival of Flight 3369.

A third agent—Ib—sat two seats back from Torres as the plane headed west on its three-hour flight. Across the aisle from Torres sat Viktor Sidorenko, Russian deputy minister for atomic energy. His responsibilities included protecting his country's nuclear arsenal. Russia now had around 130 tons of weapons-grade plutonium, enough to make sixteen thousand atom bombs, each twice the size of the one that destroyed Hiroshima.

Sidorenko had received a number of disturbing reports that detailed lax controls and low morale among the staff of hundreds of Russian institutes and research centers with access to radioactive substances. A few months before, a worker at a nuclear plant in the Urals had been arrested with radioactive uranium pellets in a plastic bag. Over five kilos of uranium had been squirreled away by workmen at another plant near Minsk and hidden in their homes. The thefts had only come to light when a kilo was sold for twenty bottles of vodka. Sidorenko was traveling to Germany to assure Chancellor Helmut Kohl's government that cases like this would never happen again; the Germans were threatening sanctions.

At 5:45 P.M., exactly on time, Flight 3369 landed at Munich's Franz Josef Strauss Airport and taxied to its terminal C stand. Minister Sidorenko was the first to deplane. He was whisked away by a waiting car and driven to a high-security area. There he was told that Tashanka had just been arrested in Moscow.

Torres entered the arrivals area. The presence of heavily armed German police would not have surprised him. Munich had always made a show of its security after the Olympic Games massacre of Israeli athletes. Torres made a telephone call to the Excelsior Hotel, and was connected to room 23. Waiting there was a Spaniard, Javier Arratibel, whose passport described him as an "industrialist." In fact, he was the broker for the plutonium. He called a man he knew only as Julio-O.

The calls had been monitored by German intelligence officers. As Torres strolled to the luggage carousel to collect his suitcase, he was observed from a nearby office by Munich police superintendent Wolfgang Stoephasios and the senior intelligence officer.

Torres picked up his suitcase and walked toward the Nothing to Declare exit. Ib and Mort followed. They could do no more. They had no power of arrest here. Stoephasios emerged from his office. It was the signal for action.

In moments Torres was surrounded and bundled away. The suitcase was taken to a room. Inside waited a white-suited figure with a Geiger counter. With him were bomb-disposal experts. They used a portable X-ray machine to see if the case was wired with explosives. It was not. Neither was there a telltale clicking from the Geiger to indicate a leak of fissionable material. The suitcase was opened. Inside, wrapped in heavy plastic, were the containers of plutonium 239. They were removed and placed in bomb-blast boxes and carried to a waiting armored truck. From there they were taken to Germany's atomic energy complex.

In the Excelsior Hotel, Arratibel was arrested. But the next link in the chain, Julio-O, had slipped across the border into Hungary. The Hungarian police said they would look for him. But no one was holding his breath in Munich. Hungary was known to be one of the entry points to the West for Russian smugglers.

The Mossad men informed Tel Aviv what had happened.

In Tel Aviv, Mossad's director general, Shabtai Shavit, saw the outcome as another small victory in the endless battle against nuclear terrorism. But he was not alone in wondering how many other suitcases had slipped through, how soon before there would be a nuclear explosion unless impossible demands were met.

A few miles away from where Shavit pondered such questions, Rafi Eitan, the man who had masterminded what the FBI and CIA still believed had been the theft of nuclear material from the Numec reprocessing plant at Apollo, continued to spend his free time carving yet more sculptures from scrap materials. Outwardly he was at peace with the world. Both the Pollard and Apollo operations had faded from memory; when pressed, he said he could not recall the first names of either Pollard or Shapiro. LAKAM had officially been closed down. Rafi Eitan insisted that his work nowadays was very different from what he had done before: he was a director of a small shipping company in Havana where he also had an interest in a company manufacturing agricultural pesticides. He claimed a close relationship with Fidel Castro, "which probably does not please the

Americans." He had never set foot in the United States since his trip to Apollo. He said he had no desire to, not least because he suspected he might still be asked "a lot of questions" about Jonathan Pollard and what exactly had happened following his visit to Apollo.

Then, in April 1997, Rafi Eitan's name began to surface in connection with a Mossad spy in Washington whom the FBI identified and code-named "Mega."

His own well-placed source within Mossad had told Rafi Eitan that the FBI had begun to explore the role Mega could have had in the way Jonathan Pollard had been run. Had Mega been the source for some of the ultrasecret material Pollard had passed on? The FBI had recently reinterviewed Pollard in prison and he had admitted that even his high security clearance had not been enough to obtain some of the documents his handler, the funereal Yagur, had requested. The FBI knew such documents had a special code word through which they had to be accessed, which changed frequently, sometimes even on a daily basis. Yet Yagur had seemed to know the code within a matter of hours to give to Pollard. Had Mega provided it? Was Mega the second Israeli spy in Washington the FBI had long suspected? How close had he been to Rafi Eitan?

These were the dangerous questions now being asked in Washington that could shatter the relationship between Washington and Tel Aviv.

After the FBI had identified him as the puppet master behind Pollard, Rafi Eitan had accepted that his time in Israeli intelligence was finally over. He had looked forward to ending his days facing no greater risk than being scorched from the blowtorch he wielded when forming his sculptures.

Instinctively he knew that events in Washington posed a threat not only to him—a CIA snatch squad could try to grab him as he came and went from Cuba and bring him to Washington for questioning, and there was no way of telling what would happen then; but the discovery of Mega's existence would also be exercising minds in the upper echelons of the Israeli intelligence community's Va'adat Rashei Hesherytin— the Committee of the Heads of Service whose primary function is to coordinate all intelligence and security activities at home and abroad.

But even they knew nothing about who Mega was. All they had been told was that he was highly placed in the Clinton administration. Whether the president had inherited him from the Bush government was another carefully guarded secret. Only the incumbent Mossad memune knew how long Mega had been in place.

The committee members did, however, know that the FBI's counterintelligence division finally believed that the lack of action against Mossad was due to the power of the Jewish lobby in Washington, and the reluctance of successive administrations to confront it. Once more that lobby could be called upon to dampen the firestorm building since Mega had first been discovered by the FBI. On February 16, 1997, the National Security Agency (NSA) had provided the FBI with an intercept of a late-night telephone conversation from the Israeli embassy between a Mossad intelligence officer identified only as Dov, and his superior in Tel Aviv, whose name had not been revealed during the short conversation.

Dov had asked "for guidance" as to whether he "should go to Mega" for a copy of a letter written by Warren Christopher, then secretary of state, to PLO chairman Yasser Arafat. The letter contained a set of assurances given to Arafat by Christopher on January 16 about the withdrawal of Israeli troops from the West Bank city of Hebron. Dov was instructed by the voice in Tel Aviv "to forget the letter. This is not something we use Mega for."

The brief conversation had been the first clue the FBI had of the importance of Mega. The code name had not been heard before in its around-the-clock surveillance of the Israeli embassy and its diplomats. Using state-of-the-art computers, the FBI narrowed the urgent search for the identity of Mega to someone who either worked there or had access to a senior official employed by the National Security Council, the body that advises the president on intelligence and defense-related matters. Its office is in the White House, and its members include the vice president and the secretaries of state and defense. The director of Central Intelligence and the chairman of the Joint Chiefs of Staff serve in an advisory role. The permanent staff is headed by the president's national security adviser.

How the Israeli embassy had learned its secure communications channel with Tel Aviv had been breached still remained as closely guarded as the identity of Mega. Like all Israeli missions, the Washington embassy was constantly updated with more sophisticated systems for encryption and burst transmissions: a significant portion of this equipment has been adapted from stolen U.S. blueprints.

On February 27, 1997, a pleasant spring morning in Tel Aviv, the members of the Committee of the Heads of Services drove from their various offices around the city along the broad road called Rehov Shaul Hamaleku to a guarded gate in a high blank wall tipped with barbed wire. All that could be seen of what lay behind the wall were the roofs of buildings. Rising above them was a massive concrete tower visible all over Tel Aviv. At various heights were unsightly clusters of electronic antennae. The tower was the centerpiece of the headquarters of the Israel Defense Forces. The complex is known as the Kirya, which simply means "place."

At a little before 11:00 A.M., the intelligence chiefs used their swipe cards to access a building near the tower. Like most Israeli government offices, the conference room they entered was shabby.

The meeting was chaired by Danny Yatom, who had recently been appointed as Mossad's latest chief by Prime Minister Benyamin Netanyahu. Yatom had a reputation as a hard-liner, very much in keeping with Netanyahu. The Tel Aviv rumor mills had it that the new Mossad chief had "baby-sat" the embattled prime minister when Netanyahu's colorful private life threatened his career. The men around the cedarwood conference table listened attentively as Yatom outlined the strategy to be adopted should the "situation" with Mega become a full-blown crisis.

Israel would deliver a strongly worded protest that its Washington embassy's diplomatic status had been violated by the bugging—a move that would undoubtedly cause embarrassment to the Clinton administration. Next, sayanim connected to the U.S. media should be instructed to plant stories that Mega was an incorrect decoding of the Hebrew slang *Elga*, which had long been Mossad-speak for the CIA. Further, the word Mega was part of one well-known to U.S. intelligence. Megawatt was a code name it had until recently used jointly with Mossad to describe shared intelligence. For good measure sayanim should add that another word, Kilowatt, was used for commonly shared terrorist data.

But, for the moment, nothing would be done, Yatom concluded.

In March 1997, on receipt of information from Mossad's *katsa* in Washington, Yatom took action. He send a yahalomin team to Washington to follow-up on the *katsa's* report that President Clinton was repeatedly indulging in phone-sex calls with a a former White House aide, Monica Lewinsky. He was making the calls from the Oval Office to her apartment in the Watergate complex. Knowing that the White House was totally protected by electronic counter-measures, the ya-halomin team focused on Lewinsky's apartment. They began to inter-cept explicit phone calls from the president to Lewinsky. The recordings were couriered by diplomatic bag to Tel Aviv.

On March 27, Clinton once more invited Lewinsky to the Oval Office and revealed he believed a foreign embassy was taping their conversations. He did not give her any more details, but shortly af-terwards the affair ended.

In Tel Aviv, Mossad's strategies pondered how to use the highly embarrassing taped conversations; they were the stuff of blackmail—though no one suggested any attempt should be made to blackmail the president of the United States. Some, however, saw the recordings as a potent weapon to be used if Israel found itself with its back to the wall in the Middle East and unable to count on Clinton's support.

There was common consensus that the FBI must also be aware of the conversations between Clinton and Lewinsky. Some strate-gists urged Yatom to use "the back-door channel" with Washington and let the FBI know Mossad was aware of the president's phone calls: it would be a not-very-subtle way of telling the agency to back off in their continuing hunt for Mega. Other analysts urged a wait-and-see policy, arguing that the information would remain explosive whenever it was released. That view prevailed.

In September 1998, the Starr report was published and Yatom had left office. The report contained a short reference to Clinton warning Lewinsky back in March 1997 that his phone was being bugged by a foreign embassy. Starr had not pursued the matter when Lewinsky had given her testimony before the grand jury about her affair with Clinton. However, the FBI could only have seen the revelations as further evidence of their inability to unmask Mega.

Six months later, March 5th 1999, the *New York Post* published in a cover story the revelations in the original edition of this book. The *Post* story began: "Israel blackmailed President Clinton with phone-tapped tapes of his steamy sex talks with Monica Lewinsky, a blockbuster new book charges. The price Clinton paid for the silence of the Mossad spy agency was calling off an FBI hunt for a top-level Israeli mole."

Within hours this complete distortion of the facts in the book (which I had carefully checked with sources in Israel), the *Post*'s version had appeared in thousands of newspapers around the world.

The essential point of my story, that public prosecutor Kenneth Starr had not fully pursued his impeachment investigation into Clinton, was lost. Starr had noted in his report that on March 29th 1997: "He (Clinton) told her (Lewinsky) that he suspected that a foreign embassy (he did not specify which one) was taping his telephones. If anyone ever asked about their phone sex, she should say that they knew that their calls were being monitored all day long, and the phone sex was a put-on."

The president's words most strongly indicated he was aware that he had become a potential target for blackmail. By talking to Lewinsky over a public phone network—there is no evidence he had attempted to secure the phone in her apartment—the president had indeed left himself open to interception by foreign eavesdroppers and, even more so, to the powerful microwave vacuum cleaners of the National Security Agency. Given that any incumbent president routinely gets NSA reports, he would also have known that his calls to Monica could well end up on the Washington rumor mills.

A sense of the panic my revelations created in the White House can be seen from its briefing to correspondents by Oval Office spokesmen Barry Toiv and David Leavy. There is a shifting-sands feeling about their responses that the official White House transcript has retained.

Q: Why did the president reportedly tell Monica Lewinsky that he was concerned about his phone conversations being taped?

TOIV: Well, as you know, other than the president's testimony in this case, we really haven't commented on specifics, on other specifics like that and we're not going to start now.

Q: When the president heard about this, was he concerned by it, was he shocked by it? What was his reaction, Mr. Toiv?

TOIV: To be honest, I haven't gotten the president's reaction to the book.

Q: Well, why did he say that to Monica Lewinsky? Why did he warn her?

TOIV: I've already not answered that question. (Laughter). I'm sorry.

Q: I know you've not answered it, but it's very valid, really.

TOIV: Well, again, we're not going to get into commenting on specifics beyond what the president has already testified to.

Q: I don't understand why you think it's legitimate for you not to comment on the president of the United States supposedly saying that he thinks a foreign government is taping his conversations. For you just to say, no comment.

TOIV: There have been questions about all sorts of comments that have been made or testified to and we have not gone beyond the president's testimony in discussing these and we're not going to do that.

Q: That's because you've said it's unseemly and it's about sex. This is about the national security of the United States and the president supposedly saying that a foreign government is taping his conversations. And you're just going to say sorry, no comment?

TOIV: I am not going to go beyond what he has already testified to.

Q: You're not denying it. You're not denying it.

LEAVY: Obviously, we're not aware of a mole at the White House. But it's the long-standing practice for people who speak at this podium to refer calls to the appropriate authorities who undertake these types of investigations.

Q: Was there any attempt by the president to intervene in any kind of investigation or search for a mole?

LEAVY: No. There is no basis in that allegation whatsoever.

Q: Well, there is a basis for it. There is a sworn testimony that Lewinsky gave that attributes to the president a comment that a foreign embassy was taping—

LEAVY: And Barry just answered that question.

Q: His answer was that he is not going to comment on it. That's not much of an answer. With all due respect.

LEAVY: Let me say two things—noted.

TOIV: I wouldn't go beyond my comments.

LEAVY: Yes, I'm definitely not going to add to Barry's comments. But let me just say this. We take all the necessary precautions to secure the president's communications. There is absolutely no basis for the allegation in the book.

Q: Are you getting that from CIA or FBI, or are you getting it out of just an automatic reflex?

LEAVY: You can take that as authoritative.

Q: I understand that you would have his communications secure. However, if he picks up the phone and calls some ordinary citizen at 2:30 A.M. in the morning at their apartment, what's to say that that person's phone couldn't be tapped? Does your security system prevent that?

LEAVY: There is some very serious allegations in this book, and what I am saying is that there is absolutely no basis for the allegation. So I have to leave it at that.

Not one serious newspaper made any attempt to follow up those revealing responses.

It turned out that Mossad was not the only organization that had taped the sex phone calls. The Republican senator for Arizona, Jon

Kyl, a member of the Select Committee on Intelligence, told his local newspaper *The Arizona Republic* that, "a U.S. intelligence agency may have taped telephone conversations between President Clinton and Monica Lewinsky. There are different agencies in the government that make it their business to tape certain things for certain reasons, and it was one of those agencies."

Kyl refused to identify to the newspaper who the agency or agencies were: "That's something I absolutely can't get into in any greater detail." Of his sources he said, "By virtue of who they are, they have credibility. You can assume that they are people who at some period in time have been in the employ of the federal government." He went on to compare the existence of the tapes to the "smoking-gun" evidence in the Watergate scandal.

These explosive allegations from a respected politician were never pursued into the public domain.

According to at least one well-placed Israeli intelligence source, Rafi Eitan had received a phone call from Yatom reinforcing the need to stay well clear of the United States for the foreseeable future.

Rafi Eitan did not need to be told how ironic it would be if he fell victim to the very technique that had made him a legend—the kidnapping of Adolf Eichmann. Even worse would be to be quietly killed by one of the methods that had burnished his reputation among men who saw assassination as part of the job.

CHAPTER 6

AVENGERS

On a warm afternoon in mid-October 1995, a technician of Mossad's internal security division, Autahat Paylut Medienit (APM), used a hand-operated scanner to check an apartment off Pinsker Street in downtown Tel Aviv for bugging devices. The apartment was one of several safe houses Mossad owned around the city. The search was an indication of the sensitivity of the meeting shortly to take place there. Satisfied the apartment was electronically clean, he left.

The apartment's furniture could have come from a garage sale; nothing seemed to match. A few cheaply framed pictures hung on the walls, views of the Israel tourists liked to visit. Each room had its own separate unlisted telephone. In the kitchen, instead of domestic appliances, were a computer and modem, a shredder, a fax, and, where an oven would be, a safe.

Usually the safe houses were dormitories for trainees from the Mossad school for spies on the outskirts of the city while they learned street craft: how to tail someone or themselves avoid surveillance; how to set up a dead-letter box, or exchange information concealed inside a newspaper. Day and night the streets of Tel Aviv were their proving ground under the watchful eye of instructors. Back in the safe houses, the lessons continued: how to brief a katsa going to a target country; how to write special-ink letters or use a computer to create information capable of being transmitted in very short bursts on specified frequencies.

An important part of the seemingly endless hours of training was how to form relationships with innocent, unsuspecting people. Yaakov Cohen, who worked for twenty-five years as a katsa under deep cover around the world, believed one reason for his success was lessons learned in those lectures:

"Everyone and anyone became a tool. I could lie to them because truth was not part of my relationship with them. All that mattered was using them for Israel's benefit. From the very beginning, I learned a philosophy: Do what was right for Mossad and for Israel."

Those who could not live by that credo found themselves swiftly dismissed from the service. For David Kimche, regarded as one of Mossad's best operatives:

"It's the old story of many think they are called, few are chosen. In that way we are a little like the Catholic Church. Those who remain, develop bonds which will carry them through life. We live by the rule of 'I help you, you help me.' You learn to trust people with your life. No greater trust can ever be given by one person to another."

By the time every man or woman who had access to the safe houses graduated to the next group, that philosophy had been engraved on their minds. They were now katsas departing on a mission or returning to be debriefed. Known as "jumpers" because they operated overseas on a short-term basis, they inevitably called the safe houses "jump sites." Too much imaginative description was frowned upon by their superiors.

Finally, the safe houses were used as meeting places for an informer, or to interrogate a suspect who had the potential to be recruited as a "mole." The only indication of their numbers has come from a former Mossad junior officer, Victor Ostrovsky. He claimed in 1991 there were "about 35,000 in the world; 20,000 of these operational and 15,000 sleepers. 'Black' agents are Arabs, while 'white' agents are non-Arabs. 'Warning agents' are strategic agents used to warn of war preparations: a doctor in a Syrian hospital who notices a large new supply of drugs and medicines arriving; a harbor employee who spots increased activity of warships."

Some of these agents had received their first instructions in a safe house like the one that had been meticulously checked for bugs on that October afternoon. Later in the day, a handful of senior members of Israel's intelligence community would meet around the apartment's dining-room table to sanction an assassination that would have the full approval of Prime Minister Yitzhak Rabin.

In the three years he had been in that office, Rabin had attended a growing number of funerals for the victims of terrorist attacks, each time walking behind pallbearers and watching grown men weep as they listened to the committal prayer. With each death he had conducted "a funeral in my own heart." Afterward he had again read the words from the prophet Ezekiel: "And the enemy shall know I am the Lord when I can lay down my vengeance on them."

This was not the first time Rabin's vengeance had been felt; Rabin had himself on more than one occasion participated in an act of revenge. Most notable had been the assassination of Yasser Arafat's deputy, Khalil Al-Wazir, known throughout the Arab world and on Mossad's Honeywell computer as Abu Jihad, the voice of holy war, who lived in Tunisia. In 1988, Rabin had been Israel's defense minister when the decision was taken in the same apartment off Pinsker Street that Abu Jihad must die.

For two months Mossad agents conducted an exhaustive reconnaissance of Abu Jihad's villa in the resort of Sidi Bou Said on the outskirts of Tunis. Access roads, points of entry, fence heights and types, windows, doors, locks, defenses, the routing employed by Abu Jihad's guards: everything was monitored, checked, and checked again.

They watched Abu Jihad's wife play with her children; they came alongside her as she shopped and went to the hairdresser. They listened to her husband's phone calls, bugged their bedroom, listened to their lovemaking. They calculated distances from one room to another, found out what the neighbors did, when they were at home, and logged the makes, colors, and registrations of all the vehicles that came and went from the villa.

The rule for preparing an assassination Meir Amit had laid down all those years ago was constantly in their minds: Think like your target and only stop being him when you pull the trigger.

Satisfied, the team returned to Tel Aviv. For the next month they practiced their deadly mission in and around a Mossad safe house near Haifa that matched the target villa. From the time they would enter Abu Jihad's house, it should take the unit just twenty-two seconds to murder him.

On April 16, 1988, the order was given for the operation to go ahead.

That night several Israeli air force Boeing 707s took off from a military base south of Tel Aviv. One carried Yitzhak Rabin and other high-ranking Israeli officers. Their aircraft was in constant touch by safe radio with the execution team already in position and led by an operative code-named "Sword." The other aircraft was crammed with jamming and monitoring devices. Two more 707s acted as fuel tankers. High above the villa the fleet of aircraft circled, following every move on the ground through a secure radio frequency. A little after midnight on April 17 the airborne officers heard Abu Jihad had returned home in the Mercedes Yasser Arafat had given him as a wedding gift. Prior to that the hit team had set up sensitive listening devices able to hear everything inside the villa.

From his vantage point near the villa, Sword announced into his lip mike that he could hear Abu Jihad climbing the stairs, going to his bedroom, whispering to his wife, tiptoeing to an adjoining bedroom to kiss his sleeping son, before finally going to his study on the ground floor. The details were picked up by the electronic warfare plane—the Israeli version of an American AWAC and relayed to Rabin's command aircraft. At 12:17 A.M. he ordered: "Go!"

Outside the villa, Abu Jihad's driver was asleep in the Mercedes. One of Sword's men ran forward, pressed a silenced Beretta into his ear, and pulled the trigger. The driver slumped dead across the front seat.

Next, Sword and another member of the hit team laid an explosive charge at the base of the villa's heavy iron front door. A new type of "silent" plastic explosive, it made little sound as it blew the doors clean off their hinges. Inside, two of Abu Jihad's bodyguards were standing in the entrance hall, too stunned by the explosion to move. They, too, were shot dead by silenced weapons.

Running to the study, Sword found Abu Jihad watching video footage of the PLO. As he rose to his feet, Sword shot him twice in the chest. Abu Jihad crashed heavily to the floor. Sword stepped quickly forward and put two more bullets through his forehead.

Leaving the room, he encountered Abu Jihad's wife. She was holding her small son in her arms.

"Get back to your room," Sword ordered in Arabic.

Then he and the team vanished into the night. From the time they had entered the villa to departure had taken them only thirteen seconds—nine vital seconds better than their best practice run.

For the first time, an Israeli assassination met with public criticism. Cabinet minister Ezer Weizman warned that "liquidating individuals will not advance the peace process."

Nevertheless the assassinations continued.

Two months later, South African police were finally forced to reveal a secret that Israel had pressed them to keep: Mossad had executed a Johannesburg businessman, Alan Kidger, who had been supplying high-tech equipment to Iran and Iraq that could be used to manufacture biochemical weapons. Kidger had been found with his arms and legs amputated. Johannesburg's chief police investigator, Colonel Charles Landman, said the killing was a "clear message from the Israeli government through its Mossad."

Six weeks before the execution of Abu Jihad, Mossad had played an important role in another controversial assassination—that of three unarmed members of the IRA shot dead on a Sunday afternoon in Gibraltar by a team of Britain's Special Air Services marksmen.

In previous years, some of their colleagues from British intelligence had been secretly brought to Tel Aviv by Rafi Eitan to witness firsthand how Mossad executed Arab terrorists in the back streets of Beirut and Lebanon's Bekáa Valley.

Four months before the Gibraltar shootings, Mossad agents had begun their own surveillance of Mairead Farrell, Sean Savage, and

Daniel McCann in the belief they were once more on a "shopping spree for Arab arms for the IRA."

Mossad's close interest in the activities of the IRA went back to the time when the Thatcher government had, in the utmost secrecy, brought Rafi Eitan to Belfast to brief the security forces on the developing links between the Irish terror groups and the Hezbollah.

"I arrived on a rainy day. It rained every day I was in Ireland. I told the British all we knew. Then I went on a tour of the province, all the way down to the border with the Republic. I was careful not to cross over. Imagine what the Irish government would have said if they'd picked me up! Before I left I arranged for the SAS to come to Israel so they could see something of our methods in handling terrorists."

From those early beginnings a close working relationship developed between the SAS and Mossad. Senior Mossad officers would regularly travel to SAS headquarters in Hereford to brief special forces on operations in the Middle East. On at least one occasion a joint Mossad-SAS unit trailed several high-ranking IRA men from Belfast to Beirut and photographed them in meetings with Hezbollah leaders.

In October 1987, Mossad agents tracked the tramp steamer *Eksund* as it made its way through the Mediterranean with 120 tons of arms, including surface-to-air missiles, rocket-propelled grenade launchers, machine guns, explosives, and detonators. All had been purchased through IRA contacts in Beirut. The *Eksund* was intercepted by the French authorities.

Unable to make headway with the Irish security authorities—at least one Mossad officer still believed this stemmed from Israel's strong opposition to Ireland's peacekeeping role in Lebanon—Mossad used Britain's SAS as a conduit to tip off Dublin about other arms shipments heading for Ireland.

The Mossad agents trailing the IRA commando unit in Spain quickly decided they were not there to meet Arab arms dealers, nor to make contact with ETA, the Basque terrorist group. Nevertheless, the Mossad team continued to dog the footsteps of Spain's International Terrorism Unit, who were also following the Irish trio.

At first there was a keep-your-distance attitude by the Spaniards. This was their operation—the first time they had become seriously involved with both M15 and the SAS in dealing with the IRA. Understandably, the Spaniards wanted to ensure the glory, if it came, would be theirs. Mossad quickly made it clear that all they wanted to do was help. Relieved, the Spaniards were soon working together with Mossad.

When the Spanish lost track of Mairead Farrell, it was a katsa who located her. He discovered that Farrell had hired another car, a white Fiesta, and parked it, loaded with sixty-four kilos of Semtex and thirty-six kilos of shrapnel, in an underground parking lot in Marbella.

The fashionable resort is not only a favorite refuge from the fierce desert sun where a number of Arab notables spend their time dreaming of the day the hated Israel will be overrun; Marbella is only a short distance from the raffish marina of Puerto Banus, where many Arab petrodollar millionaires kept their luxury yachts. Mossad had long feared that the boats traveled the length of the Mediterranean to smuggle explosives and weapons to Arab terrorists. Farrell's car was suspected of being parked for that purpose, ready to be hoisted on board a boat ostensibly bound on a cruise to the Holy Land.

The Mossad team conducted surveillance on the car. They also spotted Farrell at the wheel of another Fiesta, the one she had used to drive McCann and Savage around Spain these past weeks. Two of the Mossad team followed the IRA unit as it drove south toward Puerto Banus. Ten minutes after leaving Marbella, Farrell passed the entrance to the marina and continued on down the coast.

Using their car radio tuned to the police channel, the Mossad katsa alerted the Spanish police that the IRA trio were heading toward Gibraltar. The Spanish alerted the British authorities. The SAS team moved into position. Hours later Farrell, McCann, and Savage were shot dead. They were given no warning or chance to surrender. They were executed.

A week later, Stephen Lander, the MI5 officer officially credited with running the operation—and who would later become director general of MI5—telephoned Admoni to thank Mossad for their help with the assassination.

On that October evening in 1995, in the safe house off Pinsker Street, all was ready for the meeting to settle the next assassination. Selected for execution was the religious head of Islamic Jihad,

Fathi Shkaki. Mossad had established that his group had orchestrated the deaths of over twenty Israeli passengers in a bus destroyed the previous January by two suicide bombers outside the small town of Beit Lid.

The incident brought the number of terrorist attacks to over ten thousand in the last quarter century. In that time over four hundred Israelis had been killed and another thousand injured. Many of those responsible for this catalog of death and maiming had themselves been hunted down and killed in what katsa Yaakov Cohen, who had himself done his share of revenge taking, would describe as "all those back streets that have no names; where a knife can be more effective at times than a gun; where it's either kill or be killed."

In this pitiless world Shkaki had long been lionized by his people. It was he who had personally granted the bombers of Beit Lid absolution from the inviolable Islamic prohibition against suicide. To do so he had combed the Koran to extrapolate a philosophical assumption that oppression makes the oppressed discover new strengths; in preparing the suicide bombers he had exploited the psychological flaws in unbalanced youngsters who, like the Japanese kamikaze teenagers in World War II, went to their own end on that January day in a state of religious fervor. Afterward, Shkaki had paid for their death notices in Jihad's newspaper and, at Friday prayers, had praised their sacrifice, assuring their families their sons had found a place in heaven.

In the tension of the streets where he operated, it had become a matter of honor for a family to provide a son for Shkaki to sacrifice. Those who died were remembered each day after the muezzin wailed through the crackling loudspeakers to call the faithful to prayer. In the shadowy coolness of the mosques of south Lebanon, their memories were kept alive.

His next recruits chosen, their target selected, Shkaki would hand the youths over to his bomb makers. They were the strategists who could study a photograph of a target and decide upon the quantity of explosive needed. Like ancient alchemists, they worked by experience and instinct, and their language was filled with the words that brought death: "oxidizer," "desensitizer," "plasticines," and "freezing point depressants." These were Shkaki's people. Borrowing a phrase once used by a leader of his hated enemy, Israel, he told them all: "We fight, therefore we exist."

On that October evening when his fate was about to be settled in the Tel Aviv safe house, Shkaki was at home in Damascus with his wife, Fathia. The apartment was strikingly different from the squalor of the refugee camps where he was venerated. Expensive carpets and wall hangings were gifts from the ayatollahs of Iran. A gold-framed photograph of Shkaki with Mu'ammar Gadhafi was a present from the Libyan leader. A coffee service made of silver was a gift from the Syrian president. Shkaki's clothes were far removed from the simple gown he wore on his crusades among the impoverished masses in south Lebanon. At home he wore robes cut from the finest cloth available from London's Savile Row and his feet were shod in custom-made shoes bought in Rome, not the bazaar sandals he wore in public.

Over his favorite meal of couscous, Shkaki reassured his wife he would be safe on his forthcoming trip to Libya to seek further funds from Gadhafi; he hoped to return with one million dollars, the full amount he had requested in a fax to Libya's revolutionary headquarters in Tripoli. As usual the money would be laundered through a Libyan bank in Valletta on the island of Malta. Shkaki planned to spend less than a day on the island before catching the flight home.

News of the stopover in Malta had prompted his two teenage sons to give him their own shopping order: half a dozen shirts each from a Malta store where Shkaki had shopped previously.

Fathia Shkaki would recall: "My husband insisted if the Israelis were planning a move against him, they would have done so by now. The Jews always respond quickly to any incident. But my husband was very certain in his case they would do nothing to make Syria angry."

Until three months before, Shkaki would have correctly judged the mood in Tel Aviv. Early in the summer of 1995, Rabin had turned down a Mossad plan to firebomb Shkaki's apartment in the western suburb of Damascus. Uri Saguy, then chief of military intelligence and effectively Israel's intelligence supremo, who had authority even over Mossad, had told Rabin he detected "a sea change in Damascus. Assad is still on the surface our enemy. But the only way to overcome him is to do the unexpected. And that means giving up the Golan Heights, give it up completely. Move every one of our people out of there. It's a huge price. But it is the only way to get a proper lasting peace."

Rabin had listened. He knew how much the Golan had personally cost Uri Saguy. He had spent most of his military career defending its rugged terrain. He had been wounded four times doing so. Yet he was prepared to put all this behind him to see Israel have real peace.

The prime minister had postponed Mossad's plans to eliminate Shkaki while Saguy continued to explore the reality of his hopes.

They had withered in the heat of the region's summer, and Rabin, who was now a Nobel Peace Prize winner, had ordered Shkaki's execution.

Shabtai Shavit, in his last major operation as Mossad's chief, ordered a "black agent" in Damascus to resume electronic surveillance of Shkaki's apartment. The agent's American equipment was sophisticated enough to override the defense circuit breakers in Shkaki's Russian-built communications system.

Details of Shkaki's forthcoming visit to Libya and Malta were sent to Tel Aviv.

Now, on that October evening in 1995, the heads of Israel's three most powerful intelligence services made their way through the crowds strolling along Pinsker Street. Each one supported the conditions for executing a self-proclaimed enemy of Israel that Meir Amit had so clearly defined when he had been director general:

"There would be no killing of political leaders. They needed to be dealt with politically. There would be no killing of a terrorist's family. If its members got in the way, that was not our problem. Each execution had to be sanctioned by the prime minister of the day. And everything must be done by the book. Minutes kept of the decision taken. Everything neat and tidy. Our actions must not be seen as some act of state-sponsored murder but the ultimate judicial sanction the state could bring. We would be no different from the hangman or any other lawfully appointed executioner."

Since the successful hunting down of the nine terrorists who had killed the Israeli athletes at the Olympic Games in 1972, all subsequent assassinations had broadly observed these conditions. Almost twenty-three years to the day since Meir Amit had first formulated the rules for a state-sponsored killing, his successors headed for the safe house.

The first to arrive was Shabtai Shavit. Colleagues unkindly said he had the manner of a front-desk clerk in one of Tel Aviv's lesser hotels: the same carefully pressed clothes, the handshake that never maintained its grip for long. He had been in the job for three years and gave the impression he never quite knew how long he would remain.

Next came Brigadier General Doran Tamir, chief intelligence officer for the Israel Defense Forces. Nimble and in the prime of his life, everything about him suggested the authority that came from long years of commanding.

Finally Uri Saguy arrived, strolling into the safe house like a warrior god on his way to stardom even more glittering than his position as director of Aman, military intelligence. Soft-voiced and self-deprecating, he continued to provoke controversy among his peers by insisting that beneath its renewed bluster, Syria was still ready to talk peace.

The relationship among the three men was, in Shavit's words, "cautiously cordial."

Said Uri Saguy, "We can hardly compare with each other. As head of Aman, I tasked the other two. There was competition between us but, as long as we were serving the same aim, it's fine."

For two hours they sat around the living-room table and reviewed the plan to have Fathi Shkaki murdered. His execution would be an act of pure vengeance, the biblical "eye for an eye" principle Israelis liked to believe justified such killings. But sometimes Mossad killed a person when he stubbornly refused to provide his skills to support Israel's aspirations. Then, rather than risk those talents falling into the hands of an enemy, he too was ruthlessly terminated.

Dr. Gerald Bull, a Canadian scientist, was the world's greatest expert on barrel ballistics. Israel had made several unsuccessful attempts to buy his expertise. Each time Bull had made clear his distaste for the Jewish state.

Instead he had offered his services to Saddam Hussein to build a supergun capable of launching shells containing nuclear, chemical, or biological warheads from Iraq directly into Israel. The super-gun's barrel was 487 feet long, composed of thirty-two tons of steel supplied by British firms to Iraq. Late in 1989 a prototype had been test-fired at a gunnery range at Mosul in northern Iraq. Saddam Hussein had ordered three of the weapons to be built at a cost of $20 million. Bull was retained as a consultant at $1 million. The project was code-named Babylon.

His company, Space Research Corporation (SRC), was registered in Brussels as an armaments design company. From there it had sent out a detailed requirement list to European suppliers, including twenty in Britain, to provide high-technology components.

On February 17, 1990, a kasta in Brussels obtained copies of documents setting Babylon's technical goals: the supergun was really going to be an intermediate range ballistics missile. The core of the weapon's launch system would be Scud missiles grouped in clusters of eight to give the warheads a range of 1,500 miles. That would place not only Israel but many European cities in range. Bull believed it would be possible to eventually produce a supergun ca-pable of landing a direct hit on London from Baghdad.

Mossad's director general, Nahum Admoni, sought an immediate meeting with Prime Minister Yitzhak Shamir. A former urban guer-rilla leader who had ruthlessly fought the British during the dying weeks of the Mandate, Shamir was the kind of political leader Mos-sad liked, fully supporting the need to destroy Israel's enemies when it was critical and all else failed. During the 1960s, when Nazi rocket scientists were working with Egypt to provide long-range weapons capable of hitting Israel from across the Sinai Desert, Shamir had been called in by Mossad to provide expertise in plan-ning assassinations. His speciality during the Mandate rule had been devising means to eliminate British soldiers. Shamir had sent for-mer members of his underground forces to kill the German sci-entists. Some of these assassins later became founding members of the Mossad's kidon unit.

Shamir spent only a short time studying Mossad's file on Bull. The service had done its usual thorough job tracing Bull's career from the time, at the age of twenty-two, he had been awarded a doctorate in physics and gone to work for the Canadian govern-ment's Armaments and Research Development Establishment.

There he had clashed with senior officials, sowing the seeds for what had become a lifelong hatred of bureaucrats. He had set up as a private consultant—"literally a gun for hire," the file observed with a touch of black humor.

His reputation as an armaments inventor was established in 1976 when he designed a .45 caliber howitzer that could shell targets twenty-five miles away; at that time the only comparable weapon NATO possessed had a maximum range of only seventeen miles. But once more Bull fell foul of government attitudes. NATO members were blocked from buying the new gun because the major European weapon producers had effective political lobbies. Bull finally sold the howitzer to South Africa.

He then moved to China, helping the People's Liberation Army develop its missile capability. Bull enhanced the existing Silkworm rockets by giving them a larger range and a greater payload of explosives. Batches of the rockets were then sold by China to Saddam Hussein. Initially Iraq deployed them in the long-running war against neighboring Iran. But a sufficient quantity of Silkworms remained at Iraqi launch sites for Mossad to believe they would eventually be used against Israel.

Meanwhile, project Babylon was gathering pace. A more advanced prototype had been test-fired. Opponents of the Saddam regime who had been recruited as Mossad informers in Iraq reported that missile nose cones were being designed to hold chemical and biological weapons.

On the afternoon of March 20, 1990, in the prime minister's office, Yitzhak Shamir agreed with Nahum Admoni that Gerald Bull had to die.

Two days after the decision was taken, a two-man kidon team arrived in Brussels. Waiting for them was the katsa who had been closely monitoring Bull's activities.

At 6:45 on the evening of March 22, 1990, the three men drove in a hired car to the apartment block where Bull lived. Each kidon carried a handgun in a holster under his jacket.

Twenty minutes later, the sixty-one-year-old Bull answered the chiming doorbell of his luxury apartment. He was shot five times in the head and the neck, the kidons firing their 7.65-mm pistols in turn, leaving Bull dead outside his doorway. Later, Bull's son,

Michael, would insist his father had been warned that Mossad would kill him. He could not say who had given the warning, or why his father had ignored it.

Once the kidon team was safely back home, Mossad's Department of Psychological Warfare began to feed stories to the media, strongly suggesting that Gerald Bull had died because he had planned to renege on his deal with Saddam Hussein. Now, five years later, the tactics used to execute Bull, a scientist Israel considered as much of a terrorist as Fathi Shkaki, were once more to be implemented on the direct order of another prime minister, Yitzhak Rabin.

On October 24, 1995, two men in their late twenties—code-named Gil and Ran—left Tel Aviv on separate flights; Ran flew to Athens, Gil to Rome. At each airport they collected new British passports handed over by a local sayan. They arrived in Malta on a late-afternoon flight and checked into the Diplomat Hotel overlooking Valletta's harbor.

That evening a motorcycle was delivered to Ran. He told staff he planned to use it to tour the island.

No one at the hotel would recall the two men having any contact. They spent most of their time in their rooms. When one of the bellboys had remarked that Gil's Samsonite case was heavy, Gil had winked and said it was filled with gold bars.

That evening a freighter that had sailed the previous day from the port of Haifa, bound for Italy, radioed the Maltese harbor authorities reporting it had developed engine trouble and, while it was being fixed, the ship would remain hove to off the island. On board the freighter were Shabtai Shavit and a small team of Mossad communication technicians. They established a radio link with Gil, whose suitcase contained a small but powerful radio.

The suitcase's locks had to be opened counterclockwise to deactivate the fuses in the two charges built into the lid. They were designed to explode in the face of anyone who opened the case after turning the keys clockwise. The radio's rhombic antenna, a quarter of a mile of fiber-optic cable, was tightly coiled to form a disk six inches in diameter. Splitters connected the disk to four dipoles welded to the inside corner of the Samsonite. During the night Gil received a number of radio messages from the boat.

Fathi Shkaki had arrived earlier that day on the Tripoli-Valletta ferry, accompanied by Libyan security men who had stayed on board, their responsibilities over when Shkaki came ashore alone. Before doing so, he had shaved off his beard. He identified himself to Maltese immigration officers as Ibrahim Dawish, showing them his Libyan passport. After checking into the Diplomat Hotel, he spent the next few hours in seafront cafés, sipping endless cups of coffee and nibbling sweet Arabic cakes. He made several telephone calls.

The next morning Shkaki was returning with the promised shirts for his sons, strolling along the seafront, when two men on a motorcycle slowed beside him. One of them shot the Jihad leader at point-blank range six times in the head. Shkaki died instantly. The motorcyclists disappeared. Neither was ever found. But an hour later a fishing boat sailed out of Valletta harbor and dropped anchor in the lee of the freighter. Shortly afterward the captain informed the harbor authorities that the engine malfunction had been temporarily repaired but the ship was returning to Haifa for further repairs.

In Iran, the spiritual home of Shkaki, the mullahs declared a day of national mourning. In Tel Aviv, asked to comment on the death, Prime Minister Yitzhak Rabin said: "I am certainly not sad."

A few days later, on November 4, 1995, Rabin was assassinated at a Tel Aviv peace rally, close to the safe house where his order to execute Shkaki had been prepared. Rabin had died at the hands of a Jewish fanatic, Yigal Amir, who in many ways had the same ruthless qualities the prime minister had so admired in Mossad.

Yitzhak Rabin, the hawk who had become a dove, the powerful political leader who had come to realize the only chance of peace in the Middle East was, as he once misquoted his favorite book, the Bible, "is to turn our swords into ploughshares and till the soil with our Arab neighbors," was murdered by one of his own people because he failed to accept that his Jewish enemies would behave with the same ferocity as his old Arab foes had done—both groups determined to destroy his vision of the future.

In 1998 there were forty-eight members in the Mossad kidon unit, six of them women. All were in their twenties and superbly fit. They lived and worked outside Mossad headquarters in Tel Aviv, based in a restricted area of a military base in the Negev Desert. The facility could be adapted to approximate a street or a building where an assassination was to take place. There were getaway cars and an obstacle course to negotiate.

The instructors included former unit members who supervised practice with a variety of guns, and taught how to conceal bombs, administer a lethal injection in a crowd, and make a killing appear accidental. Kidons reviewed films on successful assassinations—the shooting of President John F. Kennedy, for example—and studied the faces and habits of scores of potential targets stored on their own highly restricted computer and memorized the constantly changing street plans of major cities as well as air and seaport layouts.

The unit worked in teams of four who regularly flew abroad on familiarization trips to London, Paris, Frankfurt, and other European cities. There were also occasional trips to New York, Los Angeles, and Toronto. During all of these outings a team was always accompanied by instructors who assessed their skills in setting up an operation without drawing attention to themselves. Targets were chosen from local sayanim volunteers who were only told they were taking part in a security exercise designed to protect an Israeli-owned facility; a synagogue or bank were usually given as the reason. Volunteers found themselves pounced upon in a quiet street and bundled into a car, or had their homes entered in the middle of the night and awoke to find themselves peering down a gun barrel.

Kidons took these training exercises very seriously, for every team was aware of what was known as the "Lillehammer Fiasco."

In July 1973, at the height of the manhunt for the killers of the Israeli athletes at the Munich Olympics, Mossad received a tip that the "Red Prince" Ali Hassan Salameh, who had planned the operation, was working in the small Norwegian town of Lillehammer as a waiter.

Mossad's then director of operations, Michael Harari, had put together a team not drawn from the kidon unit; its members were scattered across the world chasing the remaining terrorists who had carried out the Munich killings. Harari's team had no field experience, but he was confident his own background as a katsa in Europe was sufficient. His team included two women, Sylvia Rafael and Marianne Gladnikoff, and an Algerian, Kemal Bename, who had been a Black September courier before being browbeaten by Harari into becoming a double agent.

The operation had run into disaster from the outset. The arrival of a dozen strangers in Lillehammer, where there had not been a murder for forty years, aroused speculation. The local police began to watch them. Officers were close by when Harari and his team shot dead a Moroccan waiter named Ahmed Bouchiki, who had no connection to terrorism and did not even physically resemble Salameh. Harari and some of his squad managed to escape. But six Mossad operatives were captured, including both women.

They made full confessions, revealing for the first time Mossad's assassination methods and other equally embarrassing details about the service's clandestine activities. The women, together with their male colleagues, were charged with second-degree murder and received jail sentences of five years each.

Returning to Israel, Harari was fired and the entire Mossad undercover network in Europe of safe houses, dead-letter boxes, and secret phone numbers was abandoned.

It would be six years before Ali Hassan Salameh would finally die in the operation masterminded by Rafi Eitan, who said, "Lillehammer was an example of the wrong people for the wrong job. It should never have happened—and must never happen again."

It did.

On July 31, 1997, the day after two Hamas suicide bombers killed 15 and injured another 157 people in a Jerusalem marketplace, Mossad chief Danny Yatom attended a meeting chaired by Prime Minister Benyamin Netanyahu. The prime minister had just come from an emotional press conference at which he had promised that he would never rest until those who planned the suicide bombings were no longer a threat.

Publicly, Netanyahu had appeared calm and resolute, his responses to questions measured and magisterial; Hamas would not escape retribution, but what form that would take was not a matter for discussion. This was the "Bibi" from Netanyahu's days on CNN during the Gulf War, when he had earned repeated praise for his authoritative assessments of Saddam Hussein's responses and how they were viewed in Israel.

But on that stifling day, away from the cameras and surrounded only by Yatom and other senior intelligence officers and his own political advisers, Netanyahu offered a very different image. He was neither cool nor analytical. Instead, in the crowded conference room adjoining his office, he frequently interrupted to shout he was going to "get those Hamas bastards if it's the last thing I do."

He added, according to one of those present, that "you are here to tell me how this is going to happen. And I don't want to read in the newspapers anything about 'Bibi's' revenge. This is about justice—just retribution."

The agenda had been set.

Yatom, well used to the mercurial mood swings of the prime minister, sat silently across the table as Netanyahu continued to bluster. "I want their heads. I want them dead. I don't care how it's done. I just want it done. And I want it done sooner rather than later."

Tension deepened when Netanyahu demanded that Yatom provide a list of all Hamas leaders and their present whereabouts. No prime minister had ever before asked for sensitive operational details at such an early stage. More than one person in the room thought that "Bibi was sending a signal he was going to be hands-on for this one."

It deepened the unease among some Mossad officers that the service was being forced to come too close to Netanyahu. Perhaps sensing this, Yatom told the prime minister that he would provide the list later. Instead, the Mossad chief suggested that it was "time to look at the practical side of things." Locating the Hamas leaders would be "like searching for individual rats in a Beirut sewer."

Once more Netanyahu erupted. He didn't want excuses; he wanted action. And he wanted it to start "here and now."

After the meeting ended, several intelligence officers were left with the impression that Bibi Netanyahu had crossed the fine line where political expediency ended and operational requirements took over. There could not have been a man in the room who did not realize that Netanyahu badly needed a public relations coup to convince the public the act-tough-on-terrorism policy that had brought him into office was not just empty rhetoric. He had also gone from one scandal to another, each time barely wriggling clear by leaving others to carry the blame. His popularity was at an all-time low. His personal life was all over the press. He badly needed to show he was in charge. To deliver the head of a Hamas leader was one surefire way.

A senior Israeli intelligence officer undoubtedly spoke for many when he said:

"While we all agreed there could be no objection to the principle that to cut off the head kills the snake, it was the time frame which was our concern. All Bibi's talk about 'action now' was pure bullshit. Any operation of that nature requires careful planning. Bibi wanted results as if this was a computer game, or one of those old action-hero movies he likes to watch. But it just doesn't work like that in the real world."

Yatom ordered a full search of every Arab country and sent katsas into Gaza and the West Bank to discover more about the where-abouts of the shadowy figures who control Hamas. Throughout August 1997, he was summoned several times to the prime minister's office to report on his progress. There was none. The Israeli intelligence community was rife with accounts of how the prime minister had demanded that Yatom put more men into the field and had begun to hint that if he didn't see results soon, he might have to take "other actions." If Netanyahu had intended this to be a clumsy threat to his Mossad chief, it did not work. Yatom simply said he was "doing everything possible." The unspoken implication was that if the prime minister wanted to fire him, that was his prerogative; but in the public debate that would inevitably follow, there would be questions asked about Netanyahu's own role. But the prime minister continued to press for the death of a Hamas leader—and he wanted it sooner rather than later.

By September 1997, Netanyahu had begun to call Yatom at all hours of the night about progress. The pressurized Mossad chief bowed. He pulled in katsas from other stations. For one, "Yatom was rearranging the map as a knee-jerk to Bibi's demands. Yatom is one tough guy. But when it came to push-and-shove, he was just no match for Bibi, who had started to talk about how quickly his brother had helped to put together the raid on Entebbe. The comparison had no meaning. But that's Bibi all over—use anything that can push his case."

On September 9, news reached Tel Aviv that Hamas had struck

again, this time seriously wounding two Israeli bodyguards of the cultural attaché at the newly opened Israeli embassy in Amman, the Jordanian capital.

Three days later, shortly before the Friday Sabbath began, Netanyahu requested that Yatom join him for lunch at his home in Jerusalem. The two men sat down to a meal of soup, salad, and a fish course, washed down with beer and bottled water. The prime minister immediately raised the attack in Amman. How could the Hamas gunmen have come close enough to shoot? Why had there been no advance warning? What was the Mossad station in Amman doing about it?

Yatom interrupted Netanyahu in midflow: There was a Hamas leader in Amman named Khalid Meshal who ran the organization's politburo from an office in the city. For weeks Meshal had been traveling through various Arab countries, but Amman station reported that he was back in the city.

Netanyahu was galvanized. "Then go and knock him down!" he said across the table. "That's what you have to do. Knock him down! Send your people in Amman to do that!"

Stung by almost six weeks of relentless pressure from a prime minister who increasingly had appeared to have no grasp of the political sensitivity of any intelligence operation, the Mossad chief delivered a sharp lesson. Eyes glinting behind his spectacles, he warned that to launch an attack in Amman would destroy the relationship with Jordan that Netanyahu's predecessor, Yitzhak Rabin, had created. To actually kill Meshal on Jordanian soil would jeopardize Mossad's operations in a country that had yielded a continuous flow of intelligence about Syria, Iraq, and Palestinian extremists. Yatom suggested it would be better to wait until Meshal once more left Amman and then strike.

"Excuses! That's all you give me! Excuses!" Netanyahu was said to have shouted. "I want action. I want it now. The people want action. It's Rosh Hashanah soon!" he added, in a reference to the Jewish New Year. "This will be my gift to them!"

From that moment on, every move that Yatom made would be personally approved by Netanyahu. No other Israeli prime minister had taken such a close personal interest in a state-sponsored act of murder.

Khalid Meshal was forty-one years old, a full-bearded and physically strong man. He lived close to King Hussein's palace and by all accounts was a devoted husband and father of seven children. Cultured and well-spoken, he had remained a little-known figure in the Islamic fundamentalist movement. But the rapidly assembled data that Mossad's Amman station had put together indicated Meshal was the driving force behind the suicide bomb attacks against Israeli civilians.

Details of Meshal's movements had been furnished, together with a photograph the Mossad head of station had surreptitiously taken. With his report was a personal plea that Yatom should once more try to persuade Netanyahu not to go ahead with an assassination in Amman. Such a reckless action would jeopardize two years of important counterespionage work Mossad had done with Jordan's cooperation.

Netanyahu had rejected the plea, saying it sounded like a prediction of failure, something he would not tolerate.

Meantime, an eight-man kidon squad had been preparing: a two-man team would actually carry out the hit in broad daylight; the others would provide backup, including car support. The team would all drive back into Israel, crossing over at the Allenby Bridge near Jerusalem.

Mossad's weapon of choice was unusual, not a gun, but an aerosol filled with a nerve agent. It would be the first time a kidon hit team had used this method of killing, though it had long been perfected by the KGB and other Soviet Bloc intelligence agencies. Russian scientists recently emigrated to Israel had been recruited by Mossad to create a range of deadly toxins, including tabun, sarin, and soman, nerve agents that were all outlawed under international treaties. The substances were intended to produce death that could be instantaneous or lingering; in all cases the victim lost control over his internal organs and suffered pain so excruciating that death itself would be a merciful release. This form of killing had been selected as appropriate for Meshal.

On September 24, 1997, the kidon unit flew into Amman from Athens, Rome, and Paris, where they had been positioned for several days. Some members traveled on French and Italian documents. The hit men had been given Canadian passports in the names of Barry Beads and Sean Kendall. They told staff when they checked into the city's Intercontinental Hotel they were tourists. The other katsas bedded down in the Israeli embassy a short distance away.

Beads and Kendall joined them the next day. The two men once more inspected the aerosol. No one knew which nerve agent it contained. The agents speculated that it could induce anything from hallucinations to heart failure before death. They were briefed on the latest movements of Meshal by the station chief.

He had been in London in September 1978 when a Bulgarian defector, Georgi Markov, had been killed by a nerve agent. A passerby had jabbed him in the thigh with the tip of an umbrella. Markov had died an excruciating death caused by ricin, a deadly poison made from the seeds of the castor-oil plant. The passerby had been a KGB agent who had never been caught.

On that optimistic note, Beads and Kendall returned to their hotel shortly before midnight. Each ordered a room service break-fast of coffee, orange juice, and Danish pastries. Next morning, at 9:00 A.M., Beads appeared in the lobby and signed for the first of two rented cars, a blue Toyota. The second, a green Hyundai, arrived shortly afterward and was claimed by Kendall. He told one of the front-desk staff that he and "his friend" were going to explore the south of the country.

At 10:00 A.M. Meshal was being driven by his chauffeur to work; in the back of the car with him were three of his young children, a boy and two girls. Beads followed at a discreet distance in his rented car. Other team members were out on the road in other cars.

As they entered the city's Garden District, the chauffeur informed Meshal that they were being followed. Meshal used the car phone to call in the make and number of Beads's car to Amman police headquarters.

As the rented Toyota drove past, Meshal's children waved at Beads, as they had done to other motorists. The Mossad agent ignored them. Next Kendall's green Hyundai pulled ahead of the chauffeur and both cars disappeared into the traffic.

Moments later an officer at Amman police headquarters called Meshal to say the car was rented to a Canadian tourist. Meshal relaxed and watched his children once more waving at passing motorists, their faces pressed close to the windows. Every morning they took turns riding with their father to work before the chauffeur dropped them off at school.

Shortly before 10:30 A.M. the chauffeur pulled into Wasfi Al-Tal Street, where a crowd had gathered outside the Hamas office, with Kendall and Beads among them. Their presence caused no alarm; curious tourists often came to the office to learn more about Hamas's aspirations.

Meshal quickly kissed his children before leaving the car. Beads stepped forward as if to shake him by the hand. Kendall was at his shoulder, fumbling with a plastic bag.

"Mr. Meshal?" asked Beads pleasantly.

Meshal looked at him uncertainly. At that moment Kendall produced the aerosol and tried to spray its contents into Meshal's left ear.

The Hamas leader recoiled, startled, wiping his lobe.

Kendall made another attempt to spray the substance into Meshal's ear. Around him the crowd were beginning to recover from their surprise, and hands reached out to grab the agents.

"Run!" said Beads in Hebrew.

Followed by Kendall, Beads sprinted to his car, parked a little way up the street. Meshal's chauffeur had seen what was happening and began to reverse back down the street, trying to ram the Toyota.

Meshal was staggering around, moaning. People were trying to support him from falling. Others were shouting for an ambulance.

Beads, with Kendall sprawled beside him and still clutching his half-used aerosol, managed to avoid the chauffeur's car and was accelerating up the street.

Other cars were in pursuit. One of the drivers had a cell phone and was calling for roads in the area to be blocked. The chauffeur was using his car phone to contact police headquarters.

By now backup members of the kidon team had arrived. One of them stopped and waved for Beads to transfer to his car. As the two Mossad men jumped out of the Toyota, another vehicle blocked their path. From it emerged a number of armed men. They forced Beads and Kendall to lie on the ground. Moments later the police arrived. Realizing there was nothing they could now do, the remaining members of the kidon team drove away, eventually making their way undetected back to Israel.

Beads and Kendall were less fortunate. They were taken to Amman central police quarters, where they produced their Canadian passports and insisted they were victims of some "horrendous plot." The arrival of Samih Batihi, the formidable chief of Jordanian counterintelligence, ended the pretense. He told them he knew who they were; he had just gotten off the phone with the Mossad station chief. Later, according to Batihi, the spymaster had "made a clean breast. He said they were his people and Israel would deal directly with the king."

Batihi ordered that the two Mossad agents be locked in separate cells but that they not be harmed in any way.

Meantime, Meshal had been admitted to the intensive care unit at Amman's main hospital. He complained of a persistent "ringing" in his left ear, a "shivery feeling like a shock running through my body," and increasing difficulty with breathing.

The doctors put him on a life-support system.

News of the operation's failure reached Yatom in a secure telephone call from the station chief in the Israeli embassy in Amman. Both men were said to be "beyond rage" at the debacle.

By the time Yatom reached Netanyahu's office, the prime minister had received a telephone call from King Hussein on the hot line installed between the two leaders to deal with a crisis. The flavor of the call came later from an Israeli intelligence officer:

"Hussein had two questions for Bibi. What the fuck did he think he had been playing at? Did he have an antidote for the nerve gas?"

The king said he felt like a man whose best friend had raped his daughter and that if Netanyahu was thinking of denying everything, he had better understand his two agents had made a full confession on video, which was now on its way to Washington for Madeleine Albright, the U.S. secretary of state, to review. Netanyahu sat there hunched over his phone, "as white as anyone caught with his hand in the till."

Netanyahu offered to fly at once to Amman to "explain matters" to the king. Hussein told him not to waste his time. The intelligence officer recalled:

"You could hear the ice crackling on the line from Jordan. Bibi didn't even protest when Hussein told him that he now expected Israel to release Sheikh Ahmed Yassin [the Hamas leader Israel had held in prison for some time], as well as a number of other Palestinian prisoners. The call lasted only a few minutes. It must have been the worst moment in Bibi's political life."

Events now took on their own momentum. Within an hour, an antidote to the nerve gas had been flown to Amman by an Israeli military plane and administered to Meshal. He began to recover and, within a few days, was well enough to stage a press conference in which he ridiculed Mossad. The Amman station chief and Samih Batihi had a short meeting during which they also spoke to Yatom on the phone. The director general fervently promised there would never be another assassination attempt carried out by Mossad on Jordanian soil. Next day Madeleine Albright made two short calls to Netanyahu; she made it clear what she thought of what had happened, her language at times as salty as King Hussein's.

Learning how its passports had been compromised, Canada recalled its ambassador to Israel—a move that fell just short of breaking off diplomatic relations.

When details began to emerge, Netanyahu received a roasting in the Israeli and international press that would have driven other men to resign.

Within a week, Sheikh Yassin was released and returned to a hero's welcome in Gaza. By then Kendall and Beads were back in Israel, minus their Canadian passports. These had been handed over to the Canadian embassy in Amman for "safekeeping."

The two katsas never returned to the kidon unit; they were assigned to nonspecific desk duties at Mossad headquarters. As an Israeli intelligence officer said: "That could mean they would be in charge of security in the building's toilets."

But Yatom had become a lame-duck chief. His senior staff felt he had failed to stand up to Netanyahu. Morale within Mossad slumped to a new low. The prime minister's office leaked the view that it "is only a matter of time before Yatom goes."

Yatom tried to stem what one Mossad senior officer likened to "the tidal wave of dejection in which we are drowning." Yatom adopted what he called "his Prussian pose." He tried to browbeat his staff. There were angry confrontations and threats to resign.

In February 1998, it was Yatom himself who resigned in an attempt to head off what he acknowledged was "a near mutiny." Prime Minister Netanyahu did not send his fallen intelligence chief the customary letter of thanks for services rendered.

Yatom left office with the first ripples of a sensation beginning to emerge over the murder of Prime Minister Yitzhak Rabin. A dedicated Israeli investigative reporter, Barry Chamish, had privately gathered medical and ballistics reports and eyewitness accounts from Rabin's bodyguards, his widow, surgeons, and nurses, together with members of the Israeli intelligence community he had spoken to. Much of it was evidence given in closed court.

By 1999 Chamish, at risk to himself, had begun to publish his findings over the Internet. They are an eerie replay of the doubts raised about a lone gunman in the John Kennedy assassination in 1963. Chamish's closely argued conclusions are, if nothing else, intriguing. He has concluded, "The gunman theory, accepted by the Israeli Government's Shamgar Commission into the Rabin assassination, is a cover-up in what was to be a staged, unsuccessful assassination to rekindle Rabin's flagging popularity with the electorate. Yogal Amir had agreed to perform the lone gunman function for his controller or controllers in the Israeli intelligence community.

"Amir fired a blank bullet. And he fired just one shot, not the alleged three. Israeli police lab ballistic tests on a shell casing found at the scene do not match Amir's gun. No blood was seen coming from Rabin. Then there is the mystery of how Rabin's car got lost for eight to twelve minutes on what should have been a forty-five second drive to hospital on clear streets cordoned off by police for the peace rally Rabin had been attending."

Chamish's most explosive allegation—like all the others he has made, this one has yet to be refuted by any Israeli official in authority—claims: "During that strange drive to hospital by a very experienced chauffeur, Rabin was shot twice by real bullets and they came from the handgun of his own bodyguard Yoram Rubin. His gun disappeared at the hospital and has never been found. Two bullets retrieved from the prime minister's body went missing for eleven hours. Rubin later committed suicide."

Chamish spoke to the three operating room surgeons who fought to save the prime minister's life. The reporter discussed the testimony of police officers who had been present when Amir fired. The officers had all testified that when Yitzhak Rabin was placed in the car, he showed no visible wounds. The surgeons were adamant. When the prime minister finally reached the hospital, he showed clear signs of having sustained a massive chest wound and severe damage to his spinal cord in the lower neck area. The surgeons insisted there was no possible gunshot wound that would have allowed Rabin to leave the attack site showing no evidence of a wound and arrive at the hospital with multiple damage.

The Shamgar Commission concluded it had found no evidence to confirm those wounds had occurred. Subsequently the doctors have refused to discuss the matter.

Outside Chamish's own investigation, there is independent sworn testimony to support his contention that "what happened is deep and is conspiratorial."

At his arraignment hearing, Amir had told the court: "If I tell the truth, the whole system will collapse. I know enough to destroy this country."

A Shin Bet agent who was close to Amir when he fired at Rabin testified: "I heard a policeman shout to people to calm down. The shot is a blank." His evidence was given in closed court.

Leah Rabin stated at the same hearing that her husband did not stagger and fall after apparently being shot at close range. "He was standing and looking very well." She also insisted she was kept from seeing her husband for a full hour after she had arrived at the hospital and, according to Chamish, was told by a high-ranking intelligence officer that she should "not worry as the whole thing had been staged."

The prime minister's widow has steadfastly refused to make any public comment on this or any aspect of her husband's murder.

Chamish believes she had been scared into silence like seventeen nurses at the hospital where Rabin was admitted on that day. "The plan was evil and brilliant. They persuaded Rabin to let someone take a pot shot at him to help him regain his popularity. That was why he did not wear a bulletproof vest. Amir was carefully selected fro his proverbial fifteen minutes of fame. He was a dupe in the hands of his controller or controllers. What he couldn't possibly know was how they would use his blank shot to murder Rabin in his car on the way to hospital."

Barry Chamish does not fit the image of a "conspiracy nut." He is careful in what he writes and overwhelms every piece of evidence with corroborative testimony. He has been slow to rush to judgment and gives the impression there is a great deal more he can say but won't—yet. More certain, Chamish is a man who walks his own path, is beholden to no one and, most important of all, is trusted.

He has posted all the evidence he has so far obtained on the Internet, doing so partly as insurance and partly because he wants to get the truth out. He is also realistic enough to accept it may never surface in a form suitable for a court of law.

CHAPTER 7

THE GENTLEMAN SPY

On a damp spring morning in 1997, David Kimche instructed Arab landscapers how he wanted his garden rearranged in a Tel Aviv suburb. His manner was diffident, the mellifluous voice more suited to a college campus than dealing with manual workers, suggesting Kimche was descended from generations of administrators who had once raised Britain's Union Jack over far-flung lands. The English-born son of middle-class Jews, Kimche's impeccable manners deepened the image of the quintessential Englishman. Expensively tailored clothes emphasized a figure kept trim with regular workouts and a strict diet. Kimche looked twenty years younger than his close to sixty years and there was a boyish quality about him. His every gesture while briefing the gardeners—the flicking away of hair from his forehead, the lengthy pauses, the thoughtful stare— suggested a lifetime spent cloistered on a college campus.

In reality, David Kimche had been what Meir Amit called "one of the intellectual powerhouses" behind many Mossad operations. His reasoning skills had been accompanied by breathtaking nerve, catching even the wariest with some totally unexpected move that had quickly earned the respect of even cynical colleagues. But his very intellectualism had often made them keep their distance; he was too remote and abstract for their earthy ways. Several felt like Rafi Eitan, "that if you said 'good morning' to David, his mind would already be deciding how 'good' it was and how much of the morning was left."

Within Mossad, Kimche was widely regarded as the epitome of the gentleman spy with the cunning of an alley cat. His journey into the Mossad fold began after he left Oxford University with a First in Social Science in 1968. A few months later he was recruited by Mossad, then newly under the command of Meir Amit, who was seeking to introduce into its ranks a sprinkling of university graduates to complement the ruthlessness of men like Rafi Eitan who had learned their skills in the field.

How, where, and by whom Kimche was recruited was something he would forever keep under lock and key. The rumor mills of the Israeli intelligence community offered several scenarios: that he had signed on over a good dinner with a London publisher, a Jew who had long been a sayan; that the proposition came in a rabbi's office in a Golders Green synagogue; that a distant relative had made the first move.

The only certainty is that one spring morning in the early Sixties, Kimche walked into Mossad's headquarters building in Tel Aviv, the newest member of the Planning and Strategy Department. To one side was a branch of the Bank of Israel, several business offices, and a café. Uncertain what to do or where to go, Kimche waited in the cavernous lobby. How different it was from the imposing entrance of the CIA he had read about. At Langley the agency proudly proclaimed its existence in marble on the floor with an inlaid sixteen-pointed star on a shield dominated by the head of a bald eagle in profile, accompanied by the words "Central Intelligence Agency of the United States of America." Set in a wall were the words of the apostle John about people being set free by the truth. Beyond the plaque were banks of elevators, guarded by armed guards.

But here, in the somewhat shabby lobby of the building on King Saul Boulevard, were only bank tellers at their stations and people seated on the café's plastic chairs. Not one of them looked remotely likely to be a Mossad employee. In the far corner of the lobby an unmarked door opened and a familiar figure emerged, a consular officer at the Israeli embassy in London who had supplied Kimche's travel documents. Leading Kimche back to the door, he explained that his own diplomatic status protected his real work as a Mossad katsa in Britain. At the door he handed Kimche two keys and said that from now on they would be his only means to enter Mossad headquarters. One key opened the door, the second the elevators that rose through Mossad's eight floors. The headquarters was "a building within a building" with its own utilities—power, water, sanitation—separate from the rest of the tower block.

It had become Mossad's headquarters shortly after the end of the Suez War in 1956.

That year, in October, British, French, and Israeli forces had launched a joint invasion of Egypt to recapture the Suez Canal, which Egyptian president Gamal Nasser had nationalized. The invasion had the hallmark of the "gunboat diplomacy" that for so long had dominated the region. The United States had almost no prior warning of an invasion that had turned out to be the last gasp of both British and French domination of the Middle East. Washington had exerted massive diplomatic pressure to stop the fighting, fearing that it would draw the Soviet Union into the conflict on the side of Egypt, creating a superpower confrontation. When the fighting ended on the banks of the Suez Canal, Britain and France found they had been replaced by the United States as the dominating foreign power in the Middle East. But Israel insisted on retaining the land it had captured in the Sinai Desert. Richard Helms, a future director of the CIA, flew to Tel Aviv and was received by senior staff in Mossad's headquarters. They struck Helms "like a bunch of Realtors, proudly pointing out the amenities."

Riding up in the elevator, Kimche's guide explained that the lower floor housed the listening and communications center; on the next floor came the offices of junior staff. Upper floors were given over to analysts, planners, and operations personnel. Research and Development had a floor to itself. On the top floor were the offices of the director general and his senior aides.

Kimche was given space among the planners and strategists. His office was equipped like all the others: a cheap wooden desk, a steel filing cabinet with only one key, a black telephone, and an internal directory stamped "Do Not Remove." A strip of carpet completed the furnishings. The office was painted olive green and offered a fine panoramic view over the city. Thirteen years on, the headquarters showed signs of wear and tear; paint had cracked on some walls and carpeting needed replacing.

But, despite these failings, David Kimche sensed he had arrived at an eventful time. Meir Amit was about to leave, shortly to be followed by Rafi Eitan and other senior Mossad officers.

Kimche soon came to recognize the quirks of colleagues: the analyst who invariably prefaced a judgment with the words "this is a European maneuver, classic as Clausewitz in its way"; the head of department who signaled an action by stuffing black flakes of tobacco into the bowl of his pipe, and when the smoke came out white, he had made a decision; the strategist who always ended a briefing by saying espionage was a continuous education in human frailty. These were all men who had earned their dues and they welcomed Kimche's enthusiasm and his ability to turn a problem on its head. They also sensed he fully understood that solving an enemy's deceptions was as important as perpetuating Mossad's own.

Part of his work included monitoring events in Morocco; there were still a substantial number of Jews living there under the repressive regime of King Hassan. In an attempt to make their lives easier, Meir Amit had established a "working relationship" with the monarch's feared security service, finding common cause in trying to remove Egypt's President Nasser, whose own hatred of Israel was only equaled by what he felt for the king. Nasser saw the monarch as a stumbling block to his dream of establishing a powerful Arab coalition stretching from the Suez Canal to the Atlantic coast of Morocco. The potential threat to Israel of such a coalition had persuaded Meir Amit to train the king's men in counterintelligence and interrogation techniques that stopped little short of sophisticated torture.

Within Morocco, a small but equally ruthless opposition survived, led by Mehdi Ben-Barka. Kimche had charted Ben-Barka's career: the king's loyal tutor; onetime president of Morocco's national consultative assembly, a virtually toothless parliament that merely rubber-stamped Hassan's increasingly oppressive decrees against his people. Finally Ben-Barka had become the one authentic voice of opposition to Hassan. Time and again Ben-Barka had barely escaped being captured by the king's men. But knowing it was only a matter of time before he was arrested, the charismatic former schoolteacher had fled to Europe. From there he continued to plot the downfall of Hassan.

Twice Ben-Barka's small but efficient resistance movement in Morocco had come close to launching successful bomb plots against the monarch. The enraged Hassan ordered Ben-Barka tried in absentia and sentenced to death, and Ben-Barka responded by ordering fresh attacks against the king.

In May 1965, Hassan asked Mossad to help deal with Ben-Barka. The task of evaluating the request was given to David Kimche. Later that month he traveled on his British passport to London. Ostensibly he was on vacation. In reality he was finalizing his plans. Equipped with a perfectly doctored second British passport provided by a sayan, and with a Moroccan visa, Kimche flew to Rome; he spent a day there sight-seeing—a move to make sure he was not being followed—and then traveled on to Morocco.

He was met at Rabat Airport by Muhammed Oufkir, the country's fearsome minister of the interior. That night, over a dinner enlivened by the presence of some of the country's best belly dancers, Oufkir spelled out what the king wanted: Ben-Barka's head. Displaying both a crude sense of humor and an appreciation of Jewish history, Oufkir had added: "After all, your Jewish Salome asked your King Herod for the head of a troublemaker."

Kimche said that while that was indeed correct, it really was not a matter for him. Oufkir would have to come back with him to Israel.

Next day the two men flew to Rome and caught a flight to Tel Aviv. Meir Amit met them in a safe house. He was polite but cautious. He told Kimche he was "not very excited" at the prospect of doing Oufkir's dirty work and insisted our "involvement would be confined to preparatory work."

Unknown to Meir Amit, Oufkir had already made an arrangement with a faction within France's intelligence service, SDECE, to murder Ben-Barka if he could be lured out of his fortresslike home in Geneva and across the Swiss border into France. Still reluctant, Meir Amit had insisted that Prime Minister Levi Eshkol must personally sanction Mossad's involvement. The prime minister gave it.

Mossad set to work. A Moroccan-born katsa traveled to Geneva and infiltrated Ben-Barka's circle. Over several months, the agent carefully planted the idea that he had access to a sympathetic French millionaire who would like to see King Hassan topped and genuine democracy come to Morocco. Kimche had created this fiction. On October 26, 1965, he learned that Ben-Barka, "like the Scarlet Pimpernel of old," was about to travel to Paris.

Mossad's communications center sent a coded message to Oufkir in Morocco. The following day the minister and a small team of Moroccan security men flew to Paris. That night the minister was briefed by the SDECE faction. Concerned he had been excluded from the meeting, the Mossad agent who had accompanied Ben-Barka to the French capital called Kimche on a secure line for instructions. Kimche consulted Meir Amit. Both agreed, in Amit's later words, "that something nasty was cooking and we should stay well clear."

Next evening an SDECE surveillance van was positioned outside when Ben-Barka arrived for dinner at a restaurant in the St. Germaine district. He believed he had come to meet the millionaire. After he waited an hour and still no one had showed, Ben-Barka left the restaurant. As he stepped onto the sidewalk, he was grabbed by two SDECE agents and bundled into the van. It was driven to a villa in the Fontenay-le-Vicomte district that the SDECE used from time to time to interrogate its own suspects. Throughout the night, Oufkir supervised Ben-Barka's questioning and torture until, at dawn, the broken man was executed. Oufkir photographed the body before it was buried in the villa's garden. The minister flew home with the film to show the king.

When the corpse was discovered, the outcry in France reached all the way to the president's palace. Charles de Gaulle ordered an unprecedented investigation that led to a massive purging of the SDECE. Its director, anxious to maintain interservice collegiality, struggled to keep Mossad's name out of the affair. But de Gaulle, no friend of Israel, was convinced that Mossad was involved. He told aides that the operation bore the "hallmark of Tel Aviv." Only the Israelis, he had fumed, would show such total disregard for international law. A once-close relationship between Israel and France, established in the 1956 Suez War, was over. De Gaulle promptly ordered that arms supplies to Israel should stop, along with all intelligence cooperation. Meir Amit would "remember the body blows from Paris raining down."

For Kimche, "It was heroic to see the way Meir Amit handled the situation. He could have tried to blame me or the others involved in the operation. Instead he insisted on taking full responsibility. He was a true leader."

Prime Minister Eshkol's government, battered by the reaction from Paris, distanced itself from Mossad's chief. More criticism came from an unexpected source. The more Meir Amit protested that Mossad's role had been "marginal," no more than "supplying a few passports and hiring some cars," the more his predecessor, Isser Harel, insisted the Ben-Barka affair would never have happened in his day. Meir Amit warned the prime minister they would both sink under such sniping. Eshkol responded by setting up a committee of inquiry, headed by the then foreign minister, Golda Meir. The committee concluded Meir Amit should resign, but he refused until Eshkol did the same. Stalemate followed. It was not until a year later that Meir Amit accepted that the death of Ben-Barka was no longer going to trouble him. But it had been a close-run call.

By then Kimche had other matters to concern him. The Palestinians had secretly trained a commando unit to exploit a security weakness not even Mossad had anticipated: midair aircraft hijacking. Once a plane was seized between destinations, it would be flown to a friendly Arab country. There the passengers would be held for ransom—either for substantial sums of money to buy their freedom, or to be exchanged for Arab prisoners held by Israel. An additional bonus would be the worldwide publicity for the PLO cause.

In July 1968, an El Al flight from Rome was hijacked to Algeria. Mossad was stunned at the simple audacity of the operation. A team of katsas flew to Algeria while Kimche and other planners worked almost around the clock to devise a strategy to free the terrified passengers. But any attempt to storm the aircraft was hampered by the presence of the world's media crews covering the story. Kimche recommended playing for time in the hope the story would lose its momentum and the katsas could move. But the hijackers had anticipated that and began to issue bloodcurdling threats unless their demands were met: the freeing of Palestinian prisoners in Israeli jails. The Algerian government supported the hijackers. Kimche realized: "We were between the proverbial rock and a hard place." He was one of those who reluctantly recommended the prisoners should be exchanged for passengers, knowing "full well the consequences of such action. It would pave the way for further hijackings. It would ensure the PLO cause would receive from now on maximum coverage. Israel had been put on the defensive. So had Western governments who also had no answer to hijackings. Yet what could we do except to wait grimly for the next hijacking?"

And come they did, each one better prepared than the last. In a short time half a dozen more passenger aircraft were overpowered by hijackers who were not only expert in concealing weapons and placing explosives on board, but had been trained to fly the actual aircraft or know the actual workings of a flight deck crew. In the Libyan Desert, they practiced exchanging fire in the confined area of an airplane cabin, knowing that El Al had now introduced armed guards on its flights—one of the first moves Kimche had recommended. He had also correctly predicted that the hijackers would know the laws of the various countries they would be flying in and out of so that if they were captured, their colleagues could use those laws to obtain their freedom by bargaining or threatening.

Kimche knew that Mossad urgently needed an incident that would enable the service to overcome the hijackers through the two skills for which it was justifiably renowned: cunning and ruthlessness. And, just as the hijackers effectively used publicity, Kimche wanted an operation whose outcome would match the universal praise for Israel that had followed the kidnapping of Adolf Eichmann. The incident Kimche needed must have high drama, considerable risk, and an against-all-the-odds outcome. Those elements would combine to show Mossad leading the fight back.

On June 27, 1976, an Air France plane filled with Jewish passengers, en route to Paris from Tel Aviv, was hijacked after a stopover at Athens Airport, which was notorious for lax security. The hijackers were members of the extreme Wadi Haddad faction and they made two demands: the freeing of forty Palestinians in Israeli jails, together with a further dozen held in European prisons; and the release of two German terrorists arrested in Kenya when they tried to shoot down an El Al jet with a Sam-7 rocket as it took off from Nairobi Airport.

After a stopover in Casablanca, and being refused permission to land in Khartoum, the plane flew to Entebbe in Uganda. From there the hijackers announced the aircraft would be blown up along with all its passengers unless their demands were met. The deadline was June 30.

In Tel Aviv, in closed cabinet sessions, the vaunted public image of "no surrender" to terrorism wilted. Ministers favored freeing Israel's PLO prisoners. Prime Minister Rabin produced a Shin Bet report to show there was a precedent for releasing convicted criminals. Chief of Staff Mordechai Gur announced he could not recommend military action due to insufficient intelligence from Entebbe. While their anguished deliberations continued, news came from Entebbe that the Jewish passengers had been separated from the others on board—those passengers had been released and were on their way to Paris.

That had been the opening Mossad needed. Yitzhak Hofi, Mossad's chief, in what was to be his finest hour, argued powerfully and passionately for a rescue to be mounted. He dusted down the plan Rafi Eitan had used to capture Eichmann. There were similarities: Rafi Eitan and his men had worked far from home in a hostile environment. They had improvised as they went along using bluff— the renowned Jewish chutzpah. It could be done again. Soaked in sweat, his voice hoarse from pleading and arguing, Hofi had stared around the cabinet room.

"If we let our people die, it will open the floodgates. No Jew will be safe anywhere. Hitler would have won a victory from the grave!"

"Very well," Rabin had finally said. "We try."

As well as Kimche, every other strategist and planner in Mossad was mobilized. The first step was to open a safe communication channel between Tel Aviv and Nairobi; Hofi had nursed the unpublicized intelligence link between Mossad and its Kenyan counterpart introduced by Meir Amit. The link started to bear immediate results. Half a dozen katsas descended on Nairobi and were installed in a Kenyan intelligence service safe house. They would form the bridgehead for the main assault. Meantime Kimche had overcome another problem. Any rescue mission would require a fuel stop at Nairobi. Working the phone, he obtained Kenya's approval in a matter of hours, granted "on humanitarian grounds."

But there was still the formidable problem of reaching Entebbe. The PLO had established the airport as their own entry point to Uganda, from where the Organization ran its own operation against the pro-Israeli white supremacist regime in South Africa. Idi Amin, Uganda's despotic dictator, had actually given the PLO the residence of the Israeli ambassador as a headquarters after breaking off diplomatic relations with Jerusalem in 1972.

Kimche knew it was essential to know if the PLO were still in the country. Their battle-hardened guerrillas would be a formidable force to overcome in the short time allowed for the actual rescue mission: the Israeli forces could only be on the ground for minutes, otherwise they ran the risk of a powerful counterattack. Kimche sent two katsas from Nairobi by boat across Lake Victoria. They landed near Entebbe and found the PLO headquarters deserted; the Palestinians had recently moved on to Angola.

Then, with the stroke of luck any operation needs, one of the Kenyan security officers who had accompanied the katsas discovered that one of his wife's relatives was actually one of the men guarding the hostages. The Kenyan inveigled himself into the airport and was able to see that the hostages were all alive, but he counted fifteen very tense and nervous guards. The information was radioed to Tel Aviv.

Meanwhile, two other katsas, both qualified pilots, hired a Cessna and flew from Nairobi, ostensibly to photograph Lake Victoria for a holiday brochure. Their aircraft passed directly over Entebbe Airport, enabling one katsa to obtain good photographs of the runway and adjoining buildings. The film was flown to Tel Aviv. There, Kimche recommended yet another strategy to confuse the hijackers.

During several telephone conversations with Amin's palace, Israeli negotiators in Tel Aviv made it clear their government was ready to accept the hijacker's terms. A diplomat in a European consulate in Uganda was used to add credibility to this apparent surrender by being called "in confidence" to see if he could negotiate suitable wording the hijackers would accept. Kimche told the envoy, "It must be something not too demeaning to Israel but also not too impossible for the hijackers to accept." The diplomat hurried to the airport with the news and began to draft suitable words. He was still doing so as Operation Thunderball moved to the final stages.

An unmarked Israeli Boeing 707 to be used as a flying hospital landed at Nairobi Airport, flown by IDF pilots who knew Entebbe Airport. Meantime six Mossad katsas had surrounded that airport; each man carried a high-frequency radio and an electronic device that would jam the radar in the control tower. It had never before been tried under combat conditions.

Fifty Israeli paratroopers, under cover of darkness, left the hospital plane and went full speed to Lake Victoria. Inflating their rubber boats, they rowed across the water to wait close to the Ugandan shore, ready to storm into Entebbe Airport. In Tel Aviv, the rescue mission had been rehearsed to perfection; when the time came, a force of C-130 Hercules transporters crossed the Red Sea, headed south, refueled at Nairobi, and then, flying just above the African treetops, swept down on Entebbe Airport.

The radar jammer worked perfectly. The airport authorities were still trying to work out what had happened when the three Hercules transporters and the hospital plane landed. Commandos raced into the building where the hostages were held. By then they were only Jews. All other nationalities had been freed by Amin, enjoying his moment of strutting the world stage. The paratroopers waiting in support were never called into action. They rowed back across the lake and returned to Nairobi. There they would be picked up by another Israeli transporter and flown home.

Within five minutes—two full minutes less than the time allowed— the hostages were free and all the terrorists were killed, along with sixteen Ugandan soldiers guarding the prisoners. The attack force lost one officer, Lieutenant Colonel Yonatan Netanyahu, the elder brother of the future prime minister, Benyamin Netanyahu. He would say that his own hard line against all terrorists came as a result of the death of Yonatan. Three hostages also died.

David Kimche's wish for a headline-making riposte to hijackers had been more than met. The rescue at Entebbe was an episode that, even more than the capture of Adolf Eichmann, came to be seen as Mossad's calling card.

Increasingly, Kimche found himself ever more immersed in Mossad's efforts against the PLO. This deadly struggle was fought beyond the borders of Israel, on the streets of European cities. Kimche was one of the strategists who prepared the ground for Mossad's own assassins, the kidons. They struck in Paris, Munich, Cyprus, and Athens. For Kimche, the killings were remote; he was like the bomber pilot who does not see where the bombs fall. The deaths helped to foster within Mossad a continuing mood of invincibility: the superior information coming from its strategists meant the kidons were always one step ahead of the enemy.

One morning Kimche arrived at work to find his colleagues in a state of near shock. One of their most experienced katsas had been assassinated in Madrid by a PLO gunman. The assassin had been a contact the katsa was developing in an effort to penetrate the group.

But there was no time to mourn. Every available hand was turned to the task of fighting fire with fire. For Kimche it was a time when "we did not expect to be shown any mercy and showed none in return."

The relentless pressure continued to find new ways to get close to the PLO leadership and discover enough about its inner workings to assassinate its leaders. For Kimche, "cutting off the head was the only way to stop the tail wagging." Yasser Arafat was the first head on the kidon target list.

By 1973, another and more serious threat had begun to focus Kimche's mind: the possibility of a second full-scale Arab war, led by Egypt, against Israel. But Mossad was a lone voice within the Israeli intelligence community. Kimche's concerns, echoed by his superiors, were flatly rejected by Aman, military intelligence. Its strategists pointed out that Egypt had just expelled its twenty thousand Soviet military advisers, which should be interpreted as a clear-cut indication that Egypt's president, Anwar Sadat, was looking for a political solution in the Middle East.

Kimche remained unconvinced. From all the information crossing his desk, he grew more certain that Sadat would launch a preemptive strike—simply because Arab demands would be impossible for Israel to accept: Egypt wanted back conquered land and the creation of a Palestinian homeland within Israel. Kimche believed that even if these concessions were granted, the PLO would still continue its murderous campaign to drive Israel to its knees.

Kimche's alarm grew when Sadat replaced his war minister with a more hawkish figure whose first act was to reinforce Egypt's defenses along the Suez Canal. Egyptian commanders were also making regular visits to other Arab capitals to enlist support. Sadat had signed a new arms-purchasing deal with Moscow.

To Kimche the signs were all too ominous: "It was not a question of when war would come, only the day it would start."

But the intelligence chiefs of Aman continued to downplay the warnings coming from Mossad. They told the IDF commanders that, even if war looked like starting, there would be "at least a five-day warning period," more than enough time for Israel's air force to repeat its great success in the Six Day War.

Kimche countered that most certainly the Arabs would have learned from past mistakes. He found himself branded a member of "a war-obsessed Mossad," an accusation that did not sit well with a man so careful of his every word. All he could do was to continue to assess the Egyptian preparations and try to judge a likely date for an attack.

The broiling heat of that 1973 August in Tel Aviv gave way to a cooler September. The latest reports from Mossad katsas on the Sinai side of the Suez Canal showed that Egyptian preparations had gathered momentum. Army engineers were putting the final touches to pontoons for troops and armor to cross the waterway. When Mossad persuaded the Israeli foreign minister to raise the definitely worrying preparations at the United Nations, the Egyptian representative said soothingly, "These activities are routine." To Kimche the words had "the same kind of credibility" as those uttered by the Japanese ambassador in Washington on the eve of the attack on Pearl Harbor.

Yet the Egyptian explanation was accepted by Aman. All the more incredible to Kimche was that by October, wherever his probing eyes settled, there were yet more signs of brewing trouble; Libya had just nationalized Western oil companies; in the oil-producing Gulf states there was talk of cutting off all supplies to the West.

Yet the strategists in Aman continued to lamentably misread the intelligence picture. When Israeli air force jets were attacked by MiGs over Syria—resulting in victory for the IDF due to their pilots' tactical knowledge learned from the MiG stolen from Iraq—the downing of twelve Syrian aircraft was seen by Aman only as further evidence that, if the Arabs ever did go to war, they would be beaten just as soundly.

On the night of October 5–6, Mossad received the most stark evidence yet that hostilities were imminent, perhaps only hours away. Its katsas and informers in Egypt were reporting that the Egyptian Military High Command had gone to red alert. The evidence could no longer be ignored.

At 6:00 A.M. Mossad's chief, Zvi Zamir, joined Aman intelligence chiefs in the defense ministry. The building was almost deserted: it was Yom Kippur, the holiest of all Jewish holidays, the day even nonpracticing Jews rested, when all public services, including the state radio, shut down. The radio had always been the means used to mobilize reserves in the event of a national emergency.

Finally driven to action by the incontrovertible evidence Mossad presented, alarm bells began to sound all over Israel that a two-pronged attack—from Syria in the north and Egypt in the south—was about to engulf Israel.

War began at 1:55 P.M. local time while the Israeli cabinet was in emergency session—assured by Aman's strategists that hostilities would still only start at 6:00 P.M. The time turned out to have been pure guesswork.

Never in the history of the Israeli intelligence community had there been such an inglorious failure to predict an event. The mass of impeccable evidence that David Kimche and others had provided had been totally ignored.

After the war ended, with Israel once more snatching victory from the jaws of defeat, there was a massive purging of Aman's upper echelons. Mossad once more ruled supreme over the intelligence community, though there was a key change there too: Zamir was removed as director general on the grounds he had not been sufficiently assertive against his Aman counterpart. His place was taken by Yitzhak Hofi.

Kimche viewed his arrival with mixed feelings. In some ways Hofi was from a similar mold to Meir Amit: the same erect bearing, the same proven battlefield experience, the same incisive manner and total inability to suffer fools at any price. But Hofi was also blunt to the point of rudeness, and the tension between him and Kimche dated from the days they had instructed recruits, between their other duties, at the Mossad training school. Hofi, with his no-nonsense kibbutz mentality, had shown no patience with Kimche's languid intellectualism and his refined English accent when addressing students. But Kimche was not only now a seasoned operative but Hofi's deputy. He had been promoted to deputy director general shortly before Zamir left. Both Hofi and Kimche accepted they must put aside their personal differences to ensure Mossad continued operating with maximum efficiency.

Kimche was given one of the most difficult tasks in Mossad: he was put in charge of the service's "Lebanese account." The country's civil war had begun two years after the Yom Kippur War, and by the time Kimche took charge of "the account," the Lebanese Christians were fighting a losing battle. Just as years before Salman had gone to the Israeli embassy in Paris to initiate the first steps in stealing the Iraqi MiG, so in September 1975 an emissary from the Christians had gone there asking Israel to supply arms to stop them being annihilated. The request ended up on Kimche's desk. He saw an opportunity for Mossad to work its way into "the Lebanese woodwork."

He told Hofi that politically it made sense to "partly support" the Christians against the Muslims who were vowed to destroy Israel. Once more his interpretation was accepted. Israel would give the Christians sufficient arms to deal with the Muslims, but not enough to pose a threat to Israel. Mossad began to ship arms out of Israel into Lebanon. Next Kimche placed Mossad officers within the Christian command. They were ostensibly there to help maximize the use of the weapons. In reality the officers provided Kimche with a continuous flow of intelligence that enabled him to constantly chart the overall progress of the civil war. The information enabled Mossad to launch a number of successful attacks against PLO strongholds in southern Lebanon.

But the service's relationship with the Christians soured in January 1976, when Christian leaders invited in the Syrian army to lend additional support against the pro-Iranian Hezbollah. That group was seen in Damascus as a threat. Within days thousands of battle-hardened Syrian troops were in Lebanon and moving close to its borders with Israel. Too late the Christians found they had, in Kimche's words, "behaved like Little Red Riding Hood, inviting in the wolf."

Once more the Lebanese Christians turned to Mossad for help. But Kimche realized his carefully constructed network to supply arms was insufficient. What was needed was a full-scale Israeli logistical operation. Scores of IDF tanks, antitank missiles, and other weapons were sent to the Christians. Lebanon's civil war began to rage out of control.

Under its cover, Kimche launched his own guerrilla battle against Israel's bête noire, the PLO. Soon that had extended to fighting the Lebanese Shiites. Lebanon became a practice ground for Mossad to perfect its tactics, not only in assassinations, but in psychological warfare. It was a halcyon time for the men operating out of the featureless high-rise on King Saul Boulevard.

Inside the building, relations between Kimche and Hofi were deteriorating. There were whispers of violent disagreements over operational matters; that Hofi feared Kimche wanted his job; that Kimche felt he was not properly appreciated for the undoubted contribution he was making. To this day, Kimche will not discuss such matters, only to say he "would never give a rumor respectability by commenting."

On a spring morning in 1980, David Kimche used his unrestricted access card, which had replaced the two keys, to access the headquarters building. Arriving in his office, he was told that Hofi wished to see him at once. Kimche strolled along the corridor to the director general's office, knocked, and entered, closing the door behind him.

What happened there has passed into Mossad legend, a tale of increasingly raised voices, of accusation and counteraccusation. The row lasted for twenty electrifying minutes. Then Kimche came out of the office, tight-lipped. His career in Mossad was finished. But his intelligence activities on behalf of Israel were about to enter a familiar arena, the United States. This time it would not involve the theft of nuclear materials, but the scandal that eventually became known as Irangate.

After a period of considering his future, David Kimche had accepted the director generalship of the Israeli foreign ministry. The post was ideally suited to his ability to think his way into, and out of, a situation. It offered Kimche an opportunity to bring his skills to bear on the international stage far beyond Lebanon.

In the United States the saga of President Nixon and Watergate had moved to an inescapable finale, leaving the CIA tarred with suspicion, the likes of which had not been seen since the death of President Kennedy, as more and more revelations emerged about the Agency's activities during the Nixon years.

Kimche studied every facet of the drama, "absorbing the lessons to be learned from a debacle that should never have happened. The bottom line was that Nixon should never have kept those tapes. Without them he would still probably have been president."

Closer to home, what was happening in Iran, ever a matter of abiding interest to Israel, also occupied him. With Khomeini and his ayatollahs firmly in control, it came as a genuine shock to Kimche to see how badly the CIA and the State Department had failed to correctly judge the situation.

But there was a new president in the White House, Ronald Reagan, who promised a new dawn for the CIA. The Agency, Kimche learned from his own contacts in Washington, would become Reagan's "secret trump" in foreign policy. Heading the CIA was William Casey. Instinctively, Kimche sensed he was no friend of Israel—but someone who could be outmaneuvered should the need arise.

For the next two years, as part of his work, Kimche closely followed CIA operations in Afghanistan and Central America. Many of them struck him as "babe-in-the-wood stuff, old-fashioned intelligence gathering, mingled with some pretty ruthless killing."

Then, once more, Kimche's attention was brought to focus on Iran—and what had happened in Beirut.

———

A few months after Kimche took up his duties at the foreign ministry, Israel had begun to arm Iran with the tacit support of the United States. Israel had provided the help to weaken the Baghdad regime—part of Jerusalem's long-established tactic of what Kimche called "playing at both ends."

Three years later, two events had affected matters. There had been the car-bomb massacre in Beirut of 241 U.S. marines and the growing U.S. suspicion that Mossad not only had prior knowledge of the attack, but that Iran's intelligence service had helped to prepare it. Pressure was put on Israel to stop supplying Tehran. It increased with the kidnapping, torture, and subsequent death of William Buckley, the CIA station chief in Beirut. In quick succession, seven other Americans were taken hostage by Iran-backed groups.

For the tough-talking Reagan administration, which had come into office with its promise to crack down on terrorism, the idea of American citizens languishing deep beneath the rubble of Beirut demanded action. But retaliation was out of the question; to bomb Tehran, as Reagan suggested, was ruled out by even his hard-line aides. A rescue mission would also likely fail, said Delta Force chiefs.

There then occurred a conversation between the president and Robert McFarlane, a gung ho former marine who was national security adviser. Kimche was to recall that McFarlane told him that the conversation went like this:

"What do the Iranians need most, Mr. President?"

"You tell me, Bob."

"Weapons to fight Iraq."

"So we give them what they want. And we get back our people in return."

Reagan and McFarlane—against the advice of Casey and other U.S. intelligence chiefs—took the simplistic view that arming Iran would not only result in the mullahs bringing pressure to bear on the Beirut group to free the hostages, but would improve the administration's relations with Tehran. There could also be the added bonus that it was bound to weaken Moscow's position in Iran. The seeds were sown for what became known as Irangate.

Marine colonel Oliver North was put in charge of supplying the arms. North and McFarlane decided to exclude the CIA from their plans. Both were action-oriented men. Their push-and-shove mentality had served them well in Vietnam, and from all they had heard, Israelis were similar men of action. So, in North's words, "it was time to bring Israel into the fold." There was also the personal prospect of visiting the Holy Land; a committed Christian, North relished the thought of treading in the footsteps of Jesus.

Israel's new prime minister, Yitzak Shamir, decided there was only one person capable of handling the request from Washington for help—and making sure Israel's interests were fully protected. On July 3, 1983, David Kimche flew to meet with McFarlane in the White House. Kimche said he believed the arms-for-hostages deal could work. He asked if the CIA was "actively involved." He was told the Agency was not.

In turn, McFarlane asked Kimche how far Mossad would be involved: "After all," he stated, "they are the guys who do all your secret work overseas." Kimche told him that Yitzhak Rabin, then defense minister, and Shamir had decided to exclude Mossad and leave the entire matter to him. McFarlane said that was fine by him. Kimche had not told him that Mossad's chief, then Nahum Admoni, shared Casey's fears that the arms-for-hostages deal was fraught with operational hazards.

McFarlane drove to Bethesda Naval Hospital to present Kimche's views to Reagan, who was recovering from a colon operation. The president had one question: Could Kimche ensure that Israel would keep the deal secret? A leak could harm U.S. relations with more moderate Arab states already fearful of the growing radicalism of Tehran. Kimche claims that McFarlane reassured Reagan that Israel would "batten down the hatches." The deal was on. Kimche flew back to Israel. Two weeks later Kimche was back in Washington. Over dinner, he laid out his game plan to McFarlane. Kimche was to recall the conversation went like this:

"Do you want the good or bad news first?" Kimche asked McFarlane.

"The good."

"We'll ship the arms for you, using the same routes we used before."

McFarlane said "no problem."

Kimche's method would ensure that the United States had no direct contact with Iran, and so the administration's bellicose attitude about being tough on terrorism would not be compromised: the U.S. arms embargo on Iran would be intact and the hostages, when freed, would not have been directly exchanged for weapons.

"And the bad news?" McFarlane prompted.

Kimche said his own well-placed contacts in Iran were uncertain the mullahs could actually manage to procure the release of the Beirut hostages.

"The radicals there are getting beyond Tehran's control," he told his host.

If McFarlane was disappointed, he did not show it. The next day,

Secretary of State George Shultz told Reagan, back in the Oval Office, the risks were too high. Supposing the Iranians took the arms
and then revealed the deal to embarrass "the Great Satan," the mullahs called the United States? Wouldn't that draw Iraq further into
the Soviet camp? And what about the hostages? They could be even
worse off. All morning the arguments continued. By lunchtime Reagan was visibly tired. The decision, when it came, was sudden. The
president agreed to support the proposition that the United States
would replace all arms Israel sold to Iran. Once more Kimche returned home with a green light. Nevertheless, Shamir insisted that
all possible steps should also be taken so that he "could deny any
connection with the matter should there be a problem."

To ensure this, Kimche assembled a colorful cast of characters
to initiate the operation. There was Adnan Khashoggi, the Saudi
petrobillionaire, with a habit of eating caviar by the pound and an
eye for the current cover girls; Manacher Thorbanifer, a former
agent in the shah's notorious SAVAK secret service who still behaved like a spy, calling meetings for the middle of the night. There
was the equally mysterious Yakov Nimrodi, who had run agents for
Aman and had once been Israel's military attaché in Iran during the
shah's regime. He was invariably accompanied by Al Schwimmer,
the closemouthed founder of Israel Aircraft Industries.

Khashoggi brokered a deal that was to be a precursor for all that
followed. He would head a consortium that would indemnify the
United States if Iran failed to live up to its obligations, and would
similarly protect Iran if the arms were not acceptable as specified.
For these guarantees the consortium would receive a 10 percent fee
from the purchase of all the arms with cash provided by the United
States. In return it would also act as a buffer to ensure that plausible
deniability would remain intact for both the Iranian and U.S. governments if anything went wrong. Everyone understood that the
consortium would essentially be working outside any political control and would first and foremost be driven by the profit motive.

In late August 1985, the first planeload of arms landed in Tehran
from Israel. On September 14, a U.S. hostage, the Reverend Benjamin Weir, was freed in Beirut. As the pace quickened, still more
raffish players joined the consortium, including Miles Copeland, a
former CIA officer who, on the eve of the shah falling from power
in what was soon to be renamed the Islamic Republic of Iran, had

sent CIA agents into Tehran souks distributing hundred-dollar bills to anyone who dared shout "Long live the shah!" Other shadowy figures also became involved, such as a former Special Air Services officer who ran a company in London that had once provided non-specific services to Mossad. Meanwhile, the policymakers in Israel and Washington looked the other way. All that mattered was that the operation had taken off under the noses of an unsuspecting world—at least for the moment.

In all, Iran would receive 128 U.S. tanks; two hundred thousand Katysha rockets captured in south Lebanon; ten thousand tons of artillery shells of all calibers; three thousand air-to-air missiles; four thousand rifles; and close to fifty million rounds of ammunition.

From Marama Air Force Base in Arizona, over four thousand TOW missiles were airlifted to Guatemala to begin their long journey to Tel Aviv. From Poland and Bulgaria, eight thousand Sam-7 surface-to-air missiles were shipped, together with one hundred thousand AK-47s. China provided hundreds of Silkworm sea-to-sea missiles, armored cars, and amphibious personnel carriers. Sweden provided 105-mm artillery shells, Belgium air-to-air missiles.

The weapons were shipped with certificates showing Israel was the end user. From IDF military bases in the Negev Desert, the consortium arranged for chartered transport aircraft to fly the weapons to Iran. The consortium received a "handling fee" for each consignment, Iran paying the money out of funds in Swiss bank accounts. The sum eventually totaled $7 million. Israel received no financial reward—only the satisfaction of witnessing Iran improve its capability to kill more Iraqis in the long-drawn-out war between both countries. For David Kimche it was a further example of the "divide and rule" policy he strongly advocated.

Nevertheless, his well-honed instincts told him that what had started as "a sweet operation" was now in danger of running out of control. In his view: "The wrong men now had too much power in the consortium."

In creating it, he had again demonstrated Israel's realpolitik: Israel had been ready to help the United States because it recognized it could not survive without Washington's support in other areas. It was also a way to demonstrate that Israel could perform decisively on the world stage and keep matters secret.

But the longer the arms-for-hostages operation continued, Kimche sensed, the greater was the chance of discovery. In December 1985, he told the consortium that he could no longer remain involved in its activities—using the old saw of being overworked at the Ministry of Foreign Affairs.

The consortium thanked him for his help, gave him a farewell dinner in a Tel Aviv hotel, and told him that he was being replaced as the Israeli link by Amiram Nir, who was Peres's gung ho adviser on terrorism. That was the moment, Kimche would later admit, when the arms-for-hostages deal was firmly on the fast track to self-destruction. If anyone could derail it, then Nir was the man. A former journalist, Nir had shown the alarming trait of regarding real-life intelligence as being part of the same world occupied by the James Bond thrillers he so liked. He shared that fatal weakness with men in Mossad who had also decided that journalists could also serve their purpose.

In April 1999, David Kimche showed he had not lost his skills to correctly read the current political situation in the Middle East. Yasser Arafat, the man he had once plotted to murder, "because he was my blood enemy, certain that his demise would be a great victory for Israel," had now, in Kimche's view, become "Israel's best hope for long-term peace. Mr. Arafat is still hardly my idea of a perfect neighbor, but he is the only Palestine leader capable of making concessions to Israel while retaining power and domestic support."

Kimche believed he had found common ground with Arafat. He was convinced the PLO leader had finally come to recognize what Kimche had seen a quarter of a century earlier, "the real threat Islamic fundamentalism posed for the new millenium."

Sitting in his small study looking out over the garden he had seen come to fruition, Kimche was able to deliver a balanced judgment. "I cannot forgive my old enemy for endorsing the murder of my countrymen decades ago. But it would also be unforgivable to deny Arafat—and the Israelis—the chance to end the bloodshed once and for all."

CHAPTER 8

ORA AND THE MONSTER

The cavernous lobby of the Palestine-Meridian Hotel in Baghdad

was crowded as usual on that last Friday in April 1988, and the

mood was cheerful. Iraq had just won a decisive battle against Iran

in the Gulf of Basra and the consensus was that their war was finally

drawing to an end after seven bloody years.

One reason for impending Iraqi victory could be attributed to

the foreigners who sat in the lobby in their well-tailored blazers

and trousers with uniformly knife-edge creases, the permanent

smiles of successful salesmen on their faces. They were arms deal-

ers, there to sell their latest weapons, though they rarely used the word, preferring more neutral expressions: "optimum interface," "control systems," "growth capability." Between them, the salesmen represented the arms industries of Europe, the Soviet Union, the United States, and China. The common language of their trade was English, which they spoke in a variety of dialects.

Their Iraqi hosts needed no translation: what they were being offered was a range of bombs, torpedoes, mines, and other destructive gadgetry. The brochures being passed around showed helicopters with cartoonish names—Sea Knight, Chinook, Sea Stallion. One chopper, "Big Mother," could carry a small bridge; another, "the Incredible Machine," could airlift a platoon of troops. Leaflets showed guns that could fire two thousand rounds a minute or hit a moving target in pitch-black darkness with a computer-chip sight. Every and any kind of weapon was for sale.

Their hosts spoke an esoteric jargon the salesmen also understood: "twenty on the day," "thirty at half-and-half minus one": twenty million dollars on day of delivery, or thirty million dollars for a consignment, payable half down, the balance on the day before the weapons were shipped. All payments would be made in U.S. dollars, still the preferred currency in this closed world.

Watching over this ever-shifting bazaar of dealers and clients meeting over mint tea were officers from the Da'lrat Al-Mukhabarat Al-Amah, Iraq's main intelligence organization, controlled by Sabba'a, Saddam Hussein's almost as fearsome half-brother.

Some of the arms dealers had been in the hotel lobby on a very different day seven years before when their stunned hosts had told them that Israel, an enemy even more hated than Iran, had struck a powerful blow against Iraq's military machine.

Since the formation of the Jewish state, a formal state of war had existed between Israel and Iraq. Israel had felt confident its forces could win a conventional war. But in 1977, Mossad discovered the French government, which had provided Israel with its own nuclear capability, had also given Iraq a reactor and "technical assistance." The facility was Al-Tuweitha, north of Baghdad.

The Israeli air force began planning how to bomb the site before it became "hot" with the uranium rods in the reactor core. To destroy it then would cause widespread death and pollution and

turn Baghdad and a sizable area of Iraq into an irradiated desert—
and earn Israel global condemnation.

For these reasons, Yitzhak Hofi, then Mossad's chief, opposed
the raid, arguing an air strike would anyway result in a heavy death
toll among the French technicians and would isolate European
countries Israel was trying to reassure of its peaceful intentions.
Bombing the reactor would also effectively end the delicate maneuvering to persuade Egypt to sign a peace treaty.

He found himself presiding over a divided house. Several of his
department chiefs argued that there was no alternative but to neu-
tralize the reactor. Saddam was a ruthless enemy; once he had a
nuclear weapon, he would not hesitate to use it against Israel. And
since when had Israel worried unduly about winning friends in Europe? America was all that mattered, and the whisper from Washington was that taking out the reactor would result in no more than
a slap on the wrist from the administration.

Hofi tried a different tack. He suggested the United States
should bring diplomatic pressure to bear on France to stop the
export of the reactor. Washington received a curt rebuff from Paris.
Israel then chose a more direct route. Hofi despatched a team of
katsas to raid the French plant at La Seyne-sur-Mer, near Toulon,
where the core for the Iraqi reactor was being built. The core was
destroyed by an organization no one had ever heard of previously—
the "French Ecological Group." Hofi had personally chosen the
name.

While the French began to build a new core, the Iraqis sent
Yahya Al-Meshad, a member of its Atomic Energy Commission, to
Paris to arrange the shipment of nuclear fuel to Baghdad. Hofi sent
a kidon team to assassinate him. While the others patrolled the
surrounding streets, two of them used a passkey to enter Al-
Meshad's bedroom. They cut his throat and stabbed him through
the heart. The room was ransacked to look like robbery. A prostitute in an adjoining room told police she had serviced the scientist
hours before his death. Later, entertaining another client, she had
heard "unusual movement" in Al-Meshad's room. Hours after she
reported this to the police, she was killed in a hit-and-run incident.
The car was never found. The kidon team caught an El Al flight
back to Tel Aviv.

Despite this further blow Iraq, aided by France, continued with its bid to become a nuclear power. In Tel Aviv, the Israeli air force continued its own preparations while intelligence chiefs wrangled with Hofi over his continued objections. The Mossad chief found a challenge from an unexpected quarter. His deputy, Nahum Admoni, argued destroying the reactor was not essential but would teach "any other Arabs with big ideas a lesson."

By October 1980, the debate preoccupied every cabinet meeting Menachem Begin chaired. Familiar arguments were revisited. Increasingly, Hofi became a lone voice against the attack. Nevertheless he struggled on, producing well-written position papers, knowing he was writing his own professional obituary.

Admoni increasingly made no secret of his contempt for Hofi's position. The two men, who had been close friends, became cold colleagues. Nevertheless, it took a further six months of bitter conflict between the embattled Mossad chief and his senior staff before the general staff approved the attack on March 15, 1981.

The attack was a tactical masterpiece. Eight F-16 fighter-bombers, escorted by six F-15 fighter-interceptors, flew at sand-dune level across Jordan before streaking toward Iraq. They reached the target at the planned moment, 5:34 P.M. local time, minutes after the French construction staff had left. The death toll was nine. The nuclear plant was reduced to rubble. The aircraft returned unharmed. Hofi's career in Mossad was over. Admoni replaced him.

Now, on that April morning in 1988, the arms dealers in the lobby who, seven years before, had commiserated with their shocked hosts on the Israeli attack—before selling Iraq improved radar systems— would have been stunned to know that in the hotel a Mossad agent was quietly noting their names and what they were selling.

Earlier that Friday, business in the lobby had been briefly interrupted by the arrival of Sabba'a Al-Tikriti, the head of Iraqi secret police, accompanied by his own Praetorian phalanx of bodyguards. Saddam Hussein's half brother strode to the elevator, on his way to a rooftop suite. Waiting there was the tall, buxom prostitute specially flown in from Paris for his pleasure. It was highly paid, high-risk work. Some of the previous whores had simply disappeared after Sabba'a had finished with them.

The security chief left in midafternoon. Shortly afterward, from a suite adjoining the prostitute's, emerged a tall young man dressed in a blue cotton jacket and chinos. He was good-looking in a slightly effete way, with a nervous habit of stroking his mustache or rubbing his face that somehow increased his vulnerability.

His name was Farzad Bazoft. In the details on the hotel registration form—a copy of which had been routinely sent to Sabba'a's ministry—Bazoft had described himself as the "chief foreign correspondent" for *The Observer*, the London-based Sunday national newspaper. The description was inaccurate: only the newspaper's staff reporters on overseas assignments were allowed to call themselves "foreign correspondents." Bazoft was a freelance journalist who, for the past year, had contributed to *The Observer* several stories with Middle Eastern themes. Bazoft had admitted to reporters from other news organizations who were also on this trip to Baghdad that he always passed himself off as *The Observer*'s chief foreign correspondent on trips to cities like Baghdad because it ensured he had the best available hotel room. The harmless fiction was seen as another example of his endearing boyishness.

Unknown to his newspaper colleagues, there was an altogether darker side to Bazoft's personality, one that could possibly jeopardize them if they were ever suspected of being involved in the real reason he was in Baghdad. Bazoft was a Mossad spy.

He had been recruited after he had arrived in London three years before from Tehran, where his increasingly outspoken views on the Khomeini regime had put his life in danger. Like many before him, Bazoft found London alien and English people reserved. He had tried to find a role for himself in the Iranian community in exile, and for a while his considerable knowledge of the current political structure in Tehran made him a welcome guest at their dinner tables. But the sight of the same familiar faces soon palled for the ambitious and restless young man.

Bazoft began to look around for more excitement than dissecting a piece of news from Tehran. He began to establish contacts with Iran's enemy, Iraq. In the mid-1980s there were a large number of Iraqis in London, welcome visitors because Britain saw Iraq not only as a substantial importer of its goods, but also as a nation which, under Saddam Hussein, would subdue the threatening Islamic fundamentalism of the Khomeini regime.

Bazoft found himself "singing for my supper" at Iraqi parties.

His new hosts were more relaxed and ready "to let down their hair" than Iranians. In turn they were captivated by his gentle manners and endless witticisms about the ayatollahs of Tehran.

At one party had been an Iraqi businessman, Abu Al-Hibid. He had listened to Bazoft—once more, slightly tipsy by the end of the evening—endlessly proclaiming his abiding ambition to be a reporter and how his heroes were Bob Woodward and Carl Bernstein, who had brought down President Nixon. Bazoft told Abu Al-Hibid he would die happy if he could topple the Ayatollah Khomeini. By now Bazoft was contributing articles to a small-circulation Iranian newspaper for exiles in Britain.

Abu Al-Hibid was the alias for an Iraqi-born katsa. In his next report to Tel Aviv, he included a note about Bazoft, his present work, and his aspirations. There was nothing unusual about doing that; hundreds of names every week were forwarded, each to find its place in Mossad's data bank.

But Nahum Admoni was running Mossad and eager to develop his contacts in Iraq. The London katsa was instructed to cultivate Bazoft. Over leisurely dinners, Bazoft complained to Al-Hibid that his editor was not making full use of his potential. His host suggested he should try to break into mainstream English journalism. There should be an opening for a reporter with good linguistic skills and knowledge of Iran. Al-Hibid suggested the BBC would be a starting point.

Within the broadcasting organization were several sayanim whose tasks included monitoring forthcoming programs on Israel and keeping an eye on persons recruited for the BBC's Arab-language service. Whether any sayan had a direct role in the employment of Bazoft will never be known for certain, but soon after meeting Al-Hibid, he was hired by the BBC for a research assignment. He did well. Other work followed. Desk editors found they could trust Bazoft to make sense of the intrigues of Tehran.

In Tel Aviv, Admoni decided it was time to make the next move. With Irangate's revelations gathering pace in the United States, the Mossad chief deliberately decided to expose the role in the burgeoning scandal of Yakov Nimrodi, a former Aman operative. He had been a member of the consortium David Kimche had created and had used his own intelligence background to keep Mossad out of what was happening. A wily, fast-talking man, Nimrodi had, as the arms-for-hostages deal began, driven U.S. Secretary of State George Shultz to comment that "Israel's agenda is not the same as ours and an intelligence relationship with Israel concerning Iran might not be one upon which we could fully rely."

When Kimche had pulled out of the consortium, Nimrodi had remained for a while longer. But, as the reverberations from Washington grew louder and more embarrassing for Israel, the former Aman operative had disappeared back into the woodwork. Admoni, smarting at the way Nimrodi had treated Mossad, had other plans: he would publicly embarrass Nimrodi and at the same time give Bazoft a career boost that would enable him to better serve Mossad.

Al-Hibid fed sufficient details to the reporter for Bazoft to realize this could be his big break. He took the story to *The Observer*. It was published with references to "a mysterious Israeli, Nimrodi, being implicated in Irangate." Soon Bazoft was a regular contributor to *The Observer*. Finally, a coveted prize for someone who was not on staff, he was given a desk of his own. It meant he would no longer have to pay his own telephone costs to track down a story from home and he would be able to charge entertainment expenses. But Bazoft would still only be paid for what appeared in the paper. It was an incentive for him to find more stories and to push hard for any trip to the Middle East. On those occasions, he would be living on full expenses and, like all reporters, would be able to manipulate them to give him extra cash above what he had spent and could genuinely reclaim. A shortage of money had always been a problem for Bazoft, something he was careful to hide from his *Observer* colleagues. Certainly none suspected that the reporter who spent hours talking in Farsi on the phone to his contacts was a convicted thief. Bazoft had spent eighteen months in jail after raiding a building society. Passing sentence, the judge had ordered Bazoft should be deported after he was released. Bazoft appealed on the reasonable grounds he would be executed if sent back to Iran. Though the appeal was rejected, he was granted "exceptional leave" to remain in Britain indefinitely. The grounds for such an unusual step have remained locked in a Home Office vault.

Whether Mossad, having spotted Bazoft's potential, used one of its well-placed sayanim in Whitehall to facilitate matters has remained an unresolved question. But the possibility cannot be discounted.

After Bazoft was released from prison, he began to suffer bouts of depression, which he treated with homeopathic medicines. This background had been unearthed by the Mossad katsa. Later an English writer, Rupert Alison, a conservative member of Parliament and a recognized expert on intelligence recruiting methods, would say a personality like Bazoft's made him a prime target for Mossad.

A year after they had first met, Al-Hibid had recruited Bazoft. How and where this was done has remained unknown. The extra money would have certainly been a consideration for Bazoft, still short of cash. And, for someone who so often viewed life through a dramatic prism, the prospect of living out another of his dreams—to be a spy in the tradition of another foreign correspondent he admired, Philby, who had also once worked for *The Observer*, as a cover for his work as a Soviet spy—could also have been a factor.

More certain, Bazoft began to carve a small reputation for himself; what he lacked in writing style, he made up with solid research. Everything he unearthed in Iran was passed over to the London katsa. As well as stories for *The Observer*, Bazoft was also being given assignments by Independent Television News and Mirror Group Newspapers. At the time the foreign editor of the *Daily Mirror* was Nicholas Davies. In his safari-style suit, Davies might have stepped out of the pages of Evelyn Waugh's *Scoop*. He had a reporter's gift for gossip and an ability to hold his drink, and was always ready to buy his round. His north-of-England accent had all but gone: colleagues said he had spent hours perfecting the dulcet tone he now used. Women found appealing his easy good manners and the commanding way he could order dinner and select a good bottle of wine. They loved his been-there-done-that mentality, the way he spoke of faraway places as if they were part of his private fief. Late at night over another drink, he would hint at adventures that cynics said was simply Nick romancing.

Not for a moment did anyone—his colleagues at the *Mirror*, his wide circle of friends outside the newspaper world, even his wife, Janet, an Australian-born actress who had starred in the highly successful BBC Television series *Dr Who*—know that Nahum Admoni had authorized Davies should be recruited.

Davies would always insist that even if he had "been approached," he had never served as a Mossad agent and that his presence in the hotel lobby on that April Friday afternoon was purely as a journalist watching the arms dealers going about their work. He could not later recall what he and Bazoft had spoken about while in the lobby, but said, "I imagine it was about what was going on." He refused to elaborate, a position he would steadfastly maintain.

The pair had traveled to Iraq with a small group of other journalists (among them the author of this book on assignment for the Press Association, Britain's national wire service). On the flight from London, Davies had regaled the party with ribald stories about Robert Maxwell, who had finally bought Mirror Newspapers. He called him "a sexual monster with a voracious appetite for seducing secretaries on his staff." He made it very clear he was close to Maxwell, though: "Captain Bob is sheer hell to be with, he knows I know too much to sack me." Davies' claim that he personally was fireproof because of what he knew about the tycoon was dismissed by his listeners as hyperbole.

On the flight, Farzad Bazoft was quiet, saying little to the others, confining himself to talking to the flight attendants in Farsi. At Baghdad Airport his language skills helped to ease the translation difficulties with the Iraqi "minders" assigned to the party. In a stage whisper, Davies said they were really security agents. "The dozy buggers wouldn't recognize a spy if he was pointed out," Davies said prophetically.

At the Palestine-Meridian, the man from the *Mirror* informed his traveling companions he was only there because he was "bloody bored with London." But he made it clear he had no intention of following the official itinerary, which included a visit to the Basra battlefield, where the Iraqi army was eager to display the spoils of war after its victory over the Iranian forces. Bazoft said he didn't think the trip south to the gulf would interest his newspaper.

That April Friday evening in 1988, having spent hours in the hotel lobby watching the arms dealers come and go, and sharing several conversations with Davies, Farzad Bazoft ate alone in the hotel coffee shop. He declined an invitation to join other reporters from London, saying he had to "think through my schedule." During the meal he was called to take a telephone call in the lobby. He returned a few minutes later looking pensive. Having ordered dessert, he abruptly left the table, ignoring ribald jokes from some of the reporters that he had a girl stashed away.

He did not return until the next day. He appeared even more tense, saying to, among others, Kim Fletcher—a freelance journalist then working for the *Daily Mail*—that "it's all right for you lot; you're British born and bred. I'm an Iranian. That makes me different." Fletcher was not alone among the English reporters who wondered if this was "Bazoft banging on again about how hard it was to have a background like his."

Bazoft spent most of the day pacing the hotel lobby or in his suite. Twice he left the hotel for short periods. In the lobby he had several conversations with Nicholas Davies, who later said that Bazoft was "like anyone on a story, wondering if he would get what he wanted." For his part, the *Mirror* foreign editor announced he would not be writing anything, "because there is nothing here to interest Captain Bob."

Late that afternoon, Bazoft once more left the hotel. As usual he was followed by an Iraqi minder. But when Bazoft reappeared, he was alone. Reporters heard Bazoft tell Davies he wasn't "going to be followed around like a bitch in heat."

Davies' laughter, however, did little to lighten Bazoft's mood. Once more he went to his suite. When he next appeared in the lobby, he told several reporters that he would not be returning to London with them. "Something's come up," he said in the mysterious voice he liked to use at times.

"It would have to be a good story to keep me here," Fletcher said.

Hours later Bazoft left the hotel. It would be the last any of his companions would see of him until he appeared on a video distributed worldwide by the Iraqi regime seven weeks after his arrest, having confessed to being a Mossad spy.

During that time, Bazoft was on a Mossad mission that would have taxed the skills of a trained katsa. He had been ordered to try to discover how advanced were Gerald Bull's plans to provide Iraq with a supergun. That the journalist was given such a task was a clear indicator of how far his controllers were prepared to exploit him. Mossad had also taken its own steps to ensure that, if Bazoft was caught, it would appear he was working for a London-based company, Defence Systems Limited (DSL). When Bazoft was arrested close to one of the supergun test sites, the Iraqi agents also found he had in his possession a number of documents indicating that Bazoft had made several calls from the hotel to the offices of DSL. The company has denied all knowledge of Bazoft, or having any contact with Mossad.

On the videotape, Bazoft's eyes at times stared vacantly, before suddenly blinking rapidly and darting around the room, with its pleasant backdrop of a curtain patterned with flowing tendrils. He looked like a person who believed he was powerless to avoid his annihilation.

Mossad's psychologists in Tel Aviv studied every frame. For them the stages of Bazoft's disintegration followed the same pattern Israeli interrogators had noticed when they extracted confessions from a captured terrorist. First Bazoft would have experienced disbelief, an instinctive denial that what was happening was actually happening to him. Then would have come an overwhelmingly sudden and shattering realization: It *was* happening to him. At that stage, the helpless reporter may have experienced two other reactions: paralyzing fright and a compulsion to talk. This would have been the time he made his confession on the video that he was a Mossad agent.

His monotonous tone suggested he had experienced bouts of exogenous depression while in captivity, a result of being removed from familiar surroundings and having his normal lifestyle totally disrupted. He would have felt continuously tired, and what sleep he was permitted would have left him unrefreshed. That would be when self-accusation had been at its most destructive, and his sense of hopelessness maximized. Self-accusation would have gripped him. Like the prisoner in Kafka's *The Trial*, he would have felt "stupid" over the way he had behaved and put others at risk.

On the video, Bazoft's eyes showed signs he had been drugged. Mossad's pharmacologists found it impossible to decide what drugs had been used.

Nahum Admoni knew that such an abject confession as the video contained was the prelude to Bazoft's execution. The Mossad chief ordered his psychological warfare specialists to launch a campaign to deflect embarrassing questions about the service's involvement with Bazoft.

Members of Parliament in Britain soon publicly criticized *The Observer* for sending Bazoft to Iraq. At the same time, trusted reporters were fed stories that Saddam Hussein was viewing videos of every stage of Bazoft's interrogation. It may well have been true. More certain, it was an excuse to remind the world that torture and murder were instruments of state policy in Iraq. Bazoft was hanged in Baghdad in March 1990. His last reported words on the gallows were: "I am not an Israeli spy."

In London, Nicholas Davies read the report on the execution on a Reuters message that came to the *Daily Mirror* foreign desk. As instructed about all stories emanating from the Middle East he judged to be important, Davies took the report up to the office of Robert Maxwell.

Since 1974, the publisher had been the most powerful sayan in Britain. Davies would remember: "Bob read the report without comment," but could not recall "in all honesty" what he had felt about Bazoft's death.

In Tel Aviv, among those who read about the execution was one of the most colorful characters to have served Israel's spymasters, Ari Ben-Menashe. Until then he had never known of the existence of Bazoft. But typically, that did not stop the mercurial Ben-Menashe feeling a sense of grief that "another good man had been in the wrong place at the wrong time." It was emotional judgments like that which had made the darkly handsome, quick-witted Ben-Menashe such an unlikely candidate for a key position in the Israeli intelligence community. Yet, for ten years, 1977–87, he had held a sensitive post in the External Relations Department (ERD) of the Israel Defense Forces, one of the most powerful and secret organizations in the intelligence community.

ERD had been created in 1974 by then prime minister Yitzhak Rabin. Smarting over the way Israel had been completely surprised by the Syrian-Egyptian onslaught in the Yom Kippur War, he had decided the only way to avert such an intelligence failure occurring again was to have a watchdog to monitor other intelligence services and, at the same time, conduct its own intelligence gathering.

Four branches had been created to operate under the ERD umbrella. The most important was SIM; it provided "special assistance" for the growing number of "liberation movements" in Iran, Iraq, and, to a lesser extent, Syria and Saudi Arabia. The second branch, RESH, handled relationships with friendly intelligence networks. Top of those was the South African Bureau of State Security.

Mossad had a similar unit called TEVEL, which also had close links with the Republic's intelligence community. The relationship between RESH and TEVEL was often tense because of the inevitable overlapping.

A third ERD department, Foreign Liaison, dealt with Israeli military attachés and other IDF personnel working overseas. The department also monitored the activities of foreign military attachés in Israel. That brought further conflict, this time with Shin Bet, who until then had the sole prerogative to report on such activities. The fourth arm of ERD was called Intelligence Twelve. Set up to liaise with Mossad, this unit had further soured relations with the men on the upper floor of their building on King Saul Boulevard. They felt overall that ERD would diminish their power.

Ben-Menashe had been attached to RESH, with a specific responsibility for the Iranian "account." He arrived at a time when Israel was about to lose its most powerful ally in the region. For over a quarter of a century, the shah of Iran had worked diligently behind the scenes to persuade Israel's Arab neighbors to end their hostility toward the Jewish state. He was still making limited headway, notably with King Hussein of Jordan, when the shah's own Peacock Throne was swept away by Ayatollah Khomeini's Islamic fundamentalist revolution in February 1979. Khomeini promptly handed over the Israeli embassy building in Tehran to the PLO. Equally swiftly, Israel turned to helping the Kurds wage guerrilla war against the new regime. At the same time, Israel continued to supply arms to Tehran for them to use against Iraq. The "kill both sides" policy that David Kimche and others in Mossad advocated was well and truly in force.

Ben-Menashe soon found himself involved in David Kimche's grand design to trade hostages for arms with Iran. Both men traveled together to Washington, where Ben-Menashe claimed he prowled the wide corridors of the White House, met President Reagan, and was on first-name terms with his senior aides.

Charming, and with a devil-may-care attitude, Ben-Menashe was a popular figure at Israeli intelligence community parties, where senior politicians could swap stories with the spymasters to mutual benefit. Few could tell a tale better than Ben-Menashe. By the time Kimche was starting the hostages-for-arms deal, Ben-Menashe had been appointed Prime Minister Yitzhak Shamir's "personal consultant" on intelligence, having told Shamir he knew where "all the bodies were buried." Kimche decided it made Ben-Menashe the ideal choice to work with the one intelligence officer he admired above all others, Rafi Eitan. With the full approval of the prime minister, Ben-Menashe was released from all other duties to work with Eitan. The two men moved to New York in March 1981. Their purpose, Ben-Menashe would recall, was straightforward: "Our friends in Tehran were desperate to have sophisticated electronic equipment for their air force and air and ground defenses. Israel, of course, wanted to help them as much as possible in their war against Iraq."

Traveling on British passports, always a favorite of Mossad, they set up a company in New York's financial district. They quickly recruited a team of fifty brokers who scoured the U.S. electronics industry for suitable equipment. All sales were accompanied by end-user certificates that stated the equipment was to be used only in Israel. Ben-Menashe would recall: "We had packs of certificates which we would fill out and send to Tel Aviv to keep on file in case anyone ever bothered to check."

The equipment was flown to Tel Aviv. There, without going through customs, it was transferred onto aircraft chartered from Guinness Peat in Ireland and flown to Tehran. Guinness Peat, a well-regarded air-charter company, was an obvious choice. The idea of using Irish pilots had also been Rafi Eitan's. He had maintained what he called his "Irish connections. When it comes to a deal, the Irish understand the rules. The only one which matters is to pay on the day."

As the volume of the New York operation increased, it became necessary to have a central holding company to process the billions of dollars involved in the purchasing and selling-on of arms. The name chosen for the company was ORA, "light" in Hebrew.

In March 1983, Ben-Menashe was told by Rafi Eitan to recruit Nicholas Davies into ORA. How the old spymaster had heard of Davies was almost certainly through Mossad; in turn the service would have been told about Davies by Bazoft, who had done free-lance journalist work for the *Mirror* foreign editor. Later that month, Ben-Menashe and Davies met in the lobby of London's Churchill Hotel. By the time they left, Ben-Menashe knew that Davies was "our man." The next day they lunched at Davies' home.

Present was Davies' wife, Janet. Ben-Menashe quickly formed the impression that the sophisticated, smooth-talking Davies was afraid of losing her. "That was good. It made him vulnerable."

Davies' role as a consultant to ORA was finally settled over a meeting at the Dan Acadia Hotel on the beachfront north of Tel Aviv. Ben-Menashe remembered: "We agreed he would be our London conduit for arms, our contact man for various Iranian and other deals. His home address would be used on ORA stationery and during the day his direct office phone number—822-3530— would be used by our Iranian contacts."

In return, Davies would receive fees commensurate with his new-found role as a key player in the arms-for-Iran operation. In all, he would receive $1.5 million, deposited in bank accounts in Grand Cayman, Belgium, and Luxembourg. Part of the money went to settle his divorce. Janet received a single payment of $50,000. Davies cleared all his bank debts and bought a four-story house. It became ORA's European headquarters, its phone number—231-0015—another contact for the arms dealers who now had become part of the journalist's life. Through his position as foreign editor, Davies began to visit the United States, Europe, Iran, and Iraq.

Ben-Menashe noted approvingly that "on his travels he introduced himself as a representative of the ORA Group. He would set up a meeting, usually for a weekend, and he would fly to the city concerned, arrange for the number of weapons to be supplied and how payment was to be made."

In 1987, Iran's Ayatollah Ali Akbar Hashemi Rafsanjani received a cable from ORA concerning the sale to Iran of four thousand TOW missiles at a cost of $13,800 each. The cable concluded with the confirmation that "Nicholas Davies is a representative of ORA Limited, with the authority to sign contracts."

It was a champagne time for Ari Ben-Menashe, Nicholas Davies, and the powerful figure who loomed ever larger in the background of unfolding events, Robert Maxwell. But none suspected for a moment the grim truth of the Hollywood cliché Davies liked to quote, "There's no such thing as a free lunch."

CHAPTER 9

SLUSH MONEY, SEX, AND LIES

———————

Matters had looked very different on that morning in late March

1985 when Ari Ben-Menashe had caught the early-morning British

Airways flight from Tel Aviv to London. Eating his kosher airline

breakfast, he reflected that life had never been so good. He was not

only making "real money," but had learned a great deal at the elbow

of David Kimche as they trawled through the Byzantine world of

selling arms to Iran. Along the way, he had also furthered his ed-

ucation in the continuous interplay between Israel's politicians and

its intelligence chiefs.

For Ben-Menashe, "compared to my former colleagues, the average arms dealer was a choirboy." He had identified the problem: the aftereffects of Israel's Lebanon adventure, from which it had finally withdrawn, battered and demoralized. Anxious to regain prestige, the politicians gave the intelligence community an even freer hand in how it waged pitiless war against the PLO, whom they saw as the cause of all Israel's problems. The result was a succession of scandals where suspected terrorists and even their families were brutalized and murdered in cold blood. Yitzhak Hofi, the former head of Mossad, had sat on a government commission, set up after intense public pressure, to investigate the brutality. It concluded that intelligence agents had consistently lied to the court about how they obtained confessions: the methods used had too often been gross. The committee had called for "proper procedures" to be followed.

But Ben-Menashe knew the torture had continued: "It was good to be away from such awful matters." He regarded what he was doing, providing arms for Iranians to kill untold numbers of Iraqis, as "different." Nor did the plight of the Beirut hostages, the very reason for his wheeling and dealing, unduly concern him. The bottom line was the money he was making. Even with Kimche's departure, Ben-Menashe still believed the merry-go-round he was riding would only stop when *he* decided—and he would step off a multimillionaire. By his count, ORA's business was now worth "hundreds of millions"—most of it being generated through the house in the London suburb from where Nicholas Davies ran ORA's international operations.

Ben-Menashe knew Davies had continued to amass his own fortune, far in excess of the sixty-five-thousand-pound yearly salary he was paid as foreign editor of the *Daily Mirror*; Davies' commission from ORA was almost always as much in a month. Ben-Menashe didn't mind if the newspaperman took "an extra slice of the cake; it left plenty to go around. It was still champagne time."

Robert Maxwell dispensed it by the magnum from his office on top of the *Mirror* building to his guests. When the BA flight landed, Ben-Menashe would be chauffeured to see the tycoon in a limousine Maxwell would have sent, a further sign, Ben-Menashe felt, of the importance in which Maxwell now held him. In the car with him would be Nahum Admoni, Mossad's director general, traveling on board an El Al flight an hour behind the British Airways jet. Ben-Menashe planned to spend the time waiting at Heathrow Airport for Admoni by reviewing all he had put together on how a powerful press baron had become the most important sayan Mossad had recruited.

Maxwell had volunteered his services at the end of a meeting in Jerusalem with Shimon Peres shortly after Peres had formed a coalition government in 1984. One of Peres's aides would recall the encounter as "the ego meets the megalomaniac. Peres was haughty and autocratic. But Maxwell just drove on, saying things like 'I will pour millions into Israel'; 'I will revitalize the economy.' He was like a man running for office. He was bombastic, interrupted, went off on tangents and told dirty jokes. Peres sat there smiling his Eskimo smile."

Recognizing that Maxwell over the years had developed powerful contacts in Eastern Europe, Peres arranged for Maxwell to see Admoni. The meeting took place in the Presidential Suite of the King David Hotel in Jerusalem, where Maxwell was staying. Maxwell and Admoni found common ground in their central European backgrounds; Maxwell had been born in Czechoslovakia (which had led Peres to utter one of his few remembered jokes, "He's the only bouncing Czech I know with money"). Both men shared a burning commitment to Zionism and a belief Israel had a God-given right to survive. They also enjoyed a passion for food and good wine.

Admoni was keenly interested in Maxwell's view that both the United States and the Soviet Union had a similar desire to achieve global domination, but through significantly different approaches. Russia included international anarchy as part of its strategy, while Washington saw the world in terms of "friends" and "enemies" rather than nations with conflicting ideological interests. Maxwell had offered other insights: the CIA's secret contact with its Chinese counterparts was causing unease in the State Department, which found it could impinge on future diplomatic action and policies.

The tycoon had painted portraits of two men of particular interest to Admoni. Maxwell said that after meeting Ronald Reagan, he came away with the feeling that the president was an eternal optimist who used his charm to conceal a tough politician. Reagan's most dangerous failing was that he was a simplifier and never more so than on the Middle East, where his second or third thought was no better than his original shoot-from-the-hip judgment.

Maxwell had also met William Casey, and judged the CIA director as a man of narrow opinions and no friend of Israel. Casey was running a "can-do" agency with outmoded ideas about the role of intelligence in the current political global arenas. Nowhere, in Maxwell's view, was this more evident than in the way Casey had misread Arab intentions in the Middle East.

These views coincided exactly with those of Nahum Admoni. After the meeting, they drove in Admoni's unmarked car to Mossad headquarters, where the tycoon was given a personally conducted tour of some of the facilities by the director general.

Now, a year later, March 15, 1985, they would meet again.

Not until Admoni and Ben-Menashe entered Maxwell's office suite in Mirror Newspapers headquarters in London's High Holborn did their host announce there would be one other person present to share the bagels, lox, and coffee Maxwell had ordered must be available whenever he was in the building.

Like a conjurer producing a rabbit out of a hat, Maxwell introduced Viktor Chebrikov, vice chairman of the KGB, and one of the most powerful spymasters in the world. With masterful understatement, Ben-Menashe would subsequently admit that "for a KGB leader to be in a British newspaper publisher's office might seem a fanciful notion. But at the time President Gorbachev was on very friendly terms with Prime Minister Margaret Thatcher, so it was acceptable for Chebrikov to be in Britain."

More debatable is what the founder of Thatcherism and its free-trade principles would have made of the agenda for the meeting. Sprawled in Maxwell's hand-tooled leather armchairs, Admoni and Ben-Menashe led the discussion. They wanted to know if "very substantial amounts" of currency were to be transferred to banks in the Soviet Union, could Chebrikov ensure the deposits would be safe? The money was from ORA's profits in the sale of U.S. arms to Iran.

Chebrikov asked how much money was involved.

Ben-Menashe replied, "Four hundred fifty million American dollars. With similar amounts to follow. A billion, maybe more."

Chebrikov looked at Maxwell as if to ensure he had heard correctly. Maxwell nodded enthusiastically. "This is perestroika!" he boomed.

To Ben-Menashe the sheer simplicity of the deal was an added attraction. There would be no galaxy of middlemen chipping away their pieces of commission. There would just be "Maxwell with his connections and Chebrikov, because of the power he wielded. His involvement was a guarantee the Soviets would not steal the funds. It was agreed the initial $450 million would be transferred from Credit Suisse to the Bank of Budapest in Hungary. That bank would disburse the money to other banks in the Soviet bloc."

A flat fee of $8 million would be paid to Robert Maxwell for brokering the deal. Handshakes sealed matters. Maxwell proposed a champagne toast to the future capitalism of Russia. Afterward his guests were flown in the tycoon's helicopter to Heathrow Airport to catch their flights home.

Apart from Nicholas Davies, not one journalist in the *Mirror* building realized a monumental story had just escaped them. Soon another would slip from their grasp as Maxwell betrayed their journalistic skills to try to protect Israel.

At the beginning of his relationship with Mossad, it was agreed that Maxwell was too valuable an asset to be involved with routine intelligence-gathering matters. According to a serving member of the Israeli intelligence community:

"Maxwell was Mossad's high-level Mr. Fixit. He opened the doors to the highest offices. The power of his newspapers meant that presidents and prime ministers were ready to receive him. Because of who he was, they spoke to him as if he was a de facto statesman, never realizing where the information would end up. A lot of what he learned was probably no more than gossip, but no doubt some of it contained real nuggets. Maxwell knew how to ask questions. He had received no training from us, but he would have been given guidelines of areas to probe."

On September 14, 1986, Robert Maxwell called Nahum Admoni on his direct line with devastating news. A freelance Colombian-born journalist, Oscar Guerrero, had approached a Maxwell-owned Sunday tabloid newspaper, the *Sunday Mirror*, with a sensational story—one which would rip aside the carefully constructed veil disguising the true purpose of Dimona. Guerrero claimed to be acting for a former technician who had worked at the nuclear plant. During that time the man had secretly gathered photographic and other evidence to show that Israel was now a major nuclear power, possessing no fewer than one hundred nuclear devices of varying destructive force.

Like all telephone calls to and from the Mossad chief, this one was automatically recorded. That member of the Israeli intelligence community would later claim the tape contained the following exchange:

Admoni: What is the name of this technician?

Maxwell: Vanunu. Mordechai Vanunu.

Admoni: Where is he now?

Maxwell: Sydney, Australia, I think.

Admoni: I will call you back.

Admoni's first call was to Prime Minister Shimon Peres, who ordered every step be taken to "secure the situation." With those words Peres authorized an operation that once more demonstrated the ruthless efficiency of Mossad.

Admoni's staff quickly confirmed Vanunu had worked at Dimona from February 1977 until November 1986. He had been assigned to Machon-Two, one of the most secret of all the plant's ten production units. The windowless concrete building externally resembled a warehouse. But its walls were thick enough to block the most powerful of satellite camera lenses from penetrating. Inside the bunkerlike structure, a system of false walls led to the elevators that descended through six levels to where the nuclear weapons were manufactured.

Vanunu's security clearance was sufficient to gain unchallenged access to every corner of Machon-Two. His special security pass— number 520—coupled with his signature on an Israeli Official Secrets Acts document ensured no one ever challenged him as he went about his duties as a *menahil*, a controller on the night shift.

A stunned Admoni was told that almost certainly for some

months, Vanunu somehow had secretly photographed the layout of Machon-Two: the control panels, the glove boxes, the nuclear bomb-building machinery. Evidence suggested he had stored his films in his clothes locker, and smuggled them out of what was supposedly the most secure place in Israel.

Admoni demanded to know how Vanunu had achieved all this—and perhaps more. Supposing he had already shown his material to the CIA? Or the Russians? The British or even the Chinese? The damage would be incalculable. Israel would be exposed as a liar before the world—a liar with the capability of destroying a very large part of it. Who was Vanunu? Whom could he be working for?

Answers were soon forthcoming. Vanunu was a Moroccan Jew, born on October 13, 1954, in Marrakech, where his parents were modest shopkeepers. In 1963, when anti-Semitism, never far from the surface in Morocco, spilled once more into open violence, the family emigrated to Israel, settling in the Negev Desert town of Beersheba.

Mordechai led an uneventful life as a teenager. Along with every other young person, when his time came he was conscripted into the Israeli army. He was already beginning to lose his hair, making him appear older than his nineteen years. He reached the rank of first sergeant in a minesweeping unit stationed on the Golan Heights. After military service he entered Ramat Aviv University in Tel Aviv. Having failed two exams at the end of his first year in a physics-degree course, he left the campus.

In the summer of 1976 he replied to an advertisement for trainee technicians to work at Dimona. After a lengthy interview with the plant's security officer he was accepted for training and sent on an intensive course in physics, chemistry, math, and English. He did sufficiently well to finally enter Dimona as a technician in February 1977.

Vanunu had been made redundant in November 1986. In his security file at Dimona it was noted that he had displayed "left-wing and pro-Arab beliefs." Vanunu left Israel for Australia, arriving in Sydney in May of the following year. Somewhere along his journey, which had followed a well-trodden path by young Israelis through the Far East, Vanunu had renounced his once-strong Jewish faith to become a Christian. The picture emerging from a dozen sources for Admoni to consider was of a physically unprepossessing young man who appeared to be the classic loner: he had made no real friends at Dimona; he had no girlfriends; he spent his time at home reading books on philosophy and politics. Mossad psychologists told Admoni a man like that could be foolhardy, with a warped sense of values and often disillusioned. That kind of personality could be dangerously unpredictable.

In Australia Vanunu had met Oscar Guerrero, a Colombian journalist working in Sydney, while he was painting a church. Soon the garrulous journalist had concocted a bizarre story with which to regale his friends in the raffish King's Cross quarter of Sydney. He claimed he had helped a top Israeli nuclear scientist to defect with details of Israel's plans to nuke its Arab neighbors and that, one step ahead of Mossad, the scientist was now hiding out in a safe house in a city suburb while Guerrero masterminded what he called "the sale of the scoop of the century."

Vanunu was irritated by such nonsensical claims. Now a committed pacifist, he wanted his story to appear in a serious publication to alert the world to the threat he perceived Israel now posed with its nuclear capability. However, Guerrero had already contacted the Madrid office of the *Sunday Times*, and the London newspaper with a fearless reputation sent a reporter to Sydney to interview Vanunu.

Guerrero's fantasies were swiftly exposed under questioning. The Colombian began to feel he was about to lose control over Vanunu's story. His fears increased when the *Sunday Times* reporter said he would fly Vanunu to London, where his claims could be more fully investigated. The newspaper planned to have the technician questioned by one of Britain's leading nuclear scientists.

Guerrero watched Vanunu and his traveling companion board the flight to London, his misgivings deepening by the minute. He needed advice on how to handle the situation. The only person he could think of was a former member of the Australian Security and Intelligence Service (ASIS). Guerrero told him he had been cheated out of a world-shaking story, and described exactly what Vanunu had smuggled out of Dimona—sixty photographs taken inside Machon-Two, together with maps and drawings. They re-

vealed beyond a doubt that Israel was the sixth most powerful nuclear nation in the world.

Once more Guerrero's luck ran out. He had chosen the wrong
man to call. The former ASIS operative contacted his old employer
and repeated what Guerrero had told him. There was a close working relationship between Mossad and ASIS. The former provided
intelligence on Arab terrorist movements out of the Middle East to
the Pacific. ASIS informed the katsa attached to the Israeli embassy
in Canberra of the call from its former employee. The information
was immediately faxed to Admoni. By then more disturbing news
had reached him. On his backpacking trip to Australia, Vanunu had
stopped over in Nepal and had visited the Soviet embassy in Kath-
mandu. Had he gone there to show his evidence to Moscow?

It took a Mossad sayan on the staff of the king of Nepal three
days to discover that Vanunu's sole purpose in going to the embassy
was to enquire about the travel documents he would need to take
a vacation in the Soviet Union at some unspecified later date. He
had been sent on his way with a pile of brochures.

In the hours that had passed since Vanunu was being flown to London by the *Sunday Times*, Guerrero had tried to make a quick killing—
by offering copies of Vanunu's documentation to two Australian
newspapers. They had dismissed the material as forgeries.

Growing desperate, Guerrero had set off to London in pursuit
of Vanunu. Unable to find him, Guerrero had taken the documents
to the *Sunday Mirror*. Included was a photograph of Vanunu taken
in Australia. Within hours Nicholas Davies knew they were there.
He promptly told Maxwell. The publisher called Admoni. Several
hours later, when the Mossad chief again called Maxwell, Admoni
received another jolt. The *Sunday Times* was taking Vanunu's story
seriously. It was therefore critically important to know what the
technician had photographed. It was hoped a damage-limitation response could then be fashioned. The reports from Canberra suggested that Guerrero was clearly motivated by money. If Vanunu
was shown to have a similar aspiration, then it might be possible to
mount a successful disinformation campaign that the *Sunday Times*
had been swindled by two con men.

Once more the indefatigable Ari Ben-Menashe was pressed into service. Admoni ordered him to fly to London to obtain the copies that Guerrero had shown to the *Sunday Mirror*. Ben-Menashe would later recall to the veteran American investigative journalist Seymour Hersh:

"Nicholas Davies had arranged for Guerrero to meet this 'hot' American journalist—me. At the meeting, Guerrero, eager for another sale, displayed some of Vanunu's color photographs. I had no idea if they were significant. They needed to be seen by experts in Israel. I told Guerrero I needed copies. He balked. I said I had to know if they were real if he wanted money and that Nick would vouch for me."

Guerrero handed over several photographs to Ben-Menashe. They were couriered to Tel Aviv.

Their arrival created further consternation. Officials from Dimona identified Machon-Two from the photographs. One of the prints showed the area where nuclear land mines had been manufactured before being sown along the Golan Heights border with Syria. There was no longer any question of being able to destroy Vanunu's credibility. Every nuclear physicist would recognize what the equipment was for.

Prime Minister Peres set up a crisis team to monitor the situation. Some of Mossad's department heads urged that a kidon squad should be sent to London to hunt down Vanunu and kill him. Admoni rejected the idea. The *Sunday Times* would not have the space to publish everything Vanunu told the newspaper; it would require a full-length book to contain all the information to which the technician would have had access. But once the newspaper had finished with Vanunu, the likeliest possibility was he would then be debriefed by M16 and the CIA, and Israel would face even more problems. It was all the more imperative to learn how Vanunu had carried out his spying activities in Dimona and whether he had worked alone or with others—and if so, whom *they* were working for. The only way to discover all this was to bring Vanunu back to Israel to be interrogated.

Admoni needed a way to flush the technician out of wherever the *Sunday Times* had hidden him. In the open it would be easier to deal with Vanunu, and in the end, if he had to be killed, it would not be the first time Mossad had committed murder on the streets of London. In the hunt for the perpetrators of the massacre of the Israeli athletes at the Munich Olympics, Mossad had killed one of the Black September group in a carefully staged hit-and-run road accident as he walked back to his Bloomsbury hotel.

In London, the *Sunday Times*, realizing Israel would do everything possible to discredit Vanunu, had arranged for him to be questioned by Dr. Frank Barnaby, a nuclear physicist with impeccable credentials who had worked at Britain's nuclear weapons installation at Aldermaston. He concluded that the photographs and documentation were authentic and the technician's detailed recall was accurate.

The *Sunday Times* then took a fateful step. Its reporter presented the Israeli embassy in London with a summary of all that Vanunu had revealed to them, along with photostats of his passport and the photographs, together with Barnaby's assessment. The intention was to force an admission from the Israeli government. Instead, the embassy dismissed the material as "having no base whatsoever in reality."

In Tel Aviv the photocopies presented to the embassy caused further consternation. For Ben-Menashe:

"The cat was out of the bag. I was still in London when Davies said Maxwell wanted to see me. We met in the same office where I had agreed to pay him $8 million commission for hiding our money behind the Iron Curtain. Maxwell made it clear he understood what was to be done about the Vanunu story. He said he had already spoken to my boss in Tel Aviv."

As a result of that call, Admoni had finally come up with a way to drive Vanunu into the open.

The next issue of the *Sunday Mirror* contained a large photograph of Mordechai Vanunu, together with a story holding the technician and Oscar Guerrero up to ridicule, calling the Colombian a liar and a cheat, and the claim about Israel's nuclear capability a hoax. The report had been dictated by Maxwell who had also supervised the prominent positioning of Vanunu's photograph. The first shot had been fired in a major disinformation campaign orchestrated by Mossad's psychological warfare department.

After reading it, Vanunu became agitated to the point where he told his *Sunday Times* "minders"—the reporters who had watched over him since he had been brought to London—that he "wanted to disappear. I don't want anyone to know where I am."

The panic-stricken technician was staying at the latest hotel his minders had chosen, the Mountbatten near Shaftesbury Avenue in Central London.

Following the *Sunday Mirror* publication, sayanim in London were mobilized to find him. Scores of trusted Jewish volunteers had each been given lists of hotels and boarding houses to check. In each call they gave a description of Vanunu from the photograph published in the *Sunday Mirror*, each caller claiming to be a relative checking to see if he had registered.

On Wednesday, September 25, Admoni received news from London that Vanunu had been located. It was time to bring into play the next stage of his plan.

The link between intelligence work and sexual entrapment was as old as spying itself. In the fourth book of Moses, Rahab, a prostitute, saves the lives of two of Joshua's spies from the king of Jericho's counterintelligence people—the first recorded meeting between the world's two oldest professions. One of Rahab's heirs in the love-and-espionage business was Mata Hari, a Dutch seductress who worked for the Germans in World War I and was executed by the French. From the beginning Mossad had recognized the value of sexual entrapment. For Meir Amit:

"It was another weapon. A woman has skills a man simply does not. She knows how to listen. Pillow talk is not a problem for her. The history of modern intelligence is filled with accounts of women who have used their sex for the good of their country. To say that Israel has not done the same would be foolish. But our women are volunteers, high-minded women who know the risks involved. That takes a special kind of courage. It is not so much a question of sleeping with someone. It is to lead a man to believe you will do so in return for what he has to tell you. That does not begin to describe the great skills that are called into play to achieve that."

Nahum Admoni had handpicked an agent who possessed all those qualities to entice Mordechai Vanunu into Mossad's hands.

———

Cheryl Ben-Tov was a *bat leveyha*, one grade below a katsa. Born into a wealthy Jewish family in Orlando, Florida, she had seen her parents' marriage end in a bitterly contested divorce. She found solace in religious studies, which led to her spending three months on a kibbutz in Israel. There she became immersed in Jewish history and the Hebrew language. She decided to remain in Israel. At the age of eighteen she met and fell in love with a Sabra, a native-born Israeli, called Ofer Ben-Tov. He worked for Aman as an analyst. A year after they met the couple were married.

Among the wedding guests were several high-ranking members of the Israeli intelligence community, including one from Meluckha, Mossad's recruiting department. During the marriage feast he asked Cheryl the sort of questions any bride might expect. Was she going to go on working? Have a family at once? Caught up in the excitement of the celebrations, Cheryl had said her only plan was to try to find a way to give something back to her country, which had given her so much, referring to Israel as "family." A month after she returned from her honeymoon, she received a call from the wedding guest: he said he had been thinking over what they had spoken about and maybe there was a way for her to help.

They arranged to meet at a café in downtown Tel Aviv. He astonished her by citing with complete accuracy her school grades, her family history, how she had met her husband. Perhaps sensing her anger at having her privacy invaded, he explained that all the information was in her husband's file at Aman.

The recruiter understood that the relationship between himself and a potential recruit could often be tricky; it has been likened to a warlock initiating a neophyte into a secret sect with its special signs, incantations, and rites: it is the fellowship of Orpheus without a love of music. After telling Cheryl for whom he worked, the man delivered a set piece. Mossad was always on the lookout for people who wanted to serve their country. At the wedding she had compared Israel to a family. Well, Mossad was like that. Once you were accepted, you were part of its family, protected and nurtured. In return you served the family in any way asked of you. Was she interested?

Cheryl was. She was told she would have to undergo preliminary tests. During the next three months she took a number of written and oral examinations in various safe houses around Tel Aviv. Her high IQ—she consistently registered 140 in these tests—American background, general knowledge, and social skills made her an above-average recruit.

She was told she was suitable for training.

Before that, she had a further session with her recruiter. He told her she was about to enter a world in which she could share her experiences with no one, not even her husband. In such a lonely place, she would feel vulnerable to the corrupting lure of trust. But she must trust no one except her colleagues. She would be tutored in deceit, taught to use methods that violated every sense of decency and honor; she must accept new ways of doing things. She would find some of the acts she would be asked to perform highly un-pleasant, but she must always put them in the context of the mission she was on.

The recruiter leaned across the table in the interview room and said there was still time for her to change her mind. There would be no recriminations; there should be no sense of failure on her part.

Cheryl said she was fully prepared to undergo training.

For the next two years she found herself in a world which, until then, had only been part of her favorite relaxation, going to the movies. She learned how to draw a gun while sitting in a chair, to memorize as many names as possible as they flashed with increasing speed across a small screen. She was shown how to pack her Beretta inside her pants, on the hip, and how to cut a concealed opening in her skirt or dress for easy access to the handgun.

From time to time, other recruits in her class left the training school; such departures were never a subject for discussion. She was sent on practice missions—breaking into an occupied hotel room, stealing documents from an office. Her methods were analyzed for hours by her instructors. She was aroused from her bed in the dead of night and dispatched on more exercises: picking up a tourist in a nightclub, then disengaging herself outside his hotel. Every move she made was observed by her tutors.

She was asked close questions about her sexual experiences. How many men had there been before her husband? Would she sleep with a stranger if her mission demanded? She answered truthfully: There had been no one before her husband; if she was absolutely certain that the success of a mission depended on it, then she would go to bed with a man. It would purely be sex, not love. She learned how to use sex to coerce, seduce, and dominate. She became especially good at that.

She was taught how to kill by firing a full clip of bullets into a target. She learned about the various sects of Islam and how to create a *mishlashim*, a dead-letter box. A day was spent perfecting a floater, a strip of microfilm attached to the inside of an envelope. Another was devoted to disguising herself by inserting cotton wadding in her cheeks to subtly alter the shape of her face. She learned to steal cars, pose as a drunk, chat up men.

One day she was summoned to the office of the head of the training school. He looked her up and down as if he were doing an inspection, checking off each item on a list in his mind. Finally he said she had passed.

Cheryl Ben-Tov was assigned as a bat leveyha working in Mossad's Kaisrut department, which liaised with Israeli embassies. Her specific role was to provide cover—as a girlfriend or even as a "wife" for katsas on active service. She worked in a number of European cities, passing herself off as an American citizen. She did not sleep with one of her "lovers" or "husbands."

Admoni personally briefed her on the importance of her latest mission: with Vanunu now located, it would be up to her to use her skills to entice him out of Britain. This time her cover would be that of an American tourist traveling alone around Europe after a painful divorce. To give that part of her story credibility, she would make use of details from her own parents' separation. The final part of her story was to have a "sister" living in Rome. Her brief was to get Vanunu there.

On Tuesday, September 23, 1986, Cheryl Ben-Tov joined a team of nine Mossad katsas already in London. They were under the command of Mossad's director of operations, Beni Zeevi, a dour man with the stained teeth of a chain-smoker.

The katsas were staying in hotels between Oxford Street and the Strand. Two were registered in the Regent Palace. Cheryl Ben-Tov was registered as Cindy Johnson in the Strand Palace, staying in room 320. Zeevi had rented a room at the Mountbatten, close to the one Vanunu occupied, 105.

He may well have been among the first to observe the mood changes in the technician. Increasingly Vanunu was showing signs of strain. London was an alien environment for someone brought up in the small-town life of Beersheba. And, despite the efforts of his companions, he was lonely and hungry for female companionship, for a woman to sleep with. Mossad's psychologists had predicted that possibility.

On Wednesday, September 24, Vanunu insisted that his *Sunday Times* minders should allow him to go out alone. They reluctantly agreed. However, a reporter discreetly followed him into Leicester Square. There he saw Vanunu begin to talk to a woman. The newspaper would subsequently describe her as "in her mid-twenties, about five feet eight inches, plump, with bleached blond hair, thick lips, a brown trilby-style hat, brown tweed trouser suit, high heels and probably Jewish."

After a while they parted. Back in the hotel Vanunu confirmed to his minder he had met "an American girl called Cindy." He said he planned to meet her again. The reporters were worried. One of them said that Cindy's appearance in Leicester Square might be too much of a coincidence. Vanunu rejected their concerns. Whatever Cindy had said, it had been enough to make him want to plan to spend more time with her—and not in London, but in her "sister's" apartment in Rome.

Beni Zeevi and four other Mossad katsas were passengers on the flight on which Cheryl and Vanunu traveled to Rome. The couple took a taxi to an apartment in the old quarter of the city.

Waiting inside were three Mossad katsas. They overpowered Vanunu and injected him with a paralyzing drug. Late that night an ambulance arrived and Vanunu was carried on a stretcher out of the building. Neighbors were told by the concerned-looking katsas that a relative had fallen ill. Cheryl climbed into the ambulance, which drove off.

The ambulance sped out of Rome and down the coast. At a prearranged point a speedboat was waiting, to which Vanunu was transferred. The craft rendezvoused with a freighter anchored off the coast. Vanunu was taken on board. Beni Zeevi and Cheryl traveled with him. Three days later, in the middle of the night, the freighter docked at the port of Haifa.

Mordechai was soon facing Nahum Admoni's skilled interrogators. It was the prelude to a swift trial and a life sentence in solitary confinement. Cheryl Ben-Tov disappeared back into her secret world.

For more than eleven years Mordechai Vanunu remained in solitary confinement in a cell where Israel intended to keep him into the next century. His living conditions were bleak: poor food and an hour's exercise a day, and he spent his time in prayer and reading. Then, bowing to international pressure, Israel's government agreed in March 1998 that Vanunu could be moved to less restrictive conditions. However, he has remained an Amnesty International prisoner of conscience and the *Sunday Times* regularly reminds its readers of his plight. Vanunu received no money for the world-shattering scoop he provided the newspaper. In 1998 he was finally released from solitary but, despite renewed appeals by his lawyers, there seemed little prospect of him being released from prison.

Ten years later, plumper now, her once-styled hair blowing in the Florida sea breeze, Cheryl was back in Orlando, ostensibly on vacation at Walt Disney World with her two young daughters.

Confronted in April 1997 by a *Sunday Times* reporter, she did not deny her role in the kidnapping. Her only concern was that publicity would "harm" her "position" in the United States.

Ari Ben-Menashe fared less well. He had seen many good men come and go, victims of the constant manipulation within the Israeli intelligence community. But he had never thought his day would come.

In 1989 he was arrested in New York and accused of conspiring "with others" to violate the Arms Export Control Act by attempting to sell C-130 military aircraft to Iran. The planes had originally been sold to Israel.

During the preliminary court hearing the government of Israel said it had "no knowledge" of Ben-Menashe. He produced a file of references from his superiors in the Israeli intelligence community. The Israeli government said they were forgeries. Ben-Menashe satisfied the court they were not. The Israeli government then said Ben-Menashe was "a low-level translator" employed "within" the Israeli intelligence community. Ben-Menashe countered that the nub of the case against him—the sale of the aircraft—had been sanctioned by the Israeli and the U.S. governments. He spoke of "hundreds of millions of dollars worth of authorized arms deals to Iran."

In Tel Aviv there was consternation once more. Rafi Eitan and David Kimche were both questioned about how much Ben-Menashe knew and how much damage he could do. The responses could only have been less than reassuring. Rafi Eitan said that Ari Ben-Menashe was in a position to blow wide open the U.S./Israeli arms-to-Iran network whose tentacles had extended everywhere: down to Central and South America, through London, into Australia, across to Africa, deep into Europe.

Waiting for trial in the Metropolitan Correction Center in New York, Ben-Menashe was visited by Israeli government lawyers. They offered him a deal: plead guilty in return for a generous financial settlement that would assure him a good life after he came out of prison. Ben-Menashe decided to tell it how it had been. He had started to do so when suddenly, in November 1990, a federal jury acquitted him of all charges.

A number of his former associates in Israeli intelligence felt that Ben-Menashe had been lucky to escape; they would claim that in his attempts to gain freedom he had used what one Mossad officer called "a scatter-gun approach," by attacking everyone who threatened his freedom. Kimche echoed the fervent hope of many when he later recalled "all we wanted was for him to disappear from our sight. He had set out to damage us, his country and its safety. The man was, and is, a menace."

But Israel had not counted on the revenge Ben-Menashe took. He wrote a book, *Profits of War*, that he hoped would have the same effect Woodward and Bernstein achieved with their Watergate expose that had brought down President Richard Nixon. Ben-Menashe's self-stated intention was clear: "to right the terrible wrongs of the 1980s and help remove from power those who were responsible."

In Tel Aviv there were urgent meetings. The question of buying the manuscript and forever locking it away was discussed. It was pointed out that Ben-Menashe had already refused a very large sum—said to be a million dollars—to stay silent; he was unlikely to have changed his mind. The decision was taken that every sayan in New York publishing must be alerted to use every possible means to stop the book appearing. What success they had is debatable, though the manuscript was submitted to several mainstream publishers before being published by Sheridan Square Press, a small New York house.

Ben-Menashe would describe his book as:

> a tale of government by a cabal—how a handful of people in a few intelligence agencies determined the policies of their governments, secretly ran enormous operations without public accountability, abused power and public trust, lied, manipulated the media and deceived the public. Last, but not least, it is a tale of war—a war run not by generals, but by comfortable men in air-conditioned offices who are indifferent to human suffering.

Many saw the book as an outrageous act of atonement by its author; others saw it as an exaggerated version of events, with Ari Ben-Menashe at center stage.

In London, as he had done so many times before, Robert Maxwell hid behind the law, threatening to issue writs against anyone who dared to repeat Ben-Menashe's allegations about him. No English publisher was prepared to defy the tycoon; no newspaper was ready to use its investigative skills to substantiate Ben Menashe's claims.

Robert Maxwell, like Ben-Menashe had once firmly believed, remained convinced he was invincible for one simple reason. He had become a thief for Mossad. The more he had plundered for them, the greater had grown his belief he was indispensable to the service.

Again, like Ben-Menashe had once said, Maxwell liked to say on his visits to Israel that he too knew where all the bodies were buried. It was a claim that did not go unnoticed in Mossad.

CHAPTER 10

A DANGEROUS LIAISON

Robert Maxwell, who once fired a reporter who had cheated on his expenses, had been secretly stealing the pension funds of his employees to support Mossad. The wholesale thefts mirrored Mossad's own ruthless cunning and increasing willingness to take high-risk gambles.

Maxwell had personally removed the money through a series of interlinked financial maneuvers which, years later, would leave fraud investigators awed by his skilled duplicity. Maxwell had given mass-scale swindling a whole new dimension, transferring hundreds of thousands of dollars at a time into the special account Mossad main-

GORDON THOMAS

tained at the Bank of Israel in Tel Aviv. The funds had sometimes been laundered through an account the Israeli embassy in London had with Barclays Bank. Other banks Maxwell used for his fraud, unbeknown to them, included Credit Suisse in Geneva, the bank from which Ben-Menashe had transferred $450 million of ORA profits, with Maxwell's connivance. Sometimes the stolen pension funds traveled around the world, touching down at Chemical Bank in New York, Australia's First National Bank, and banks in Hong Kong and Tokyo. Only Robert Maxwell knew the money was purloined and where it was at any given time in its journey. What made matters worse was that he frequently ordered his newspapers to attack "white-collar crime."

Victor Ostrovsky, a Canadian-born Israeli who served as a Mossad case officer from 1984 to 1986, was the first to discover what had been happening:

"Mossad was financing many of its operations in Europe from money stolen from Maxwell's newspaper pension fund. They got their hands on the funds almost as soon as Maxwell made the purchase of the Mirror Newspaper Group with money lent to him by Mossad, together with expert advice he received from its financial analysts. What was sinister about it, aside from the theft, was that anyone in his news organisation, travelling anywhere in the Middle East, was automatically suspected of working for Israel, and was only one rumor away from the hangman's noose."

On visits to Israel, Maxwell was feted like a head of state; he was a regular guest of honor at government banquets, and was given the finest accommodations. But Mossad had taken the precaution of being prepared should the proverbial "hand that fed it" suddenly withdraw its largesse. Discovering Maxwell had a strong sexual appetite and, because of his massive size, favored oral sex, Mossad arranged that during the tycoon's visits to Israel he was serviced from one of the stable of prostitutes the service maintained for blackmail purposes. Soon Mossad had acquired a small library of video footage of Maxwell in sexually compromising positions. The bedroom suite of the hotel where he stayed had been rigged with a concealed camera.

Ostrovsky's allegations had surfaced in two personal books that still inflame the entire Israeli intelligence community. *By Way of Deception* and *Other Side of Deception* tore aside the veil of secrecy about his time in Mossad. He described operational methods and named numerous serving officers, and may well have compromised some of them in a classic exposé by a whistle-blower who believed he had been unfairly treated when he was dismissed from Mossad.

Ironically, the Israeli government had ignored the advice of Maxwell to say nothing about Ostrovsky's claims. In a meeting in Tel Aviv with Prime Minister Yitzhak Shamir, the tycoon cited what happened when the Thatcher government tried to halt publication of a book by a former MI5 officer, Peter Wright. His *Spycatcher* also contained similarly embarrassing details about Britain's security service. Pursuing its campaign to stop publication, the British government had been finally routed in the Australian courts, where Wright's prime publisher was based. *Spycatcher* had become a world best-seller and Britain had looked foolish.

The same fate had befallen the Israeli government. Pressured by serving and former members of Mossad—Meir Amit and Isser Harel had been particularly vocal in demanding action against Ostrovsky—Shamir ordered his attorney general to take legal action to halt the former katsa's first book.

The case also stoked Shamir's virulent anti-Americanism, rooted in a fixed belief that the United States was partially responsible for the Holocaust. There were claims that he believed that President Roosevelt should have come to an "arrangement"—one of Shamir's favorite words—with Hitler to replace Britain, then the dominant power in the Middle East, with the Third Reich. In turn, Hitler would have allowed the Jews to travel to Palestine, and the Holocaust would never have happened.

Nonsensical as the idea was, it had colored Shamir's views of the United States to the point of near hatred. He had personally authorized, "as a gesture of goodwill" (another favorite phrase of Shamir's) to pass on to the Soviet Union a portion of the estimated five hundred thousand pages of documents Jonathan Pollard had stolen. Shamir hoped this would improve Israel's relationship with Moscow. The documents included current U.S. intelligence on Soviet air defenses and the CIA's annual review of the entire Russian capability to make war. One document included satellite photographs, communication intercepts, radar intelligence, and reports from CIA agents in the Soviet Union. When Shamir had been told by Nahum Admoni that the data would almost certainly enable

Soviet counterintelligence to discover the spies, he had reportedly shrugged.

At their meeting to discuss what to do about Ostrovsky, Shamir repeated to Robert Maxwell what he had told others: he would do anything to reduce American influence in the world, and was convinced that Washington had encouraged Ostrovsky to publish his books as an act of retaliation.

Shamir asked Maxwell to mobilize his powerful media resources to destroy Ostrovsky's credibility. Maxwell pointed out that before employing him, Mossad would surely have checked his background.

Nevertheless, Ostrovsky became the object of a smear campaign in the Maxwell media, including the Tel Aviv tabloid *Maariv*, which Maxwell had bought. He was attacked as a fantasist, a liar, and, unlike Maxwell, not a true friend of Israel.

Having studied Ostrovsky's books, senior members of the Israeli intelligence community knew much of what he claimed was true.

The New York court refused to accept the Israeli government's argument that Israel's national security was endangered by Ostrovsky's revelations. His book became a best-seller.

Though the first person to publicly identify Robert Maxwell's links to Mossad, Ostrovsky had by no means revealed the full story. Like so much else, it had its roots firmly entangled in the activities of Shamir's old and valued friend, Rafi Eitan.

The two men had known each other since the 1950s, when they had served in Mossad, sharing an equal determination to fight to achieve Israel's place in the world.

Thirty years on, in 1986, it had been Shamir who had stood by Rafi Eitan during the crushing criticism he had faced in the aftermath of the Pollard affair, condemned as the leader "of a group of renegade intelligence officers acting without authorization."

The lie was a desperate attempt by the Israeli government to distance itself from an episode from which the intelligence community had hugely benefited, as had those of the Soviet Union and South Africa. With the full connivance of Israel, both countries had received valuable information about U.S. spying activities.

Nevertheless, with the concurrent unraveling of his role in the arms-to-Iran scandal, Rafi Eitan was professionally severely damaged. Though deeply hurt and angry at the way his own peers had singled him out for blame, the old spymaster had remained stoically silent in public; and for those trusted friends who had once sat in his living room and listened enthralled to his account of the capture of Adolf Eichmann, he had a new story to tell: how Israel turned on its own.

Increasingly fewer people rang Rafi Eitan's doorbell on Shay Street, or joined him in admiring his latest creations fashioned from scrap metal. For hours he would stand alone before his furnace brandishing his fiery torch, his mind filled no longer purely with anger over the way he had been treated, but with plans to find a way not only to "get back into the game," but also to make himself some "real money." His decision to continue to help his country despite the ignominy poured on him contained a touching simplicity: "Patriotism is not a fashionable word anymore. I am a patriot. I believe in my country. Right or wrong, I will fight anyone who threatens it or its people."

That had been the wellspring for a scheme he had secretly nurtured during the height of his involvement in Irangate. Like so many of Rafi Eitan's plans, this one required him to use his undoubted talent to exploit the original idea of someone else. It would be a plan that would eventually find him no longer remembered only as the man who captured Adolf Eichmann, but as someone who became a close associate of Robert Maxwell.

In 1967, communications expert William Hamilton returned to the United States from Vietnam, where he had devised a network of electronic listening posts to monitor the Vietcong as its forces moved through the jungle. Hamilton was offered a job with the National Security Agency. His first task had been to create a computerized Vietnamese-English dictionary that proved to be a powerful aid to translating Vietcong messages and interrogating prisoners.

It was an era when the revolution in electronic communications—satellite technology and microcircuitry—was changing the face of intelligence gathering: faster and more secure encryption and better imagery were coming online at increasing speed. Computers grew smaller and faster; more sophisticated sensors were able to separate thousands of conversations; photographic spectrum analysis lifted from millions of dots only the ones that were of interest; microchips made it possible to hear a whisper a hundred yards away; infrared lenses let one see in the black of night.

The fiber-optic sinews of a new society had contributed to operational intelligence: to amass and correlate data on a scale far beyond human capability offered a powerful tool in searching for a pattern and a modus operandi in terrorist actions. Work had started on the computer-driven Facial-Analysis Comparison and Elimination System (FACES) that would revolutionize the system of identifying a person from photographs. Based on forty-nine characteristics, each categorized on a 1 to 4 scale, FACES could make 15 million binary yes/no decisions in a *second*. Interlinked computers did simultaneous searches to eventually make a staggering 40 million binary decisions a second. Computers themselves had begun to reduce in size but retained a memory that contained the equivalent information of a five-hundred-page reference book.

Still working for the NSA, Hamilton saw an opening in this ever-expanding market; he would create a software program to interface with data banks in other computer systems. Its application in intelligence work would mean that the owner of the program would be able to interdict most other systems without their users' being aware. A patriotic man, Hamilton intended his first client for the system would be the United States government.

Just as NASA had given the country an unassailable lead in space technology, so William Hamilton was confident he would do the same for the U.S. intelligence community. Encouraged by the NSA, the inventor worked sixteen-hour days, seven days a week. Obsessive and secretive, he was the quintessential researcher; the NSA was full of them.

After three years, Hamilton was close to producing the ultimate surveillance tool—a program that could track the movements of literally untold numbers of people in any part of the world. President Reagan's warning to terrorists, "You can run, but you can't hide," was about to come true.

Hamilton resigned from the NSA and purchased a small company called Inslaw. The company's stated function was to cross-check court actions and discover if there was common background to litigants, witnesses and their families, even their attorneys—anyone involved or becoming involved in an action. Hamilton called the system Promis. By 1981, he had developed it to the point where he could copyright the software and turn Inslaw into a small, profit-making company. The future looked promising.

The NSA protested that he had made use of the agency's own research facilities to produce the program. Hamilton hotly rejected the allegation but offered to lease Promis to the Justice Department on a straightforward basis: each time the program was used, Inslaw would receive a fee. The proposed deal itself was unremarkable; Justice, like any government department, had hundreds of contractors providing services. Unknown to Hamilton, Justice had sent a copy of Hamilton's program to the NSA for "evaluation."

The reasons this was done would remain unclear. Hamilton had already demonstrated to Justice that the Promis program could do what he claimed: electronically probe into the lives of people in a way never before possible. For Justice and its investigative arm, the FBI, Promis offered a powerful tool to fight the Mafia's money-laundering and other criminal activities. Overnight it could also revolutionize the DEA's fight against the Colombian drug barons. To the CIA, Promis could become a weapon every bit as effective as a spy satellite. The possibilities seemed endless.

In the meantime, one of those characters the world of international wheeling and dealing regularly produces had heard about Promis. Earl Brian had been California's secretary of health during Reagan's time as state governor. Largely because Brian spoke Farsi, Reagan had encouraged him to put together a Medicare plan for the Iranian government. It was one of those quixotic ideas the future president of the United States loved: a version of Medicare would show Iran a positive side of America and at the same time improve the United States' image in the region. In a memorable phrase to Brian, the governor said, "If Medicare works in California, it can work anywhere."

During his visits to Tehran, Brian had come to the attention of Rafi Eitan, who was then one of the helmsmen steering the arms-for-hostages deal ever closer to the rocks. He invited Brian to Israel. They immediately struck up a rapport. Brian was captivated by his host's account of capturing Eichmann; Rafi Eitan was equally fascinated by his guest's description of Californian life in the fast lane.

Rafi Eitan soon realized that Brian could not widen his own circle of contacts in Iran and privately thought Reagan's idea for a Medicare program in Iran was "just about the craziest thing I had heard for a long time." Over the years the two men had stayed in touch; Rafi Eitan had even found time to send Brian a postcard from Apollo, Pennsylvania, where he was checking out the Numec plant. It contained the message, "This is a good place to be—from." Brian had kept Rafi Eitan informed about Promis.

In 1990 Brian arrived in Tel Aviv. He was more than weary from his long flight; the paleness on his face came from anger that the Justice Department was using a version of the Promis program to track money-laundering and other criminal activities.

Rafi Eitan's instincts told him that his old friend could not have arrived at a more opportune time. Once more conflict had flared between Mossad and the other members of the Israeli intelligence community. The cause was a new Arab uprising, the Intifada. Promis could be an effective weapon to counter its activities.

The revolution had spread with remarkable speed, stunning the Israelis and galvanizing the Palestinians in the West Bank and Gaza Strip. The more people the Israeli army arrested, shot, beat, and uprooted from their homes, the swifter the Intifada spread. There was something close to grudging understanding outside Israel when a young Arab boy used a hang glider to evade Israel's sophisticated border defenses with Lebanon and land in scrubland close to the small northern town of Kiryat Shmona. In a few minutes the youth killed six heavily armed Israeli soldiers and wounded seven more before he was shot dead.

The incident became enshrined in Palestinian minds; within the Israeli intelligence community there was furious finger-pointing. Shin Bet blamed Aman; both blamed Mossad for its failure to provide advance warning from Lebanon. Worse followed. Six dangerous terrorists escaped from the maximum-security jail in Gaza. Mossad blamed Shin Bet. That agency said the escape plot had been organized from outside the country—which made Mossad culpable.

Almost daily, Israeli soldiers and civilians were shot dead in the streets of Jerusalem, Tel Aviv, and Haifa. Desperate to regain authority, Defense Minister Yitzhak Rabin announced he was implementing a policy of "force, might and beatings," but it had little effect.

Beset by deepening interservice strife, the Israeli intelligence community was unable to agree on a coordinated policy to deal with mass Arab resistance on a scale not seen since the War of Independence. An added thorn was the criticism from the United States over the growing evidence on TV screens of the brutal methods deployed by Israeli soldiers. For the first time U.S. networks, normally friendly to Israel, began to screen footage which, for sheer brutality, matched what had happened in Beijing's Tiananmen Square. Two Israeli soldiers were filmed relentlessly smashing a rock against the arm of a Palestinian youth; an IDF patrol was caught on camera beating a pregnant Palestinian mother; children in Hebron were shown having IDF rifle butts smashed against their bodies for throwing stones.

The Intifada coalesced to form the United National Leadership of the Uprising. Every Arab community was postered with instructions in Arabic on how to stage strikes, close shops, boycott Israeli goods, refuse to recognize the civil administration. It was reminiscent of the resistance in the last days of the German occupation of France in World War II.

Desperate to reestablish Mossad's preeminent role among the intelligence community, Nahum Admoni took action. On February 14, 1988, a kidon team was sent to the Cypriot port of Limassol. They planted a powerful bomb on the chassis of a Volkswagen Golf. It belonged to one of the leaders of the Intifada, Muhammad Tamimi. With him were two senior PLO officers. They had met with Libyan officials who had handed over $1 million to continue bankrolling the Intifada. All three men were killed in the massive explosion that rocked the entire port.

The following day, Mossad struck again—planting a limpet mine on the hull of the *Soi Phayne*, a passenger ship the PLO had just bought for an intended public relations exercise. With the world's press on board, the ship would have sailed to Haifa as a poignant reminder of the Palestinians' "right to return" to their homeland— and a more pointed reminder of the Jewish boats, immortalized by the *Exodus*, which, forty years before, had defied the British navy to bring the survivors of the Holocaust to Israel, also under their "right to return." The *Soi Phayne* was destroyed.

The operations had done nothing to daunt Arab determination. At every turn guerrillas were able to outsmart the Israelis, whose only response seemed to be violence and more violence. The world watched as Israel not only failed to stop the Intifada but also lost the propaganda war. Commentators made the comparison that here was a modern-day David-versus-Goliath conflict, with the IDF cast in the role of the Philistine giant.

Yasser Arafat used the Intifada as an opportunity to regain control over his dispossessed people. Around the world his voice cracked with fury on radio and television that what was happening was the direct result of Israel's policy of stealing Arab land. He urged every Arab to rally in support. One day Arafat was in Kuwait urging Hamas, the terrorist group backed by Iran, to provide its deadly skills. The next he was in Lebanon, meeting with the leaders of Islamic Jihad. Arafat was achieving what had, only a short time before, seemed impossible—uniting Arabs of all persuasions in a common cause. To them all he was "Mr. Palestine" or "Chairman."

Mossad was constantly flummoxed by Arafat's strategies as he flitted between Arab capitals. It had little or no warning where he would turn up, or whom he would next rally to his side.

All this and more Rafi Eitan explained to his houseguest, Earl Brian. In turn Brian described how Promis worked. In his view, there was still work to be done to bring the program up to speed. Rafi Eitan realized that Promis could then have an impact on the Intifada. For a start, the system could lock on to computers in the PLO's seventeen offices scattered around the world to see where Arafat was going and what he could be planning. Rafi Eitan put aside his foraging for scrap metal and focused on how to exploit the brave new world Promis offered.

No longer, for instance, would it be necessary to rely solely on human intelligence to understand the mind-set of a terrorist. With Promis it would be possible to know exactly when and where he would strike. Promis could track a terrorist's every step.

To achieve such a breakthrough would once more undoubtedly make him a powerful figure in the Israeli intelligence community. But the wounds inflicted on him by his former peers had gone deep. He had been turned out into the cold with little more than a modest pension. He was getting on in years; his first obligation was to his family, whom, through his work, he had been forced to neglect for long periods. Promis offered an opportunity to make amends; handled properly, it could make his fortune. However, for all his brilliance, Rafi Eitan was no computer genius; his skills in that area extended to little more than switching on his modem. But his years at LAKAM had given him access to all the experts he would need.

When Earl Brian returned to the United States, Rafi Eitan put together a small team of former LAKAM programmers. They deconstructed the Promis disc and rearranged its various components, then added several elements of their own. There was no way for anyone to be able to claim ownership of what Promis had become. Rafi Eitan decided to keep the original name because it was "a good marketing tool to explain what the system was."

Intelligence operatives, untrained in computer technology beyond knowing which keys to tap, would be able to access information and judgments far more comprehensive than they could ever carry in their own heads. A Promis disc could fit a laptop computer and choose from a myriad of alternatives the one that made most sense. It would eliminate the need for deductive reasoning because there were too many correct but irrelevant matters to simultaneously take into account for human reasoning alone to suffice. Promis could be programmed to eliminate all superfluous lines of inquiry and amass and correlate data at a speed and scale beyond human capability.

But before it could be sold, according to Ben-Menashe, Rafi Eitan needed to add one further element. Ben-Menashe claims he was summoned a played a large part in inserting a "trapdoor," a built-in chip that, unknown to any purchaser, would allow Rafi Eitan to know what information was being sought.

Ben-Menashe knew someone who could create a trapdoor that even the most sophisticated scanners would be unable to detect. The man ran a small computer research and development company in Northern California. He and Ben-Menashe had been schoolboy friends, and for five thousand dollars he agreed to produce the microchip. It was, Ben-Menashe admitted, cheap at the price. The next stage would be to test the system.

Jordan was selected as the site, not only because it bordered on Israel, but because it had become a haven for the leaders of the Intifada. From the desert kingdom, they directed the Arab street mobs on the West Bank and Gaza to launch further attacks inside Israel. After an atrocity, PLO terrorists would slip across the border into Jordan, doing so often with the connivance of the Jordanian army.

Consequently, long before the Intifada, Jordan had become a proving ground for Mossad to develop its electronic skills. In the 1970s, Mossad technicians had tapped into the computer IBM had sold to the country's military intelligence service. The information gained had supplemented that provided by the deep-cover katsa Rafi Eitan had placed inside King Hussein's palace. Promis would offer much more.

To sell it directly to Jordan was impossible because normal business links between both countries were still some years away. Instead, Earl Brian's company, Hadron, made the deal. When the company's computer experts installed the program in Amman's military headquarters, they discovered the Jordanians had a French-designed system to track the movements of PLO leaders. Promis was secretly wired into the French system. In Tel Aviv, Rafi Eitan soon saw results as the trapdoor showed which PLO leaders the Jordanians were tracking.

The next stage was to prepare the sales pitch for Promis. Yasser Arafat was selected as the ideal example. The PLO chairman was renowned for being security-conscious; he constantly changed his plans, never slept in the same bed two nights in succession, altered his mealtimes at the last moment.

Whenever Arafat moved, the details were entered on a secure PLO computer. But Promis could hack into its defenses to discover what aliases and false passports he was using. Promis could obtain his phone bills and check the numbers called. It would then cross-check those with other calls made from those numbers. In that way, Promis would have a "picture" of Arafat's communications.

On a trip he would inform the local security authorities of his presence, and steps would be taken to provide protection. Promis could obtain the details by interdicting police computers. Wherever he went, Yasser Arafat would be unable to hide from Promis.

Rafi Eitan realized that neither Earl Brian nor his company had the resources to market Promis globally. That would require someone with superb international contacts, boundless energy, and proven negotiating skills. There was only one man Rafi Eitan knew who had those requirements: Robert Maxwell.

Maxwell needed little convincing and, in his usual ebullient manner when there was a deal to be profited from, said he had a computer company through which to sell Promis. Degem Computers

Limited was based in Tel Aviv and was already playing a useful role in Mossad's activities. Maxwell had allowed Mossad operatives, posing as Degem employees, to use the company's suboffices in Central and South America. Now Maxwell saw an opportunity not only to make a healthy profit from marketing Promis through Degem, but to further establish his own importance to Mossad and ultimately Israel.

On recent visits to Israel he had begun to display disturbing traits. Maxwell told Admoni he should start employing psychics to read the minds of Mossad's enemies. He began to suggest targets for elimination. He wanted to meet kidons and inspect their training camps. All these requests were firmly but politely parried by the Mossad chief. But within Mossad, questions began to be asked about Maxwell. Was his behavior only that of a megalomaniac throwing about his weight? Or was it a precursor of something else? Could the time eventually come when, despite all he had done for Israel, Robert Maxwell became sufficiently mentally unstable and unpredictable to create a problem?

But there was no doubting Maxwell was a brilliant marketeer of Promis—or, as far as Mossad was concerned, of the effectiveness of the system. The service had been the first to obtain the program and it had been a valuable tool in its campaign against the Intifada. Many of its leaders had left Jordan for safer hideouts in Europe after several had been assassinated in Jordan by kidons.

A spectacular success came when an Intifada commander who had moved to Rome called a Beirut number that Mossad's computers already had listed as the home of a known bomb maker. The Rome caller wanted to meet the bomb maker in Athens. Mossad used Promis to check all the travel offices in Rome and Beirut for the travel arrangements of both men. In Beirut, further checks revealed the bomber had ordered the local utility companies to suspend supplies to his home. A further search by Promis of the local PLO computers also showed the bomber had switched flights at the last moment. It did not save him. He was killed by a car bomb on the way to Beirut airport. Shortly afterward, in Rome, the Intifada commander was killed in a hit-and-run accident.

Meantime, Mossad was using Promis to read the secret intelligence of a number of services. In Guatemala, it uncovered the close ties between the country's security forces and drug traffickers and their outlets in the United States. Names were passed on to the DEA and FBI by Mossad.

In South Africa, a katsa in the Israeli embassy used Promis to track the country's banned revolutionary organization and their contacts with Middle Eastern groups. In Washington, Mossad specialists at the Israeli embassy used Promis to penetrate the communications of other diplomatic missions and U.S. government departments. The same was happening in London and other European capitals. The system had continued to yield valuable information for Mossad. By 1989, over $500 million worth of Promis programs had been sold to Britain, Australia, South Korea, and Canada. The figure would have been even bigger but for the CIA marketing its own version to intelligence agencies. In Britain, Promis was used by MI5 in Northern Ireland to track terrorists and the movements of political leaders like Gerry Adams.

Maxwell had also managed to sell the system to the Polish intelligence service, the UB. In return the Poles, according to Ben-Menashe, allowed Mossad to steal a Russian MiG-29. The operation was a reminder of the theft of the earlier version of the MiG from Iraq. A Polish general in charge of the UB office in Gdansk, in return for $1 million paid into a Citibank account in New York, had arranged for the aircraft to be written off as no longer airworthy, though the plane had only recently arrived from its Russian aircraft factory. The fighter was dismantled, placed in crates marked "Agricultural Machinery," and flown to Tel Aviv. There the plane was reassembled and test-flown by the Israeli air force, enabling its pilots to counter the MiG-29s in service with Syria.

It was weeks before the theft was discovered by Moscow during a routine inventory of aircraft supplied to Warsaw Pact countries. A strong protest was made by Moscow to Israel—backed by the threat to stop the exodus of Jews from the Soviet Union. The Israeli government, its air force having discovered all the MiG's secrets, apologized profusely for the "mistaken zeal of officers acting unofficially" and promptly returned the aircraft. By then the UB general had joined his dollar fortune in the United States. Washington had agreed to give him a new identity in return for the USAF being allowed to conduct its own inspection of the MiG.

Shortly afterward Robert Maxwell flew to Moscow. Officially he was there to interview Mikhail Gorbachev. In reality he had come to sell Promis to the KGB. Through its secret trapdoor microchip, it gave Israel unique access to Soviet military intelligence, making Mossad one of the best-briefed services on Russian intentions.

From Moscow Maxwell flew to Tel Aviv. As usual he was received like a potentate, excused all airport formalities and welcomed by an official greeter from the Foreign Office.

Maxwell treated him the way he did all his staff, insisting the official carry his bags and sit beside the driver. Maxwell also demanded to know where his motorcycle escort was, and when told it was not available, he threatened to call the prime minister's office to have the greeter fired. At every traffic stop, Maxwell harangued the hapless official, and he continued to do so all the way to his hotel suite. Waiting was Maxwell's favorite prostitute. He sent her running; there were far more pressing matters than satisfying his sexual needs.

In London Robert Maxwell's newspaper empire was in grave financial trouble. Soon, without a substantial injection of capital, it would have to cease operations. But, in the City of London, where he had previously always found funding, there was a reluctance to go on providing it. Hard-nosed financiers who had met Maxwell sensed that behind his bluster and bully-boy tactics was a man who was losing the financial acumen that in the past had allowed them to forgive so much. In those days he had raged and threatened at the slightest challenge. Bankers had curbed their anger and caved in to his demands. But they would no longer do so. In the Bank of England and other financial institutions in the City, the word was that Maxwell was no longer a safe bet.

Their information was partially based on confidential reports from Israel that Maxwell was being pressed by his original Israeli investors to repay them the money that had helped him to acquire the Mirror Group. The time limit on repayments had long gone and the demands from the Israelis had become more insistent. Trying to fend them off, Maxwell had promised them a higher return on their money if they waited. The Israelis were not satisfied: they wanted their money back now. This was why Maxwell had come to Tel Aviv: he hoped to cajole them into granting him another extension. The signs were not good. During the flight, he had received several angry phone calls from the investors, threatening to place the matter before the City of London regulatory body.

There was a further matter for Maxwell to be concerned over. He had stolen some of the very substantial profits from ORA that he had been entrusted to hide in Soviet Bloc banks. He had used the money to try to prop up the Mirror Group. Maxwell had already stolen all he could from the staff pension fund, and the ORA money would not stretch very far.

And, unlike the Israeli investors, once that theft was uncovered, he would find himself confronting some very hard men, among them Rafi Eitan. Maxwell knew enough about the former Mossad operative to realize that would not be a pleasant experience.

From his hotel suite, Maxwell began to strategize. His share of the profits from Degem's marketing of Promis would not be able to stem the crisis. Neither would profits from *Maariv*, the Israeli tabloid modeled on his flagship *Daily Mirror*. But there was one possibility, the Tel Aviv–based Cytex Corporation he owned, which manufactured high-tech printing equipment. If Cytex could be sold quickly, the money could go some way to solving matters.

Maxwell ordered Cytex's senior executive, the son of Prime Minister Yitzhak Shamir, to his suite. The executive had bad news: a quick sale was unlikely. Cytex, while holding its own, faced increasing competition. This was not the time to take it to the market. To sell would also throw skilled people out of work at a time when unemployment was a serious problem in Israel.

The reaction provoked a furious outburst from Maxwell as his last hope of rescue faded. Tactically he made an error in lambasting the prime minister's son, who now told his father that Maxwell was in serious financial trouble. The prime minister, aware of the tycoon's links to Mossad, informed Nahum Admoni. He called a meeting of senior staff to see how to deal with what had become a problem.

Later it emerged that several options were discussed.

Mossad could ask the prime minister to use his own considerable influence with the Israeli investors not only to wait a while longer for their money, but to mobilize their own resources and contacts to find money to bail out Maxwell. This was rejected on the grounds that Maxwell had managed to upset Shamir with his cavalier attitude. Everyone knew that Shamir had a strong sense of self-preservation and would now wish to distance himself from Maxwell.

Another option was for Mossad to approach its highly placed sayanim in the City of London and urge them to support a rescue package for Mossad. At the same time Mossad-friendly journalists in Britain could be encouraged to write supportive stories about the troubled tycoon.

Again those suggestions were discounted. Reports Admoni had received from London suggested that many of the sayanim would welcome the end of Maxwell and that few journalists outside Mirror newspapers would dream of writing favorable stories about a tycoon who had spent years threatening the media.

The final option was for Mossad to break off all contact with Maxwell. There was a risk there: Maxwell, on the evidence of his present unpredictable state of mind, could well use his newspapers to actually attack Mossad. Given the access he had been given, that could have the most serious consequences.

On that somber note, the meeting concluded that Admoni would see Maxwell and remind him of his responsibility to both Mossad and Israel. That night the two men met over dinner in Maxwell's hotel suite. What transpired between them would remain a secret. But hours later, Robert Maxwell left Tel Aviv in his private plane. It would be the last time, it would turn out, that anyone in Israel would see him alive.

Back in London, Maxwell, against all the odds, seemed to be succeeding in holding on to his newspaper group. He was likened to an African whirling dervish as he went from one meeting to another seeking financial support. From time to time he called Mossad to speak to Admoni, always informing the director general's secretary that the "little Czech" was on the line. The sobriquet had been bestowed on Maxwell after he had been recruited. What was said in those calls would remain unknown.

But a clue would later emerge from the former katsa, Victor Ostrovsky. He believed Maxwell was insisting it was payback time; that the huge sum of money he had stolen from the *Mirror* pension fund should now be returned to him. At the same time, Maxwell also proposed that Mossad should, on his behalf, lobby for Mordechai Vanunu to be freed and handed over to him. Maxwell would then fly the technician to London and personally interview him for the *Daily Mirror*. The story would be Vanunu's "act of atonement," written in a way that would show Israel's compassion. With the chutzpah characteristic of so many of his actions, Maxwell added it would be a huge circulation booster for the *Mirror* and would unlock those doors still closed to him in the City of London.

Ostrovsky was not alone in believing that the preposterous plan finally decided Mossad that Robert Maxwell had become a dangerous loose cannon.

On September 30, 1991, further evidence of Maxwell's bizarre behavior came when he telephoned Admoni. This time there was no disguising the threat in Maxwell's words. His financial affairs had once more taken a turn for the worse, and he was being investigated in Parliament and the British media, so long held at bay by his posse of high-priced lawyers and their quiver of writs. Maxwell then said that unless Mossad arranged to immediately return all the stolen *Mirror* pension fund money, he could not be sure if he would be able to keep secret Admoni's meeting with Vladimir Kryuchkov, the former head of the KGB. Kryuchkov was now in a Moscow prison awaiting trial for his role in an abortive coup to oust Mikhail Gorbachev. A key element of the plot had been a meeting Kryuchkov had on Maxwell's yacht in the Adriatic shortly before the coup was launched.

Mossad had promised that Israel would use its influence with the United States and key European countries to diplomatically recognize the new regime in Moscow. In return, Kryuchkov would arrange for all Soviet Jews to be released and sent to Israel. The discussion had come to nothing. But revealing it could seriously harm Israel's credibility with the existing Russian regime and with the United States.

That was the moment, Victor Ostrovsky would write, when "a small meeting of right wingers at Mossad headquarters resulted in a consensus to terminate Maxwell."

If Ostrovsky's claim is true—and it has never been formally denied by Israel—then it was unthinkable that the group was acting without the highest sanction and perhaps even with the tacit knowledge of Israel's prime minister, Yitzhak Shamir, the man who had once had his own share of killing Mossad's enemies.

The matter for Mossad could only have become more urgent with the publication of a book by the veteran American investigative reporter Seymour M. Hersh, *The Samson Option: Israel, America and the Bomb*, which dealt with Israel's emergence as a nuclear power. News of the book had caught Mossad totally by surprise and copies were rushed to Tel Aviv. Well researched, it could nevertheless still have been effectively dealt with by saying nothing; the painful lesson of the mistake of confronting Ostrovsky's publisher (also the publisher of this book) had been absorbed. But there was one problem: Hersh had identified Maxwell's links to Mossad. Those ties mostly involved the Mirror Group's handling of the Vanunu story and the relationship between Nick Davies, ORA, and Ari Ben-Menashe. Predictably, Maxwell had taken refuge behind a battery of lawyers, issuing writs against Hersh and his London publishers. But, for the first time, he met his match. Hersh, a Pulitzer Prize winner, refused to be cowed. In Parliament, more pointed questions were asked about Maxwell's links to Mossad. Old suspicions surfaced. MPs demanded to know, under parliamentary privilege, how much Maxwell knew about Mossad's operations in Britain. For Victor Ostrovsky, "the ground was starting to burn under Maxwell's feet."

Ostrovsky would claim that the carefully prepared Mossad plan to kill Maxwell hinged on being able to persuade him to keep a rendezvous where Mossad could strike. It had a striking similarity to the plot that had led to the death of Mehdi Ben-Barka in Paris.

On October 29, 1991, Maxwell received a call from a katsa at the Israeli embassy in Madrid. Maxwell was asked to come to Spain the next day, and, according to Ostrovsky, "his caller promised that things would be worked out so there was no need to panic." Maxwell was told to fly to Gibraltar and board his yacht, the *Lady Ghislaine*, and order the crew to set sail for the Canary Islands "and wait there for a message."

Robert Maxwell agreed to do as instructed.

On October 30, four Israelis arrived in the Moroccan port of Rabat. They said they were tourists on a deep-sea fishing vacation and hired an oceangoing motor yacht. They set off toward the Canary Islands.

On October 31, after Maxwell reached the port of Santa Cruz on the island of Tenerife, he dined alone in the Hotel Mency. After dinner a man briefly joined him. Who he was and what they spoke about remain part of the mystery of the last days of Robert Maxwell. Shortly afterward, Maxwell returned to his yacht and ordered it back to sea. For the next thirty-six hours, the *Lady Ghislaine* sailed between the islands, keeping well clear of land, cruising at various speeds. Maxwell had told the captain he was deciding where to go next. The crew could not recall Maxwell showing such indecision.

In what it claimed was a "world exclusive," headlined "How and why Robert Maxwell was murdered," Britain's *Business Age* magazine subsequently claimed that a two-man hit team crossed in a dinghy during the night from a motor yacht that had shadowed the *Lady Ghislaine*. Boarding the yacht, they found Maxwell on the afterdeck. The men overpowered him before he could call for help. Then, "one assassin injected a bubble of air into Maxwell's neck via his jugular vein. It took just a few moments for Maxwell to die."

The magazine concluded the body was dropped overboard and the assassins returned to their yacht. It would be sixteen hours before Maxwell was recovered—enough time for a needle prick to recede beyond detection as a result of water immersion and the skin being nibbled by fish.

More certain, on the night of November 4–5, Mossad's problems with Maxwell were laid to rest in the cold swell of the Atlantic. The subsequent police investigation and the Spanish autopsy left unanswered questions. Why were only two of the yacht's eleven-man crew awake? Normally five shared the night watch. To whom did Maxwell send a number of fax messages during those hours? What became of the copies? Why did the crew take so long to establish Maxwell was not on board? Why did they delay raising the alarm for a further seventy minutes? To this day no convincing answers have emerged.

Three Spanish pathologists were assigned to perform the autopsy. They wanted the vital organs and tissue to be sent to Madrid for further tests. Before this could be done, the Maxwell family intervened, ordering the body embalmed and flown forthwith to Israel for burial. The Spanish authorities, unusually, did not object.

Who or what had persuaded the family to suddenly act as it did?

On November 10, 1991, Maxwell's funeral took place on the Mount of Olives in Jerusalem, the resting place for the nation's most revered heroes. It had all the trappings of a state occasion, attended by the country's government and opposition leaders. No fewer than six serving and former heads of the Israeli intelligence community listened as Prime Minister Shamir eulogized: "He has done more for Israel than can today be said."

Those who stood among the mourners included a man dressed in a somber black suit and shirt, relieved only at the throat by his Roman collar. Born into a Lebanese Christian family, he was a wraithlike figure—barely five feet tall and weighing little over a hundred pounds. But Father Ibrahim was no ordinary priest. He worked for the Vatican's Secretariat of State.

His discreet presence at the funeral was not so much to mark the earthly passing of Robert Maxwell, but to acknowledge the still-secret ties developing between the Holy See and Israel. It was a perfect example of Meir Amit's dictum that intelligence cooperation knows no limits.

CHAPTER 11

UNHOLY ALLIANCES

From the beginning, successive Israeli prime ministers had been fascinated by the concept of the pope as an absolute ruler elected for life, a leader not held accountable to any judiciary or legislative control. Using a pyramidic and monarchical structure, the supreme pontiff wielded extraordinary influence to shape the economic, political, and ideological outlook of not only the Catholic faithful but the world at large. David Ben-Gurion once growled: "Never mind that nonsense about how many divisions does the pope have—just look at how many people he can summon to his aid."

For Mossad, the appeal was the sheer secrecy with which the

Vatican operated. It was a well-defined mechanism, strictly enforced, and it cloaked everything the Holy See did. Often months passed before the first hints emerged of papal involvement in some diplomatic initiative; even then the full story rarely surfaced. Each Mossad chief wondered how to penetrate the veil. But various attempts by both the government of Israel and Mossad to establish a good working relationship with the Vatican had been politely but firmly rejected.

The reality was that within the Holy See's Secretariat of State—the equivalent of a secular foreign office—there existed a powerful anti-Israeli faction. These soutaned monsignors would invariably refer to the West Bank and the Gaza Strip as "occupied territories" and the Golan Heights as having been "annexed" from Syria. In the evenings, they would drive out of their tiny city-state to the apartments of wealthy Arabs on Rome's Via Condotti, or join them for cocktails in the Piazza Navona, dispassionately listening to dreams of removing Israel from the face of the earth.

The priests were careful what they said; they believed the Jewish state had its agents everywhere, watching, listening, perhaps even recording and photographing. One of the first warnings a newcomer to the Secretariat received was to be aware of being "spied or enveigled upon, especially by agents from countries the Vatican firmly refuses to diplomatically recognize." Israel was high on that list. Upon his election in 1978, Pope John Paul II had reaffirmed it would remain there; only well into his pontificate would he finally agree to grant full diplomatic status to Israel.

The information the pope received about Israel continued to be influenced by contacts his priest-diplomats made with Arabs. Their forays into Rome were followed by the monsignors returning to the third floor of the Apostolic Palace, the overcrowded, artificially lit, and poorly ventilated headquarters of the papal diplomatic service. Known as the Extraordinary Affairs Section, it was responsible for implementing the foreign policy of the Holy See. Its twenty "desks" dealt with almost as much paperwork as other major foreign ministries, a measure of the Vatican's ever expanding worldwide diplomatic interests.

The Middle East desk was housed in cubbyhole offices overlooking the San Damaso Courtyard, a magnificent piazza in the heart of the great palace. One of the first papers the desk presented to the new Polish pontiff was a closely argued case for Jerusalem to have international status and be patrolled by United Nations forces with the Vatican having responsibility for all the city's Christian shrines. News of the proposal reached Tel Aviv early in 1979, having been photocopied from a document passed by a monsignor to a wealthy Lebanese Christian living in Rome. The man's staff included a Mossad sayan. The prospect of internationalizing Jerusalem angered Prime Minister Menachem Begin, who ordered Mossad's chief, Yitzhak Hofi, to redouble his efforts to establish contact with the Vatican.

Both knew what had happened the last time Mossad tried to do that under cover of a state visit by Begin's predecessor, the redoubtable Golda Meir.

Late in 1972, Golda Meir finally received a response from Pope Paul VI that he would be prepared to receive her in a short private audience. In December of that year she told cabinet members at their weekly session who had wondered if the meeting would produce anything worthwhile that she was fascinated by the "Marxist structuralism of the papacy. First it has financial power which is almost unprecedented. Then it operates without political parties or trade unions. The whole apparatus is organised for control. The Roman Curia controls the bishops, the bishops control the clergy, the clergy control the laity. With its multitude of secretariats, commissions and structures, it is a system tailor-made for spying and informing!"

The date for the papal audience was set for the morning of January 15, 1973; Golda Meir was informed she would have precisely thirty-five minutes with the pontiff; at the end they would exchange gifts. There was no specific agenda for the meeting but Golda Meir hoped to persuade the pope to visit Israel. The official reason would be for him to celebrate Mass for the hundred thousand or so Christian Arabs in the country. But she also knew his presence would give the country a huge boost on the international stage.

For security reasons there would be no prior announcement about the meeting. At the end of her visit to a conference of international socialists in Paris, Golda Meir would fly on to Rome in her chartered El Al plane. Only on the flight would journalists accompanying her be told she was going to the Vatican.

Zvi Zamir, Mossad's chief, flew to Rome to check security arrangements. The city was a hotbed for terrorist factions from both the Middle East and Europe. Rome had also become an important listening post for Mossad's current preoccupation, locating and killing the perpetrators of the Munich Olympics massacre.

Zamir had based Mark Hessner, one of his ablest katsas, in Rome to probe the city's large Arab community. In Milan, another center for terrorist activity, the Mossad chief had stationed Shai Kauly, another experienced katsa. After Zamir briefed both men on the forthcoming visit, they accompanied him to the Vatican.

On January 10, 1973, as the three men were chauffeured across Rome to the Vatican, they knew far more about the Holy See's long relationship with another intelligence service than their hosts may have realized.

In 1945, the wartime Office of Strategic Services (OSS)—the forerunner to the CIA—had been welcomed into the Vatican, in the words of James Jesus Angleton, the head of the OSS Rome station, "with open arms." Pope Pius XII and his Curia asked Angleton to help the Church's militant anti-Communist crusade by getting the Italian Christian Democratic Party into power. Angleton, a practicing Catholic, used all the considerable resources at his disposal to bribe, blackmail, and threaten voters to support them. He had been given full access to the Vatican's unparalleled information-gathering service through Italy; every curate and priest reported on the activities of Italian Communists in their parishes. When the Vatican had assessed the information, it was passed to Angleton, who sent it on to Washington.

There it was used to support the now deeply entrenched State Department fear that the Soviet Union presented a real and long-term threat to the West. Angleton was told to do anything that would stop the wartime resistance activists of Italy's Communist Party from taking over. Like the pope, Angleton was haunted by the specter of a worldwide Communist threat that would split the globe into two systems—capitalism and socialism—which could never peacefully coexist. Stalin had himself said no less.

The pope was convinced that the Italian Communists were at the spearhead of a campaign to destroy the Church at every opportunity. The regular meetings between Pius and the pious Angleton became sessions where the bogey of Communism loomed ever larger. The pope urged Angleton to tell the United States it must do all possible to destroy the threat. The pontiff who represented peace on earth became an enthusiastic proponent of U.S. foreign policy which led to the cold war.

By 1952, the Rome station of what was now the CIA was being run by another devout Catholic, William Colby—who went on to mastermind the CIA's activities in Vietnam. Colby had established a powerful network of informers within the Secretariat of State and every Vatican congregation and tribunal. He used them to help the CIA fight Soviet espionage and subversion across the globe. Priests regularly reported to the Vatican what was happening. In countries like the Philippines, where Communists were trying to make inroads into what had long been a devout Catholic nation, the CIA was able to launch effective counterattacks. The pope saw the violence as necessary and shared the view that if the United States did not perform what he once called "sad, but necessary actions," the world would have to endure decades of further suffering.

In 1960, the CIA achieved another breakthrough when Milan's Cardinal Montini—three years later to become Pope Paul VI—gave the CIA the names of priests in the United States deemed by the Vatican to be still soft on Communism. The cold war was at its peak; paranoia ran rife in Washington. The FBI hounded the priests, and many left the country, heading for Central and South America. The CIA had a substantial slush fund, called "project money," used to make generous gifts to Catholic charities, schools, and orphanages to pay for the restoration of church buildings the Vatican owned. All-expenses-paid holidays were given to priests and nuns known to be staunchly pro-American. Italian cardinals and bishops received cases of champagne and hampers of gourmet delicacies in a country still recovering from the food shortages of World War II. Successive CIA station chiefs were regarded by the Vatican as being more important than America's ambassadors to Italy.

When John XXIII was elected supreme pontiff in 1958, he stunned the Curia (the Vatican civil service) by saying that the crusade against Communism had largely failed. He ordered the Italian bishops to become "politically neutral." The CIA was frantic when Pope John ordered its free access to the Vatican must stop. The

Agency's panic increased when the CIA learned the pope had begun to nurture the seeds of an embryonic Ostpolitik and started a cautious dialogue with Nikita Khrushchev, the Soviet leader. For the CIA's station chief in Rome, "the Vatican was no longer totally committed to the American system. The Holy See is hostile and we must from now on see its activities in that light."

CIA analysts in Washington prepared exhaustive assessments with such grandiose titles as *The Links between the Vatican and Communism*. In the late spring of 1963, the Rome station reported that the Holy See was to establish full diplomatic relations with Russia. The CIA's director, John McCone, flew to Rome and bulldozed his way into a meeting with Pope John, saying he had come at the insistence of America's first Catholic president, John F. Kennedy. McCone told the pontiff that the Church "must stop this drift toward Communism. It is both dangerous and unacceptable to dicker with the Kremlin. Communism is a Trojan horse as the recent left-wing victories in the Italian national elections indicate. In office the Communists have dismantled many of the policies Catholic parties supported."

For ten full minutes, McCone spoke in this blunt manner without interruption. Silence finally settled over the audience chamber in the Apostolic Palace. For a moment longer the old pope studied his tall, ascetic visitor. Then, speaking softly, John explained that the Church he led had an urgent duty: to end abject poverty and the denial of human rights, to close down the slum dwellings and the shantytowns, to end racism and political oppression. He would talk to anybody who would help him do that—including the Soviets. The only way to meet the challenge of Communism was to confront it with reasoned argument.

McCone, unable to contain his anger any longer—"I had not come to debate"—said the CIA had ample evidence that, while the pope pursued his détente with Moscow, Communism was persecuting priests through the Soviet Bloc, Asia, and South America: Pope John realized that was all the more reason to seek a better relationship with the Soviets. Defeated, McCone returned to Washington convinced that Pope John was "softer on Communism than any of his predecessors."

John's not unexpected death—he had a rapidly progressing cancer—was greeted with relief by McCone and President Kennedy.

When Montini of Milan became Paul VI in late 1963, Washington relaxed. Two days after his inauguration, the pope received Kennedy in private audience. Outside, McCone strolled through the Vatican gardens like a landowner who had returned home after a long absence.

Paul's long pontificate was blighted on the personal front by his declining health and, on the international stage, by the Vietnam War. He came to believe that the escalation President Lyndon Johnson had ordered in 1966 was morally wrong and that the Holy See should be given the role of peacemaker. Three months after Richard Nixon came into the Oval Office, he flew to Rome to meet the pope. The president told him he proposed to increase America's commitment in Vietnam. Once more the CIA found itself out of favor in the Vatican.

All this, Zvi Zamir had learned from his Washington katsa. Now, on this brilliantly sunny morning on January 10, 1973, as he and his two colleagues were driven into the Vatican to check the security arrangements for Golda Meir's visit, Zamir hoped it would result in Mossad taking the place of the CIA in the Vatican's long flirtation with the intelligence world.

Waiting for them outside the Apostolic Palace was the head of Vatican security, a tall, pinch-faced man wearing a dark blue suit, the uniform of the Vigili, the Vatican security service. For several hours he had taken them on a tour of the small city-state, checking possible places where an Arab gunman could hide before trying to assassinate Golda Meir. Unknown to the Vatican security chief, Zvi Zamir was also looking for places where Mossad could plant bugging devices once it had established a working relationship with the Holy See. Zamir flew back to Tel Aviv satisfied with the city-state's security presentations. More important, he believed he had detected a softening in the attitude of the Holy See toward Israel.

Even before Zamir had landed in Israel, details of Golda Meir's visit were in the hands of Black September, almost certainly leaked by a pro-Arab priest in the Secretariat of State. For Ali Hassan Salameh, the group's leader, though he was on the run from Mossad after masterminding the Munich atrocity, Golda Meir's visit was an opportunity he could not ignore. He began to plan a missile attack against her plane as it landed at Rome's Leonardo Da Vinci Airport.

He hoped to kill not only her, but key government ministers who would be accompanying the prime minister and the senior Mossad men who would also be on board. By the time Israel had recovered from these blows, Salameh hoped, he and his men would be ensconced in the hideout they were negotiating with the Russians to provide.

Since 1968, when a generation born after World War II launched its own war on society—under such disparate names as Italy's Red Brigades, Germany's Red Army Faction, the Turkish People's Liberation Army, Spain's ETA, and the PLO—the Kremlin had recognized their value in helping to destroy imperialism—and Israel.

Arab terrorists had struck a special cord with the KGB: they were more daring and more successful than most other groups. And they faced a most powerful enemy, Mossad, long a service the KGB both loathed and admired for its sheer ruthlessness. The KGB arranged for selected Arab activists to receive training at the Patrice Lumumba University in Moscow. This was no ordinary campus, but a finishing school for terrorists. They received not only political indoctrination, but also instruction in the latest KGB terrorism target selection and assassination techniques. It was at Patrice Lumumba that Salameh put together the finishing touches to the Munich massacre. After the murderous attack, the surviving members of the group asked Russia to give them sanctuary. But the Soviets were reluctant to do so: the firestorm of fury the Munich attack had generated had made even the Kremlin unwilling to be discovered shielding the killers. They had told Salameh his request for asylum for himself and his men was still being considered.

Nevertheless, the Russians had done nothing to cooperate in the hunt for Black September—and certainly had not revealed that the group had a cache of Soviet missiles hidden in Yugoslavia. These rockets would be used to shoot down Golda Meir's aircraft.

The plan, like all those created by Salameh, was bold and simple. The missiles would be loaded onto a boat at Dubrovnik and taken across the Adriatic to Bari on Italy's east coast. From there they would be brought by road into Rome shortly before Golda Meir's plane arrived. Salameh had also not forgotten the lessons on strategy his KGB instructor at Patrice Lumumba had given: Always make the enemy look the other way. Salameh needed to direct Mossad's vigilance away from Rome in the run-up to the attack.

On December 28, 1972, a Black September unit attacked the Israeli embassy in Bangkok. The PLO flag was hoisted over the building and six Israelis were taken hostage. Soon five hundred Thai police and troops surrounded the building. The terrorists demanded that Israel release thirty-six PLO prisoners, or they would kill the hostages.

In Tel Aviv, a familiar scenario unfolded. The cabinet met in emergency session. There was the usual talk of standing tough or surrendering. It was left to Zvi Zamir to say that getting to Bangkok would require logistical support that was simply not there along a hostile route. And the Israeli embassy was in the center of busy Bangkok. The Thai government would never allow even the possibility of a shoot-out to occur. Then, after only brief negotiations, the terrorists unexpectedly agreed to a Thai offer of safe conduct out of the country in return for freeing the hostages. Hours later the Black September unit were on a flight to Cairo, where they disappeared.

In Tel Aviv, Zamir's relief that no Israelis had died turned to suspicion. Black September were highly trained and motivated and well financed, and had shown they had strategic cunning. They understood the methods and pressure points to bring any government to its knees. So why had they given in so quickly this time? The Bangkok embassy was a perfect target to gain them further publicity and so attract others to their cause. Almost certainly there was nothing random in their choice of target. Everything the group did was part of its concentrated assault on democracy. Within the embassy's compound the terrorists had followed the advice of their guru, Che Guevara, to keep hatred alive. The helpless hostages had been subjected to a tirade of anti-Semitic abuse—but was it all a diversionary tactic? Was another operation somewhere in the world being planned against Israel? Where and when? Zamir was still pondering these questions when he flew with Golda Meir to the Paris conference. From there he continued to search for answers.

In the early hours of January 14, 1973, the break came. A sayan working in Rome's central telephone exchange handled two telephone calls from a pay phone in an apartment block where PLO

GORDON THOMAS

terrorists sometimes stayed. The first was to Bari, the second to Ostia, the port that served Rome. The calls were made in Arabic, a language the sayan spoke. The caller said that it was time "to deliver the birthday candles for the celebration."

The words convinced Zamir this was a coded order connected to a forthcoming terrorist attack. "Birthday candles" could refer to weapons; the most likely one with a candle connotation was a rocket. And a rocket would be the perfect way to destroy Golda Meir's aircraft.

To warn her would be pointless. She was a women without fear. To alert the Vatican could well lead to the visit being canceled: the last thing the Holy See would want was to be caught up in a terrorist incident, especially one that would involve it having to condemn its Arab friends.

Zamir telephoned Hessner and Kauly, the two katsas who originally accompanied him to the Vatican, and moved Kauly from Milan to Rome. Then Zamir, accompanied by the small Mossad team traveling with Golda Meir, took the first flight to the city. Their mood was reflected in Zamir's gallows humor that it could be the city of eternity for Golda Meir.

In Rome, Zamir laid out his fears to the head of DIGOS, the Italian antiterrorist squad. Its officers raided the apartment block from where the calls had been made to Bari and Ostia. A search of one of its apartments turned up a Russian instruction manual for launching a missile. Throughout the night, DIGOS teams, each accompanied by a Mossad katsa, carried out a series of raids on other known PLO apartments. But nothing more was found to confirm Zamir's fears. With dawn breaking and Golda Meir's plane due in a few hours, he decided he would concentrate his search in and around the airport.

Shortly after sunrise, Hessner spotted a Fiat van parked in a field close to the flight path. The katsa ordered the van driver to step out of the cab. Instead, the back door of the vehicle opened and there was a burst of gunfire. Hessner was unhurt but two terrorists in the back of the van were seriously wounded when he fired back. Hessner set off in foot pursuit of the driver, catching up with him as he tried to hijack a car—driven by Kauly. The two Mossad katsas bundled the luckless terrorist into the car and drove off at high speed to where Zamir had his mobile command post, a truck.

230

The Mossad chief had already received a radio message that the Fiat van contained six rockets. But he still had to know if there were more positioned elsewhere. The van driver was severely beaten before he revealed the whereabouts of the second set of rockets. Zamir suspected he was one of the men who had provided backup for the Munich massacre. Driving at full speed in the truck, Zamir, Hessner, and Kauly, with the now-battered terrorist slumped between them, headed north.

They spotted a van parked on the side of the road. Protruding from its roof were three unmistakable nose caps of missiles. In the distance, descending by the second, was the equally unmissable shape of Golda Meir's 747, the sun illuminating its markings. Without slowing, Zamir used the truck as a battering ram, hitting the van side-on and toppling it onto its side. The two terrorists inside were half-crushed as the missiles fell on them.

Stopping only to toss the senseless driver out onto the road beside the van, Zamir drove off, alerting DIGOS that there had been "an interesting accident they should look into." Zamir had briefly considered killing the terrorists, but he felt their deaths would serve as a serious embarrassment to Golda Meir's audience with the pope.

Meir had the feeling that the weight of the world bore down on the pope's narrow shoulders, threatening to crush his diminutive white-clad figure. At the end of the audience, in reply to her question, Paul said he would visit the Holy Land, and spoke of his pontificate being a pilgrimage. When she asked him about the possibility of Israel establishing formal ties with the Holy See he sighed and said the "time is not yet appropriate." Golda Meir gave him a leather-bound book depicting the Holy Land; he handed her an inscribed copy of *Humanae Vitae*, the encyclical in which he had spelled out the consecration of his pontificate.

On her way out of the Vatican, Golda Meir told Zamir that the Holy See seemed to have a clock different from the rest of the world's.

The Black September terrorists—who had taken part in the Munich massacre of Israel's Olympic athletes—were taken to a hospital and, after they recovered, were allowed to fly to Libya. But within months they would all be dead—killed by Mossad's kidon.

The biblical eye-for-an-eye retribution Golda Meir had authorized met with distaste from Pope Paul, whose entire pontificate was rooted in the power of forgiveness. It also strengthened the Vatican's ties to the PLO, which John Paul II continued following his own election in 1978.

Since then the pope had received Yasser Arafat and senior aides in several lengthy private audiences, during which John Paul had each time reiterated his commitment to actively pursue a search for a Palestinian homeland. The PLO, now based in Tunisia, had a permanent liaison officer attached to the Secretariat of State, and the Holy See had its own envoy, Father Idi Ayad, assigned to the organization.

With his frayed cassock trailing in the desert dust, padre's hat planted squarely above his pinched face, Ayad served with equal devotion pontiff and the PLO, even to having his bedroom wall decorated with framed and signed photographs of John Paul and Yasser Arafat. Ayad had helped Arafat draft a letter in 1980 to the pope that had delighted him:"Please permit me to dream. I am seeing you going to Jerusalem, surrounded by returning Palestinian refugees, carrying olive branches and spreading them at your feet."

Ayad had suggested Arafat and the pontiff should exchange courtesies on their respective holy days: Arafat began to send John Paul a Christmas card, while the pope sent Arafat greetings on the prophet Muhammad's birthday. The tireless priest had also brokered the meeting between the PLO foreign minister and Cardinal Casaroli, the Holy See's secretary of state. Afterward the Middle East desk had been expanded and the papal nuncios, the Holy See's ambassadors, were instructed to persuade governments to which they were accredited to support the PLO's aspirations to nationhood. All these moves had dismayed Israel. Its official contacts were still limited to infrequent visits by a government official who would be granted only a few minutes in the papal presence.

The chilly relationship on both sides stemmed partly from a bizarre incident following the creation of Israel in 1948. The then secretary of state had sent an emissary to Israel's attorney general, Haim Cohn, carrying a request that Israel should restage the trial of Christ and, of course, reverse the original verdict. Once that was done, the Vatican would formally recognize Israel. The importance of such a diplomatic tie was not lost on Cohn. But to achieve it in such a way he had found "capricious almost beyond belief. Such a trial would be pointless and anyway we had more pressing matters to settle—surviving against the onslaughts of our Arab neighbours. Rattling the bones of Christ's biography was very low down on my list of priorities."

After the monsignor was brusquely seen off by Cohn, the Vatican all but turned its back on Israel.

Since then there had been a glimmer of hope only when John Paul's immediate predecessor, the frail Albino Luciano, hinted during his thirty-three days on the Throne of Saint Peter that he would consider establishing diplomatic ties with Israel. His death from a heart attack, allegedly brought about by the responsibility of his high office, had led to the election of Karol Wojtyla. Under his pontificate the Bronze Door of the Apostolic Palace remained all but closed to Israel as the papacy moved even further into international politics, encouraged to do so by its reestablished links with the CIA.

In 1981, William Casey, a devout Catholic, was the CIA director. He had been among the first men the pope received in private audience after being elected. Casey had knelt before the charismatic Polish pope and kissed the Fisherman's Ring on his finger. In every word and gesture, the CIA director was a humble supplicant, not like the bombastic, hard-bitten men his predecessors had been. But Casey shared their and the pope's deep distrust and fear of Communism.

For over an hour the two men discussed issues dear to them. Where should Ostpolitik go now? How would the Polish regime, indeed the whole of the Soviet Bloc, respond to the change in direction the Church must now take? Casey left the audience chamber sure of one thing: John Paul was not a man to seek easy accommodations. That was what made him so charismatic. His clean-cut beliefs were the best possible answer to that tired old question, the one Stalin was supposed to have posed about how many divisions a pope had. John Paul, Casey believed, was a pontiff who single-handedly would prove that faith could be more effective than any force.

Casey returned to Washington to brief President Reagan, who told the CIA director to return to Rome and tell the pope, under a secret arrangement the president approved, that from now on he would be kept fully informed on all aspects of U.S. policy—military, political, and economic.

Every Friday evening the CIA station chief in Rome brought to the Apostolic Palace the latest secrets obtained from satellite surveillance and electronic eavesdropping by CIA field agents. No other foreign leader had access to the intelligence the pope received. It enabled the most political of all modern pontiffs to stamp his distinctive style and authority on both the Church and the secular world. Papal diplomacy, the political core of a highly centralized Vatican bureaucracy, had, more than at any time in its five hundred years of very active history, become deeply involved with international events. As a world leader, this involvement had nearly cost the pope his life when he was almost assassinated in St. Peter's Square on May 13, 1981.

Two years later, on November 15, 1983, a cold winter's night in Rome, John Paul was about to learn the answer to a question that still consumed him: Who had ordered the assassination? Every moment of what had happened had been seared forever into his memory and remained as vivid as the scar tissue from his bullet wounds.

There had been about one hundred thousand people in St. Peter's Square on that Wednesday afternoon, May 13, 1981. They were packed within the three-quarter circle encompassing Bernini's colonnades—284 columns and 88 pilasters, themselves supporting 162 statues of the saints. A fenced-off route indicated the path the popemobile would travel to the platform from which John Paul delivered his weekly address. There was a festive air and some of the onlookers speculated what the pontiff would be doing in the Papal Apartments while they waited.

What went on in the mind of a swarthy young Turk, Mehmet Ali Agca, would not be known. He had arrived in the square in midafternoon and worked his way close to the path along which the popemobile would trundle. Agca had been a member of a terrorist group based in Turkey that called itself the Gray Wolves. But he had left their ranks and traveled through the Middle Eastern training camps of even more extreme Islamic fundamentalist groups. Now he was almost at the end of his journey. Agca was in St. Peter's Square not to praise but to kill the pope.

At four o'clock John Paul had changed into a freshly pressed pristine white silk cassock. On the advice of the CIA, the garment had been cleverly modified to enable a flak jacket to be worn undetected beneath the garment. On his last visit to the Apostolic Palace, Casey had warned John Paul that "in these crazy times, even the pope was not above attack. I told him we had no hard evidence he was in danger. But John Paul was a very controversial figure and a fanatic could try to kill him."

John Paul had refused to wear the protection. The very idea, he had told his English-language secretary, Monsignor John Magee, went against all his papacy represented.

John Paul descended to the San Damaso Courtyard inside the Apostolic Palace at 4:50 P.M. The Vatican's security chief, Camillo Cibin, ticked off the pontiff's approach on his copy of the minute-by-minute schedule that governed the pope's working day. In the jacket of Cibin's custom-made steel gray suit was a small but powerful cellular phone linking him to Rome police headquarters. But the immediate protection of the pontiff was in the hands of blue-suited Vigili. The Vatican's small but highly trained security force were the sharp eyes behind the ceremonial Swiss Guards already positioned in St. Peter's Square.

Parked in the courtyard was the popemobile, or *campagnola*, with its white-leather padded seat and handrail for the pope to grip during his progress through the vast piazza. Gathered around the vehicle were senior members of his staff. Magee would remember that John Paul was in "unusually good form."

At five o'clock precisely, the popemobile drove out of the courtyard. Ahead, from St. Peter's Square, the cheering began. As the *campagnola* approached the Arch of the Bells, the Vigili were joined by Rome city policemen, who walked ahead and immediately behind the vehicle. As the popemobile emerged into the piazza, the crowd noise rose to a roar. John Paul waved and smiled; his time as an actor in his youth had given him a powerful stage presence.

At two miles an hour, the pope turning from one side to the other, the vehicle moved toward the Egyptian obelisk in the center of the piazza. At exactly 5:15 P.M. the *campagnola* began a second circuit of the square under the watchful eyes of Cibin; the security chief was trotting behind the popemobile. The crowd's cheering was even wilder. Impetuously, John Paul did something that always made Cibin nervous. The pope reached into the crowd and plucked out a child. He hugged and kissed the little girl and then handed her back to her ecstatic mother. It was part of the pontiff's routine. Cibin's concern was that a child would wriggle free of the pope's grasp and fall, creating a nasty accident. But John Paul had dismissed all such concerns.

At 5:17 P.M. he once more reached out to touch the head of another little girl, dressed in communion white. Then he straightened and looked about him, as if wondering who else he might greet. It was his way of personalizing the papacy in even the largest of crowds.

Furthest from his mind at that moment were the dangers he had faced in other crowds. Only three months before—in Pakistan, on February 16, 1983—a bomb had exploded in Karachi's municipal stadium shortly before he began his journey among the faithful. In January 1980 the French secret service had warned of a Communist plot to kill him. It was just one of scores of threats the Vatican had received against the pope's life. All had been investigated as far as was possible. Later Magee said: "In reality we could only sit and wait. Short of enclosing the Holy Father in a bulletproof cage whenever he appeared in public, something he would never agree to, there was not much else we could do."

At 5:18 P.M. the first shot rang out in St. Peter's Square.

John Paul remained upright, his hands still gripping the handrail. Then he started to sway. Mehmet Ali Agca's first bullet had penetrated his stomach, creating multiple wounds in the small intestine, the lower part of the colon, the large intestine, and the mesentery, the tissue that holds the intestine to the abdominal wall. Instinctively, John Paul placed his hand over the entry wound to try to stop the spurting blood. His face increasingly filled with pain and he slowly began to collapse. Only seconds had passed since he had been hit.

Agca's second bullet struck the pontiff in his right hand, which fell uselessly to his side. Bright red blood spurted over his white cassock. A third 9-mm bullet hit John Paul higher up on the right arm.

The *campagnola* driver twisted in his seat, his mouth open, too stunned to speak. Cibin was screaming at him to move. A papal aide shielded the pope with his own body. The vehicle began to lurch forward. The crowd itself was swaying as if buffeted by a giant wind. One shocking sentence rippled outward from the scene of carnage. In a score of different languages came the same disbelieving words, "The pope has been shot."

Cibin and his Vatican security men and city of Rome policemen were waving their guns, shouting orders and counterorders, looking for the gunman. Agca had burst through the crowd, running very fast, holding his gun in his right hand. The crowd continued to open before his waving pistol. Suddenly he tossed the gun away. At the same moment, his legs were cut from beneath him. A Rome police officer had made the arrest. In a moment both men were buried beneath other policemen in a scene that resembled a rugby scrum. Several policemen kicked and punched Agca before he was dragged away to a police van.

The popemobile had continued at an agonizingly slow speed toward the nearest ambulance stationed by the Vatican's Bronze Door. But the ambulance had no oxygen equipment, so the pope was transferred to a second ambulance nearby. Vital moments were lost.

Lights flashing and sirens wailing, the ambulance raced to Rome's Gemelli Hospital, the nearest to the Vatican, completing the journey in a record eight minutes. During the drive the pope uttered no sound of despair or resentment, only words of profound prayer, "Mary, my mother! Mary, my mother!"

At the hospital, he was rushed to a ninth-floor surgical suite that comprised an induction room, an operating room, and a recovery area. Here, at the center of the crisis, there was no panic, no wasted movement or word. All was quiet urgency and tightly controlled discipline. Here the stricken pontiff could have felt the beginning of hope.

His bloodstained cassock, vest, and underpants were expertly cut away, and the bloodstained cross on its solid gold chain was removed. Surgical towels were draped over his nakedness. Gloved hands reached for, fetched, and carried the first of the instruments needed in a struggle the surgical team was only too familiar with.

When he had recovered after almost six hours of surgery, John Paul believed he had been saved by the miraculous intervention of one of the most revered apparitions in the Catholic world, the Virgin of Fatima, whose feast day was the same one as the attempt on his life.

During his long months of recovery, John Paul became increasingly preoccupied with who had ordered him to be assassinated. He tried to read every scrap of evidence that came from police and intelligence agencies as diverse as the CIA, West Germany's BND, and the security services of Turkey and Austria. It was impossible to read it all: there were millions of words of reports, statements, and assessments.

Not one document answered fully John Paul's question: Who had wanted him killed? He was still no wiser when Agca stood trial at the Rome assize court in the last week of July 1981. The brisk three-day hearing cast no light on the gunman's motives. Agca was sentenced to life imprisonment; with good behavior he would be eligible for parole in the year 2009.

Two years after Agca had been convicted, John Paul had finally been promised the answer to the question that still festered in his mind. It would come from a priest he trusted above all others. His title was *Nunzio Apostolico Con Incarichi Speciali*. The words offered no real clue that Archbishop Luigi Poggi was the natural heir to the world of secret papal politics, with special responsibility for gathering intelligence from Communist Europe. People in the Vatican simply called him "the pope's spy."

For many months Poggi had been involved in very secret contacts with Mossad. Only recently, when they were sufficiently advanced, had he informed the pope what he had been doing. John Paul had told him to continue. Since then there had been meetings with a Mossad officer in Vienna, Paris, Warsaw, and Sofia, Bulgaria. Both priest and katsa wanted to make sure what was on offer, what was expected. After each contact both had gone away to ponder the next move.

A few days before, there had been another meeting, again in Vienna, a city both Poggi and the officer liked as a background for their clandestine contacts.

It was from that meeting that Poggi was returning to the Vatican on that icy November night in 1983. He was bringing with him the answer to the pope's question: Who had ordered Agca to try to murder him?

CHAPTER 12

BLESSED ARE THE SPYMASTERS

One of the massive gates of the Arch of the Bells was already closed—the prelude to the nightly ritual of locking all the entrances to the Vatican on the stroke of midnight—when the dark blue Fiat limousine crunched across the cobblestones, its lights picking out the two Swiss Guards caped against the chill. Behind them stood a Vigili. One of the guards stepped forward, arm raised half in salute, half in command to stop. The car was expected and the figure behind the wheel was the familiar one of a Vatican chauffeur. But after the assassination attempt on the pope, no one was taking any chances.

The chauffeur had waited an hour at Rome's airport for the flight from Vienna, which had been delayed by bad weather. The guard stepped back after raising his arm in full salute to the passenger in deep shadow on the rear seat. There was no return acknowledgment.

The car drove past the side of St. Peter's Basilica and bounced over the cobblestones of San Damaso Courtyard before stopping outside the main entrance to the Apostolic Palace. The driver jumped out and opened the door for his passenger. Archbishop Luigi Poggi emerged, dressed in severe black, a scarf covering the white flash of his collar. Physically he bore a resemblance to Rafi Eitan: the same powerful shoulders and biceps, the same rolling gait, and eyes that could be as cold as this night.

As usual, Poggi had traveled with a small leather suitcase for his personal effects and a briefcase fitted with a combination lock. He sometimes joked he spent more time dozing in aircraft seats than asleep in his bed in the spacious suite he occupied at the rear of the Apostolic Palace.

Few recent trips matched the importance of what Poggi had finally been told at the meeting in Vienna's old Jewish Quarter. There, in a narrow steep-roofed building a few blocks from Nazi hunter Simon Wiesenthal's offices, the archbishop had listened raptly to a man they had agreed would only be called by his first name—Eli.

Poggi was now well used to such precautions in his dealings with Mossad. None carried security to such lengths as did its operatives. The only personal detail he knew about Eli was that he spoke several languages, and had finally answered the question of who had orchestrated the attempt on John Paul's life.

For his part, Luigi Poggi's own work was so secret that the Annuario Pontificio, the Vatican register that listed the names and duties of all its employees, contained no clue that for over twenty years, the archbishop had developed his own tried and tested and very secret contacts, which reached all the way into the Kremlin, Washington, and the corridors of power in Europe. He had been among the first to learn that Soviet leader Yuri Andropov was dying from chronic hepatitis, a disease of the kidneys. It was Poggi who had sat in the Russian mission in Geneva, a palatial nineteenth-century mansion stocked with the finest vodka and caviar the archbishop so relished, and learned firsthand that Moscow was prepared to eventually withdraw its nuclear warheads pointing at Europe if Washington would stop playing hardball in the disarmament talks. The news had been given to the CIA station chief at his next Friday-night briefing with the pope. Over two decades, Poggi had provided pontiffs with details that enabled them to better evaluate information from other sources. The archbishop had that ability, rare even among diplomats, to produce a balanced and swift assessment of material from a dozen sources and in almost as many languages, most of which he spoke fluently.

In his next meeting with Eli, Poggi had spoken in the soft voice that was long his trademark, his brown eyes watchful, lips pursed before putting a new question, his composed appearance never changing.

But on that cold winter's night, no doubt physically tired from his travels, he could be forgiven a bounce in his step. Walking into the Apostolic Palace, past the duty Vigili and the Swiss Guards who sprang to attention as he passed, Poggi took the elevator to the Papal Apartments.

The pope's butler showed Poggi into John Paul's study. The room's bookshelves offered clues to the pope's expanding interests. Along with leather-bound Polish editions of the classics and the works of theologians and philosophers were copies of the *International Defence Review* and books with such arresting titles as *The Problems of Military Readiness* and *Military Balance and Surprise Attack*. They reflected the pontiff's unswerving conviction that the main enemy the world still faced in 1983 was Soviet Communism.

John Paul had never lost an opportunity to tell his personal staff that before the new millennium dawned, something "decisive" would sweep the world. To all their questions as to what the event would be, he had refused to amplify, shaking his massive head and saying they must all pray that the Church would not lose more ground to Communism or the secularism sweeping countries like the United States, Germany, and Holland. He insisted his life had been spared in St. Peter's Square to lead the fight back.

Poggi knew that it was this concern, more than any other, which had affected John Paul both mentally and physically. Greetings over, Poggi could not have failed to notice that away from public gaze, John Paul had become more withdrawn. Agca's bullets had not only shattered bone and tissue, but had created emotional scars that had left the pope introspective and at times remote.

Seated with both hands on his knees, the position Poggi always assumed when there was grave news to impart, the archbishop began to unfold a story that had begun in those first weeks after Agca had shot John Paul.

When news of what had happened in St. Peter's Square on the afternoon of May 13, 1981, reached Tel Aviv, the immediate reaction of Mossad's director general, Yitzhak Hofi, was that the shooting had been the work of a crank. Shocking though the incident in Rome had been, it had no direct bearing on Mossad's current concerns.

Israeli Arabs were becoming ever more radical while, at the same time, Jewish extremists—led by members of the Kahane Kach Party—were becoming more violent. A plot had been discovered just in time to stop them blowing up the most holy Muslim shrine in Jerusalem, the Dome of the Rock. The consequences if they had succeeded were too nightmarish to contemplate. The Lebanon war dragged on despite endless U.S. shuttle diplomacy between Damascus, Beirut, and Jerusalem. In the cabinet, Prime Minister Begin led a party eager for a full-scale "final" showdown with the PLO. Killing Yasser Arafat was still a standing order for Mossad; during the very month the pope was shot there were two unsuccessful attempts to assassinate the PLO chairman.

The fact that seemingly every Western intelligence service was investigating the papal shooting also influenced Hofi's decision to keep Mossad from becoming involved. In any event, he eventually expected to learn from one of them the background to the incident.

He was still waiting to be told when he was replaced by Nahum Admoni in September 1982. With his Polish background—his parents had been middle-class immigrants from near Gdansk—Admoni had more than a passing curiosity about the Catholic Church. In his time abroad working under cover in the United States and France, he had seen how powerful the Church's influence could be. Rome had helped elect John F. Kennedy, a Catholic, to the White House and, in France, the Church continued to perform an important role in politics.

Once he had settled into office, Admoni sent for Mossad's file

on the attempted papal assassination. It contained mostly news clips
and a report from a katsa stationed in Rome that did not go much
further. Unusually, the six security services who had conducted
their own inquiries—including interviewing Agca in his high-
security cellblock of Rome's Rebibbia Prison—had failed to pool
their knowledge. Admoni decided to conduct his own investigation.

William Casey, then director of Central Intelligence, would later
say the likeliest reason appeared to be "Mossad sniffing that maybe
here was a way into the Vatican. Admoni had to be thinking he
could come up with something to trade off with the Holy See."

In the wake of Golda Meir's unsuccessful attempt to establish
diplomatic ties with the Vatican, Zvi Zamir had established a permanent Mossad presence in Rome to try to penetrate the Vatican.
Working out of a building close to the Israeli embassy, the katsa
had tried and failed to recruit priest informers. Most of what he
learned was gossip overheard in the bars and restaurants frequented
by Vatican staff. He achieved little more than enviously watching
the CIA's head of Rome station drive into the Vatican for his
Friday-night briefings to the pope; these had resumed as soon as
John Paul had recuperated from his surgery.

During that convalescence, Agostino Casaroli, cardinal secretary
of state, had run the Vatican. The katsa had heard that Casaroli
had expressed some very blunt sentiments about the shooting: the
CIA should have known about Agca and the entire plot. He had
sent on the secretary's views to Tel Aviv.

Within the U.S. intelligence community was a prevailing view that
Agca had been a trigger for a KGB-inspired plot to kill the pontiff.
In a paper stamped "Top Secret" and titled "Agca's Attempt to Kill
the Pope: The Case for Soviet Involvement," the argument was
made that Moscow had come to fear how the pontiff could ignite
the flames of Polish nationalism.

Already by 1981, Solidarity, the country's workers' movement
under the leadership of Lech Walesa, was increasingly flexing its
industrial muscles, and the authorities were under mounting pressure from Moscow to curb the union's activities.

The pope had urged Walesa to do nothing that would precipitate
direct Soviet military intervention. John Paul had urged Poland's
dying cardinal, Stefan Wyszinski, to also reassure the country's

Communist leaders that the pontiff would not allow Solidarity to overstep the mark. When the union scheduled a general strike, Cardinal Wyszinski prostrated himself before Walesa in his office, grabbed the bemused shipyard worker's trouser leg, and said he would cling on until he died. Walesa called off the strike.

In Tel Aviv, Mossad analysts concluded that the pontiff fully understood the importance of appeasing the Soviets over Poland so as to avoid losing the considerable ground Solidarity had achieved. It seemed increasingly unlikely Moscow would have wanted the pope killed. There was still the possibility that the Soviets had subcontracted the assassination to one of its surrogates. In the past, the Bulgarian secret service had carried out similar missions for the KGB when it was necessary to keep its own involvement hidden. But the analysts thought this time it would be unlikely the KGB would have delegated such an important mission. The Bulgarians would never have conducted the assassination of their own volition.

Nahum Admoni began to explore the CIA's current involvement with the papacy. In between Casey's regular visits to the pope, an important player in the relationship between the Vatican and the CIA was Cardinal John Krol of Philadelphia, who shuttled between the White House and the Apostolic Palace. To Monsignor John Magee, the pope's English-language secretary, Krol was "the Holy Father's extra-special pal. Both came from a similar background, knew the same Polish songs and stories and could joke across the Pope's dining table in a local Polish dialect. The rest of us just sat there and smiled, not understanding a word."

It had been Krol who had accompanied Casey to the CIA director's first audience with John Paul after his convalescence. Later, the cardinal had introduced Casey's deputy, Vernon Walters, to the pontiff. Since then, the list of subjects the CIA officer and the pope discussed ranged from terrorism in the Middle East to the internal politics of the Church and the health of Kremlin leaders. For Richard Allen, a Catholic, who was Ronald Reagan's first national security adviser: "The relationship between the CIA and the pope was one of the great alliances of all time. Reagan had this deep conviction the pope would help him to change the world."

More certain, common goals were established. The president and pontiff had proclaimed their united opposition to abortion. The United States blocked millions of dollars of aid to countries that ran family-planning programs. The pope, through a "purposeful silence," supported U.S. military policies, including supplying NATO with a new generation of cruise missiles. The CIA regularly bugged the phones of bishops and priests in Central America who advocated liberation theology and opposed U.S.-backed forces in Nicaragua and El Salvador; the phone transcripts formed part of the pope's Friday briefing by the Rome CIA station chief. Reagan had also personally authorized Colonel Oliver North, then working for the National Security Council, to make regular and substantial payments to priests the Vatican deemed "loyal" in Central and South America, Africa, and Asia. The money was used to support their often lavish lifestyles and promote the Holy See's opposition to birth control and divorce.

One of the duties of the pope's personal secretary, Monsignor Emery Kabongo, was to keep the list of approved priests updated. Another task was to file the documents provided by the CIA and act as note taker to their clandestine meetings with the pope.

Kabongo had first encountered the Washington spymasters on November 30, 1981, shortly after John Paul returned to work after being shot. After Kabongo joined John Paul for the first prayers of his day—5:15 A.M. on the longcase clock in the corridor outside the private chapel in the Papal Apartments—the two men had gone to the paneled study to receive CIA deputy director Vernon Walters. Kabongo would recall:

"I took up my usual position in the corner of the room, a notebook on my knee. There was no interpreter present. General Walters asked what language should he use. His Holiness said he would be comfortable with Italian. Walters began by saying he brought greetings from President Reagan. The pope returned the felicitations. Then it was down to business. Walters produced satellite photographs and His Holiness was fascinated to see how clear they were. Walters spoke for over an hour about the CIA's view of the latest Soviet intentions. His Holiness thanked him. At the end of the meeting, Walters produced a number of rosaries and asked the pope to bless them, explaining they were for relations and friends and His Holiness did so."

Intrigued by the pope's ability to switch from temporal to spiritual matters, Admoni used his personal friendship with Secretary of State Alexander Haig—they had met when Admoni worked out of the Israeli embassy in Washington—to obtain a copy of the CIA's psycho-profile of John Paul.

It was a portrait of a man whose religious fervor could be so intense that he would cry out when praying and would often be found on the marble floor of his private chapel, face down, arms extended to form a cross, as still as in death. He could spend hours in that prone position. Yet his anger could be eruptive and fearful to behold; then he would storm and shout. His grasp of geopolitics was formidable and he could be as unflinching as any dictator. John Paul was also not afraid to confront the Curia, the Vatican's civil service, or his long-serving secretary of state, Agostino Casaroli. The profile concluded that John Paul was "highly politicized from his Polish experiences and that he relishes being a player on the world stage."

For Nahum Admoni, one matter was clear: the close and self-serving ties between the CIA and the pope had played a crucial role in John Paul coming to accept the American view that the attempt on his life had been organized by the Kremlin.

Yet, supposing that standpoint could be demonstrated to be wrong? How would the pope react? Would that shatter his faith in the CIA? Make him wary of all intelligence services? And would it allow Mossad—if it could show there was another hand behind the attempted assassination—to finally find a way past the Vatican's Bronze Door and, if not be admitted as a fully fledged secret secular adviser to the papacy, at least be granted a hearing for its information and, in return, hopefully be able to revise the Holy See's attitude to Israel?

Six months later the answer to Admoni's first question—had someone else masterminded the attempted assassination?—was established to his satisfaction.

The plot had been prepared in Tehran with the full approval of Ayatollah Ruholla Khomeini. Killing the pope was intended as the opening move in a jihad, holy war, against the West and what Khomeini saw as its decadent values being approved by the largest Christian Church.

A report prepared for Admoni said: "Khomeini remains the classic example of religious fanaticism. He has cast himself in the role of God-instructor to his people. To maintain that myth, he will need to act increasingly in a manner more dangerous to Israel, the West and the whole world."

Anticipating that Agca could fail, his Iranian controllers had ensured he would be seen as a fanatical loner by leaking details of his background. Mehmet Ali Agca had been born in the remote village of Yesiltepe in eastern Turkey and had been raised in a hotbed of Islamic fundamentalism. At the age of nineteen he joined the Gray Wolves, a pro-Iranian terrorist group responsible for much of the violence in a Turkey clinging to democracy. In February 1979, Agca murdered the editor of an Istanbul newspaper renowned for its pro-West policies. Arrested, Agca escaped from prison with the help of the Gray Wolves. The next day the newspaper received a chilling letter about the pope's visit to Turkey, then three days away:

"Western imperialists, fearful that Turkey and her sister Islamic nations may become a political, military and economic power in the Middle East, are sending to Turkey at this delicate moment the Commander of the Crusades, John Paul, designed as a religious leader. If this visit is not called off, I will deliberately kill the Commander Pope."

Admoni became convinced the letter had been composed in Tehran: in style and content it was certainly far above the writing skills of the almost illiterate Agca. Mossad's computer search of Khomeini's speeches revealed he had previously referred to the "Commander of the Crusades" and "Commander Pope" in describing John Paul.

In the end the pontiff's visit passed without incident. Agca's name and photograph went on to the computers of a number of intelligence services, though not Mossad's. Otto Kormek, a case officer with the Austrian security service who had been in charge of its inquiries into the papal shooting, felt it was "not necessary to inform Mossad. Israel would be the last place Agca would go."

Mossad's investigation had discovered that after his prison escape, Agca was spirited into Iran, where he spent months in various training camps being indoctrinated. From its own sources in those camps, Mossad had pieced together a picture of Agca's life at that time.

He arose before dawn, his small, red-rimmed eyes set deep in a long face, watchful as the other recruits awoke. The first light of day showed posters on the walls of their hut: photographs of the Ayatollah Khomeini and revolutionary slogans, each designed to fire their fantasies. Songs piped through the huts' loudspeakers reinforced this.

Clad in vest and shorts, Agca was an unprepossessing figure; large hands and feet were all out of proportion to his body with his concave chest, protruding shoulder blades, and skinny arms and legs. The first thing he did each morning, like the other recruits, was to spread his prayer rug and prostrate himself three times, each time touching his forehead to the ground, murmuring the name of Allah, Master of the World, the All-Meaningful and All-Compassionate, the Supreme Sovereign of the Last Judgment. Afterward he began to recite his long list of hatreds, which his instructor had encouraged him to write down. The list had grown long and diverse and included all imperialists, NATO, and those Arab countries that had refused to cut off oil from the West. He especially called upon Allah to destroy the United States, the most powerful nation on earth, and its people, praying that their way of life, their values and customs, the very wellspring of their existence, would be squeezed from them.

Finally only his religious hatreds remained. They were the most virulent, consuming him like a cancer, eating into his brain. He saw all other faiths as threatening to overthrow the one to which he subscribed. His instructors had taught him to reduce that hatred to one instantly recognizable image: a man, dressed in white, living in a huge palace far beyond the mountains. From there he ruled like a caliph of old, issuing decrees and orders many millions obeyed. The man spread his hated message the way his predecessors had done for over nineteen centuries. Supported by pomp and glory, rejoicing in even more titles than Allah, the man was known variously as Servant of the Servants of God, Patriarch of the West, Vicar of Christ on Earth, Bishop of Rome, Sovereign of the State of Vatican City, Supreme Pontiff, His Holiness Pope John Paul the Second.

Mehmet Ali Agca had been promised that, when the time came, he would be given a chance to kill the pope. His instructors drummed into him that it was no coincidence the pope had come to office at almost the same time as their beloved Khomeini delivered Iran from the shah's regime. The "infidel in Rome," as Agca was taught to refer to John Paul, had come to destroy the revolution the ayatollah had proclaimed in the name of the Holy Koran.

There was a grain of truth in the accusation. John Paul had increasingly spoken harshly about Islam and the dangers he believed it contained in its fundamentalist form. Visiting the Olivetti factory at Ivrea, Italy, John Paul had astonished the workers by inserting into his speech an impromptu passage:

"What the Koran teaches people is aggression; what we teach our people is peace. Of course, you always have human nature which distorts whatever message religion is sending. But even though people can be led astray by vices and bad habits, Christianity aspires to peace and love. Islam is a religion that attacks. If you start by teaching agression to the whole community, you end up pandering to the negative elements in everyone. You know what that leads to: such people will assault us."

In January 1981, Agca had flown to Libya. Initially Mossad had been puzzled by that part of his journey, until an informer in Tripoli discovered that a renegade CIA officer, Frank Terpil, had been in the country at that time. Terpil had been indicted by a grand jury in Washington for supplying arms to Libya, conspiring to assassinate one of Gadhafi's opponents in Cairo, recruiting former U.S. military pilots to fly Libyan aircraft, and Green Berets to run Gadhafi's training camps for terrorists. In Libya he was instructing terrorists how to evade detection by Western security agencies. Terpil had moved on to Beirut—where he had disappeared. Mossad believed he had been murdered when he had outlived his usefulness.

Mossad knew Agca's contact with Terpil had been arranged by Agca's controllers in Tehran and leaked to the KGB after the attempted John Paul assassination, allowing for the Russians to claim the plot had been orchestrated by the CIA. Like Mossad, the KGB had an effective psychological warfare department. The fiction about the CIA filled thousands of column inches and many hours of broadcast time. To further muddy the waters, the Tehran mullahs arranged for Agca, after he left Libya in February 1981, to travel to Sofia, Bulgaria, to meet men who told him they were members of the country's secret service: no convincing proof ever emerged they were. Furious at the KGB's attempts to smear the

Agency, the CIA countered by claiming the Bulgarians had controlled Agca on behalf of the Kremlin.

For Mossad the situation was perfectly poised to exploit the adage "We divide to rule." Not only would Mossad be able to discredit the CIA with the Vatican, but at long last, by promoting their version of the plot as the correct one, Mossad had found a way to gain the pope's ear. All else would flow from that: its officers could have access to the secretary of state's own formidable information-collecting network; it would enable katsas to work with, and if need be, exploit priests and nuns; and, when the opportunity arose, those electronic bugs could finally be planted in all those holy places in the Vatican Zvi Zamir had indicated.

When Mossad's account of Mehmet Ali Agca's odyssey had been fully pieced together in Tel Aviv, Nahum Admoni set out to answer the one question that would make all that happen. Once more a computer search found the solution. One of Rafi Eitan's "survivor spies," a Catholic living in Munich, had described the extraordinary role Luigi Poggi played in the papacy. Nahum Admoni had sent for Eli and told him to make contact with Poggi.

Now, a full two years after Agca had shot the Pope, the archbishop sat far into the night, explaining completely to John Paul what Eli had told him.

A month later, on December 23, 1983, at 4:30 A.M., almost three hours before the lights on the Christmas tree in St. Peter's Square would be switched off for the day, the pope was awoken by his valet.

The bedroom was surprisingly small, its walls still lined with the pastel linen covering his predecessor favored. The wooden floor, gleaming from being polished, was partly covered by a rug woven by Polish nuns. On the wall above the bed, in which four of John Paul's predecessors had lain waiting for death, was a crucifix. On another wall was a fine painting of Our Lady. Both were gifts from Poland. In addition to the pope's valet, those who saw him at this hour—usually one of his administrative priests with news that could not wait—were relieved to see John Paul had regained some of his old vigor and vitality.

As always, the pope began his day by going to his prie-dieu to kneel in private prayer. Afterward he shaved and showered and dressed in the clothes the valet had laid out: a heavy woolen white cassock caped around the shoulders, white clerical shirt, knee-high white stockings, brown shoes, and white skullcap. He was ready to go to see Agca in Rome's Rebibbia Prison.

The meeting was arranged at the pope's request, intended, he said, as "an act of forgiveness." In reality, John Paul wanted to find out if what Mossad had said was true. He was driven to the prison by the very man who was at the wheel of the popemobile in St. Peter's Square when Agca shot him. Accompanied by a Roman police escort, the limousine sped northeastward across the city to the prison. In a backup car was a small group of journalists (they included the author of this book). They had been invited to witness the historical moment when the pope and his assassin came face-to-face.

Two hours later, John Paul was admitted to Rebibbia's maximum-security wing. He walked alone down the corridor to the open door of cell T4, where Agca stood waiting inside. The reporters waited farther up the corridor. With them were prison guards, ready to run to Agca's cell should he make any threatening move to his visitor.

As the pope extended his ring hand, Agca moved to shake it, hesitated, then bent to kiss the Fisherman's Ring. Next he took the pope's hand and placed it briefly against his forehead.

"Lei è Mehmet Ali Agca?" The pope framed the question softly. He had been told Agca had learned Italian in prison.

"Sì." A quick smile accompanied the word, as if Agca was embarrassed to admit who he was.

"Ah, lei abita qui?" John Paul looked around the cell, genuinely interested in the place where his would-be killer might well spend the rest of his life.

"Sì."

John Paul sat on a chair positioned just inside the door. Agca sank onto his bed, clasping and unclasping his hands.

"Come si sente?" The pope's question as to how Agca felt was almost paternal.

"Bene, bene." Suddenly Agca was speaking urgently, volubly, the words coming in a low torrent only the pope could hear.

John Paul's expression grew more pensive. His face was close to Agca's, partially shielding him from the guards and journalists.

Agca whispered into the pope's left ear. The pope gave an almost imperceptible shake of the head. Agca paused, uncertainty on his face. John Paul indicated, with a quick chopping motion of his right hand, that Agca should continue. Both men were so close their heads almost touched. Agca's lips barely moved. On John Paul's face there was a pained look. He closed his eyes, as though it would help him to better concentrate.

Suddenly, Agca stopped in midsentence. John Paul did not open his eyes. Only his lips moved; only Agca could hear the words.

Once more Agca resumed speaking. After a few more minutes, the pope made another little chopping motion of the hand. Agca stopped talking. John Paul placed his left hand to his forehead, as if he wanted to shield his eyes from Agca.

Then John Paul squeezed the younger man's upper arm, almost as if to thank him for what he had said. The exchanges lasted for twenty-one minutes, and then the pope slowly rose to his feet. He held out a hand, encouraging Agca to do the same. The two men stared into each other's eyes. The pope ended this moment of near perfect drama by reaching into a cassock pocket and producing a small white cardboard box bearing the papal crest. He handed it to Agca. Puzzled, Agca turned the box over in his hand.

The pope waited, the gentlest of smiles on his lips. Agca opened the box. Inside was a rosary crafted in silver and mother-of-pearl.

"Ti ringrazio," thanked Agca. "Ti ringrazio."

"Niente. Niente," responded the pope. Then he leaned forward and spoke again words only for Agca.

Then, saying no more, the pontiff walked from the cell.

Later, a Vatican spokesman said, "Ali Agca knows only up to a certain level. On a higher level, he doesn't know anything. If there was a conspiracy, it was done by professionals and professionals don't leave traces. One will never find anything."

Not for the first time, the Vatican had been economical with the truth. Agca had confirmed what Luigi Poggi had been told by Mossad. The plot to kill the pope had been nurtured in Tehran. The knowledge would color John Paul's attitude toward both Islam and Israel. Increasingly, he told his staff that the real coming conflict in the world was not going to be between the East and West, the United States and Russia, but between Islamic fundamentalism and

Christianity. In public he was careful to separate Islam, the faith, and Islamic fundamentalism.

In Israel, Mossad's analysts saw the pontiff's new attitude as the first sign that the evidence presented to Poggi had been accepted. But while there was no immediate move made to invite Mossad to contribute to John Paul's understanding of the world, the pope had become convinced of the value of Poggi's dialogue with Eli. In Tel Aviv, Admoni told Eli to remain in contact with Poggi. They continued to meet in various European cities, sometimes at an Israeli embassy, other times in a papal nunciature. Their discussions were wide-ranging, but almost always focused on two issues: the situation in the Middle East and the pope's wish to visit the Holy Land. Linked to this was John Paul's continued effort to find a permanent homeland for the PLO.

Poggi made it clear the pope had both a liking for, and a fascination with, Yasser Arafat. John Paul did not share the views of men like Rafi Eitan, David Kimche, and Uri Saguy, that the PLO leader, in Eitan's words, was a ruthless killer and "a butcher of our women and children, someone I would kill with my own bare hands."

To the pontiff, raised against the background of the heroic Polish resistance against the Nazis, Arafat was an appealing underdog, a charismatic figure continuously able to escape Mossad's various attempts to kill him. Poggi recounted to Eli how Arafat had once told John Paul he had developed a sixth sense—"and some measure of a seventh"—when he was in danger. "A man like that deserves to live," Poggi had said to Eli.

Through such glimpses, Eli obtained a clearer view of the pope's mind-set. But John Paul also paid more than lip service to the historical truth that the Jewish roots of Christianity must never be forgotten, and that anti-Semitism—so rife in his own beloved Poland—must be eradicated.

In May 1984, Poggi invited Eli to the Vatican. The two men talked together for hours in the archbishop's office in the Apostolic Palace. To this day no one knows what they spoke about.

In Israel, this was once more a time of scandal involving the nation's intelligence community. A month before, April 12, four PLO terrorists had hijacked a bus with thirty-five passengers as it headed for the southern town of Ashqelon. The official version of the incident was that Shin Bet agents had stormed the bus, and in the ensuing gunfight, two terrorists were shot dead and the two who had been wounded died on their way to the hospital.

Newspaper reports showed them being led from the bus, visibly not seriously injured. It emerged they had been so severely beaten in the ambulance by Shin Bet officers that both men died. Mossad, although not directly involved, was tarnished by the international condemnation of the incident.

Against this background, Poggi explained to Eli, there could be no question of John Paul establishing diplomatic relations with Israel. Until he did, Eli reiterated, there could be no question of the pope being allowed to visit the Holy Land.

Yet it was a measure of the bridge building they were engaged upon that both men agreed the issue was not dead.

On April 13, 1986, John Paul did something no other pontiff had done. He entered the Synagogue of Rome on Lungotevere dei Cenci, where he was embraced by the city's chief rabbi. Each dressed in their regalia, the two men walked side by side through the silent congregation to the *teva*, the platform from where the Torah is read.

In the back of the congregation sat Eli, who had played his part in bringing about this historic moment. Yet it still did not achieve what Israel wanted—papal diplomatic recognition.

That would only finally come in December 1993, when, despite the continuing objections of the Secretariat hard-liners, diplomatic ties were established.

By then, Nahum Admoni was no longer Mossad's chief. His successor, Shabtai Shavit, continued the delicate process of trying to bring Mossad closer to the Vatican. Part of that maneuvering was to show the pope that both Israel and the PLO at long last had a genuine interest in reaching a settlement, and recognized the common threat of Islamic fundamentalism. Pope John Paul bore the physical scars of the truth of that.

Meanwhile, Mossad had been busy on a continent where the Vatican pinned so many hopes for the future—Africa. From there the Holy See one day expected to see emerge the Church's first black pope. But it was there that Mossad had already shown itself the past master at the black art of playing off one intelligence service against another to secure its own position.

CHAPTER 13

AFRICAN CONNECTIONS

A few blocks from Nairobi's venerable Norfolk Hotel, the Oasis

Club had long been a favorite among Kenya's business community.

They could drink all night in its gloomy interior and take a bar girl

to one of the rooms out back after checking her current medical

certificate confirmed she was free of venereal disease.

Since 1964, the club had also received other visitors, Chinese in

safari suits, slab-faced Russians, and men whose nationality could

have been of any country around the Mediterranean basin. They

were not there for the cold beer or what the club advertised as "the

hottest girls in all-Africa." These men worked for intelligence services fighting to gain a foothold in central Africa, where once only Britain's MI6 had secretly operated. The newcomers represented the Chinese Secret Intelligence Service (CSIS), the Soviet KGB, and Mossad. Each service had its own agenda, playing one off against the other. No one had become better at this than Mossad.

All told, there were a dozen katsas scattered along the equator, operating from Dar es Salaam on the Indian Ocean to Freetown on the shore of the Atlantic. Possessing an impressive number of false passports, young and superbly fit, the operatives, as well as all their normal skills, had acquired the basics of field medicine and surgery to enable them to survive in the bush, where predatory lions and leopards roamed, as well as hostile tribesmen.

Mossad's African adventure had begun shortly after Fidel Castro came to power in Cuba in 1959 and started to export his revolution. His first success began when his surrogate, John Okello, a self-styled "field marshal," was plucked out of the jungle by a Castro recruiter, given a short course in guerrilla warfare in Havana, and told to go and seize the small island of Zanzibar off the East African coast. His sheer height and bulk—he was three hundred pounds—terrified the island's small police force into submission. Okello's ragtag army stamped their brutal authority on a population whose only weapons were the primitive tools they used to harvest the spices that made Zanzibar world famous. The island became Castro's launchpad for penetrating the African mainland. There was a Chinese ethnic population in the port of Dar es Salaam, and their reports home about what was happening came to the notice of the Beijing government. Realizing the opportunity the embryonic revolution offered for China to gain a greater hold on the continent, the CSIS was ordered to establish itself in the region and to provide all possible support for the revolutionaries.

Meantime, Castro had set up a full-scale operation to Cubanize the now burgeoning black liberation movement. The focus was the port of Casablanca on the West African coast. Shiploads of Cuban weapons arrived and on the return voyages to Havana the boats were filled with guerrilla trainees from all over central Africa. Soon the CSIS was helping to select them.

The prospect of thousands of trained and well-armed revolutionaries being within a few hours' striking distance of Israel was alarming to its politicians and intelligence services. But to provoke this guerrilla army when they had offered no direct threat could lead to a confrontation Israel did not want. With its hands already full fighting off the threat from Arab terrorists, to become embroiled in direct action against black revolutionaries was to be avoided. Meir Amit ordered his katsas in Africa to keep a close watch but not to become actively involved.

The arrival of the KGB on the scene changed all that. The Russians brought an offer would-be terrorists could not refuse: the opportunity to be trained at the Patrice Lumumba University in Moscow. There they would receive the wisdom of the KGB's best instructors in guerrilla tactics and how to exploit them under the guise of helping the dispossessed, powerless, and unelectable in democratic states. To help sell the idea, the KGB brought along some of the most successful graduates of Patrice Lumumba: Arab terrorists.

Meir Amit reinforced his African katsas with kidons. His new orders were to disrupt by all means possible the relations between the Russians and their African hosts and between the KGB and the CSIS; to kill Arab activists when the opportunity arose; and to foster relations with black African revolutionaries by promising them that Israel would assist their movements to progress beyond guerrilla tactics and allow their organizations to achieve political legitimacy. All Israel wanted in return was a guarantee it would not be attacked by these movements.

The Oasis Club had become part of the battle for the hearts and minds of African revolutionaries. The nights were filled with long discussions of how, without publicity, terrorism was a weapon firing only blanks, and of the need to never lose sight of the ultimate goal: freedom and independence. Within the club's stifling atmosphere plots were hatched, deals made, targets identified for execution or destruction. Some victims would be ambushed driving on a dirt road, others killed in their beds. One day it would be a KGB agent, the next a CSIS spy. Each side blamed the other for what Mossad had done.

Back at the Oasis, the nights would continue as before, with new plans being made around the bamboo tables, with the rain rolling off the hills and beating on the tin roof. There was no need to whisper, but old habits died hard.

Meir Amit had briefed his agents on all he had learned of the CSIS. The service had a tradition of espionage extending back over 2,500 years. For centuries it had been a creature of the ruling emperor spying on his subjects. But with the arrival of first Mao and then Deng Xiaoping, China's intelligence gathering, like so much else in the country, had taken a new direction. The CSIS began to expand its networks across the Pacific into the United States, Europe, the Middle East, and finally Africa.

These networks were used for more than espionage purposes: they were major routes for drug running and money laundering. With about half the world's opium grown on the doorstep of the People's Republic, in the Golden Triangle—Thailand, Laos, and Myanmar—the CSIS worked alongside Triad gangs to smuggle drugs into the West. Given Hong Kong's position as one of the world's major centers for money laundering, the CSIS had a perfect cover for concealing China's profits from drug trafficking. That money helped to finance its operations in Africa. Those were, since 1964, ultimately under the control of the CSIS's director general, Qiao Shi. A tall, stooped man with a taste for French cognac and Cuban cigars, he was a chief with hundreds of spies and a budget for bribery and blackmail rivaled only by that of the KGB. The labor camps of central China were filled with those who had dared challenge Qiao. Mossad's psycho-profile described a man whose entire career consisted of adroit, low-key moves.

CSIS activities in Africa were under the local command of Colonel Kao Ling, already a legendary figure in the service, having made his reputation in Nepal and India with his subversive tactics. Based in Zanzibar, Kao Ling had a lavish lifestyle and a succession of nubile young African women as mistresses. He moved across central Africa like a predator, disappearing for weeks at a time. His visits to Nairobi became occasions for wild parties at the Oasis. Sweet-smelling smoke from bundles of joss sticks filled the club. Delicacies imported directly from China were served. The African whores were dressed up in cheongsams; there were indoor fireworks and cabarets flown in from Hong Kong.

Guerrillas who had returned from Cuba were feted before disappearing into the African bush to wage war. One of them had a party trick of drinking a glass of the human blood he drained from executed enemies he had killed.

Meantime, Kao Ling was expanding his operations not only across the width of Africa, but also northward toward Ethiopia,

South Yemen, and Egypt. He provided its terrorists with substantial sums of money to launch attacks on Israel. The CSIS regarded Israel as a pawn in the hands of Washington and a legitimate target for what Kao Ling called "my freedom fighters."

Meir Amit decided Mossad should go head-to-head against the CSIS. First it wrecked a Chinese plot to overthrow the pro-West Hastings Banda regime in Malawi. Next it informed the Kenyan authorities about the full extent of the Chinese network in its midst. Later the Nairobi government would show its gratitude by granting overfly rights for Israeli air force planes to carry out their mission to Entebbe. The Oasis Club was closed down and its Chinese patrons put on planes out of the country, loudly protesting they were only businessmen. They were lucky; several CSIS operatives would remain permanently in Africa, killed by Mossad katsas and left out on the savannas for lions and leopards to consume.

The more the Chinese tried to fight back in other African countries, the more ruthless Mossad became. Kidons stalked CSIS operatives wherever they set up shop. In Ghana, a CSIS agent was shot dead as he left a discotheque with his girlfriend. In Mali another died in a car bomb; in Zanzibar, still the jewel in the CSIS crown, a fire consumed an apartment block where CSIS staff lived. On one of his field trips, Kao Ling himself narrowly escaped death when some instinct made him switch cars in Brazzaville in the Congo. The other vehicle exploded minutes later, killing its driver. In Zambia, a CSIS agent was left bound to a tree for lions to consume.

When Kwame Nkrumah, the pro-Chinese ruler of Ghana, was on a state visit to Beijing, Mossad orchestrated the uprising that led to both Nkrumah's overthrow and the destruction of the CSIS infrastructure in the country.

For three years Mossad waged its deadly war of attrition against the CSIS over the length and breadth of Africa. There was no mercy on either side. When a CSIS hit team ambushed a Mossad katsa in the Congo, they fed him to crocodiles, filming his last moments in the water and sending the footage to the local Mossad station chief. He retaliated by personally firing a rocket into the building from where the CSIS operated. Three Chinese were killed.

Finally, through an intermediary, President Mobutu of Zaire, the CSIS let Mossad know it had no wish to fight anymore; rather, they shared a common interest in stemming Russian influence on the continent. The approach perfectly suited Mossad's policy toward all superpowers, articulated in Meir Amit's dictum: "Dividing them helps Israel to survive."

While the CSIS and Mossad had battled each other, the KGB had taken further steps to take over Castro's plans to Cubanize Africa. KGB chiefs and the politburo had met in the Kremlin and agreed that Russia would underwrite the entire Cuban economy. The terms were enough to ensure that a nation of seven million people became in hock to the Soviet Union. In return, Castro agreed to accept that Moscow's brand of Communism rather than Beijing's was the correct one for Africa. He also agreed to receive five thousand advisers who would "instruct" Cuba's own security service, the DGI, on how to operate "correctly" in Africa.

The KGB began to work alongside Cubans throughout black Africa. Within six months every act of terrorism in Africa was controlled by the Russians. From the Middle Eastern camps it had set up to train terrorists, the KGB brought the very best to Africa to wage war against the apartheid regime of South Africa. Terrorists from Europe, Latin America, and Asia were also soon providing their expertise in Angola, Mozambique, and countries bordering South Africa.

According to Meir Amit, "Matters were really heating up below the equator." He realized it could only be a matter of time before these battle-hardened mercenaries would turn their attention to Israel. The offer from the CSIS to collaborate against a common enemy, the KGB and its terrorists, was one the Mossad chief gratefully accepted. The Chinese began to provide details about Arab movements in and out of Africa. Some were killed by the usual Mossad methods of car bombs or explosives placed in hotel rooms. On one occasion, Mossad placed a bomb in the toilet of a mercenary suffering from "Congo stomach," a particularly unpleasant form of dysentery. The lower half of his body was blown to pieces when he pulled the flush in a Khartoum hotel.

Mossad kept its side of the bargain, tipping off the CSIS that Moscow intended to offer a massive financial aid package to one of the poorest countries on earth, Somalia. Beijing promptly doubled the offer. Next Mossad helped China in Sudan, where Moscow had established a bridgehead through President Nimeri's military government. But when the dictator refused to become completely dependent on the Russians, the KGB planned a coup. Mossad

informed the CSIS, who told Nimeri. He expelled all Russian diplomats and suspended Soviet Bloc aid schemes.

Having set the two bastions of Communism at each other's
throat while at the same time, as Meir Amit later put it, "working
our way into the African woodwork," Mossad turned its attention
to the one intelligence service in Africa it had come to look upon
as a friend: the Bureau of State Security, BOSS, the most feared
arm of South Africa's security apparatus. BOSS matched Mossad in
blackmail, sabotage, forgery, kidnapping, prisoner interrogation,
psychological warfare, and assassinations. Like Mossad, BOSS had
a free hand in how it dealt with its opponents. The two services
quickly became bedfellows. Often operating in tandem, they moved
through Africa, enjoined by a secret "understanding" between Israel's prime minister, Golda Meir, and the Pretoria regime.

The first result had been the export of uranium ore to Dimona.
The shipments were carried on commercial El Al flights from Johannesburg to Tel Aviv, and listed on manifests as agricultural machinery. South African scientists traveled to Dimona and were the only
outsiders who knew the true purpose of the facility. When South Africa tested a crude nuclear device on a remote island in the Indian
Ocean, Israeli scientists were present to monitor the blast. In 1972,
Ezer Weizman, then a senior official in the Israeli defense ministry,
met Prime Minister P. W. Botha in Pretoria to ratify a further "understanding." If either country was attacked and required military assistance, the other would come to its aid. Israel supplied the South
African army with substantial quantities of U.S.-manufactured arms
and in return was granted permission to test the first nuclear devices
produced by Dimona at the site in the Indian Ocean.

By then, Mossad had deepened its own relationship with BOSS.
While never able to wean the bureau's agents from their brutish
methods of interrogation, Mossad instructors introduced them to a
range of other methods that had worked in Lebanon and elsewhere:
sleep deprivation; hooding; forcing a suspect to stand at a wall for
long periods; squeezing genitals; a variety of mental torture ranging
from threats to mock executions. Mossad katsas traveled with BOSS
units into neighboring black African countries on sabotage missions.
Kidons showed the South Africans how to carry out killings that left
no embarrassing trails. When Mossad offered to locate African National Congress (ANC) leaders living in exile in Britain and Europe

for BOSS to kill, the bureau welcomed the idea. The Pretoria government finally vetoed the proposal, fearing it would lose what support it had among die-hard Conservative politicians in London.

Both Mossad and BOSS were driven by an obsessive belief that Africa was lurching leftward toward a revolution that would eventually engulf both their countries. To avoid that happening, any method was permissible. Feeding off each other's fears, both services gave no quarter and shared a self-perpetuating concept that only they knew how to deal with the enemy. Between them, BOSS and Mossad became the two most feared foreign intelligence services in Africa.

This alliance did not sit well with Washington. The CIA feared it could affect its own efforts to maintain a hold on the black continent. The decolonization of Africa in the early 1960s had produced a new interest in Africa within the Agency—and a huge increase in its clandestine activities. An African division was formed, and by 1963, CIA stations had been established in every African nation.

One of the first to serve in Africa was Bill Buckley, later to be kidnapped and murdered by Hezbollah terrorists in Beirut. Buckley would recall, shortly before his capture, "These were really crazy times in Africa with everybody jockeying for position. We were late to the party, and the Mossad looked at us as if we were gate-crashers."

In Washington, the State Department made discreet but determined efforts to reduce Israeli influence in Africa. It leaked details of how several hundred Jews from South Africa had flown north to help Israel during the Suez War. Twenty black African nations broke off diplomatic relations with Jerusalem. Among them was Nigeria. The severance could have been a severe blow to Israel: Nigeria provided over 60 percent of Israel's oil supplies in return for arms that had originally been supplied by the United States to Israel. Despite the diplomatic breach, Prime Minister Yitzhak Shamir agreed to continue secretly arming Nigeria in return for the continued flow of oil. To Buckley it was a "prime example of realpolitik." Another was how Mossad set about shoring up its longtime partner BOSS. In the aftermath of the Israeli invasion of Lebanon in 1982, Mossad found a substantial quantity of documents revealing close links between the PLO and the ANC, long BOSS's bête noire. The incriminating material was turned over to the bureau, enabling its agents to arrest and torture hundreds of ANC members.

The eighties were halcyon days for Mossad's great African safari.

As well as playing off the Chinese against the Russians, it made matters difficult for the CIA, MI6, and other European intelligence agencies operating on the continent. Whenever one threatened Mossad's own position, Mossad exposed its activities. In Kenya an MI6 agent was blown. In Zaire, a French network was wrecked. In Tanzania a German intelligence operation was hurriedly aborted after being uncovered by Mossad through a tip to a local reporter.

When terrorist leader Abu Nidal—who had masterminded the assassination of Israel's ambassador to Britain, Shlomo Argov, on June 3, 1982, outside London's Dorchester Hotel—tried to seek shelter in Sudan, Mossad promised the regime Israel would pay one million U.S. dollars for his capture, dead or alive. In the end Nidal fled to the safety of Baghdad.

In a dozen countries, Mossad exploited newfound African nationalism. Among agents who had served in several of those countries was Yaakov Cohen, who would recall: "We gave them an intelligence capability to remain on top of the opposition. In countries like Nigeria, tribal rivalries had led to civil war. Our policy was to work with anyone who would work with us. That enabled us to know everything that was happening in a country. The slightest mood change which could affect Israel was reported back."

Before going to Africa, Cohen had distinguished himself in undercover missions in Egypt and elsewhere. As part of his disguise, Mossad had changed Cohen's physical appearance by arranging for a plastic surgeon to alter his distinctive ethnic feature—his nose. When he returned from the hospital, his own wife barely recognized Cohen and his new nose.

On New Year's Day, 1984, Nahum Admoni's daily intelligence summary contained news of a coup d'état in Nigeria. A military cabal led by Major General Muhammad Buhari had seized power. Prime Minister Shamir's first question was to ask what effect this would have on Israel's oil supplies. No one knew. Throughout the day, urgent efforts were unsuccessfully made to establish contact with the new regime.

On his second day in office, Buhari issued a list of former members of the government accused of a variety of crimes. At its top was Umaru Dikko, the ousted transport minister, charged with embezzling several million U.S. dollars in oil profits from the government treasury. Dikko had fled the country and, despite strenuous efforts to find him, had vanished.

Admoni saw his opening. Traveling on a Canadian passport—another Mossad travel document of choice for undercover missions—he flew to the Nigerian capital, Lagos. Buhari received him late at night. The general listened as Admoni delivered an offer that had the full approval of Rabin. In return for a guarantee of no interruption in oil supplies, Mossad would find Dikko and return him to Nigeria. Buhari had a question: Would Mossad also be able to locate where Dikko had hidden the embezzled money? Admoni said the cash was almost certainly in numbered Swiss bank accounts and would be virtually impossible to trace unless Dikko volunteered to reveal its whereabouts. Buhari smiled for the first time. Once Dikko was back in Nigeria, there would be no problem getting him to talk. Buhari had a final question: Would Mossad agree to work with Nigeria's own security service and, once Dikko was found, take no credit for his capture? Admoni agreed. There were no kudos to be gained for Mossad in an operation that should be simple enough.

Rafi Eitan's "survivor spies" were mobilized throughout Europe. Katsas were sent to trawl from Spain to Sweden. Sayanim in a dozen countries were alerted: doctors were told to be on the lookout in case Dikko needed medical attention or even consulted a plastic surgeon to change his appearance; hotel concierges at Dikko's old playgrounds in St.-Moritz and Monte Carlo watched for him. Clerks at car rental agencies from Madrid to Munich were instructed to report if he hired a car; airline agents were asked to call in if he bought a ticket. Sayanim working for all the credit card companies were asked to watch if he used his cards. Waiters memorized Dikko's description, tailors his measurements, and shirtmakers his collar size. Shoemakers from Rome to Paris were given details of Dikko's size-twelve fitting for the customized shoes he wore. In London, Robert Maxwell was asked to probe his high-level contacts among African diplomats in London for any whisper of where Dikko had gone. Like everyone else, he drew a blank.

Nevertheless, Admoni decided that Dikko was hiding out in London—the city had become a haven for Nigerian opponents of the new regime—and he moved his ablest katsas to the city. With them came agents from Nigerian security led by Major Muhammad Yusufu. They rented an apartment in the city's Cromwell Road. The katsas chose hotels catering to tourists from Africa.

Working separately, the two groups moved among London's sizable Nigerian community. Yusufu's men posed as refugees from the new regime, the katsas as sympathetic to black Africans' aspirations to overthrow the regime in South Africa. Gradually they narrowed down the search to West London, to the area around Hyde Park where many wealthy Nigerians lived in exile. They began to comb electoral registers freely available in the area's town halls. Each time they drew a blank.

Then, seven months to the day after Dikko had fled from Lagos, he surfaced. On June 30, 1984, a katsa driving down Queensway, a busy thoroughfare off Bayswater Road, spotted a man who fitted the description of Umaru Dikko. He looked older and thinner but there was no mistaking the broad face and the coal black eyes that did not give the katsa's car a second glance.

Spotting a parking place, the katsa set off on foot to tail Dikko to a house in nearby Dorchester Terrace. Admoni was immediately informed. He ordered the only step to be taken for the moment was full-time surveillance of the house. For the first three days of July 1984, two operatives maintained continuous surveillance on Dikko. Meantime the Nigerians used their embassy as a base to prepare a kidnap operation closely modeled on the one Rafi Eitan had used to snatch Adolf Eichmann.

Unusually, a key role had been assigned to an outsider, a much respected doctor, Levi-Arie Shapiro, a consultant anesthetist and director of the intensive care unit at Hasharon Hospital in Tel Aviv. He had been recruited by Alexander Barak, a katsa who had appealed to the doctor's patriotism. The doctor agreed to travel to London and spend the thousand dollars Barak had given him to pay for medical equipment, which included anesthetics and an endotracheal tube. He would receive further instructions in London. Shapiro refused to accept a fee for his services, saying he was proud to serve Israel. Another katsa, Felix Abithol, had arrived in London on a flight from Amsterdam on July 2. He checked into the Russell Square Hotel. His first instruction to the head of the Nigerian team, Major Yusufu, was to rent a transit van. One of Yusufu's men chose one that was a bright canary yellow color. That may well have been the moment the plan started to unravel.

Late in the evening of July 3, a Nigerian Airways 707 freighter landed at Stansted Airport, thirty miles northeast of London. It had flown from Lagos empty. The pilot informed the airport authorities he had come to collect diplomatic baggage from the London embassy. Traveling with the aircrew were several Nigerian security men who openly identified themselves and said they were there to protect the baggage. Their presence was reported to Scotland Yard's Special Branch. There had been several claims in the past month that the Lagos military regime was threatening exiles in London. The security men were told they must not leave the airport. Apart from visits to the terminal coffee shop, they remained on board the aircraft.

Around midmorning the next day, the canary yellow van drove out of a garage in Notting Hill Gate that had been rented by one of the Nigerians. At the wheel was Yusufu. In the back squatted Dr. Shapiro beside a crate. Crouching with him were Barak and Abithol. At noon out at Stansted, the 707 captain filed a departure time for Lagos of three o'clock that afternoon. The flight manifest listed the cargo as two crates of "documentation" for the Ministry of External Affairs in Lagos. The paperwork claimed diplomatic immunity for both containers.

Shortly before noon, the van drove through traffic and parked outside the house in Dorchester Terrace. Soon afterward, Umaru Dikko emerged on his way to meet a friend for lunch at a nearby restaurant. Watching from a window was his private secretary, Elizabeth Hayes. As she turned away, the back door of the van burst open and "two dark-skinned men grabbed Mr. Dikko and forced him into the back of the van. He just managed to scream something before they jumped in after him and the van was driven away at high speed."

Recovering, the secretary dialed emergency—999. Within minutes police were on the scene, closely followed by Commander William Hucklesby of Scotland Yard's Anti-Terrorist Squad. He suspected what had happened. Every port and airport was alerted. For Hucklesby, the situation had its own special difficulties. If Dikko had been kidnapped by the Nigerian regime, that could present tricky political questions. The Foreign Office was alerted, as was Downing Street. Hucklesby was ordered to take what action he thought appropriate.

Shortly before 3:00 P.M. the van arrived at Stansted's freight terminal. Yusufu waved a Nigerian diplomatic passport at airport customs officers. They watched the two crates being loaded on board the aircraft. One of the officers, Charles Morrow, would recall: "There was something about one of the containers that was just not right. Then I heard noise coming from one. I thought, sod this. Diplomatic immunity or not, I needed to see inside."

The cases were taken off the plane and brought to a hangar despite Yusufu's furious protest that they were protected by diplomatic privilege. In the first crate, Umaru Dikko was discovered tied and unconscious from an anesthetic. Sitting beside him was Dr. Shapiro, a syringe in his hand ready to increase Dikko's drug intake. There was an endotracheal tube in Dikko's throat to stop him from choking on his own vomit. In the other container crouched Barak and Abithol.

At their trial, both agents stuck stoically to the fiction that they were mercenaries acting on behalf of a group of Nigerian businessmen who wanted to return Dikko to face trial. One of Britain's most eminent and expensive lawyers, George Carmen, QC, had been retained for their defense. In his closing speech he told the court, "Perhaps the most plausible explanation is that the Israeli intelligence service was never far removed from the entire operation."

The prosecution offered no evidence to implicate Mossad. It was left to the judge to do so in his summing-up. He told the jury, "The finger of involvement almost certainly points to Mossad."

Barak received a fourteen-year sentence, Dr. Shapiro and Abithol ten years apiece. Yusufu was given twelve years' imprisonment. All were subsequently released after remission for good conduct and quietly deported to Israel. As it had for others before them who had served Mossad well, the service made sure they would remain out of the limelight and not have to answer such troubling questions as to whether Dr. Shapiro, who had so flagrantly broken his Hippocratic oath, still practiced medicine—and for whom.

Nahum Admoni was told by MI5 that if there was a further lapse, Mossad would be treated as an unfriendly service. By then the Mossad chief was planning yet another operation designed to remind Britain of who the real enemies were—and at the same time gain sympathy for Israel.

CHAPTER 14

THE
CHAMBERMAID'S
BOMB

On a cloudless morning in February 1986, two Israeli air force

fighter aircraft swooped down on a Libyan-registered Learjet flying

from Tripoli to Damascus. The civilian plane was in international

airspace, thirty thousand feet over the Mediterranean and about to

begin its descent into Syrian airspace. On board were delegates

returning from a conference of Palestinian and other radical groups

that Mu'ammar Gadhafi had convened to discuss new steps to

achieve the Libyan leader's burning obsession to see Israel driven

from the face of the earth.

The sight of the fighters taking up stations on either side of the

Learjet created near panic among its fourteen passengers, and for good reason. Four months before, on Tuesday, October 1, 1985, Israeli F-15 fighter-bombers had destroyed the headquarters of the Palestinian Liberation Organization southeast of Tunis, flying a round-trip of almost three thousand miles, which had involved air-to-air refueling and the kind of precise intelligence that always sent a collective shiver throughout the Arab world.

That raid was a direct response to the murder by PLO gunmen of three middle-aged Israeli tourists as they sat aboard their yacht in the Cypriot port of Larnaca only days before, basking in the sunshine of late summer. The killings had occurred on Yom Kippur and, for many Israelis, the slaughter rekindled memories of the onset of the war on the Day of Atonement when the nation itself had been caught as unaware as the tourists.

Despite having endured almost four decades of terrorism, the murders caused widespread horror and fear among Israelis: the tourists had been held for some time on board their boat and allowed to write down their final thoughts before they were killed: first to die was the woman, fatally shot in the stomach. Her two male companions were made to throw her overboard. Then one after another, they were shot at point-blank range in the back of the head.

In the black propaganda war that had long been a feature of the intelligence war between the PLO and Israel, the former claimed that the three victims were Mossad agents on a mission. So well did the PLO plant the story that several European newspapers identified the woman as one of the agents caught in the Lillehammer affair in 1973. That woman was still alive and had long given up her Mossad activities.

Since then the Arab press had been full of dire warnings that Israel would retaliate. Many of the stories had been planted by Mossad's psychological warfare department to fray still further the nerves of millions of Arabs.

The passengers in the Learjet, who only a few hours before had chanted for the destruction of Israel at the Libyan conference, saw the grim faces of their enemy peering at them. One of the fighters waggled its wings, the follow-me signal recognized the world over by pilots. To reinforce the message, an Israeli pointed a gloved hand straight ahead and then downward toward Galilee. The women on board the jet began to wail; some of the men started to pray. Others stared ahead fatalistically. They all knew this had always been a possibility; the accursed infidels had the capability to reach out and snatch them from the sky.

One of the Israeli aircraft fired a short warning burst from its cannon, warning the Learjet's captain not to contemplate radioing for help from the Syrian air force—only minutes' flying time away. The passengers' fear increased. Were they, too, about to suffer the same fate that had befallen one of the authentic heroes of the Arab world?

Just a month before the Tunis air raid, an Israeli naval patrol boat with Mossad agents on board had stopped a small ship called *Opportunity* on its regular shuttle between Beirut and Larnaca. From the bilges they had dragged out Faisal Abu Sharah, a terrorist with blood on his hands. He had been bundled on board the patrol boat, the prelude to ruthless interrogation in Israel, followed by a quick trial and a long term in jail. The swiftness and audacity of the operation had yet again enhanced the image of invincibility Israel presented to the Arab world.

Such incidents were not uncommon. Working closely with Israel's small but highly trained navy, Mossad had since then intercepted several boats and removed passengers suspected of terrorist activities. Not only Israel's long Mediterranean coast called for vigilance; the Red Sea also presented a constant vulnerability. A Mossad agent in Yemen had been the source for an operation that had thwarted a PLO plot to sail a fishing boat up the Red Sea to the Israeli resort of Elat and detonate its cargo of explosives close to the shore, lined with hotels. An Israeli gunboat had intercepted the fishing boat and overpowered its two suicide bombers before they could detonate the cargo.

As the Learjet descended toward northern Israel, the passengers also feared this was a further retaliation for what had happened when another of their heroes, Abu Al-Abbas, had, only a few months before, on October 2, 1985, taken over the Italian cruise liner *Achille Lauro* in what was the most spectacular act of maritime piracy the world could recall. Al-Abbas had murdered one of the passengers, Leon Klinghoffer, an American Jew in a wheelchair, by throwing him into the sea.

The crime had become a floating diplomatic incident that had embroiled an outraged Israel and the United States, Egypt, Italy, Syria, Cyprus, Tunisia, and the stateless PLO; for days the crisis had drifted around the Mediterranean, gathering publicity for the hijackers and revealing the self-interest which, in the Middle East, governed attitudes toward terrorism. The hijacking of a cruise liner that was bringing much-needed foreign tourists and hard currency to Israel, followed by the murder of a passenger, provoked a wave of indecision. The murder had technically taken place on Italian soil, the Genova-registered *Achille Lauro*. But Italy was highly vulnerable to terrorism and wished to see a quiet end to the incident. The United States wanted justice for its murdered citizen. Across the nation appeared stickers proclaiming, "Don't get mad, get even." Finally the hijackers, having held the world's headlines for several days, surrendered to the Egyptian authorities, who then allowed them to leave the country—to the fury of Israel.

More than one of the Learjet's passengers wondered whether they would now be held in some Israeli jail in an act of revenge. With the fighters still flying almost wingtip to wingtip, the executive jet landed at a military airfield in northern Galilee. A waiting team of Aman interrogators had been told by Mossad that on board were two of the most wanted terrorists in the world, the notorious Abu Nidal and the equally infamous Ahmed Jibril. Instead the interrogators found themselves questioning a bunch of badly frightened Arabs, none of whose names appeared on Israel's computers. The Learjet was allowed to depart with its passengers.

Israel would insist that the prospect of catching terrorists was the only reason for intercepting the aircraft. But within Mossad was a mood that no opportunity should be lost to create fear and panic in Arab minds. The Aman interrogators had some satisfaction in knowing that the passengers would further the image of an all-powerful Israel.

The head of Aman, Ehud Barak, believed the operation was yet another example of Mossad shooting from the hip, and he made his feeling very clear to Nahum Admoni.

Never a person to suffer a mistake or a rebuke lightly, the Mossad chief set about devising an operation that would not only put an end to the mocking of Mossad on Arab radio stations for being reduced to forcing down an unarmed civilian plane, but one that would also end the sniping within Israel's own intelligence community that the service he commanded should next time be very sure before it made a fool of them all.

So began an operation which, among much else, would ruin the life of a pregnant Irish chambermaid and send her Arab lover to prison to serve one of the longest sentences given by a British court; cause huge embarrassment to German chancellor Helmut Kohl and French prime minister Jacques Chirac; once more reveal Robert Maxwell in full manipulative fury; cause Syria to be exiled from the world's diplomatic table; and force all those Arab radio stations that had so gleefully ridiculed Mossad to change their tune.

Like all operations, there were moments of high tensions and periods of patient waiting. It had its quota of human despair, useful anger, and betrayal, but for men like Nahum Admoni, such a plot was the very substance of his life. It went with asking himself the same questions over and over again. Could it work? Would other people actually believe that it had been like that? And, of course, would the real truth remain buried forever?

More certain, Mossad had enlisted the very different skills of two men for the operation. One was a katsa who had served in Britain under the alias of Tov Levy. The other was a Palestinian informer, code-named Abu. The Palestinian had been recruited after being discovered by Mossad stealing from a PLO fund he had been administering in a village on the Israeli-Jordanian border. Playing on his fear that the crime could be revealed through an anonymous tip to the village head, resulting in Abu's death, Mossad had dragooned him to leave for London. He had been provided with fake documents stating he was a businessman and given living expenses commensurate with his role as a high-flying big spender. His assigned controller was Tov Levy.

In every way Abu fitted the classic definition by Uzi Mahnaimi, a former member of the Israeli intelligence community, of what an agent should be: "You spend hours with him, days even; you teach him everything he needs to know, you go through his courses with him, help him, socialize with him, look at his family photographs, you know the names and ages of his children. But the agent is not a human being; you must never think of him as one. The agent is just a weapon, a means to an end, like a Kalashnikov—that is all. If you have to send him to the hanging tree, don't even think about it. The agent is always a cipher, never a person."

Abu had played his part to perfection and had become a familiar figure around the gambling tables of Mayfair. Given his success, his sexual appetites and bouts of drinking were tolerated. Moving in the haunts of arms dealers and wealthy PLO supporters, Abu picked up information that enabled Mossad to strike against its enemies. Fifteen PLO men were killed by Mossad over a few weeks as a result of Abu's information.

Some of his meetings with Tov Levy had taken place in the bars and restaurants of the Hilton Hotel on Park Lane. Working there was an Irish woman from Dublin, Ann-Marie Murphy.

Like many others, she had been tempted across the Irish Sea by the lure of making good money in London. All she had been able to get was a chambermaid's job. The pay was low, the hours long. Ann-Marie's little free time was spent in bars in the Shepherds Bush district, long a refuge for Irish expatriates. She joined in the rebel songs and made a glass of Guinness last. Then it was back to her lonely room, ready for another long day of changing bedsheets, scouring lavatory bowls, and leaving each hotel room sparkling in the prescribed Hilton manner. Her career was going nowhere.

Shortly before Christmas, 1985, close to tears at the thought of having to spend it alone in a city so different from the carefree Dublin she longed for, Ann-Marie met a dark-skinned Arab who was handsome in her eyes. In his silk suit and flashy tie he also exuded affluence. When he smiled at her, she smiled back. His name was Nezar Hindawi, and he was a distant cousin of Abu. Hindawi was thirty-five years old, though he lied about that to Ann-Marie, lopping three years from his age to make him the same as her, thirty-two. He would go on lying to a trusting, naive woman.

They had met in a bar close to the BBC Theatre in Shepherds Bush Green. She had never been to this pub before and was surprised to find Hindawi among the ruddy-faced building-site navvies whose accents echoed every county in Ireland. But Hindawi seemed to know many of the drinkers, joining in their rough humor and standing a round when it was his turn.

For weeks, Hindawi had been coming to the bar hoping to make contact with the IRA. Abu had asked him to do so, though typically his cousin had not explained why. Hindawi's few attempts to discuss the political situation in Ireland had been brushed aside by men more interested in sinking pints. Whatever scheme Abu was concocting would remain a secret as far as Hindawi was concerned. The arrival of Ann-Marie had also given him something else to think about.

Captivated by his good manners and charm, Ann-Marie soon found herself laughing at Hindawi's stories about his life in the Middle East. To a woman who had never traveled farther than London, he made it sound like an Arabian Nights fantasy. Hindawi drove her home that night, kissed her on both cheeks, and left. Ann-Marie wondered if the giddy feeling she experienced was the first stage of falling in love. The following day he took her to lunch at a Syrian restaurant and introduced her to the delights of Arabic cooking. Tipsy from a fine Lebanese wine, she put up only token resistance when he took her back to his apartment. That afternoon they made love. Until then Ann-Marie had been a virgin. Raised in the strong Irish Catholic tradition opposed to contraception, she had taken no precautions.

In February 1986, she found she was pregnant. She told Hindawi. He smiled reassurance; he would take care of everything. Alarmed, Ann-Marie said she would never agree to an abortion. He told her the idea had never crossed his mind. In truth he was panic-stricken at the prospect of having to marry a woman he regarded as beneath his social class. He also feared she would go to the authorities and complain. With little understanding of how indifferently officialdom would view such matters, he thought his permission to stay in Britain would be revoked, resulting in his being deported as an undesirable alien. Hindawi turned to the only source of help he knew, his cousin Abu.

Abu had his own problems, having lost a good deal of money gambling. He bluntly told Hindawi he couldn't loan him the money Hindawi had decided he would offer Ann-Marie to return to Dublin, have the baby, and place it out for adoption. She had told him that was common in Ireland.

Next day Abu met Tov Levy. Over dinner the katsa told Abu he needed to do something to cause the British government to close down the Syrian embassy in London and order out its staff, long suspected of being involved in terrorist activities. Levy said he needed a "hook" that would achieve that. Could Abu tell him about anyone, anything, that might be useful? Abu mentioned he had a cousin with an Irish girlfriend who was pregnant in London.

The plot began to coalesce after the aftershocks rocking the Israeli intelligence community from the disclosures tumbling out of Washington about the arms-for-hostages deal with Iran. Israel's tough image for dealing with terrorism had taken a pounding. There was anger within Mossad that the Reagan administration had allowed matters to go so badly wrong as to allow Israel's role in Irangate to surface.

The revelations had made it that much more difficult to maintain even the minimum support of cautiously friendly neighbors like Egypt and Jordan at a time when they were both finally growing tired of the PLO and the histrionics of Yasser Arafat. Increasingly the PLO leader had become a political captive of his own extremists. No Marxist himself, he found himself cornered into spouting its rhetoric, calling for "the liquidation of the Zionist entity politically, culturally, and militarily."

The vituperation did nothing to improve his position among the various breakaway factions of the PLO. To them, Arafat was the man who had been forced to make a humiliating withdrawal from Beirut under cover of UN protection from the watchful eye of the Israelis. Some fifteen thousand Palestinian fighters had boarded boats for Tunis. Others had deserted Arafat on the promise of support from Syria and had become even more militant against both him and Israel from their new bases outside Damascus.

Yet for Mossad, Arafat remained the key obstacle to peace. Killing him was still a priority; at the Mossad target range the silhouettes were all of Arafat. Until he was dead, he would continue to be held ultimately responsible for all the acts of savagery committed by the disparate Palestinian groups in Syria.

Then two incidents happened which, momentarily at least, moved the focus from Arafat, and ultimately settled the plot in which Abu was to become a key figure.

A growing problem Syria had with the PLO factions under its wing was the need to satisfy their constant demands for action. As one of the world's prime exponents of state-sponsored terrorism, Syria was more than prepared to finance any operation that did not further blight its own already seriously tarnished image. Many of the schemes the PLO factions placed before Syrian intelligence were too risky for the Syrians to endorse. One had been to poison Israel's water supply. Another was to send an Arab suicide bomber, posing as an Orthodox Jew, to blow himself up at the Wailing Wall in Jerusalem. Either was guaranteed to draw draconian retaliation from Israel.

Then came an audacious plot that Syrian intelligence recognized could not only work, but would strike a telling blow at the very heart of Israel's military supremacy. The first step had been to buy a ship. After several weeks of searching ports around the Mediterranean, a Panama-registered merchantman, *Atavarius*, was purchased and sailed to the port of Algiers.

A week after it arrived, a detachment of Palestinian commandos arrived from Damascus on a Syrian air force transport plane. With them they brought a small arsenal of weapons: machine guns, antitank weapons, and boxes of Kalashnikov rifles so beloved of terrorists. That night, under cover of darkness, the commandos and arms were placed on board the *Atavarius*.

At daybreak the ship set sail, its captain having told the port authorities he was bound for Greece to undergo an engine overhaul. The commandos were belowdecks. But their arrival had not gone unnoticed. A Mossad informer employed in the harbormaster's office had become sufficiently suspicious to inform the katsa stationed in the city. He sent a message to Tel Aviv.

Its arrival triggered a "condition yellow" alert that was sent to the entire Mossad network stationed around the Mediterranean. Memories were still fresh of the unsuccessful attempt to blow up the seafront at Elat, and it was assumed this could be a similar attack, only this time against Haifa. The busy port on the Mediterranean seaboard was an obvious target. Two naval gunboats were stationed offshore ready to deal with any attempt by the *Atavarius* to enter the harbor that was Israel's main trading sea link with the world.

The *Atavarius*'s destination was the beaches north of Tel Aviv. In a plan that could have been plucked from a Hollywood movie, the *Atavarius* would lower the commandos into rubber boats, which they would row ashore. Then they would fight their way into Tel

Aviv to their target, the Kirya, the fortresslike headquarters of the Israel Defense Forces, whose tower dominated the skyline and would serve as a beacon for the commandos. The plan depended on total surprise and the ruthless courage the Israelis had themselves made a byword.

The attack had been set for Israel's Independence Day celebrations, when a carnival mood would prevail, and the Kirya, according to Syrian intelligence, would have fewer men than usual guarding it. The commandos did not expect to escape with their lives, but they had been chosen for the mission because they had all shown the same mentality as the Beirut suicide bombers.

Meantime, they could relax and enjoy the short cruise that took them past Tunisia to their next landfall, the island of Sicily. No one on board probably paid any attention to the fishing trawler wallowing in the swell as the *Atavarius* passed. The boat contained sophisticated electronic equipment capable of monitoring radio conversations on board the merchantman. A short transmission in Arabic announced that the ship was on schedule. One of the trawler's two-man crew, both Mossad sayanim, radioed the news to Tel Aviv. For the next twenty-four hours, the *Atavarius* was shadowed by other Mossad-operated vessels as it passed Crete and then the island of Cyprus.

A fast motor yacht crossed its path. It, too, was equipped with detection gear, including a powerful camera concealed in the side of the wheelhouse. On deck were two young women, sunbathing. They were cousins of the Cypriot sayan who owned the yacht and were being used as bait to attract interest from those on board the *Atavarius*. As the yacht cruised alongside, several of the commandos appeared at the deck rail, shouting and smiling at the women. In the wheelhouse, the sayan activated the camera to photograph the gesticulating men. His part in the surveillance over, he raced back to Cyprus. In his home the film was developed, and the prints were wired to Tel Aviv. Mossad's computers identified three of the faces as known Arab terrorists. Condition yellow moved to red.

Prime Minister Shimon Peres ordered that the *Atavarius* be attacked. A plan to bomb it was considered and rejected. An air attack might be mistaken by Egypt as part of a preemptive strike; though diplomatic relations between Israel and its neighbor had survived a number of incidents, there was considerable tension and suspicion in Cairo about Tel Aviv's activities. Peres agreed that the attack should be seaborne.

Six Israeli navy gunboats were fueled and armed with rockets. On board were units of the IDF Special Forces and Mossad operatives who were to interrogate any of the commandos taken alive. The gunboats set off in the early hours for Haifa, heading west out into the Mediterranean. They raced through the waters in stern-to-prow formation, so as to reduce the possibility of detection by radar on board the *Atavarius*. The Israelis had timed their attack to be launched with the rising sun immediately behind them.

At a little after 6:30 A.M., the *Atavarius* was sighted. In a textbook maneuver, the gunboats fanned out, attacking the merchantman from both sides, raking the hull and decks with rockets. On deck the commandos fired back. But their heavy armaments were still crated below, and their automatic rifles were no match for the superior firepower of the Israelis. In minutes the *Atavarius* was on fire and its crew and commandos began to abandon ship. Some were shot as they plunged into the sea.

In all, twenty crew and commandos were killed. Their bodies were all recovered. Eight survivors were taken prisoner. Before the gunboats raced back to Israel, they sank the *Atavarius* with rockets whose nose cones were filled with extra-powerful explosives.

The bodies of the dead were unceremoniously buried in the Negev Desert. The prisoners were tried in secret and sentenced to lengthy terms of imprisonment. During their interrogation, they had totally implicated Syria as the guiding force behind the incident. But, rather than launch an attack on its neighbor, the Israeli government, acting on the advice of Mossad, kept the incident secret. Mossad's psychologists had predicted that the disappearance of the ship and its crew and passengers would become the subject of intense and increasingly fearful speculation among the Syrian-based PLO groups. Mossad also warned Prime Minister Peres that the one thing he could be certain of was that the terrorists, knowing their operation had failed, would be eager to regain face with their Syrian benefactors.

Meanwhile, the Palestinians continued to fulminate against Arafat and applaud the deadly war being waged against him by his onetime associate, Abu Nidal. Long deemed terrorism's "grand master of the unexpected," Nidal had fallen out with Arafat over tactics.

Arafat was slowly coming around to the idea that a movement that had nothing at its disposal but terrorism would ultimately fail; it needed a political program and a sense of diplomacy. Arafat had been trying to demonstrate that in his recent public statements, earning encouragement from Washington to continue on this new path. In Israel, Arafat's words were seen as a sham. For Abu Nidal they were nothing but a betrayal of all he personally stood for—naked, unadulterated terrorism.

For months, Nidal had been biding his time. When he heard about the failure of the *Atavarius* mission and the way the ship had subsequently disappeared from the face of the earth, he decided the time had come to remind Israel he was still around. With the full connivance of his protectors in Syrian intelligence, Abu Nidal struck with horrific effect. At the Rome and Vienna airports in December 1985, his gunmen opened fire on helpless Christmas travelers. In as many seconds nineteen passengers, among them five Americans, were slaughtered at the El Al check-in counters at both airports. How had those terrorists been able to move unhampered around Italian police to reach their targets? Where were El Al's own security men?

While answers to these urgent questions were being sought, Mossad's strategists were also looking at other areas. Though Britain had joined in the total condemnation of the attacks, the country still maintained full diplomatic ties with Syria—despite Mossad having furnished MI5 with ample evidence of Damascus's role in state-sponsored terrorism. It was not enough for the prime minister, Margaret Thatcher, to deliver forceful denunciations in Parliament of terrorism. There was a need for more direct action. However, in the past MI5 had reminded Mossad that even Israel had from time to time shown expedient self-interest, and accepted the need to trade with its sworn enemies. There had been its decision to free over a thousand Palestinian detainees—many convicted terrorists—only months before the Rome and Vienna airport bombings, in exchange for three Israeli soldiers held in Lebanon.

But now Mossad was determined to strike a telling blow to force Britain to sever all diplomatic ties with Damascus by closing down its London embassy, long regarded by Mossad as one of the core missions in Europe for plotting against Israel. Central to the plot would be Abu, the cousin of Nezar Hindawi.

After his dinner with Tov Levy, Abu sought out Hindawi, apologizing for his previous indifference about Ann-Marie. Of course he would help, but first he needed to have some answers. Was she going to keep the baby? Was she still pressing him to marry her? Did Nezar really love the girl? They came from different cultures and mixed marriages rarely worked.

Hindawi replied if he had ever loved Ann-Marie, he did not now. She had become shrewish and weepy, asking all the time what was going to happen. He certainly did not want to marry the chambermaid.

Abu gave his cousin ten thousand dollars—money enough, he said, for Hindawi to be rid of Ann-Marie and continue to live a bachelor's life in London. The money had been provided by Mossad. In return Hindawi would have to do something for the cause they both believed in: the overthrow of Israel.

On the evening of April 12, 1986, Hindawi visited Ann-Marie in her rooming house in the Kilburn area of London. He brought flowers and a bottle of champagne, purchased with some of the money Abu had provided. He told Ann-Marie he loved her and wanted to keep the baby. The news brought tears to her eyes. Suddenly her world seemed a far better place.

Hindawi said there was one final hurdle to clear. Ann-Marie must get the blessing of his parents for them to marry. It was an Arabic tradition no dutiful son could flout. She must fly to the Arab village in Israel where his family lived. He painted a picture of their lifestyle having changed little since Christ had walked the earth. To a girl educated by nuns and for whom Mass had been an important part of her life, the imagery was final confirmation that she was making the right decision in marrying her lover. He and his family might not be Christians, but that did not matter; they came from the land of her Lord. In her eyes that made them God-fearing people. Nevertheless, Ann-Marie hesitated. She couldn't just walk out of her job. And where would she get the money to pay the airfare? And for such an important meeting, she would need new clothes. Hindawi stilled her concerns by producing from his pocket a bundle of notes. He told her it was more than enough for her to buy a new wardrobe. With another flourish, Hindawi produced an El Al ticket for a flight on April 17, five days away. He had bought it that afternoon.

Ann-Marie laughed. "You were sure I would go?"

"As sure as I am of my love for you," Hindawi replied.

He promised that once she returned to London they would be married. The next few days passed in a whirl for the pregnant chambermaid. She quit her job and visited the Irish embassy in London to collect a new passport. She shopped for maternity dresses. Every night she made love to Hindawi. Each morning, over a leisurely breakfast, she planned their future together. They would live in Ireland, in a little cottage by the sea. Their baby would be christened Sean if it was a boy. Sinead if a girl.

On the day of Ann-Marie's departure, Hindawi told her he had arranged for her to collect a "gift" for his parents from a "friend" who was one of the cleaners on the air side of the airport.

Ari Ben-Menashe, who subsequently claimed to have detailed knowledge of the plot, insisted that "because Hindawi didn't want to risk her being stopped for having too much carry-on luggage he had arranged for his friend to pass her the bag when she entered the El Al departure lounge."

Her gullibility in not asking any questions about the "gift" was the reaction of a woman head over heels in love and completely trusting her lover. She was the perfect patsy in the accelerating plot.

In the taxi to the airport, Hindawi was the loving, concerned father-to-be. Would she make sure to do her breathing exercises during the long flight? She must drink plenty of water and sit in an aisle seat to avoid developing the cramps she had started to complain of. Ann-Marie had laughingly shushed him: "Holy be to God, you'd think I was flying to the moon!"

She had lingered at the door to the flight departure area, not wishing to be separated from him, promising to phone from Tel Aviv, saying she would love his parents like her own. He kissed her one last time, then gently pushed her into the line making its way toward the immigration-control desk.

Watching her until she was out of sight, Hindawi continued to follow the instructions given to him by Abu and boarded a Syrian Arab Airlines bus for the ride back into London. Meantime, the unsuspecting Ann-Marie had safely passed through passport control and UK security checks. Next she made her way to the high-security area reserved for the El Al flight. Shin Bet–trained agents carefully questioned her and inspected her hand baggage. She was assigned a seat and motioned through to the final departure lounge to join the other 355 passengers.

According to Ari Ben-Menashe, she was handed the "gift" for Hindawi's parents by a man dressed in the blue coveralls of an airport cleaner. The man disappeared as mysteriously as he had appeared. Ben-Menashe would write: "Within seconds, Ann-Marie was asked to submit to a search. The El Al security people found plastic explosives in a false bottom in the bag."

The explosives consisted of over three pounds of Semtex. Ann-Marie sobbed out her story to waiting Special Branch and MI5 officers. It was the tale of an ill-starred woman not only crossed in love but double-crossed by her partner. The officers concentrated on establishing Hindawi's contacts with Syria after they realized Ann-Marie had been an innocent dupe.

As the airlines bus entered London, Hindawi ordered the driver to divert to the Syrian embassy. When the driver protested, Hindawi said he had the "authority" to do so. At the embassy, he asked consular officials to grant him political asylum. He told them he feared the British police were about to arrest him because he had tried to blow up an El Al plane for the "cause." The astonished officials handed Hindawi over to two embassy security men. They asked him to remain in an embassy staff apartment after they questioned him. They might well have been suspicious that this was some sort of trap to embarrass Syria. If so, those fears would only have deepened when Hindawi left the apartment shortly after.

Hindawi had gone in search of Abu. Failing to find him, he checked into the London Visitors' Hotel in the Notting Hill district, where he was arrested shortly afterward.

The BBC broadcast news of how the police had foiled the plot. The details were unusually precise: the Czech-made Semtex had been concealed in the false bottom of Ann-Marie's bag and was primed to explode at thirty-nine thousand feet.

For Ben-Menashe, the operation had swiftly moved to a satisfying conclusion. "Margaret Thatcher closed down the Syrian embassy. Hindawi was jailed for forty-five years. Ann-Marie went home to Ireland where she gave birth to a daughter." Abu returned to Israel, his role over.

After Hindawi's trial, Robert Maxwell unleashed the *Daily Mirror:* "The bastard got what he deserved," screamed an editorial. "Ambassador of Death," shrieked a headline on the day of the expulsion of Syria's ambassador to the Court of St. James's. "Get Out, You Syrian Swine," screamed another. Ari Ben-Menashe would be the first to claim that Mossad had pulled off a "brilliant coup which cast Syria into the political wilderness."

But there were intriguing questions behind that clear-cut sentiment. Had Ann-Marie Murphy really been handed a working bomb, or had it been part of an elaborate scam? Was the man in blue coveralls—Hindawi's supposed "friend"—a security officer? How much foreknowledge of the plot did MI5 have? And would it not have been unthinkable for Mossad and Britain's security services to actually allow Semtex to be taken on board an airliner when there was even the remotest chance the bomb could have detonated on the ground? Such an explosion would certainly have devastated a sizable area of the world's busiest airport at a time when thousands of people would have been in the area. Had the real brilliance of the coup been that Mossad had achieved the diplomatic castration of Syria at no risk at all to El Al and Heathrow by using a harmless substance resembling Semtex? To all such questions, Prime Minister Shimon Peres would only intone: "What happened is usually known to those who should know and whoever does not know should continue not knowing."

From Britain's high-security jail at Whitmoor, Hindawi has continued to protest he was a victim of a classic Mossad sting operation. White-haired and no longer slim, he says he expects to die in prison. He refers to Ann-Marie only as "that woman." In 1998, she lives in Dublin raising their daughter, who, she is thankful, does not look like her lover. She never speaks of Hindawi.

There is one puzzling footnote to the story. Two weeks after Hindawi was sentenced to a prison sentence that would see him incarcerated well into the twenty-first century, Arnaud de Borchgrave, the respected editor of the *Washington Times,* placed his tape recorder on the desk of France's prime minister, Jacques Chirac, in Paris. De Borchgrave was in Europe to attend the European Com-

munity foreign ministers' meeting in London, and the interview
with Chirac was to obtain a briefing on the French position. The
interview had moved along predictable lines, with Chirac making it
clear that France and Germany had been dragooned into a show of
loyalty to the British government, which was proving to be increasingly intransigent over Common Market policies. De Borchgrave
raised the question of France's own relationship in another area.
The editor wanted to know what stage Chirac's negotiations had
reached with Syria to end the spate of terrorist bombs in Paris, and
of France's efforts to free the eight foreign hostages held by the
Hezbollah in Lebanon. The prime minister paused and looked
across his desk, seemingly oblivious of the recorder. He then said
that the German chancellor, Helmut Kohl, and foreign minister,
Hans-Dietrich Genscher, had both told him that the Syrian government was not involved in Hindawi's plan to blow up the El Al
airliner; that the plot "was engineered by Mossad, the Israeli Secret
Service."

The resulting diplomatic furor nearly ruined Chirac's career. He
found himself being attacked on one side by his own president,
François Mitterand, and on the other fending off furious telephone
calls from Helmut Kohl demanding he must retract. Chirac did
what politicians often do. He said he had been misquoted. In London, Scotland Yard said the matter had been fully dealt with by the
courts and there was no need for further comment. In Paris, the
office of Jacques Chirac—in 1997 president of France—said he had
no recall of the interview with the *Washington Times*.

Soon another sting would leave Mossad with a further stain on
its reputation.

CHAPTER 15

THE EXPENDABLE CARTOONIST

Nahum Admoni's demise as director general of Mossad began on

a July afternoon in 1986, the result of an incident on one of those

Bonn streets built in the post–World War II building boom in

Germany. Forty years later the street had become a mature avenue

with small but well-kept front gardens and maids' quarters in the

rear. Security systems were discreetly hidden behind wrought-iron

gates and the lower windows were mullioned, the result of using

bottle glass.

No one saw the person who left a plastic carrier bag in the tele-

phone booth at the end of the street. A police patrol car spotted it and stopped to investigate. The bag contained eight freshly minted blank British passports. The immediate reaction of the local office of the Bundeskriminal Amt (BKA), the equivalent of the FBI, was that the passports were for one of the terrorist groups who had brought terrorism to the streets of Europe with a series of violent and brutal bombings and kidnappings.

Representing causes and minorities from all corners of the world, they were determined to force their way to a role in setting the agenda for international policy. They had found ready support from the radical student politics that had swept Britain and the Continent. Since 1968, when Leila Khaled, a young Palestinian woman revolutionary, hijacked a jet plane to London and was promptly released because the British government feared further attacks, naive students had chanted the agitprop slogans of the PLO. Those middle-class young radicals had a romanticized view of the PLO as "freedom fighters" who, instead of taking drugs, took the lives of the bourgeoisie, and instead of holding sit-ins, held hostages.

The BKA assumed that the passports had been left by a student acting as a courier for a terrorist group. The list of groups was dauntingly long, ranging from the IRA or Germany's own Red Army Faction to foreign groups like the INFS, Islamic National Front of Sudan; the ELN, the National Liberation Army of Colombia; the MDRA, the Angola Liberation Movement; or the LTTE, the Tamil Tigers. These and many more had cells or cadres through the Federal Republic. Any one of them could be planning to use the passports to attack one of the British military bases in Germany or travel to Britain and stage an outrage there.

Despite being Western Europe's leading former imperial power, initially Britain had only encountered continued terrorism at the hands of the IRA. But its intelligence services had warned it was only a matter of time before other foreign groups, allowed to operate against their own countries from London, would drag Britain into their machinations. A foretaste of what could happen came when a group opposed to the Tehran regime took over the Iranian embassy in 1980. When negotiations failed, the Thatcher government sent in the SAS, who killed the terrorists. That well-publicized action had led to a sudden decline in Middle Eastern plots hatched in London. Instead, Paris had become the battleground for bloody internal conflicts between various foreign organizations, most notably Yasser Arafat's PLO and Abu Nidal and his gunmen. Mossad had also done its share of killing Arab enemies on the streets of the French capital.

The BKA believed the passports found in the Frankfurt telephone kiosk were the precursor of more slaughter. The agency called in the BundesNachrichten Dienst (BND), the republic's equivalent of the CIA, who informed the MI6 liaison officer attached to BND headquarters in Pullach, in southern Germany. In London, MI6 established that the passports were expert forgeries. That ruled out the IRA and most other terrorist groups. They did not have the capability to produce such high-quality documents. Suspicion switched to the KGB; their forgers were among the best in the business. But the Russians were known to have a stockpile of passports and certainly it was not their style to use a phone booth as a pickup point. The South African security service, BOSS, was also ruled out. It had virtually stopped operating in Europe, and false British passports were hardly needed in the unsophisticated African countries where BOSS now concentrated its activities. MI6 turned to the only other intelligence service who could make good use of the passports—Mossad.

Arie Regev, an attaché at the Israeli embassy in London who was also the resident katsa, was invited to meet a senior MI6 officer to discuss the matter. Regev said he knew nothing about the passports but agreed to raise the matter with Tel Aviv. Back came the swift response from Nahum Admoni: the passports had nothing to do with Mossad. He suggested that they could be the work of the East Germans; Mossad had recently discovered that the Stasi, the East German security service, was not above selling fake passports to Jews desperate to travel to Israel, in return for hard currency. Admoni knew the passports had been created by Mossad forgers—and were intended to be used by katsas working under cover in Europe and to enable them to more easily enter and leave Britain.

Despite an "understanding" with MI5 that Rafi Eitan had originally helped hammer out, in which Mossad agreed it would keep MI5 informed of all operations inside Britain, the agency was secretly running an agent in England in the hope it would lead to a double triumph for Mossad: killing the commander of the PLO's elite Special Forces unit—Force 17—and ending Yasser Arafat's increasing success in establishing a relationship with the Thatcher government.

In London, no longer was Arafat's name synonymous with terrorism. Mrs. Thatcher had slowly become convinced that he could bring about a just and lasting peace in the Middle East that would both recognize the legitimate rights of the Palestinian people and assure the security of Israel. Jewish leaders were more skeptical. They argued it was only terrorism that had brought the PLO to the stage at which it was now, and that the organization would continue to use the threat of more terrorist actions unless all its demands were met. Not for the first time, London was unmoved by Tel Aviv's protestations. Mossad continued to regard Britain as a country which, despite the outcome of the Iranian embassy siege, was becoming too ready to support the Palestinian cause. There was already concern within Mossad over the way the PLO had managed to cozy up to the CIA.

Contacts between the United States and the PLO would later be precisely dated by former secretary of state Henry Kissinger. He would reveal in his memoirs, *Years of Upheaval*, that six weeks after the U.S. ambassador to Sudan was shot dead in Khartoum by Black September gunmen, a secret meeting took place, on November 3, 1973, between CIA deputy director, Vernon Walters, and Yasser Arafat. The outcome was a "nonaggression pact" between the United States and the PLO. Kissinger subsequently wrote: "Attacks on Americans, at least by Arafat's faction of the PLO, ceased."

When he learned of the pact, Yitzhak Hofi fumed that in the long history of expediency, there had never been a worse example. Using his back channel to the CIA, Hofi tried to have Walters cancel the agreement. The CIA deputy director said that was not possible and warned Hofi that Washington would regard it as an "unfriendly act" if news of the pact became public. It was a shot across the bow not to let loose Mossad's Department of Psychological Warfare on friendly journalists.

Hofi's anger became apocalyptic when he discovered whom Arafat had put in charge of administering the PLO end of the pact: Ali Hassan Salameh, the Red Prince, the Black September group leader who had planned the Munich massacre of the Israeli Olympic athletes and the murder of the U.S. ambassador in Khartoum; Salameh, the man whose life would finally end the way it had been lived, in a powerful explosion arranged by Rafi Eitan. But that was still some years away. In 1973, Salameh was a revered figure within the PLO and Arafat had no hesitation about appointing him to liaise with the CIA. What genuinely shocked Mossad was that the CIA had accepted the Red Prince barely a year after the Munich killings and the murder of the U.S. envoy in Khartoum.

Soon Salameh was a regular visitor to CIA headquarters at Langley. Usually accompanied by Vernon Walters, the Red Prince would stride across the Agency's marble-floored entrance, past the guards, and ride in the elevator to the seventh floor, where Walters had his spacious office. Their meetings would be interrupted to join CIA's senior officers in their special dining room. Walters would unfailingly pay for the Red Prince's meal; there was no such thing as a free lunch at Langley.

What passed between Salameh and the CIA has remained secret. Bill Buckley, who later died at the hands of terrorists in Beirut when he was CIA station chief, would claim that "Salameh played a large part in winning the hearts and minds of the U.S. for the PLO. He was charismatic and persuasive and knew when to argue and when to listen. And, in intelligence terms, he was a super informer."

An early example was when Salameh warned the CIA of an Iran-brokered plot to shoot down Kissinger's plane when it next flew into Beirut during the secretary's shuttle for peace. Next, Salameh brokered a deal in which the PLO escorted 263 westerners in West Beirut to safety during the height of the Lebanese civil war. Shortly afterward, the Red Prince gave the CIA warning of an attempt to assassinate the U.S. ambassador to Lebanon. Then, in yet another meeting with the CIA, the Red Prince wrote and signed a "non-assassination guarantee" for all U.S. diplomats in Lebanon. In Beirut the repeated joke was "It pays to live in the same building as American diplomats because the PLO security is so good."

Yitzhak Hofi, then head of Mossad, had demanded the CIA break off all contacts with the Red Prince. The request was ignored. Around CIA headquarters at Langley, Salameh was increasingly known as "the bad guy who has come good for us." He continued to provide intelligence and operational information that kept the CIA fully briefed on the Middle East and had become its most important asset in the region. When he was finally killed, the CIA was enraged, and its relations with Mossad were cool for a considerable time.

One U.S. ambassador to Lebanon, Hermann Eilts, later said after Salameh's own assassination: "I know that on a good many occasions, in a nonpublic fashion, he was extraordinarily helpful, assisting with security for American citizens and officials. I regard his assassination as a loss."

Now, six years later, the PLO was once more beguiling the government of Margaret Thatcher while its Force 17, under a new leader, continued to kill Israelis. Nahum Admoni decided he would succeed where his predecessors had failed. He would disrupt the PLO's relationship with Britain and, at the same time, kill the Force 17 commander. The success of the operation would turn out to depend on a young Arab who, as a boy, had prayed in his village mosque that Allah would give him the strength to murder as many Jews as possible.

Ismail Sowan's potential had been spotted ten years before. In 1977, when Sowan was still a teenager living in a West Bank village, an Israeli army intelligence officer had interviewed him as part of a routine updating of the IDF's profile of the area.

The Sowan family had settled there in the 1930s, a time when the revolt against the British mandate and the Jews had heated the blood of all Arabs. Everywhere there was violence; bloodshed had begotten bloodshed. Ismail's father had joined the Palestine Arab Party, organizing protests and raising nationalist feeling in his community. At first his fury had been against the British. But when they withdrew from Palestine in 1948, the new Jewish state became a prime target. Ismail's first remembered words were to chant hatred for the Jews.

Throughout his childhood the one word that he heard most often was "injustice." It was force-fed to him at school; it filled the conversations around the family dinner table: the terrible injustice done to his people, his family, himself.

Then, shortly after his fifteenth birthday, he witnessed a brutal attack on a bus filled with Jewish pilgrims on their way to Jerusalem. Women and children had been slaughtered by Arabs. That night Ismail had asked a question that would change forever his thinking: Supposing the Jews were entitled to defend what they had? All else had flowed from that: his steady alienation from the violence of his companions, his belief that Jew and Arab *could* live together, *must* live together. With this came a conviction that if he could do anything to achieve that, he would.

Two years later, barely seventeen, he had sat down and told the IDF intelligence officer what he still felt. The officer had first listened intently, then thoroughly questioned Ismail. How could he have turned his back on all his people's beliefs, which were like a tocsin sounding a single note: that *Arabs* were the wronged ones, that *they* must fight to the death for what *they* believed was right? The officer's questions had been many and Ismail's answers long.

The officer noted that, unlike other young Arabs living under Israeli rule, Sowan had few objections to the stringent security the army imposed. Refreshingly, the slightly built youth with an engaging smile seemed to understand why the Israelis had to do this. All that really concerned him was that the regular army clampdown meant he could not go to school in East Jerusalem to study his favorite subject, science.

Sowan's file made its way through the IDF intelligence community, flagged as someone worth further investigation, finally reaching the desk of a Mossad officer. He passed it over to recruitment.

Ismail Sowan was invited to travel to Tel Aviv, ostensibly to discuss his future education; he had recently applied to go to Jerusalem to study. Ismail was questioned for an entire afternoon. First his interrogator explored Ismail's knowledge of science and was satisfied with the answers. Then the whole Sowan family history was laid bare and Ismail's answers checked against those given to the IDF intelligence officer. Finally, Ismail was told what was on offer. Mossad would pay for his education, provided he came through its training course. He must also understand that if he spoke a word of any of this to anyone; his life would be in danger.

It was a standard warning, given to all Arabs Mossad recruited. But to the idealistic Ismail Sowan, it was the chance he had been waiting for: to bring together Jew and Arab.

Sowan went through all the interview processes in safe houses before being sent to the training school on the outskirts of Tel Aviv. He excelled in a number of subjects, showing a natural aptitude for computer skills and shaking off a tail. Not surprisingly, he scored high in the subjects dealing with Islam, and his paper on the role of the PLO in the Middle East conflict was sufficiently interesting to be shown to Mossad's then chief, Yitzhak Hofi.

On completion of his training, Sowan became a *bodel*, a courier between headquarters and Israel embassies from where katsas operated under diplomatic cover. He began to shuttle around the Mediterranean, regularly visiting Athens, Madrid, and Rome, carrying documents in diplomatic pouches. Occasionally he traveled to Bonn, Paris, and London. The chance to see the world and be paid for it—he was getting five hundred dollars a month—was an exciting feeling for someone barely out of his teens.

What Sowan did not realize was the documents had no importance. They were part of yet another test—to see if he made any attempt to show them to an Arab contact he might have in any of the cities he visited. During each trip Sowan was shadowed by other newly qualified Israeli-born Mossad officers, practicing their own skills at surveillance. The person Ismail handed over the documents to at some prearranged meeting in a café or hotel lobby was not, as he imagined, an Israeli diplomat, but a Mossad officer.

After weeks of spending his free time abroad strolling around Rome's Pantheon, visiting the Sistine Chapel, and exploring London's Oxford Street, he was ordered to go to Beirut and join the PLO.

Enlisting was easy. He simply walked into a PLO recruiting office in West Beirut. The recruiter was intelligent and extremely well informed in political matters. He spent time exploring Ismail's attitude toward the need for violence and whether Sowan was ready to eschew all previous affiliations—family and friends—in favor of becoming dependent upon the PLO for emotional support. He was told if he was accepted, it would mean a great change in his life: the organization would be his only protection against a hostile world. In return, the PLO would look to him to give unswerving loyalty.

His Mossad controller had prepared Sowan to give the correct responses, and he was sent to a training camp in Libya. There the indoctrination continued. He was taught in a dozen different ways that Israel was out to destroy the PLO, so it first must be destroyed. His tutors preached an acute hostility to everything and everyone outside the PLO. The lessons learned at the Mossad training school about role-playing were remembered; Sowan had spent many hours absorbing from his Mossad instructors the dynamics of terrorist groups, their likely behavior and tactics. In Libya, he was harangued that a murder was no more than a means to win liberation; a car bomb represented another step toward freedom; a kidnapping was a way to achieve justice. Ismail continued to show the skills Mossad had instilled. He accepted all the PLO training but never let it affect his core belief. He also displayed sufficient persistence, resourcefulness, and physical toughness to be singled out as more than a foot soldier. When he left the training camp, a place was found for him in the PLO operation echelons. Step by step he moved up the chain of command.

He met the organization's leaders, including Yasser Arafat; he traveled to PLO training camps throughout the Middle East. Back in Beirut he learned to live under the Israeli air force raids, avoiding hiding underground because of the risk the building would be bombed and collapse on top of him. But somehow he managed never to miss an appointment with his Mossad controller, who regularly slipped into Lebanon to collect Sowan's latest news.

Always he maintained his cover. When Ali Hassan Salameh was killed, Ismail Sowan led the chanting against the hated Israelis. Each time a PLO sniper shot an IDF soldier, he was among the cheerleaders. In all he said and did he appeared a fiercely committed militant.

In 1984, with Arafat driven out of Lebanon and regrouping in Tunis, the PLO sent Sowan to Paris to learn French. Nahum Admoni, who had by this time replaced Hofi, saw Sowan's transfer as a golden opportunity to have an agent on the inside of the PLO's burgeoning activities in Europe.

Arab ghettos in Paris's Eighteenth and Twentieth Arrondissements had become a haven for terrorists; in the narrow streets where people lived on the edge of legality, there was ready shelter for the gunmen and bomb makers. From here had been launched the attacks on Jewish restaurants, shops, and synagogues. It was in Paris that the first joint communiqué had been signed by various terrorist organizations pledging united support to attack Israeli targets in all Europe.

Mossad had fought back with its renowned ruthlessness. Kidons had entered the Arab enclaves and killed suspected terrorists in their beds. One had his throat cut from ear to ear, another his neck wrung like a chicken. But these were small victories. Mossad knew that the terrorists retained the upper hand, largely because they were so well directed by the PLO. The prospect of having his own man inside the organization's Paris operational headquarters was an exciting one for Admoni.

Within days of arriving in the French capital, Sowan made contact with his case officer, working out of the Israeli embassy at 3, rue Rabelais. He would only ever know him as Adam. They set up regular meeting points in cafés and on the Metro. Usually, Sowan would carry a copy of that day's newspaper in which he had inserted his information. Adam would have a similar copy in which was concealed Sowan's instructions and his monthly salary, now raised to one thousand dollars. In a technique they had both perfected at the Mossad training school, one would bump into the other and offer profuse apologies, and they would go their separate ways, having exchanged newspapers.

By this simple means, Mossad tried to regain the upper hand in a city that had long relished its reputation for offering sanctuary to political extremists—providing they left France alone. Only Mossad had chosen to break that understanding by launching an operation that delivered a blow to French pride that even now, almost twenty years later, France can neither forgive nor forget. The episode began three thousand miles away, at the Mediterranean mouth to the Suez Canal, designed by Ferdinand de Lesseps, the French visionary.

In a few shattering minutes on the afternoon of October 21, 1967, Israel had discovered its vulnerability to modern warfare. One of its flagships, an old World War II British destroyer renamed *Eilat*, on patrol off the Egyptian coast, was hit by three Russian Styx missiles fired from Port Said. Forty-seven Israeli sailors were killed and another 41 seriously injured out of a complement of 197 officers and men. The *Eilat* was sunk. It was not only the biggest sea disaster Israel had ever suffered, but the first time in the long history of naval warfare that a ship had been destroyed by long-range missile attack.

When the immediate magnitude of the calamity passed, Levi Eshkol's government ordered a crash program to provide its navy with a new kind of ship to replace the outdated *Eilat*. In weeks, designers had come up with a gunboat that would be fast, highly maneuverable, and equipped with electronic countermeasures to provide the precious seconds needed to take evasive action against any future missile attack. An order to build seven of the boats was placed with the Chantiers de Construction Mecanique de Normandie, CCM, shipyard in Cherbourg, France.

While they were being constructed, scientists at Dimona were manufacturing the missiles the boats would carry, together with the sophisticated equipment to be fitted once they arrived in Israel.

Matters progressed uneventfully at Cherbourg until President de Gaulle introduced a total French arms embargo after Israel commandos attacked the Beirut airport on December 26, 1968, and destroyed thirteen parked Lebanese aircraft—a reprisal for a Palestinian attack on an El Al Boeing 707 at the Athens airport two days previously. The embargo meant the gunboats would not be handed over to Israel.

The French response ended a decade-long alliance with Israel. It had been forged during the Algerian revolution, which had finally led to the colony's independence from France in 1962, and was partly rooted in a common hostility to Gamal Abdel Nasser's Egypt. During that time, Mossad had supplied intelligence about the anti-French FLN organization, and France had sold Israel arms and frontline Mirage fighter aircraft.

With the loss of Algeria, de Gaulle had quickly restored France's traditional links with other Arab countries, and the PLO was allowed to open an office in Paris. The Beirut airport raid was seen by de Gaulle as a very public slight to his demand that Israel should not carry out what the president called "revenge attacks" against its Arab neighbors.

The French arms embargo effectively meant Israel would no longer have sufficient replacement Mirage aircraft to dominate the Middle East's skies, or be able to effectively defend itself from seaborne attack. Perversely, the embargo came at a time when Israel was grappling with the price of its stunning victory in the Six Day War. In those few days in 1967, it had brought the West Bank, East Jerusalem, and the Gaza Strip under its control. With the land came almost a million Arabs, the great majority imbued with hatred for their conquerors.

For Meir Amit, the problem Israel faced "could not be over-stated. Within our borders were thousands of *mehabelim*—the He-brew for terrorist—and they had the support of the general Arab population who, at minimum, would give them succor and shelter: my first job was to increase Mossad's targeting and penetration of all Palestinian organizations."

Meir Amit was told by Israel's new prime minister, Golda Meir, to devise a plan to get the completed boats out of France. He would recall: "The first suggestion was we should sail into Cherbourg with sufficient armed sailors and just take the boats and head back for Israel. Moshe Dayan, then minister of defense, sat on that—hard. He correctly pointed out that the international reaction would create huge repercussions and see Israel branded a thief. Whatever we did had to be done legally. We had to come up with a watertight right to sail out of French territorial waters. Once we were on the high seas, it would be a different matter."

The legality of what was to follow would be in the eyes of the beholder. Despite Dayan's insistence on the letter of the law being obeyed, what was contemplated was pure and simple trickery.

By November 1969, Meir Amit had the first stage of Operation Noah's Ark in place. A London-based firm of lawyers had been briefed by Israel's largest shipping company, Maritime Fruit—which freighted produce around the world—to register a new firm named Starboat, after the Star of David. Its principal shareholder was Mila Brenner, a director of Maritime Fruit. The other share-holders were proxies for Meir Amit. The second part of the oper-ation went equally smoothly. For months Admiral Mordechai Limon, the Israeli navy liaison officer at Cherbourg for the gunboat project, had been discussing compensation with the shipyard for breach of contract; each time the French came close to an agree-ment, Limon had found a new point to argue. On November 10, he informed the shipyard that Israel was once more ready to discuss the matter.

In Tel Aviv, Mila Brenner had contacted one of the most re-spected shipping magnates in the world, Ole Martin Siem, based in Oslo. He agreed to join the board of Starboat for the specific pur-pose of purchasing the gunboats.

Limon, with a sleight of hand worthy of a card player, made his move. On November 11, he met with shipyard officials. He listened to their improved offer of compensation and said he was still not satisfied. The officials were astonished; their new offer was a generous one. While they contemplated what to do next, Limon hurried to Paris. Waiting there was Ole Siem. After the two men met, Limon telephoned the shipyard officials to say he would be in touch with them "in a few days." Within the hour, Siem was seated in the office of General Louis Bonte, the French government's arms salesman. Siem said he had heard that there "are some gunboats for sale that can be converted to drill for oil."

Timing his intervention to perfection, Limon at that moment called Bonte to say he was in Paris and was ready to accept a final offer in compensation. The figure he proposed was the one the Cherbourg shipyard officials had offered. Bonte told Limon he was "in negotiation" and would call back. The general then turned to Siem and revealed the offer Limon had agreed to accept but said it was too high for the government to agree to pay. Siem promptly increased Limon's offer by 5 percent. Bonte called back Limon and said his offer was most agreeable. Bonte believed he had made a good deal in ridding France of a thorny problem. Israel would get its compensation and France would have made a 5 percent profit.

He only had two questions for Ole Siem. Were the boats going to Norway? Could Siem guarantee they would not be reexported after their oil-exploration activities? Siem gave an unequivocal guarantee on both counts. Bonte accepted that, to avoid press inquiries about the site of the oil fields—a sensitive commercial matter in an industry renowned for its secrecy—the removal of the boats from Cherbourg would be done discreetly. A departure date was set for Christmas Eve, 1969, when Cherbourg would be celebrating the start of the holiday season.

There was still a month to go—and Meir Amit was only too well aware that that was more than enough time for things to go wrong. There would be a need to provide 120 Israeli sailors to crew the boats for the three-thousand-mile voyage from Cherbourg to Haifa. To send that many men at one time would most certainly alert the French security service. Once more the inventive Meir Amit had the answer.

He decided only two sailors at a time would travel together to cities all over Europe before going on to Cherbourg. The sailors were instructed not to stay in the port's hotels for more than a night before moving to another one. They all traveled on Israeli passports so that, in case they were caught, they could not be charged with possessing forged travel documents. Nevertheless, Meir Amit knew the risks were still high. "It just needed one suspicious French policeman to ask why so many Jews were coming to Cherbourg for Christmas and the whole operation could be blown."

By December 23, the sailors had all arrived in Cherbourg. Scattered around the town, they listened to the incessant carols; some who had been born and raised in Jerusalem joined in the singing.

In Tel Aviv, a relieved Meir Amit watched other problems come and go. The question of providing enough supplies for eight days at sea had been solved by the operation's supply officer visiting every shop in Cherbourg. But whenever shopkeepers pressed on him Christmas *jambon*, he politely refused. The quarter of a million liters of fuel had been smuggled on board in drums and hidden belowdecks. The one great imponderable was the weather. The boats would have to sail across the Bay of Biscay in winter conditions that could sink them. Meir Amit would recall that in Tel Aviv: "What we prayed for was Dunkirk weather. We had sent a meteorologist to Cherbourg and he monitored every forecast out of England, France, in Cherbourg and Spain."

The hours ticked slowly by until finally it was Christmas Eve. The forecast in Cherbourg was for rain gusting out of the southwest. Nevertheless, the order was given to sail at 8:30 that night. By 7:30 P.M. the crews were all on board. But the weather worsened. A new departure time was set for 10:30 P.M. That came and went, halted again by the weather. From Tel Aviv came urgent coded signals: Sail no matter what the conditions.

In Cherbourg, the ranking Israeli naval officer ignored the pressure; for him the lives of his men were more important at that moment. In his command boat, he sat silently watching the meteorologist feverishly studying his weather charts. At midnight the weatherman announced: "The winds will drop and veer northerly in two hours. They will not be so strong and be behind us. We can go."

At exactly 2:30 A.M. on Christmas Day, the boats' engines started and the crafts headed slowly out to sea. Seven days later, on New Year's Day, they sailed into Haifa Harbor.

Among those waiting on the quayside was Meir Amit. For him the New Year could not have had a better start. But he also knew President Charles de Gaulle would never forgive Israel for what had happened.

So it had proven to be the case. When Mossad came hunting Middle Eastern terrorists in Paris and other French cities, its katsas were as closely watched as any terrorist by the French security service. Worse, pro-Arab officers in the SDECE often tipped off the PLO that Mossad was about to launch a counterstrike. Too often a terrorist would slip away.

The most notorious of these was Ilich Ramirez Sanchez, whose activities had earned him the nickname "Carlos the Jackal." In Paris, he was the proverbial gun for hire in the service of one of the PLO breakaway groups based in Syria. His exploits had made him an admired figure in the Marxist underground press that flourished in Europe. Women found his playboy habits thrilling— the more so when he seemed able to flit at will in and out of the traps Mossad set to kill him. One day he would be on the Riviera sunning himself with a girl, the next he would be spotted in London with a group of Middle Eastern terrorists, helping them lay their plans against other Arab groups and, of course, Israel. Carlos and they operated without interference from Britain's police and intelligence services on the understanding they would do no harm to British citizens. By the time Mossad was in a position to kill Carlos, he was back on the Continent, or had flown to Damascus, Baghdad, or other Arab countries to stoke up further mischief making.

Keeping track of Carlos long enough for Mossad to be able to assassinate him had become yet another task assigned to Ismail Sowan during his time in Paris.

His overall contribution to the war Mossad waged in France was considerable, allowing its katsas and kidons to claim spectacular successes: a PLO forgery factory producing false documents was firebombed; weapons caches were destroyed; couriers were intercepted and murdered; explosives smuggled in from Eastern Europe were blown up; in a dozen and more ways, Mossad fought fire with fire as a result of the intelligence Sowan provided.

In January 1984, Sowan was told by Adam, his Mossad controller, he was being sent to England, where he would pose as a mature student studying for a science degree. His new task would be to penetrate the PLO in London and discover everything he could about its active service unit, Force 17. It was now run by Abdul-Rahid Mustapha, who was using Britain as a base. Mustapha was on Mossad's assassination list.

Ismail Sowan told the PLO office manager in Paris he had completed his French studies—a French sayan had produced a forged diploma to confirm this in case he was asked for proof, though no one did—and he wished to go to England to continue his quest for an engineering science degree. He even managed to slip in a reminder that the qualification would make him "even more useful when it came to bomb making."

The prospect of adding another bomb maker to the PLO's team of such experts was always welcome, and never more so than in 1984. The PLO leadership needed to show the Palestinians in the West Bank and Gaza Strip that they were not forgotten. Tens of thousands were suffering increasing hardship under Israeli occupation; they could not understand why Yasser Arafat did not do more to help them in a practical way: rhetoric was one thing, action another.

Mossad knew that Arafat was under growing pressure to support the peace overtures that Egypt's president, Hosni Mubarak, had started to make toward Israel. In Syria, the always unpredictable regime had decided to cool its relationship with the various Palestinian factions, and had imprisoned hundreds of its fighters. President Assad wanted to show the Americans he was not the troublemaker the world believed.

That only increased the feeling among the rank-and-file PLO in the camps that they would be cast adrift by the Arab world, shunted from place to place, left to fend for themselves. There was ugly talk of being betrayed by their own leadership. The Israelis continued to exploit this, broadcasting throughout the occupied territories that the PLO had assets of $5 billion, invested all over the world. Arafat had also become the victim of a separate smear campaign, created by Mossad's experts in psychological warfare, which claimed he used some of the money to satisfy his liking for nubile young boys. The rumor was fed into the refugee camps and though not widely believed, it did have some effect. Arafat, in a shrewd move, ordered the seventeen PLO offices to leak a story that he had a healthy appetite for women—which was true.

For the PLO office manager in Paris, the idea that Sowan would use his hoped-for degree to become a bomb maker was indeed welcome news, and sufficient reason to provide Ismail's train fare to England and a week's living expenses. Sowan was also given five hundred pounds by Adam and told he must find a job to pay for his studies in Britain to avoid any suspicion.

Ismail arrived in London on a blustery day in February 1984, traveling on a Jordanian passport provided by Mossad. He had a second Canadian passport concealed in the false bottom of his suitcase. He had been told to use it only if he had to leave Britain in a hurry. Concealed with the passport was Mossad's briefing about Abdul-Rahid Mustapha and the Force 17 he commanded.

The unit had originally been created as Yasser Arafat's personal security force. Its name came from the number of Arafat's telephone extension in the old PLO headquarters in Beirut. At one stage in Lebanon, Force 17 had grown to a ragtag army of over a thousand fighters; one of its units had been the notorious Black September group that had carried out the massacre of the Israeli athletes at the Munich Olympics. Shortly before the PLO was forced to leave Lebanon and resettle in Tunis, Force 17's original commander, Ali Hassan Salameh, was killed by the car bomb arranged by Rafi Eitan. In Tunis, Arafat had faced hard realities. He was not only hunted by Mossad, but had become increasingly threatened by other Arab extremists. Abu Nidal, who claimed he was the authentic voice of the armed struggle, said there could be no victory until Arafat was eliminated. Arafat's response had been to restructure Force 17 into a close-knit unit with a dual purpose: to continue to protect him, and to launch well-prepared attacks against its enemies, beginning with Israel. Mustapha was given command of Force 17. In Tunis, his men were trained by both Chinese and Russian Special Forces in guerrilla warfare. In 1983, Mustapha began to travel to Britain to recruit mercenaries.

London was awash with former SAS men and regular army veterans who had seen service in Northern Ireland and were looking for a new outlet for their killing skills. The pay as PLO instructors was good and many of the mercenaries had a strong anti-Semitic attitude. A number signed on and traveled to Tunisia to work in PLO training camps. Other instructors were drawn from the ranks of former French foreign legionnaires and, at one stage, even included a former CIA officer, Frank Terpil, who would later become briefly involved with Mehmet Ali Agca, the fanatic who shot Pope John Paul II.

For a whole year Mustapha had slipped in and out of Britain without MI5 or the Special Branch even realizing who he was. When Mossad informed them, the only action taken was for an MI5 officer to remind the PLO office in London it would be closed and its staff expelled at the first hint they were engaged in terrorist activity against Britain. But they could continue to fulminate against Israel.

An intriguing sidelight to the propaganda war came when Bassam Abu-Sharif, then Arafat's chief media spokesman, was invited to meet novelist Jeffrey Archer. The PLO man would remember that Archer had explained "how we should develop and manage our media relations, how to organize our political activity, how to set about building contacts with British politicians and mobilize public opinion. I am extremely impressed."

That meeting ensured that Archer's name found its way onto Mossad's computers.

To the furious Israelis it appeared Mustapha was under the protection of the British authorities and that any attempt to deal with him in Britain could have repercussions for Mossad.

Ismail Sowan's task was to try to lead Mustapha into a trap outside the country, preferably in the Middle East, where waiting Mossad kidons could execute him. Sowan had been told by Adam in Paris he would work under the guidance of his Mossad controllers based at the Israeli embassy in London. The first was Arie Regev. The other was Jacob Barad, who looked after Israel's commercial interests. A third London-based katsa, not working under diplomatic cover, was Bashar Samara, who would be Sowan's main contact. Samara had asked a sayan employed by a London house-letting agency to rent an apartment for Sowan in the Maida Vale district of the city.

A few days after arriving in London, Sowan set up his first contact with Samara. The couple met beneath the Eros statue in Piccadilly Circus. Each carried a copy of the *Daily Mirror*, newly acquired by Robert Maxwell. Using the technique of exchanging newspapers that had worked in Paris, Sowan obtained his six hundred pounds first month's salary, together with instructions on how to find office work at the PLO office in London.

Many of those who worked there wanted to be on the cutting edge of the action, such as carrying messages to various PLO cells around Europe, flying to the Organization's Tunis headquarters with particularly important information, and afterward waiting for hours for the chance just to glimpse Arafat. These young, committed revolutionaries had no interest in routine office work, clerking or filing, reading the newspapers, manning the phones. When Sowan volunteered for this work, he was promptly taken on at the London office.

Within a few days he had met Mustapha. Over tiny cups of sweet mint tea, they quickly developed a rapport. Both had a common background of having lived through the Israeli bombardment of Beirut. They had walked the same streets with the same quickness of eye and mind, passed the same gutted buildings pocked with so many holes they looked like latticework. Both had slept in a different bed each night and waited for the dawn when, over the crackling loudspeakers, the muezzin called the faithful to prayer. Each of them had taken his turn on PLO checkpoint duty in Beirut, waving the Palestinian ambulances through, stopping everyone else, and only running for cover when the whine of Israeli aircraft once more filled their ears. They had laughed over the memory of the old Beirut saying, "If you hear the bomb explode, you're still alive." So many memories; the cries of the dead and dying, the wail of the women, their looks of helpless hatred at the sky.

Sowan and Mustapha spent a whole day in communion with their past. Finally, Mustapha asked what Sowan was doing in London. To further his education so as to better serve the PLO, Ismail replied. In turn, he asked Mustapha what had brought him to England.

The question unleashed a flow of revelations. Mustapha described Force 17 exploits: how its commandos had been about to hijack an Israeli aircraft filled with German tourists when Arafat canceled the mission for fear of antagonizing German opinion. But

Mustapha had carried the war against Israel into Cyprus and Spain. Ismail knew that everything his companion boasted of would only make Mossad more determined to kill him.

They agreed to meet in a few days at Hyde Park's Speakers' Corner, London's traditional venue for all kinds of opinion to be freely aired. Ismail Sowan called the special number he had been given if he had urgent news. Bashar Samara answered. They arranged to meet in Regent Street. Strolling among the lunchtime office workers, Sowan reported what Mustapha had told him. Samara said he would be at Speakers' Corner to photograph Mustapha and then tail him wherever he went.

Mustapha did not keep the appointment. It would be weeks before Sowan saw him again. By that time, Ismail had been accepted as a student by a college in Bath, the spa resort. Twice a week he traveled to London to visit the PLO office to carry out his clerking. On one trip, Mustapha was there.

Once more the two men spoke over endless cups of mint tea. From his briefcase, Mustapha produced an illustrated book recording the history of Force 17. He boasted over one hundred thousand copies were to be distributed to Palestinians. Leafing through it, Ismail saw a picture of Mustapha taken in Lebanon. With a flourish, Mustapha signed it and presented the book to Ismail. Once more they arranged to meet, but Mustapha again broke the appointment.

Meanwhile, Sowan had handed over the book to Samara at what became a regular meeting place, the Bath railway station. The katsa would travel down on one train and return to London on the next, taking with him anything Sowan had learned at the PLO office and handing over his monthly stipend of six hundred pounds to the informer.

For almost a year their relationship continued in this manner. By then, Sowan had met an English girl named Carmel Greensmith. She agreed to marry him. But on the eve of the ceremony, Sowan had still not settled on a best man.

Making another trip to the PLO office, he again met Mustapha, who, as usual, did not explain where he had been. Mustapha had with him a bundle of tear sheets from the London-published Arab newspaper, *Al-Qabas*. Each page contained a biting cartoon mocking Yasser Arafat. The newspaper was subsidized by the Kuwaiti ruling family, long an enemy of the PLO.

The cartoons were the work of the Arab world's most celebrated political artist, Naji Al-Ali. Based in London, he had waged a one-man war against Arafat, portraying the PLO leader as venal, self-serving, and politically inept. The cartoons had established *Al-Qabas* as the voice of opposition to Arafat.

Mustapha threw the tear sheets on the table and said Al-Ali deserved to die and his Kuwaiti paymasters taught a lesson.

Sowan smiled noncommittally. Mossad welcomed anything that undermined Arafat's position. He also brought up a matter of more immediate personal concern, finding a best man for his wedding. Mustapha immediately offered himself for the role. They embraced each other in Arab fashion. That may well have been the moment when Ismail Sowan wished he could somehow remove himself from the clutches of Mossad.

In Tel Aviv, Nahum Admoni had begun to wonder how long it would be before MI5 discovered the truth about the eight forged British passports left in the telephone booth in Germany in July 1986. Shimon Peres, no admirer of Mossad, was, in the closing months of his coalition government, asking pointed questions. The prime minister was saying the debacle would ruin Israel's relationship with the Thatcher government; that it was better to make a clean breast of the matter, in keeping with the well-known Peres sentiment, "The sooner said, the sooner mended."

Admoni opposed the idea. It could lead to MI5 and the Special Branch beginning an investigation into just what else Mossad was doing in Britain. That could result in Ismail Sowan being expelled; he had proven to be a mine of useful information. Further, to admit the truth about the passports would be to reveal a piece of incompetent bungling by Mossad.

The passports had been intended for the Israeli embassy in Bonn. The job of couriering them from Tel Aviv had been given to a bodel who was new to the job and had never been to Bonn before. He had driven around the city for a while, not wishing to ask directions for fear of drawing attention to himself. Finally he had used the pay phone to call the embassy. An official had berated him for his tardiness. Either through panic or sheer carelessness, the bodel had left the carrier bag in the phone booth. Arriving at the embassy he realized his mistake but, even more panic-stricken, he couldn't remember exactly the location of the street from where he had made the call. Accompanied by the embassy's furious head of security, they had finally found the phone box. The bag was gone. The bodel had been posted to the Negev. But the problem of the passports had continued to trouble Admoni. The Foreign Office, through Britain's Tel Aviv ambassador, was raising the matter with the Israeli government.

One of the passports had been intended for Sowan's use to enable him to travel more easily between London and Tel Aviv; a British passport meant he would be subjected to fewer checks by immigration at Heathrow than with his Canadian one.

In the time Sowan had been in London, he had made occasional trips to Israel to visit his family; it was part of his cover to do so. To them he was still a PLO activist. He played the role so convincingly that his elder brother, Ibrahim, finally warned him the Israelis would arrest him. He jokingly suggested Ismail should preempt matters by offering to work for the Organization. Ismail pretended to be horrified at the idea and returned to London to continue his work.

Soon matters were taking an unexpected turn. Sowan's new wife had urged her husband to accept a post as a researcher at Humberside College in Hull. For her it would mean more money to supplement his office work for the PLO. She knew nothing of her husband's relationship with Mossad, or the six hundred pounds it paid him every month. For Ismail the move to Hull could be an opportunity to escape the ever-increasing demands of his Mossad controller.

Like many an informer who had taken the Mossad shekel, Ismail Sowan had become badly frightened by the risks he faced. After performing his duties as best man, Mustapha had become even friendlier. He regularly dropped in to see Ismail and his wife, bringing gifts from the Middle East for the couple. Over dinner, Mustapha told stories of how he had dealt with the latest enemy of the PLO. Over the months, he boasted of killing several "traitors to the cause." Sowan had sat mesmerized, hoping "my heart beat wasn't thumping too loud." He was becoming equally frightened after his meetings with Samara; the katsa was asking him to access the PLO office computer and photocopy sensitive documents; he was also to try to arrange to go on "holiday" with Mustapha to

Cyprus, where a kidon team would be waiting. So far, Sowan had managed to come up with excuses—he was never able to be alone in the computer room, or the pressure of his studies meant he had to forgo holidays—but he had sensed a growing threat behind Samara's demands. In Hull, he hoped he would be in less contact with both Mustapha and Samara, and be allowed to have an academic life without further pressures. Mossad had very different plans for him.

On Friday, March 13, 1987, Mossad's headquarters on King Saul Boulevard buzzed with the rumor that Admoni was expecting an important visitor. Shortly before noon, the MI6 liaison officer was escorted up to the director general's ninth-floor office. Their meeting was short. Admoni was told that MI6 was satisfied that the forged passports found in Germany were the work of Mossad. A Special Branch officer who had been involved in the operation recalled in June 1997 how "the man from Six just walked in, said 'Good morning,' declined a cup of tea or coffee, and spelled it out. He then nodded and walked out again. It probably took less than a minute for him to deliver the message."

In London, the Foreign Office called in the Israeli ambassador and delivered a strong protest accompanied by a demand that such behavior would not happen again. The only small comfort for Admoni was that no one had mentioned Ismail Sowan.

In the early evening of July 22, 1987, Ismail Sowan turned on the BBC early-evening television news in his Hull apartment. He had not heard from Mossad since April, when Bashar Samara had traveled to Hull for a meeting at the city's railway station and told Sowan to keep a low profile until further notice—unless Mustapha made contact.

Now, the face of the man Mustapha had said deserved to die filled the screen; Naji Al-Ali, the cartoonist, had been shot as he left the offices of *Al-Qabas* in London. The gunman had fired once and disappeared. The bullet had entered through the cartoonist's cheek and lodged in his brain. Sowan's first reaction was that the assailant was not from Mossad or Force 17. Both organizations used the same professional way of killing: several shots in the head and the upper body. This looked like an amateur attack. The TV report said a massive police hunt was under way and that the cartoonist's colleagues were hinting the attack was because of the unnamed "powerful enemies" Naji had made.

Sowan remembered a previous conversation with Mustapha. He became increasingly certain Yasser Arafat had ordered the shooting. He suddenly wondered if he was the only person Mustapha had confided in about the need for the cartoonist to die. Sowan decided it would be best for him and his wife to fly to Tel Aviv. But even as they packed, there was a knock on the front door. Sowan would recall:

"The man had two suitcases. He said Mustapha needed to hide them urgently. When I said I wanted to know what was inside, he just smiled and told me not to worry. 'He who asks no questions is told no lies,' was all he would say. When he was gone, I looked inside the cases. They were full of arms and explosives: enough Semtex to blow up the Tower of London; AK-47s, pistols, detonators, the works."

Ismail called the special Mossad contact number in London. It had been disconnected. He telephoned the Israeli embassy. He was told that Arie Regev and Jacob Barad were not available. He asked to speak to Bashar Samara. The voice at the other end of the phone asked him to wait. A new voice came on the line. When Ismail gave his name, the voice said, "This is a good time for a holiday in the sun." The words were a signal for Sowan to travel to Tel Aviv.

There, in the Sheraton Hotel, he met Jacob Barad and Bashar Samara. He explained what he had done after discovering the contents of the suitcase. They told him to wait while they reported to their superiors. Later that night, Samara returned and told Sowan to fly to London on the next plane. When he arrived he would find everything had been taken care of.

Not suspecting what lay ahead, Sowan flew to London on August 4, 1987. He was arrested by armed Special Branch officers at Heathrow and charged with the murder of Naji Al-Ali. When he protested he was a Mossad agent, the officers laughed at him. Sowan had become as expendable as the cartoonist who had died after two weeks clinging to life in hospital. Sowan would be sacrificed in an attempt to regain favor with the Thatcher government. The presence of the arms cache in Sowan's apartment would destroy any effort he made to claim he was employed by Mossad. The arms had been brought there by a Mossad sayan.

In London, Arie Regev had turned over to MI5—who passed it on to Scotland Yard—all the "evidence" Mossad had "accumulated" of Sowan's "involvement" with terrorism. The file detailed how Mossad had tailed Sowan through the Middle East, Europe, and Britain, never able to obtain enough proof until now. The moment the arms cache had been discovered, Mossad decided, "in the name of common security," to turn in Sowan.

The decision to do so was a grim reminder of Mossad's unwritten law of expediency. A great deal of time and money had been invested by the service in training and supporting Sowan in the field. But when the time came, all that counted for nothing when weighed against the greater need for Mossad to cover its own tracks in Britain. Sowan would be the sacrificial victim, served up to the British as an example of the kind of terrorist Mossad was always warning about. There would be a loss, of course: Sowan had done a good enough job—even if he had failed to deliver all that was asked of him. But the arms cache had been too good an opportunity to miss. It would wreck the PLO's relationship with the Thatcher government and allow Israel to present Yasser Arafat as the double-dealing terrorist Mossad still said he was. And there would always be another Ismail Sowan ready to be seduced by men in Israel who reveled in broken promises.

For a full week Mossad relaxed, convinced that whatever Sowan told his British interrogators could be shrugged off.

But Admoni had not counted on Sowan's desperate efforts to stay out of jail. He gave Special Branch interrogators detailed descriptions of his controllers as well as everything he had been taught by Mossad. The police gradually realized Ismail could be telling the truth. The MI6 liaison officer in Tel Aviv was recalled. He questioned Sowan. Everything he said about Mossad's headquarters and its methods fitted what the officer knew. The full extent of Mossad's role began to unravel.

Regev, Barad, and Samara were expelled from Britain. The Israeli embassy in London issued a defiant statement: "We regret that Her Majesty's Government saw fit to take measures of the kind adopted.

Israel did not act against British interests. The struggle against terrorism was its one and only motive."

Telling the truth did not save Ismail Sowan. In June 1988, he was sentenced to eleven years' imprisonment for possessing firearms on behalf of a terrorist organization.

Five years after the expulsion of the three katsas, which had effectively closed down Mossad's station in Britain, the service was back. By 1998, five katsas worked out of the Israeli embassy in Kensington, liaising with MI5 and the Special Branch in targeting Iranian factions in Britain.

Three years previously, in December 1994, Ismail Sowan had been released from Full Sutton Prison, handed back his Jordanian passport, and deported on a plane to Amman. The last anyone saw of him was walking out of the airport carrying the suitcase Mossad had given him all those years ago when he had traveled to London. But its false bottom had been removed.

From the desert kingdom he had a ringside seat at the gathering storm in the Persian Gulf, which was preceded by a change of watch commander on the Mossad bridge. Nahum Admoni's eight years at the helm finally ended on the eve of the Jewish New Year, Rosh Hashanah. Into his place stepped Shabtai Shavit, who inherited a series of failures: the Pollard affair, Irangate, and, of course, those blank, forged British passports found in that Frankfurt phone box, which had heralded the end of Admoni's tenure. But, for his successor, beyond Jordan more than a sandstorm blew. Saddam Hussein had finally decided the time had come to take on the world.

CHAPTER 16

.

SPIES IN THE SAND

On December 2, 1990, well to the south of Baghdad, a figure in the dirty robes of a desert dweller lay motionless just below the lip of a wadi. It was dawn and the sand ice-cold; during the night the temperature had dropped to well below zero. The man's head was covered with a sheep's wool *hupta*, a hat that identified him as a tribesman of the Sarami, the oldest of the Islamic Sufi sects, who roamed the vast Iraqi desert and whose fanaticism was matched by a code of honor unequaled by other tribes'. But the man's loyalty lay some six hundred miles to the west, in Israel; he was a katsa.

His clothes came from a Mossad storeroom where garments from all over the world were kept and regularly updated. Most were obtained by sayanim and delivered to local Israeli embassies and sent on to Tel Aviv in diplomatic bags. Other garments were brought out of hostile Arab countries by pro-Israeli visitors. A few were actually made by the wardrobe mistress who presided over the storeroom. Over the years she and her small team of seamstresses had developed a reputation for detail, even using the right sewing cotton for adjustments.

The katsa's code name—Shalom—came from a list of aliases kept on file in the Operations Division; Rafi Eitan had introduced the idea of a list after the Eichmann operation. Shalom Weiss had been one of the best forgers in Mossad before he had joined the team to help capture Adolf Eichmann. Shalom Weiss had died of cancer in 1963 but his name lived on and had been used on several occasions by katsas. Only a handful of senior IDF officers, Shabtai Shavit, and Shalom's own section head knew why he was in the desert.

In August 1990, Saddam Hussein had invaded Kuwait, an action that became the precursor to the eventual Gulf War. Iraq's move against Kuwait had been a spectacular intelligence failure for all the West's services; not one had anticipated it would happen. Mossad had tried to verify reports that Saddam had actually stockpiled chemical weapons at secret sites south of Baghdad, which would place the weapons well within range not only of Kuwait City but also cities in Israel.

Within Mossad there remained doubt as to whether Iraq possessed the rockets needed to fire the warheads. Gerald Bull had been removed from the scene, and his supergun, after its initial testing, according to U.S. satellite surveillance, was now in bits. Shavit's analysts suggested that even if Saddam possessed the warheads, there was no certainty they were actually filled with chemicals; he had done that kind of posturing before.

Shabtai Shavit, displaying the caution of a new man in charge, had said that on what he had been told, to raise the alarm could only create needless panic. Shalom had been given the mission to discover the truth. He had carried out several previous operations in Iraq, once going into Baghdad, where he had posed as a Jordanian businessman. In Baghdad there had been sayanim who could have helped him. But here, in the vast, empty desert, he had to depend on his own resources—and the skills his instructors had once more tested.

Shalom had undergone survival training in the Negev Desert, mastering "memory training," how to recognize the target even in a sandstorm; and "self-image protection," how to blend in with his surroundings. He wore his garments day and night to give them a lived-in look. He spent a full day on the shooting range, demonstrating instinctive and rapid-aim firing for close-quarter combat. An hour was spent with a pharmacist learning when to use his emergency medicine in the desert; a morning was devoted to memorizing the maps that would lead him across the sands.

To all his instructors he was identified only by a number; they neither demeaned him nor offered praise. They gave Shalom no clue as to how he was doing; they were like robots. Part of each day was given over to testing his sheer physical stamina with a forced march in the fierce noon heat, carrying a rucksack weighted with rocks. He was constantly on the clock, but no one told him if he was meeting his times. Another test was to haul him out of an ongoing exercise to get his responses to such questions as: "A Bedouin child spots you: do you kill her to preserve your mission?" "You are about to be taken prisoner. Do you surrender or kill yourself?" "You come across a wounded Israeli soldier who has been on another mission: do you stop to help or leave him, knowing he will certainly die?" Shalom's answers were not intended to be definitive: the questions were designed as another way to test his ability to decide under pressure. How long did he take to respond? Was he flustered or confident in making it?

He ate only the food he would live on in the desert: concentrates that he mixed with the brackish water he could expect to find at watering places in the sand. He had attended a one-to-one class with a Mossad psychiatrist on handling stress and how to relax. The doctor also wanted to make sure Shalom still thought for himself, so that he could draw on the right amount of resourcefulness and ruthlessness for the unpredictable situations he would encounter in the field. Aptitude tests determined his present emotional stability and his self-confidence. He was assessed to see if he had developed signs of becoming a "lone wolf," a worrying trait that had ended other promising careers for katsas.

A dialect coach sat with him for hours, listening to him repeat the Sufis' patois. Already fluent in Farsi and Arabic, Shalom quickly grasped the dialect of the tribesmen. Every night he was driven to a different part of the Negev to sleep. Burrowing into the ground, he would rest for a short while, never more than dozing, then move to another place to avoid the instructors he knew were hunting him. Discovery would almost certainly mean his mission would be either postponed for further training, or assigned to another katsa.

Shalom had escaped detection. On the evening of November 25, 1990, he had boarded a CH-536 Sikorsky helicopter of the Israel Defense Forces Central Regional command.

Its crew had also been separately trained for the mission. In another area of the Negev base, they had practiced low-level weaving through an aerial obstacle course in the dark. Turbines had blasted the chopper with sand so that they could improve their techniques for flying through the unstable air currents of the Iraqi desert. The pilot had continuously stayed as close to the ground as he could without crashing. In another exercise, instructors had straddled the landing struts, firing weapons at target silhouettes, while the pilot kept his machine steady. In between, the crew had studied their flight path.

Only their commanding officer, Major General Danny Yatom, knew the route they would fly to the border with Iraq. Yatom had been a member of the elite Sayeret Matkal commando unit, Israel's Green Berets, who in 1972 had successfully stormed a hijacked Belgium airliner at Tel Aviv airport. Other commandos in the operation included Benyamin Netanyahu. The friendship with Israel's future prime minister would lead to Yatom later being given command of Mossad, a position that would also end his relationship with Netanyahu. But that was all in the future.

On that December morning, while Shalom continued to peer out over the rim of the wadi, he had no inkling that the long and dangerous journey that had brought him deep into hostile territory had been decided in a conference room in the Kirya, the Israel Defense Forces headquarters in Tel Aviv.

As well as Yatom, present had been Amnon Shahak, the head of Aman, military intelligence, and Shabtai Shavit. They had convened to discuss the latest information from a deep-penetration informer inside Iran's terrorist network in Europe. The person—only Shavit knew if the informer was a man or a woman—was known by the letter "I." All that Shahak and Yatom would have deduced was that the informer must have access to the fortified complex on the third floor of the Iranian embassy in Bonn, Germany. The complex contained six offices and a communications room. The entire area had been reinforced to withstand a bomb blast and it was permanently manned by twenty Revolutionary Guards, whose task it was to coordinate Iran's terrorist activities in western Europe. They had recently tried to ship a ton of Semtex and electronic detonators out of Lebanon into Spain. The shipment was to replace explosives for a number of pro-Iranian terrorist groups in European countries. On a tip-off from Mossad, Spanish customs had boarded the ship as it sailed into territorial waters.

But by the summer of 1990, Iran was also providing through the Bonn embassy huge cash disbursements to increase the influence of Islamic fundamentalism and terrorism in Europe. The amounts involved were all the more surprising given that Iran had been economically crippled by its eight-year war with Iraq, which had ended in a cease-fire in 1988.

But on that November day in the Kirya's guarded conference room, it was not a new threat from Iran that the double agent had discovered. It was one from Iraq. "I" had obtained a copy of a detailed Iraqi battle plan stolen by Iran's own secret intelligence service from Baghdad military headquarters outlining how Scud missiles would be used to launch chemical and biological weapons against Iran, Kuwait, and Israel.

Uppermost in the mind of each man in the conference room was one question: Could the information be trusted? "I" had proven to be sound in all the previous data he had provided. But, important though the information had been, it paled against what "I" had now sent. Yet was the battle plan part of a plot by Iranian intelligence to drive Israel into launching a preemptive attack against Iraq? Had "I" been unmasked and was he being used by Iran?

Trying to answer that question was also fraught with risk. It would need time to brief a katsa to make contact with "I." It might be weeks before that was possible; bringing an informer out of deep cover was a slow and delicate process. And if "I" proved to have remained loyal, his safety could have still been jeopardized. Yet, the consequences of acting on the Iraqi document without checking could be calamitous for Israel. A preemptive strike would certainly lead to an Iraqi retaliation—and could destroy the coalition being laboriously cobbled together in Washington to drive Saddam out of Kuwait. Many of its Arab members were likely to support Iraq against Israel.

The only way to discover the truth about the stolen battle plan had been to send Shalom into Iraq. Skimming above the desert, his helicopter had flown across a strip of Jordan in the deep black of night. Coated with stealth paint, its engine noise muffled, the Sikorsky was virtually undetectable to even the most sophisticated Jordanian radars. Flying on silent mode so that its rotor blades made almost no sound, the helicopter had reached its dropping point at the Iraqi border.

Shalom had disappeared into the night. Despite all his training, nothing had quite prepared him for that moment: he was on his own; to survive he had to respect his surroundings. A desert was like no other place on earth for surprises. A sandstorm could appear in moments, changing the landscape, burying him alive. One kind of sky meant one thing, another something quite different. He would do his own weather forecasting; he would have to do everything by himself and learn to let his ears adjust to the silence, to remember that the silence of the desert was like no other. And always he must remember that his first mistake could be his last.

Three days after leaving the helicopter, on that cold December dawn, Shalom lay prostrate in the Iraqi wadi. Beneath his *hupta* he wore goggles; their lenses gave the dark landscape a crepuscular definition. The only weapon Shalom carried was one the Sarami would expect to find on him: a hunting knife. He had been taught to kill with that in a number of ways. Whether he would bother to use it against a superior force, he did not know—any more than whether he could turn it on himself. Or simply commit suicide with the lethal pill he carried. Since Eli Cohen's torture and death, a katsa operating in Iran, Iraq, Yemen, or Syria had been given the right to kill himself rather than fall into the hands of barbaric interrogators. Meanwhile, Shalom continued to watch and wait.

The nomads in their camps half a mile away beyond the wadi had begun to recite their first prayers of the day. Already the bark of their dogs carried faintly on the wind, but the animals would not venture beyond the camp until the sun was above the horizon: behavioral patterns were among the first lessons Shalom had learned in desert survival.

According to the information he had been given at his briefing, the convoy should appear between the encampment and the hills to his left. To an untutored eye, the track they would travel over was invisible. To Shalom it was as clear as a well-signposted road: the tiny rumplings of sand were created by desert moles burrowing between vehicle tracks.

The sun was high when the convoy finally appeared: a Scud missile launcher and its support vehicle. It was still about half a mile away when it stopped. Shalom began to photograph and time what he saw.

It took the Iraqi crew fifteen minutes to launch the Scud. It rose in an arc and disappeared over the horizon. Minutes later the convoy was moving at speed toward the hills. In a few minutes that Scud could have hit Tel Aviv or any other Israeli city if the launch had not been a practice. Shalom then began the long journey back to Tel Aviv.

Six weeks later, on January 12, 1991, Shalom was among a joint team of Mossad and Aman intelligence officers who sat around the conference table at the United States Joint Special Operations Command, JSOC (its staff called it "jaysock"), at Pope Air Force Base, Georgia. JSOC commanded the Green Berets and the SEALs, and had maintained a close working relationship with Mossad.

After Shalom had returned from Iraq, Shavit had informed General Earl Stiner, operations commander of JSOC, that Saddam was doing more than posturing. The hard-charging general had a folksy style and a salty language the Israelis liked. But in a war room, his Tennessee drawl swiftly gave way to shrewd decisions. As the nation's top commando, he knew the value of good intelligence, and his own experience of the Middle East had convinced him Mossad offered the best.

Since Saddam's incursion into Kuwait, Stiner had regularly communicated with his Israeli contacts. Some of them went back to 1983, when, as a newly promoted brigadier general, he had been secretly sent by the Pentagon to Beirut to report directly to the Joint Chiefs of Staff on how far the United States should become embroiled in the Lebanon war.

Later, he had worked closely with Mossad during the *Achille Lauro* hijacking, swooping down with his Delta Force commandos on an Italian air force base in Sicily where the hijackers had stopped over in an airliner on their way to freedom out of Egypt. Italian troops had stopped Stiner from capturing the hijackers, and there had nearly been a shoot-out. Thwarted, Stiner had flown in hot pursuit of the airliner in his own military transport, only abandoning the chase when both planes entered Rome's airspace and its air traffic controllers threatened to shoot down the Delta Force aircraft for "air piracy." In 1989 Stiner had been the ground commander for the invasion of Panama, and had been responsible for the swift capture of Manuel Noriega.

Only Joint Chiefs chairman General Colin Powell and General Norman Schwarzkopf, in charge of the coalition forces, knew about Stiner's relationship with Mossad. While Schwarzkopf battled to create a defensive line along the Saudi border to deal with a thrust out of Kuwait by Iraqi forces, Stiner's intelligence officers were working closely with Mossad to form resistance movements inside Iraq to try to topple Saddam.

When Major General Wayne Downing, commander of JSOC, called the meeting to order in the conference room, everyone knew that, as the hours ticked by to the deadline for war set by the United Nations for Tuesday, January 15, 1991, the world was conducting a dialogue with the deaf in Baghdad. Saddam continued to welcome what he predicted would be "the mother of all wars."

Downing began by reminding his listeners that Washington still required Israel to remain out of the war. In return there would be long-term political and economic benefits for doing so.

The immediate response from the Israelis was to produce a set of Shalom's enlarged photographs of the Scud launch. Then came their questions. Supposing Saddam fitted a nuclear warhead to a Scud? Mossad was satisfied Iraq had already built the facilities needed to manufacture a crude device. It also had the capability to fit chemical or biological warheads to its Scuds. Was Israel supposed to wait for that to happen? What was the coalition force's plan to deal with the Scuds before they were launched? Did the Americans have any idea just how many Scuds Saddam had?

One of Downing's intelligence officers said their "best estimate" was about fifty.

"We think Saddam has about five times that number, maybe even five hundred in all," replied Shabtai Shavit.

The stunned silence in the room was broken by Downing's question. Could he pinpoint them? Shavit could not be more specific than to suggest the Scuds were sited in the Iraqi western desert and in the east of the country. The Americans agreed with Downing that "that was a lot of desert to hide them in."

"Then the sooner you start, the better," Shavit said, not bothering to conceal his frustration.

Downing promised to pursue the matter vigorously, and the meeting closed with the repeated reminder that Israel must stay out of the coming conflict—but all the intelligence Mossad and Aman could gather would be welcomed. In the meantime, they could be reassured the United States and its partners would deal with the Scuds. The Israeli team flew home feeling they had gotten the worst end of the deal.

Shortly after 3:00 A.M. on the morning of January 17, 1991—hours after the start of the Desert Storm conflict—seven Scuds hit Tel Aviv and Haifa, destroying 1,587 buildings and injuring forty-seven civilians.

Later that morning Prime Minister Yitzhak Shamir icily asked over a hot line to Washington how many Israelis had to die before President Bush did something. The short call ended with Bush pleading for restraint and Shamir warning that Israel would not remain much longer on the sideline.

Shamir had already ordered Israeli jets to patrol the northern airspace with Iraq. Bush immediately promised that if the aircraft were recalled, he would send "in double quick time" two Patriot antimissile batteries "to further defend your cities," and the coalition forces "will destroy the remaining Scuds in days."

Missiles continued to fall on Israel. On January 22, one landed in the Tel Aviv suburb of Ramat Gan. Ninety-six civilians were injured, several seriously; three died of heart attacks. The sound of the explosions carried to Mossad headquarters. In the Kirya, Amnon Shahak called a direct line number to the National Military

Command Center on the second floor of the Pentagon. His call was even shorter than Shamir's; the gist was: Do something or Israel will.

Hours later, Downing and his commandos were on their way to Saudi Arabia. Waiting for them in the tiny Iraqi border village of Ar Ar was Shalom. He was dressed in British army fatigues. He never explained, and no one asked, how he had gotten them. The news he brought was electrifying. He could confirm there were four Scud launchers less than thirty minutes' flying time away.

"Let's go!" Downing said. "Let's go fry some butts!"

Chinooks helicoptered the team into the Iraqi desert, together with their specially adapted Land Rover to operate in a terrain that mostly resembled a moonscape. In an hour, they had located the Scud launchers. Over a secure radio the commando leader called up U.S. fighter-bombers armed with cluster munitions and thousand-pound bombs. A hovering Black Hawk helicopter videoed the kills.

Hours later a copy of the tape was being viewed by Shamir in his office in Tel Aviv.

In another telephone call from Bush, the prime minister conceded he had seen enough to keep Israel out of the war. Neither man mentioned the role Mossad had played.

In the remaining days of the Gulf War, the Scuds killed or injured almost 500 people—including 128 Americans dead or wounded from a missile that landed in Saudi Arabia; over 4,000 Israelis were left homeless.

The aftermath of the Gulf War saw Mossad and Aman under fierce attack during secret sessions of the Knesset Foreign Affairs and Defense Oversight Intelligence Subcommittee. Both services were roundly condemned for failing to predict the invasion of Kuwait or to provide "sufficient warning" of the Iraqi threat. Leaks from within the committee room spoke of slanging matches involving Amnon Shahak, head of Aman, and Shabtai Shavit, and committee members. After one clash, the Mossad chief had come close to resigning. But all was not lost for the embattled Shavit.

Mossad's Department of Psychological Warfare, LAP, usually called upon to spread disinformation and blacken the character of Israel's enemies with foreign journalists, focused its skills on the local media. Favored reporters were called and told it was not a question of there having been too little intelligence, it was a matter of the Israeli public having grown accustomed to being spoiled for choice in that area.

Familiar truths were trundled out by LAP: no other country proportionate to its size and population analyzed or used as much intelligence as did Israel; no service could match Mossad in understanding the mind-set and intentions of the country's enemies, or equal its record for frustrating the plans of those who had plagued Israel for almost fifty years. It was rousing stuff and found ready space in a media only too grateful to be given "inside track" information.

A rush of articles appeared reminding readers that, despite defense cuts introduced shortly before the Gulf War, Mossad had continued to manfully battle on in Lebanon, Jordan, Syria, and Iraq. People had been able to read between the lines: Mossad was being hampered because the politicians had mishandled the defense budget. It was a familiar theme, and always guaranteed to work. To a still badly frightened population recovering from the Scud attacks, claims that a lack of funding lay at the root of what they had suffered turned criticism away from Mossad back onto the politicians. Money suddenly became available. Israel, so long dependent on U.S. satellite data, put its own spy satellite program on the fast track. The first priority was to launch a military satellite to specifically monitor Iraq. A new antimissile missile, the Hetz, was put into mass production. Several Patriot batteries were ordered from the United States.

The intelligence subcommittee wilted in the face of the barrage of pro-Mossad publicity. Shavit emerged triumphant—and set about reaffirming Mossad's position. Deep-penetration katsas in Iraq were ordered to try to discover how much of Saddam's arsenal of chemical and biological weapons had survived allied bombardment.

They discovered that Iraq still possessed quantities of anthrax, smallpox, the Ebola virus, and chemical nerve agents capable of killing not only every man, woman, and child in Israel, but a sizable proportion of the entire population on earth.

The question that faced Shabtai, the other heads of the Israeli intelligence communities, and Israel's politicians was deciding whether to make public the information. To do so would certainly create fear and panic in Israel, and could provoke other widespread negative effects. The country's tourist industry had been virtually wiped out by the Gulf War; the Israeli economy was close to rock bottom and new foreign investment was slow in coming. To reveal that Israel was still in range of deadly weapons would hardly attract tourists or money into the country.

Further, the breakup of the Gulf War coalition, whose Arab members had never been less than cool to waging war against fellow Arabs, had resulted in growing sympathy for the undoubted plight of Iraqis. The evidence of mass destruction caused by coalition bombing and the continued suffering of innocent civilians had stoked up powerful emotions elsewhere in the Middle East, and renewed Arab enmity against Israel. Moreover, if Tel Aviv were to publish details of Iraq's still-intact chemical and biological weapons, it would be seen in those pro-Arab Western countries as an attempt by Israel to persuade the United States and Britain to stage new assaults on Iraq.

The issue of going public about Saddam's arsenal was also influenced by the carefully orchestrated secret discussions to bring an end to hostilities between the PLO and Israel. By 1992, these discussions had moved to Norway, and were progressing well, though it would be a full year before an agreement was reached and publicly ratified in October 1993, when Yasser Arafat shook hands with Prime Minister Yitzhak Rabin on the White House lawn, under the benevolent smile of President Clinton. For each man it was a diplomatic triumph.

However, not everyone in Mossad shared the hope that the "land for peace" formula—a Palestinian homeland in exchange for no more fighting—would work. Islamic fundamentalism was on the march, and Israel's neighbors, Jordan, Egypt, and Syria, were being buffeted by the extremist forces of Iran. For the Tehran mullahs, Israel remained a pariah state. Within Mossad, and indeed, for many Israelis, the prospect of a lasting peace with the PLO was an unrealistic dream. Zionist Israel had little wish to accommodate itself with Arabs: everything about their religion and culture was seen by Zionists as inferior to their own beliefs and history; they could not accept that the Oslo accord guaranteed the future of their Promised Land and that both races would live together, if not always happily, at least with respect for each other.

All this was carefully weighed by Shabtai Shavit as he considered the question of whether to publicize Iraq's arsenal. In the end, he decided to keep the information secret so as not to disturb the wave of optimism outside Israel that had followed the Washington accord. Besides, if things went wrong, the information about Iraq's stockpile of deadly poison could still be made public. The image of a ruthless Saddam poised to have one of his agents place a canister of anthrax in the New York subway, or a terrorist dispersing the Ebola virus into the air-conditioning system of a fully-laden Boeing 747, so that each passenger became a biological time bomb who could spread the virus to thousands of people before the truth was discovered, were scenarios perfectly suited for Mossad's experts in psychological warfare to exploit whenever the time came to fan public opinion against Iraq.

Two other incidents, the facts of which had been hidden by Mossad, could also cause massive damage and embarrassment to the United States.

On a December evening in 1988, Pan American Airways Flight 103 from London to New York exploded in the air over Lockerbie in Scotland. Within hours, staff at LAP were working the phones to their media contacts, urging them to publicize that here was "incontrovertible proof" that Libya, through its intelligence service, Jamahirya, was culpable. (The author of this book received a call making such a claim from a LAP source hours after the disaster.) Sanctions were swiftly imposed by the West against the Gadhafi regime. The United States and Britain issued indictments against two Libyans, charging them with the destruction of the Pan Am flight. Gadhafi refused to hand over the men for trial.

LAP next accused Syria and Iran of being coplotters in the Lockerbie disaster. The case against the Damascus regime turned on no more than its well-known support for state-sponsored terrorism. With Iran, the accusation was more specific: Pan Am 103 had been destroyed as an act of revenge for the shooting down on July 3, 1988, by the USS *Vincennes* of an Iranian passenger plane in the Persian Gulf, killing 290 people. It had been a tragic error for which the United States had apologized.

LAP then named the Popular Front for the Liberation of Palestine as having conspired to destroy the airline. None of the journalists who widely published this story stopped to think why Libya, accused as the original perpetrator, would have needed to call for help from Syria or Iran, let along a Palestinian group.

According to one British intelligence source, "LAP was on a roll. Lockerbie was the perfect opportunity to remind the world that there existed the terror network that LAP always liked to promote. Lockerbie didn't need that. In fact putting in too many names in the pot was actually counterproductive. We knew only the Libyans were responsible." However, there were facts that did not make Pan Am 103 such an open-and-shut case.

The loss of the airliner had occurred at the time when George Bush was president-elect and his transition team in Washington was updating itself on the current Middle East situation so Bush could "hit the ground running" when he entered the Oval Office.

Bush had been CIA director in 1976–77, a period when Secretary of State Henry Kissinger had largely dictated Washington's pro-Israeli policy. While Bush publicly maintained Reagan's glad-handing toward Israel, his years at the helm of the CIA had convinced him that Reagan had been "too dewy-eyed about Israel." Waiting to become president, Bush needed no reminding how, in 1986, the United States had been forced to cancel a $1.9 billion arms deal with Jordan when the Jewish lobby in Congress had intervened. Bush had told his transition team that as president he would not tolerate interference in the right of "God-fearing Americans to do business with whom and where they wished." This attitude would play its part in the destruction of Pan Am 103.

On board the aircraft as it left London on that December night in 1988 were eight members of the U.S. intelligence community returning from duty in the Middle East. Four of them were CIA field officers, led by Matthew Gannon. Also on board were U.S. Army major Charles McKee and his small team of experts in hostage rescue. They had been in the Middle East to explore the possibility of freeing the Western hostages still held in Beirut. Though the Lockerbie disaster investigation was under the jurisdiction of a Scottish team, CIA agents were on the scene when McKee's still closed and miraculously intact suitcase was located. It was taken away from the scene for a short time by a man believed to be a CIA officer, though he would never be positively identified. Later the suitcase was returned to the Scottish investigation team, who logged its contents under "empty."

No one queried what had happened to McKee's belongings, let alone why he had been traveling with an empty suitcase. But at the time, no one suspected that the CIA officer might have removed from the suitcase data that explained why Pan Am 103 had been destroyed. Gannon's luggage was never accounted for—giving rise to the belief that the actual bomb had been placed in his suitcase. No satisfactory explanation would ever emerge as to how or why a CIA officer was carrying a bomb in his suitcase.

The PBS investigative television program *Frontline* subsequently claimed to have solved the cause of the disaster. Pan Am 103 had begun its journey in Frankfurt, where U.S.-bound passengers from the Middle East transferred on to Flight 103. Among them were Gannon and his CIA team, who had traveled on an Air Malta flight to make the connection. Their baggage was similar to thousands of suitcases that passed through the hands of Frankfurt baggage handlers every day. One of them was in the pay of terrorists. Somewhere in the airport baggage bays the handler had concealed a suitcase already containing the bomb. His instruction was to spot a matching suitcase coming off a connecting flight, and substitute his suitcase, and then let it continue on into the hold of Pan Am 103. It was a plausible theory—but only one of many advanced to explain the bombing.

Understandably desperate to show the destruction of Pan Am 103 had been an act of terrorism for which it could not be culpable, the airline's insurers hired a New York firm of private investigators called Interfor. The company had been founded in 1979 by an Israeli, Yuval Aviv, who had immigrated to the United States the previous year. Aviv claimed to be a former desk officer with Mossad—a claim the service would deny. Nevertheless, Aviv had satisfied the insurers he had the right connections to unearth the truth.

When they received his report, they could only have been stunned. Aviv had concluded that the attack had been planned and executed "by a rogue CIA group, based in Germany, who were providing protection to a drug operation which transported drugs from the Middle East to the U.S. via Frankfurt. The CIA did nothing to break up the operation because the traffickers were also helping them send weapons to Iran as part of the arms-for-hostages negotiations. The method of drug smuggling was quite simple. One person would check a piece of luggage on the flight, and an accomplice working in the baggage area would switch it with a piece of identical luggage containing the narcotics. On the fatal night, a Syrian terrorist, aware of how the drug operation worked, had switched a suitcase with one containing the bomb. His reason was to kill the U.S. intelligence operatives whom Syria had discovered would join the flight."

Aviv's report claimed McKee had learned about the "CIA rogue team," which had worked under the code name of COREA, and that its members also had close ties to another of those mysterious figures who had found his niche on the fringes of the intelligence world. Monzer Al-Kassar had built a reputation as an arms dealer in Europe, including supplying Colonel Oliver North with weapons for him to pass on to the Nicaraguan Contras in 1985–86. Al-Kassar also had links to the Abu Nidal organization, and his family connections were equally dubious. Ali Issa Duba, head of Syrian intelligence, was his brother-in-law, and Al-Kassar's wife was a relative of the Syrian president. Aviv's report claimed Al-Kassar had found in COREA a ready partner for the drug-smuggling operation. This had been going on for several months before the destruction of Pam Am 103. The report further claimed McKee had discovered the scam while pursuing his own contacts in the Middle East underworld in an attempt to find a way to rescue the Beirut hostages. Aviv stated in his report that "McKee planned to bring back to the U.S. proof of the rogue intelligence team's connection to Al-Kassar."

In 1994, Joel Bainerman, the publisher of an Israeli intelligence report and whose analyses have also appeared in the *Wall Street Journal*, the *Christian Science Monitor*, and Britain's *Financial Times*, wrote: "Twenty-four hours before the flight, Mossad tipped off the German BKA that there could be a plan to plant a bomb on flight 103. The BKA passed on their tip to the COREA CIA team working out of Frankfurt who said they would take care of everything."

Pan Am's attorney, Gregory Buhler, subpoenaed the FBI, CIA, FAA, DEA, NSC, and NSA to reveal what they knew, but, he later claimed, "the government quashed the subpoenas on grounds of national security."

Neither the *Frontline* program makers, Yuval Aviv, nor Joel Bainerman had been able to provide satisfactory answers to troubling questions. If there was a cover-up to COREA's activities, how high did it extend within the CIA? Who had authorized it? Had that person or persons ordered the removal of embarrassing data from within McKee's suitcase? Why had the German BKA police agency tipped off the COREA unit? Was it purely by chance? Or had it been motivated by a decision that the activities of COREA had become unacceptably dangerous for others in the CIA? And just what were the "national security grounds" that had led to Pan Am's attorney receiving a blanket refusal for his subpoenas?

Over the years, these questions have surfaced within the closed ranks of various intelligence agencies, and the answers have been kept closely guarded—not least the truth about a final mystery. Why had Mossad sent a London-based katsa north to Lockerbie within hours of the downing of Pan Am 103?

So far the service has kept to itself all it knows about the destruction of the flight. There are sources, who ask not to be named because their lives would be endangered, who claim that Mossad is holding on to its knowledge as a trump card should Washington increase its pressure for Mossad to cease its intelligence activities within the United States.

More certain, there was another episode that could turn out equally as embarrassing to the U.S. intelligence community. It concerned the death of Amiram Nir, the man with a taste for James Bond thrillers who had replaced David Kimche as Israel's point man in Irangate.

Amiram Nir was ideally suited to be Prime Minister Shimon Peres's antiterrorism adviser. Exploitive, inquisitive, acquisitive, manipulative, and ruthless, Nir had a raffish charm, a lack of self-restraint, an ability to ridicule, to take imaginative leaps, to break the rules to work against a background of blending fact and fiction. He had been a journalist.

His previous knowledge of intelligence sprang from his work as a reporter with Israeli television, and then from working for the country's largest daily newspaper, *Yediot Aharonot*; it was owned by the Moses dynasty, into which he had married. The publishing empire was everything Robert Maxwell's had never been: the epitome of respectability and securely financed; it treated its employees on the old adage of a fair day's pay for a hard day's work. Nir's marriage not only had made him the husband of one of the wealthiest women in Israel, but had also provided him with ready access to the higher echelons of the country's political hierarchy.

Nevertheless, there was astonishment when he became one of the most important members of Israel's intelligence community in 1984, when Peres appointed him to the ultrasensitive post of his adviser on combating terrorism.

Nir was thirty-four years old, and the only hands-on experience he had had of intelligence work was a short IDF course. Even among his friends, the general consensus was he needed more than rugged good looks for his new job.

Mossad's chief, Nahum Admoni, was the first to react to Nir's appointment: he changed the structure of the Committee of the Heads of Services to exclude Nir from its deliberations. Unperturbed, Nir spent the first weeks in the job speed-reading everything he could lay his hands on. He quickly came to focus on the arms-to-Iran operation that was still ongoing. Sensing a chance to prove himself, Nir persuaded Peres he should take over the role David Kimche had relinquished. With the indefatigable Ari Ben-Menashe as his mentor, Nir found himself also working with Oliver North.

Soon the two men were hand in glove, wheeling and dealing across the globe. Along their travels they created a plan to bring the arms-for-hostages deal to a stunningly successful conclusion. They would fly to Tehran and meet the Iranian leadership and negotiate the release of the hostages.

On May 25, 1986, posing as technicians employed by Aer Lingus, the Irish national airline, Nir and North flew from Tel Aviv to Tehran on an Israeli aircraft painted with Aer Lingus's distinctive shamrock logo. On board were ninety-seven TOW guided missiles and a pallet of Hawk missile spare parts. Nir was traveling on a false U.S. passport. It had been provided by North.

North, ever the evangelizing Christian, had somehow persuaded President Reagan to inscribe a Bible to be presented to Ayatollah Rafsanjani, a devout Muslim. He had also brought a chocolate cake and sets of Colt pistols for their hosts. It was all reminiscent of the days when traders had bartered for land with the Indians on Manhattan.

The first Mossad knew of the mission was when the aircraft entered Iranian airspace. Nahum Admoni's reaction was described as "incandescent rage."

Luckily the Iranians simply ordered the visitors out and used the mission to score a massive propaganda coup against the United States. Reagan was furious. In Tel Aviv, Admoni cursed Nir as "a cowboy." Nevertheless, Nir managed to remain in government service for another ten months, until the sniping from within the intelligence community calling for his removal had grown to a relentless fusillade. In those months the cases of Hindawi, Vanunu, and Sowan crossed his desk, but any contributions he offered on how matters should be handled were icily rejected by Mossad.

No longer welcome in Washington and isolated in Tel Aviv, Amiram Nir resigned as the prime minister's counterterrorism adviser in March 1987. By then his marriage was in trouble, and his circle of friends had shrunk. Ari Ben-Menashe remained one of Nir's few remaining links with his past. Early in 1988 Nir left Israel to live in London.

Then he set up house with a pretty, raven-haired Canadian, Adriana Stanton, a twenty-five-year-old who claimed to be a secretary from Toronto, whom Nir had met on his travels. Several Mossad officers believed she was connected to the CIA, one of the women it used for entrapment operations. In London, Nir acted as the European representative of a Mexican avocado purchasing company, Nucal de Mexico, based in Uruapan. The company controlled a third of the country's avocado export market.

But it was not avocados that brought Ari Ben-Menashe to Nir's door on a rainy November night in 1988. He wanted to know exactly what Nir intended to reveal when he was a major witness in Oliver North's forthcoming trial over his role in the Iran-Contra scandal. Nir made it clear his testimony would be highly embarrassing not only for the Reagan administration, but also to Israel. He intended to show how easy it had been to sidestep all the usual checks and balances to run illegal operations that would also implicate a number of countries, including South Africa and Chile. He added he was planning a book that he believed would make him the greatest whistle-blower in the history of the State of Israel. Ari Ben-Menashe arranged to meet Nir after he had made another visit to Nucal in Mexico. In the meantime, his visitor cautioned Nir to be "careful of that woman!" after Adriana Stanton had left them alone. Ben-Menashe refused to reveal what had prompted the warning except to say, in his all-too-often mysterious manner: "I know her from before and, though Nir didn't know it, Adriana Stanton wasn't her real name."

On November 27, 1988, Nir and Stanton traveled together to Madrid under false names. He called himself "Patrick Weber," the identity he had last assumed on his ill-fated trip to Tehran. Stanton was listed on the Iberia passenger manifest as "Esther Arriya." Why they had chosen aliases for the flight tickets when they both traveled on their real passports—Israeli and Canadian—would never be explained. Another mystery was why they took a flight first to Madrid when there were several scheduled direct ones to Mexico City. Was Nir trying to impress his lover with how easy it was to fool most people most of the time? Or was there already a nagging fear at the back of his mind after Ari Ben-Menashe's visit? Like so much else of what followed, those questions were to remain unanswered.

They arrived in Mexico City on November 28. Waiting at the airport was a man who would never be identified. The three of them traveled on to Uruapan, arriving there in the afternoon. Nir then chartered a T 210 Cessna from the small Aerotaxis de Uruapan.

Once more Nir behaved with strange inconsistency. He rented the aircraft in the name of "Patrick Weber," using a credit card in that name to pay the charges, and arranged with a pilot to fly them to the Nucal processing plant in two days' time. In the local hotel where they shared a room, Nir registered under his own name. The man who had accompanied them from Mexico disappeared as mysteriously as he had appeared.

On November 30, Nir and Stanton turned up at the small Uruapan airport, this time with another man. On the passenger manifest he was listed as Pedro Espionoza Huntado. Whom he worked for would remain yet another mystery. Another would be why, when they came to enter their own names on the manifest, both Nir and Stanton used their real identities. If the pilot noticed the discrepancy between the name Nir had given to charter the Cessna, it passed without comment.

The plane took off in good flying conditions. On board were the pilot, a copilot, and their three passengers. One hundred miles into the flight, the Cessna suddenly developed engine trouble and moments later crashed, killing Nir and the pilot. Stanton was seriously injured, the copilot and Huntado less so. By the time the first rescuer, Pedro Cruchet, arrived on the scene, Huntado had disappeared—another of those figures never to be seen again. How exactly Cruchet came to be first on the scene was yet another twist. He claimed to work for Nucal—but the company's plant was a considerable distance away. He could not explain why he had been so close to the crash site. Asked by police to prove his identity, he pleaded he had lost his ID at a bullfight. It turned out Cruchet was an Argentinian living in Mexico illegally. By the time that had been established he, too, had vanished. At the crash site, Cruchet had recovered and identified Nir's body, and he had accompanied Stanton to the hospital. He was with her when a local reporter called seeking further details.

Joel Bainerman, the publisher of the Israeli political intelligence digest, would claim: "A young woman indicated Cruchet was present. When she went to get him, another woman appeared at the door and told the journalist that Cruchet wasn't there and that she had never heard of him. The second woman reiterated that Stanton's presence on the Cessna was purely a coincidence and that she had no connection with 'the Israeli.' She refused to identify herself other than to say she was in Mexico as a tourist from Argentina."

Stanton added to the mystery. She told crash investigators, according to Israeli journalist Ran Edelist in 1997: "While injured and shocked, she saw Amiram Nir a few meters away, waving and comforting her in a normal voice. 'Everything will be okay. Help is on the way!' She was twice assured in the days following that Nir was alive."

Nir's body was flown back to Israel for burial. Over one thousand mourners attended his funeral and, in his eulogy, Defense Minister Yitzhak Rabin spoke of Nir's "mission to as-yet-unrevealed destinations on secret assignments and of secrets which he kept locked in his heart."

Had Amiram Nir been murdered to make sure he never revealed those secrets? Was it even Nir's body in the coffin? Or had he been killed before the crash? And if so, by whom? In Tel Aviv and Washington, a blanket of silence continues to greet all such questions.

Two days after the crash, Ari Ben-Menashe emerged from a post office in downtown Santiago, Chile. He was accompanied by two of the bodyguards he now felt it important to have to protect him. Suddenly:

"The window I was walking past shattered. Then something smashed into the metal custom-built briefcase I was carrying. The two bodyguards and I dived to the floor, realizing someone was shooting at us."

Stanton was the next to believe her life was in danger. According to Edelist, his intelligence contacts had told him she "became a recluse, underwent plastic surgery, and changed her appearance."

Increasingly, Mossad believed the CIA had murdered Nir. According to Ari Ben-Menashe, "Israeli intelligence has always believed it was a well-executed CIA operation. Nir's death ensured there would be no embarrassment for Reagan and Bush at the trial of Oliver North."

Support for this theory came from a U.S. Navy commander who had accompanied Nir to Tehran on the fruiterer's mission to free the Beirut hostages. The commander's story revolved around his claim that Nir had met with George Bush, then vice president, on July 29, 1986, at the King David Hotel in Jerusalem, to brief him about the ongoing sale of U.S. arms via Israel to Iran. According to the writer Joel Bainerman, "Nir was secretly taping the entire conversation. And this provided him with evidence linking Bush to the arms-for-hostages deal. At the meeting were McKee and Gannon, who would die in the Pan Am flight over Lockerbie."

Bainerman would describe a visit the commander had made to CIA headquarters in Langley where he had met Oliver North some months before the colonel faced trial. In the writer's words, the commander asked North "what had happened to Nir. North told him that Nir was killed because he threatened to go public with the recording of the Jerusalem meeting."

Journalists who have tried to question North on the matter have been brushed aside. Bush's aides have over the years maintained a similar attitude: anything the former president of the United States has to say on Irangate has already been stated.

In late July 1991, the home of Nir's widow, Judy, was burgled. His recordings and documents were the only items stolen. Police said the break-in was "highly professional." Judy Nir said she was certain the stolen material contained "information that would attack certain people." She refused to be drawn beyond that. The material has never been recovered. The question of who stole it has remained unanswered.

For the next four years, Shabtai Shavit continued to run Mossad, making every effort to keep it out of the headlines and free of the attention of the mythmakers as it continued to pursue its information gathering.

Away from the public gaze, the old jockeying for power within the Israeli intelligence community had lost none of its energy. Politicians who still sat on the oversight subcommittee on intelligence remembered how Shavit had bested them after the Gulf War. Memories are as long in Israel as anywhere else, and the whispering campaign against Shavit had continued: his focus was too narrow; the back channel to the CIA was barely ajar; he wasn't good at delegating; he was too aloof from the rank and file, among whom morale was falling.

Shabtai Shavit chose to ignore the warning signs. Suddenly, on a pleasant spring morning in 1996, he was summoned to the office of Prime Minister Benyamin Netanyahu and told he was being replaced. Shavit made no attempt to argue; he had seen enough of Netanyahu to know that would be pointless. He had only asked one question: Who was his successor?

Netanyahu had replied: Danny Yatom. The day of the Prussian had arrived for Mossad.

CHAPTER 17

BUNGLEGATE

Dawn was breaking on Thursday, January 16, 1998, when the government car pulled away from the white-painted house in an exclusive suburb close to the electrified fence marking the border between Israel and Jordan. In one of those twists of history that abound in Israel, the house stood on grounds where the spies of Gideon, the great Jewish warrior, had prepared their intelligence-gathering missions to enable the Israelis to defeat overwhelmingly superior forces. Now, Danny Yatom was setting off to finalize an operation that could save his career.

Beginning with the debacle on the streets of Amman in July

1997, when a *kidon* team failed to assassinate the Hamas leader Khalid Meshal, the past seven months had been, Yatom had told friends, "like living on the edge of the block waiting for the ax to fall."

His executioner-in-waiting was Prime Minister Benyamin Netanyahu. Their once-close friendship had soured to the point where not a day passed without snipers in the prime minister's office targeting the Mossad chief with the same whisper: It was only a matter of time before he was sacked. Other men would have resigned. But not Yatom. Proud and imperious, he was prepared to stand on his record. There were so many successful operations he had ordered that no outsider knew about. "It's only the failures that get publicly dumped on my doorstep," he had bitterly told his friends.

They, together with his family, had seen the strain in him: the sleepless nights; the sudden, unexpected bursts of anger, quickly extinguished; the restless pacing; the long silences; all the outward signs of a man under huge strain.

Two years into the job, he still faced pressures no other Mossad director had. Consequently, his own staff were increasingly demoralized, and he could no longer count on their loyalty. The media were circling, sensing he was wounded, but holding back, waiting to see when the one man Yatom had trusted, but no longer, would finally wield the ax. So far Benyamin Netanyahu had only kept an icy distance.

But on this cold February morning, Yatom knew his time was running out. That was why he needed the operation he had nurtured these past weeks to work. It would show the prime minister his spymaster had not lost his skills. But none of this showed on Yatom's face; despite all he had endured, he kept his emotions under lock and key. Seated in a corner of the backseat of the Peugeot, in repose Yatom looked genuinely intimidating in black leather bomber jacket, open-neck shirt, and gray pants. It was how he usually dressed for work; clothes had never interested him.

His receding hair, steel-framed glasses, and thin lips went well with his nickname—the Prussian. He knew he still commanded by something close to fear. Beside him on the seat were the morning newspapers: for once there had been no speculation about his future.

The Peugeot made its swift way down through the hills toward

Tel Aviv, the sun reflecting off the burnished bodywork; morning and evening the chauffeur polished the vehicle to mirror perfection. The Peugeot had bulletproof windows, armor-plated coachwork, and anti-mine flooring. Only the official car of the prime minister had similar protection.

Benyamin Netanyahu had Yatom confirmed in the post of director general of Mossad within minutes of Shabtai Shavit's going. In Yatom's first weeks in office, he had spent at least one evening a week with the prime minister. They had sat over cold beers and olives and put the world to rights, and remembered the times when Yatom had commanded "Bibi" in an IDF commando unit. Afterward Netanyahu had gone on to become Israel's ambassador to the United Nations and then, during the Gulf War, a self-styled expert on international terrorism, even broadcasting with a gas mask over his face in case a Scud should fall nearby. Yatom, for his part, had said how much he relished the role of the outsider who had been given the most important post in the country's intelligence community: the quintessential career soldier, he had served as military attaché to Prime Minister Yitzhak Rabin.

Yatom and Netanyahu had seemed inseparable until two embarrassments had left a seemingly unbridgeable gulf. There had been the bungled affair in Amman. The operation had been ordered by Netanyahu. When the attack failed and Mossad had been caught in the spotlight of the world's media, the prime minister blamed Yatom for the debacle. He had taken the criticism without flinching; privately he had told friends that Netanyahu had "the courage of other people's convictions."

A second and, in many ways, a graver embarrassment surfaced. In October 1997, a senior Mossad officer, Yehuda Gil, was discovered to have invented, for the past twenty years, top secret reports from a nonexistent "agent" in Damascus. Gil had drawn substantial sums from Mossad's slush fund to pay the man, pocketing the money for himself. The scam had only come to light when a Mossad analyst studying the "agent's" latest report that Syria was about to attack Israel, had become suspicious. Gil had been confronted by Yatom and made a full confession.

Netanyahu had pounced. In a stormy meeting in the prime minister's office, Yatom had been brutally questioned over the way he ran Mossad. Netanyahu had brushed aside the argument that Gil had successfully carried off his deception under four previous directors. Yatom should have known, Netanyahu had shouted. It was another foul-up. Staff in the prime minister's office could not recall such a dressing-down. The details had been leaked to the media, causing further embarrassment to Yatom.

How different it had been when he had come into office and his name had been splashed across the world's media. Reporters had called him a safe pair of hands and there had been speculation that he would assume the mantle of the great spymasters of yesteryear—Amit, Hofi, and Admoni—and once more rekindle the fire Shabtai Shavit had deliberately damped down.

The proof was not long in coming. Despite the Oslo accord giving the PLO a homeland—the Gaza Strip and the West Bank—Yatom had increased the number of Arab agents to spy on Yasser Arafat. He had ordered Mossad programmers to develop new software to hack into PLO computers, and create electronic "microbes" to destroy, should the need arise, its communication systems. He had asked scientists in research and development to focus on "infowar" weapons that could insert black propaganda into enemy broadcasting systems. He wanted Mossad to be part of the brave new world where the weapons of the future would be in keyboards that shut down an enemy's ability to mobilize its military forces.

Yatom had returned to Mossad's old stomping ground, Africa: in May 1997, the service had provided important intelligence that had helped rebel forces to topple President Mobutu of Zaire, who for so long had dominated central Africa. Mossad also increased its ties with Nelson Mandela's security service, helping it to target white extremists, many of whom it had previously worked with. Yatom also increased the budget and strength of the special Mossad unit, Al, responsible for stealing the latest U.S. scientific research.

At fifty-one years of age, there was something unstoppable about Danny Yatom; tireless and ruthless, he had the chutzpah of a street fighter. That was typified by his response to the discovery by the FBI in January 1997 of Mega—the high-level Mossad deep-penetration agent within the Clinton administration. He had told the Committee of the Heads of Services, whose role included preparing a fallback position in the event of an operational failure, all that needed to be done was to make sure that the powerful Jewish lobby in the United States countered demands from Arab organizations that the hunt for Mega must be pursued as vigorously as the FBI dealt with spies from other countries. Jewish dinner guests at the White House dinner table—Hollywood stars, attorneys, editors—all lost no opportunity to remind the president of the damage an ill-conceived manhunt would produce—even more if one of his own staff was arrested. In a presidency already besieged by scandal, that could be an opening that could finally destroy Clinton. Six months later, on July 4, 1997, Independence Day in the United States, Yatom had learned that the FBI had quietly downgraded its hunt for Mega.

Then two months later had come the disaster on the streets in Amman, swiftly followed by the scandal of the agent-who-never-was. Danny Yatom had begun to seek a new operation that would reestablish his authority. Now, on that January morning in 1998, he was on his way to put the finishing touches in place.

Planning for the operation had begun a month before, when an Arab informer in southern Lebanon had met his Mossad controller and told him that Abdullah Zein had made a brief visit to Beirut to meet with Hezbollah leaders in the city. Afterward Zein had driven south to see his parents in the small town of Ruman. The occasion had been one for celebration: Zein had not been home for a year. He had shown his relatives photographs of his young Italian wife and their apartment in Europe.

The controller had steeled himself not to rush the informer; the Arab way was to give his information in all its fine detail: how Zein had left his parents' home the next day laden with Arab delicacies and gifts for his wife, how Hezbollah had escorted him all the way to Beirut Airport to catch the flight back to Switzerland.

Was that Zein's final destination? the controller had finally asked. Yes, Bern, in Switzerland. And that was where Zein lived? The informer thought so, but could not be certain.

Nevertheless, it was Mossad's first positive news about Zein since he had left Lebanon to organize Hezbollah's fund-raising activities among wealthy Shiite Muslims in Europe. Their money, along with that from Iran, funneled through its embassy in Bonn, paid for Hezbollah's war of attrition against Israel. In the past year, Zein had been variously reported as operating from Paris, Madrid, and Berlin. But each time Yatom had sent someone to check, there had been no trace of the slim thirty-two-year-old with a taste for snappy Italian-cut suits and customized shoes.

Yatom had dispatched a katsa to Bern from Brussels, where Mossad had recently transferred its control center for European operators from Paris. The katsa had spent two fruitless days in Bern searching for Zein. He decided to extend his inquiries. He drove south to Liebefeld, a pleasant dormitory town. The katsa had last passed through its streets five years before, on his way out of Switzerland after being part of a team that had destroyed metal vats in a bioengineering company near Zurich; the vats were designed to manufacture bacteria and had been ordered by Iran. The team had destroyed the vats with explosive devices. The company had canceled all its contracts with Iran.

In Liebefeld, the katsa had shown that good intelligence work often depended on patient footwork. He had walked the streets, looking for anyone who could be from the Middle East. He had checked the phone book for a listing for Zein. He had telephoned house-leasing agencies to see if they had rented or sold a property to anyone of that name. He had called the local hospitals and clinics to see if a patient of that name had been admitted. Each time he had said he was a relative. With still nothing to show for a day's work, the katsa had decided to make another sweep of the town, this time in his car.

He had driven for some time through the streets when he spotted a dark-skinned man, wrapped against the night cold, driving a Volvo in the opposite direction. There had been only the briefest of glimpses, but the katsa was convinced that the driver was Zein. By the time the katsa had found an intersection to turn his car, the Volvo had disappeared. Next evening, the katsa was back, this time parked in a position to follow. Shortly afterward, the Volvo appeared. The katsa fell in behind. A mile later, the Volvo parked outside an apartment block and the driver emerged and entered the building, 27 Wabersackerstrasse. The katsa had no doubt the man was Abdullah Zein.

The katsa followed Zein into the apartment block. Beyond the plate-glass door was a small lobby with mailboxes. One of them identified the owner of a third-floor apartment as "Zein." A door off the lobby led to a basement service area. The katsa opened the door and went down to the basement. Fixed to a wall was a junction box for all the telephones in the building. Moments later he was back in his rental car.

Next day he leased a safe house half a mile from Wabersacker-strasse. He told the letting company he was expecting friends to join him for a skiing holiday.

Danny Yatom had continued planning. He had sent a communications specialist to Liebcfeld to examine the junction box. The technician had returned to Tel Aviv with a set of photographs he had taken of the inside of the box. The prints were studied in the research and development department and adjustments made to the devices being prepared. One was a sophisticated bug capable of monitoring all calls in and out of Zein's apartment. The bug would be linked to a miniature recorder capable of storing hours of phone calls. The recorder had a built-in capacity to be electronically emptied by a pre-arranged signal from the safe house. There the recordings would be transcribed and sent by secure fax to Tel Aviv.

By the first week of February 1998, all the technical plans were in place. Yatom moved to the most crucial part of the operation: choosing the team who would carry it out. The operation had two stages. The first was to gather sufficient evidence to show that Zein continued to be a key player in Hezbollah's activities. The second part was then to kill him.

By mid February 1998 everything was ready.

Shortly before 6:30 A.M. on that Monday, February 16, Yatom's Peugeot entered the parking lot in the basement of Mossad headquarters in Tel Aviv, and he took the elevator to a fourth-floor conference room. Waiting there were two men and two women. Seated around a table, they had already paired off as couples, the role they would assume in Switzerland. Each was in his late twenties, suntanned, and superbly fit-looking. For the past few days they had been up in the snow of northern Israel brushing up on their skiing.

The previous evening, they had been fully briefed on the mission and had selected their cover identities. The men were to pose as successful stock-market traders taking a short break from the trading floor with their girlfriends, but never quite able to put work behind them: that would explain the laptop computer one of them would carry. The laptop had been wired to provide the link between the concealed recorder to be installed in the apartment basement and the safe house. One couple were to monitor the recorder around the clock once it began working. The other pair were from the kidon unit. Their job was to find the best means to kill Zein. They would travel unarmed to Switzerland; their guns would be provided later by the Brussels office.

On the conference table were the listening device and the recorder. Yatom inspected them, saying the gadgets were far more sophisticated than any he had seen before. His final briefing was short. He asked each for the alias he or she had chosen from the list kept in operations. The men had selected "Solly Goldberg" and "Matti Finklestein"; the women were "Leah Cohen" and "Rachel Jacobson." Because they were flying directly out of Tel Aviv on an El Al flight, they would travel on Israeli passports. They would resume their aliases in Switzerland, where false passports would be waiting.

All four, in the later words of an Israeli intelligence source, had "earned their stripes." But the truth was that, after the debacle in Jordan, there was a limited selection of agents available for such a mission. The Amman team had been the best Mossad had been able to field, and its members had been able to pass themselves off as Canadians; all had experience operating on the international stage. The quartet chosen for the Swiss mission had only operated in Cairo—nowadays a relatively safe Mossad target—and none of them had had firsthand knowledge of working under cover in Switzerland.

That may have accounted for why, according to the London *Sunday Times*, Yatom ended the briefing with a reminder that the Swiss who lived in German-speaking cantons where Liebefeld was situated had a "tendency to call the police if they saw anything improper."

Yatom had shaken their hands and wished them luck, the standard benediction for any team leaving on a mission. The group had picked up their airline tickets and spent the next twenty-four hours in a Mossad safe house in the city.

Next Tuesday morning, February 20, they boarded El Al Flight 347 to Zurich, obediently arriving at Ben-Gurion Airport, as requested by the airline, two hours before takeoff. They joined the lines of passengers, mostly Swiss nationals or Israelis, making their way through the security checks. By 9 A.M., the two couples were in their business-class seats and sipping champagne and discussing their forthcoming holiday. In the hold of the aircraft were their skis.

Waiting for them at Kloten Airport in Zurich was the katsa from the Brussels station with a minibus. He had assumed the role of their guide and had adopted the alias of "Ephrahim Rubenstein."

By late afternoon they were installed in the safe house in Liebefeld. The two women cooked dinner and they all settled down to watch television. Early in the evening two rental cars arrived from Zurich, driven by sayanim. They left in the minibus, their role over. At around 1:00 A.M. on Saturday, February 20, the team left the safe house, each couple in a separate car. Rubenstein was in the first car, leading the way to Wabersackerstrasse. Reaching there, the two vehicles parked almost directly opposite the apartment block. There was no light from Zein's apartment. The persons who called themselves Solly Goldberg, Rachel Jacobson, and Ephrahim Rubenstein walked quickly toward the glass door of the building. Rubenstein carried a roll of plastic, Goldberg the laptop, Jacobson a carrier bag containing the listening devices. Meantime, Leah Cohen and Matti Finklestein had enthusiastically begun to act out their lookout role, pretending to be lovers.

Across the street an elderly woman who suffered from insomnia—Swiss police would later insist on referring to her only as "Madam X"—was once more unable to sleep. From her bedroom window, she stared out at a strange sight. A man—Rubenstein—was draping plastic across the glass door to stop anyone's looking into the apartment block opposite. Behind the sheet, she could see two other figures. Out in the street in a parked car was another shadowy couple. Just as Danny Yatom had warned, what she saw was certainly improper. The woman called the police.

At a little after 2:00 A.M., a BMW squad car arrived in the street, catching Cohen and Finklestein in midembrace. They were ordered to remain in the car. Meantime, police backup had arrived and the trio inside the lobby were asked to explain what they were doing. Goldberg and Jacobson said they had mistaken the building for one where friends lived and Rubenstein insisted he was taking down, not putting up the plastic.

Matters then became farcical. Goldberg and Jacobson asked permission to go to their car and check the address of their friends. No policemen accompanied them. At the same moment, Rubenstein fell to the ground, appearing to have suffered a heart attack. All the policemen gathered around to help and summon medical assistance. No one moved to stop the two cars as they raced out of Wabersackerstrasse into the frosty night. Shortly afterward, the cars stopped to transfer one couple into the other car. The foursome crossed the border into France in the small hours of the morning.

Meanwhile Rubenstein had been taken to the hospital. Doctors said he had not suffered a heart attack. He was taken into custody.

At 4:30 A.M. Tel Aviv time, Yatom was awoken at home by the night watch officer in Mossad headquarters and told what had happened. Not bothering to call his chauffeur, Yatom drove himself to headquarters.

After the Amman fiasco, a plan had been put in place to deal with further such disasters. The first step was for Yatom to call the senior duty officer at the foreign ministry. The officer telephoned the head of the prime minister's office, who informed Benyamin Netanyahu. He called Israel's ambassador to the European community in Brussels, Efraim Halevy. The English-born diplomat had spent nearly thirty years as a senior Mossad officer with responsibility for maintaining good relations with security services of foreign states that had diplomatic relations with Israel. He had also played an important role in patching up relations with Jordan after the bungled operation in Amman.

"Fix this, and you'll be my friend for life," Netanyahu was later quoted as saying to Halevy.

The ambassador had consulted the Filofax he carried everywhere before deciding whom to call first: Jacob Kellerberger, a senior officer at the Swiss foreign ministry. Halevy was at his diplomatic best: there had been a "regrettable incident" involving Mossad. How "regrettable"? Kellerberger had demanded. "Most regrettable," Halevy had replied. The tone had been set, an understanding in the wind. Or so Halevy believed, until Kellerberger telephoned Switzerland's federal prosecutor, Carla del Ponte.

With a jutting lower lip and steel-rimmed spectacles that

matched those of Danny Yatom, del Ponte was a figure within the Swiss legal system as formidable as Yatom had once been in the Israeli intelligence community. Her first question set the tone she would maintain: Why had the Liebefeld police not arrested all the Mossad agents? Kellerberger did not know. Del Ponte's next question raised a specter he was all too familiar with: Could the Mossad operatives have had a "Tehran connection"? Since the Gulf War, Israel had repeatedly claimed that several Swiss companies were supplying technology to Iran to produce missiles. Could the operation even be somehow connected with Israel's other preoccupation over what had become known as the "Jewish gold scandal"? Swiss banks had concealed for their own profit huge sums of money deposited in their vaults before World War II by German Jews who later became victims of the Nazis.

Throughout the weekend of February 21–22, her questions continued while Halevy struggled to keep matters quiet.

He had not counted on the forces arraigned against Danny Yatom in Israel. Within Mossad, as news of the incident percolated through the organization, morale plunged even lower. This time Yatom could not blame Netanyahu for what had happened in Liebefeld. The prime minister had known nothing beforehand of the operation. From within the prime minister's office whispers began to reach the Israeli media that Yatom was now doomed. For three more days, Efraim Halevy continued to plead and argue with Kellerberger to keep the incident quiet. But Carla del Ponte would have none of it. On Wednesday, February 25, she called a press conference to denounce Mossad: "What happened was unacceptable and disconcerting between friendly nations."

Within hours, Danny Yatom had resigned. His career was over and Mossad's reputation even more in tatters. In his last moments as director, he surprised staff who had assembled in the Mossad canteen. The cold Prussian image was replaced by an emotional tone: he was sorry to be leaving them at such a time, but he had tried to give them the best possible leadership. They should always remember Mossad was bigger than anyone. He ended by wishing whoever took over his place the very best of luck; he would need it. It was the nearest Yatom came to saying what he thought about a prime minister who continued to believe Mossad could be ultimately controlled from his office. Yatom walked out of the silent canteen. Only when he was in the corridor did the applause start, and it died as swiftly as it began.

A week later Efraim Halevy agreed to take over the service after Benyamin Netanyahu publicly acknowledged, the first time any Israeli prime minister had done so, "that I cannot deny that Mossad's image has been affected by certain failed missions."

Ever the consummate politician, Netanyahu made no mention of the role he had played.

Efraim Halevy became the ninth director general of Mossad on Thursday, March 5, 1998. He broke with tradition and did not summon his senior staff to hear his views on how the service should be run for the next two years. In appointing Halevy, Netanyahu had also announced that, on March 3, 2000, the new deputy director of the service, Amiram Levine, would take over running the service. The news was greeted with some surprise. No other director general had been given a fixed tenure; no other deputy had been assured he would step into the top job.

By 1999, Yatom had found himself a niche in Israel's thriving arms industry. He became a salesman for one of the country's biggest manufacturers of arms; the company not only provides a range of weapons for internal use but has a thriving export industry to Third World countries. Yatom makes regular visits to African countries and South American nations. From time to time he turns up in Washington.

Like Meir Amit, Levine had no previous intelligence experience, but he had commanded with distinction the Israeli army in northern Israel and south Lebanon.

Halevy's first task was to reduce the tremendous tension and resentments inside Mossad that had so seriously damaged its image both within Israel and beyond. In routine congratulatory telephone calls from both the CIA and MI6, the new director had been told those services would prefer to wait and see how he dealt with the crisis within Mossad before wholeheartedly committing their own services to no-secrets-based collaboration. One factor would be how Halevy dealt with the hard-liners in the Israeli government, especially its prime minister.

Would the urbane Halevy, only a year away from his pension and, by many years, the oldest to be given the office, be able to

keep Netanyahu at a proper distance? And for all Halevy's undoubted diplomatic skills—he had played a central role in the negotiations that led to the 1994 peace treaty with Jordan—he had
been away from the coalface of intelligence for several years. Since
his time with Mossad the agency had increasingly shown signs of
being out of control as senior officers had tried to stake their own
claims for promotion. Most of those middle-aged men remained in
office. Could Halevy deal firmly with them? Would the new director have the essential hands-on skills to raise morale? Mingling on
the cocktail circuit in Brussels had hardly been the best preparation
for the task of leading agents away from the brink of resignation.
Critically, Halevy had no personal operational field experience. He
had always been a desk man in his previous time with Mossad. And
what could he really achieve in two years? Or was he really there
to rubber-stamp what Netanyahu wanted done, or, for that matter,
what Netanyahu's wife, Sara, wanted done? Speculation continued
within the Israeli intelligence community over the part she had
played in the removal of Yatom, a man to whom she had never
warmed.

Halevy found a way to charm her. He presented Sara with a
microchip that Mossad research scientists had developed. It could
be implanted under her skin and allow her to be rescued in the
unlikely event she ever fell into the hands of terrorists. Using natural body energy, the bleep was linked to one of Israel's new space
satellites, enabling a person who wore it to be swiftly tracked to his
or her hiding place. No one knows if Sara has had the implant
inserted in her body.

But soon there were more pressing matters than beguiling the
prime minister's wife. The first major operation Halevy had enthusiastically approved, an attempt to set up a spy base in Cyprus, came
disastrously unstuck. Two Mossad agents, posing as teachers on
vacation, were swiftly unmasked by the small but efficient Cypriot
security service. They raided the apartment the agents had rented
and discovered it was filled with high-tech equipment, capable of
spying-out Cypriot plans to stiffen its defenses against neighboring
Turkey.

Halevy sent his deputy to Cyprus to negotiate the release of the
two men. He might well have wished he had gone himself. Israel's
president, Ezer Weizman, was a close personal friend of the Cypriot

president, Biafcos Clerides. (in their youth both men had served together in the Royal Air Force). Weizman dispatched his chief of staff to "eat humble pie in Cyprus" and then lambasted Halevy in a manner that even Netanyahu would have hesitated to have used against Yatom.

Further public embarrassment followed when, having approved a plan to assassinate Saddam Hussein during a visit to his mistress, it was cancelled after details were leaked to an Israeli journalist. Netanyahu learned what had happened when the reporter called his office for comment. Once more the hapless Halevy found himself facing a severe dressing-down.

For weeks the mercurial prime minister avoided all but essential contact with the Mossad chief, until late November 1998. Then the Turkish prime minister, Bulent Ecevit, telephoned Netanyahu and asked if Mossad would help capture Abdullah Ocalan, the Kurdish leader, long designated as a terrorist by other countries. Turkey held him responsible for 30,000 deaths on its soil. For over twenty years Ocalan's Kurdish Workers Party, the PKK, had waged a guerrilla war to get autonomy for Turkey's 12 million Kurds who have no minority rights such as education or permission to broadcast in their own language.

Ocalan had constantly evaded Turkey's own security service with effortless ease. He was a leader who inspired messianic fervor in his people. Whether a man, woman, or child, they were ready to die for him. To many he was the epitome of the legendary Scarlet Pimpernel; his deeds of derring-do endlessly recited where two or more Kurds met. There was a raw passion about his speeches, an unnerving defiance in his challenge to Turkey.

That November—after flitting through Moscow—Ocalan turned up in Rome. The Italian government refused to extradite him to Turkey—but also refused his request for political asylum. Earlier Ocalan had been arrested on a German warrant for traveling on a false passport. He was freed when Bonn withdrew its extradition demand for fear of inflaming its large Kurdish communities. That was the moment that Turkish Prime Minister Bulent Ecevit telephoned Netanyahu.

For Israel, a close working relationship with Turkey is an important element in its strategic and diplomatic survival in the region. Netanyahu agreed and ordered Halevy to find Ocalan. It would be a "black" operation—meaning Mossad's own involvement would never surface publicly. If successful, all the credit would go to Turkish intelligence.

The plan was given the code-name "Watchful." It reflected Halevy's own concern to do as little as possible to disturb his own running operation inside Iraq. There, Mossad *katsas* were working alongside Kurdish rebels to destabilize Saddam's regime.

Six Mossad agents were dispatched to Rome. They included a *bat leveyha*, a woman, and two technicians from Mossad *yahalomin*, its communications unit.

Working out of a Mossad safe house near the Pantheon, the team set up surveillance on Ocalan's apartment close to the Vatican. The woman agent was briefed to try and make contact with him. She followed the well-established guidelines that had been used by another Mossad female agent to entice Mordechai Vanunu to his doom in this same city over a decade before. But a plan to do the same with Ocalan failed when the Kurdish leader suddenly left Italy.

The Mossad team began to scour the Mediterranean basin for him: Spain, Portugal, Tunis, Morocco, Syria. Ocalan had been to all those countries—only to move on when refused sanctuary. On February 2, 1999, the Kurdish leader was discovered trying to enter Holland. The Dutch government refused him permission to do so. A Dutch security officer at Amsterdam's Schipol Airport informed the head of the local Mossad station that Ocalan had caught a KLM flight to Nairobi. His Mossad pursuers set off for the Kenyan capital, arriving on Thursday morning, February 5.

Kenya and Israel had developed over the years a close "understanding" on intelligence matters. As part of Mossad's "safari" in Central Africa it had exposed to the Kenyans the activities of other foreign spy networks. In return, Kenya continued to grant Mossad "special status," allowing it to maintain a safe house in the city and providing ready access to Kenya's small but efficient security service.

The Mossad team soon located Ocalan in the Greek embassy compound in Nairobi. From time to time Kurds—whom the team assumed were his bodyguards—came and went from the compound. Every night the head of the Mossad team reported to Tel Aviv.

The order was the same: Watch—do nothing. Then the order dramatically changed. By "all means available," Abdullah Ocalan was to be removed from the embassy compound and flown to Turkey.

The order was Halevy's.

Luck played into the team's hands. One of the Kurds came out of the embassy and drove to a bar close to the venerable Norfolk Hotel. In what is a classic Mossad tactic, one of the team "came alongside" the Kurd. With his dark skin and fluent Kurdish patois, the agent passed himself off as a Kurd working in Nairobi. He learned that Ocalan was getting restless. His latest application for political asylum in South Africa had received no response. Other African countries had been similarly loath to grant the Kurdish leader an entry visa.

Mossad's eavesdropping team were using their equipment to monitor all communications in and out of the compound. It was clear that Greece would also refuse Ocalan sanctuary.

The Mossad agent who had met the Kurd in the bar made his move.

He telephoned the Kurd in the embassy compound and asked for "an urgent meeting." Once more they met in the bar. The agent told the Kurd that Ocalan's life was in danger if he remained in the compound. His only hope was to return to join his fellow Kurds, not in Turkey, but in northern Iraq. In its mountain vastness, Ocalan would be safe and could regroup for another day. The plan was something that Ocalan had actually begun to consider—and had been overheard doing so by the Mossad surveillance team. The agent persuaded the Kurd to return to the embassy and try and persuade Ocalan to come out and discuss the proposal.

Simply—and lethally—the trap was set. It was now only a matter of waiting to see how long Ocalan could hold out from taking the bait.

Based on its intercepts of radio traffic from the Greek Foreign Ministry to the compound, the Mossad team know it was only a matter of days before Ocalan's increasingly reluctant hosts would show him the door. In an "eyes only for ambassador" message, Greek prime minister Costas Simitis had said that Ocalan's continued presence in the compound would trigger "a political and possibly military confrontation" in Greece.

Next morning a Falcon-900 executive jet landed at Nairobi's

Wilson Airport. The pilot said he had come to collect a group of businessmen flying to a conference in Athens.

What happened then is still a matter of intense debate. Ocalan's German lawyer later claimed that "based on a misrepresentation of the situation by the Kenyan authorities," Ocalan was "effectively dragged out of the compound." But the Kenyan government and the Greek Embassy in Nairobi strongly denied the charge. The Greeks insisted that the Kurdish leader left the compound against the advice of his hosts.

One thing is certain.

The executive jet took off from Nairobi with Ocalan on board. As the aircraft cleared Kenyan air space the questions began:

Had the Mossad team followed its normal practice and injected Ocalan with an incapacitating drug as he stepped out of the compound? Had they snatched him off the street—as another team had snatched Adolf Eichmann all those years ago in Buenos Aires? Had Kenya turned a blind eye to an action that broke all international laws?

Hours after Ocalan had been incarcerated in a Turkish jail, an exultant Prime Minister Bulent Ecevit appeared on television to speak of an "intelligence triumph . . . a brilliant surveillance operation conducted in Nairobi over a twelve-day period." He made no mention of Mossad. He was sticking to the rules.

For Efraim Halevy the success of the operation was measured against the loss of a spy network in Iraq that had depended so much on Kurdish support. He was not the first Mossad chief to wonder if Prime Minister Benjamin Netanhyahu's readiness to place Mossad in the role of "gun for hire" would have long-term repercussions in the wider business of intelligence gathering.

The success of the operation was undoubtedly muted by another fiasco that Halevy had inherited.

On October 5, 1992, an El Al cargo jet had plunged into an apartment block near Amsterdam's Schipol Airport, killing forty-three persons and injuring dozens. Since then hundreds of people living in the area had fallen ill. Despite a relentless campaign to conceal that the aircraft had been carrying lethal chemicals—including the components to produce Sarin, the deadly nerve agent—the facts had emerged, drawing unwelcome attention to a secret research center in the suburbs of Tel Aviv where scientists had, among much else, produced a range of chemical and biological weapons for Mossad's *kidon* unit.

Twelve miles southeast of downtown Tel Aviv is the Institute for Biological Research. The plant is at the cutting edge of Israel's multilayered defense system. Within its laboratories and workshops are manufactured a wide range of chemical and biological weapons. The Institute's chemists—some of whom once worked for the Soviet KGB or East German Stasi intelligence service—created the poison used to try and kill Khaled Meshal, the leader of the Hamas Islamic fundamentalist group.

The Institute's current research programs include developing a range of pathogens which would be, according to a secret CIA report for William Cohen, U.S. defense secretary, "ethnic-specific." The CIA report claims that Israeli scientists are "trying to exploit medical advances by identifying distinctive genes carried by some Arabs to create a genetically modified bacterium or virus."

The report concludes that, "still at the early stages, the intention is to exploit the way viruses and certain bacteria can alter the DNA inside their host's living cells." The Institute research mimics work conducted by South African scientists during the apartheid era to create a "pigmentation weapon that will target only black people."

The research was abandoned when Nelson Mandela came to power but at least two of the scientists who worked in the program in South Africa later moved to Israel.

The idea of the Jewish State conducting such research has triggered alarm bells—not least because of the disturbing parallel with genetic experiments conducted by the Nazis. Dedi Zucker, a member of the Israeli Parliament, the Knesset, is on record as saying "We cannot be allowed to create such weapons."

It was the raw materials for such weapons that the El Al jet was carrying on that October night in 1992 in its 114 tons of cargo that also included Sidewinder missiles and electronics. Most lethal of all were twelve barrels of DMMP, a component of Sarin gas. The chemicals had been bought from Solkatronic, the New Jersey–based chemical manufacturer. The company has steadfastly insisted that it had been told by Israel that the chemicals were "to be used for testing gas masks." No such testing is carried out at the Institute for Biological Research.

Founded in 1952 in a small concrete bunker, today the Institute sprawls over ten acres. The fruit trees have long gone, replaced by a high concrete wall topped with sensors. Armed guards patrol the perimeter. Long ago the Institute disappeared from public scrutiny. Its exact address in the suburbs of Nes Ziona has been removed from the Tel Aviv telephone book. Its location is erased from all maps of the area. No aircraft is allowed to over-fly the area.

Only Dimona in the Negev Desert is surrounded by more secrecy. In the classified directory of the Israeli Defense Force, the Institute is only listed as "providing services to the defense Ministry." Like Dimona, many of the Institute's research and development laboratories are concealed deep underground. Housed there are the biochemists and genetic scientists with their bottled agents of death: toxins that can create crippling food poisoning and lead to death; the even more virulent Venezuelan equine encephalomyelitis and anthrax.

In other laboratories, reached through air locks, scientists work with a variety of nerve agents: choking agents, blood agents, blister agents. These include Tabun, virtually odorless and invisible when dispensed in aerosol or vapor form. Soman, the last of the Nazi nerve gases to be discovered, is also invisible in vapor form but has a slightly fruity odor. The range of blister agents include chlorine, phosgene, and diphosgene which smells of new-mown grass. The blood agents include those with a cyanide base. The blister agents are based upon those first used in World War I.

Outwardly featureless, with few windows in its dun-colored concrete walls, the Institute's interior has state-of-the-art security. Code words and visual identification control access to each area. Guards patrol the corridors. Bombproof sliding doors can only be opened by swipe-cards whose codes are changed every day.

All employees undergo health checks every month. All have been subject to intense screening. Their families have also undergone similar checks.

Within the Institute is a special department that creates lethal toxin weapons for the use of Mossad to carry out its state-approved mandate to kill without trial the enemies of Israel. Over the years at least six workers at the plant have died but the cause of their deaths is protected by Israel's strict military censorship.

The first crack in that security curtain has come from a former

Mossad officer, Victor Ostrovsky. He claims that "we all knew that a prisoner brought to the Institute would never get out alive. PLO infiltrators were used as guinea pigs. They could make sure the weapons the scientists were developing worked properly and make them even more efficient."

Israel has so far issued no denial of these allegations.

The start of the NATO spring offensive against Serbia in 1999 gave Halevy an opportunity for Mossad to provide an intelligence input to the nineteen countries that formed the Alliance. Mossad had long-established contacts in the region—out of real concern that the Balkans could eventually become a Muslim enclave, so providing a back door from which to launch terrorist attacks against Israel. It gave Halevy a welcome opportunity to visit NATO headquarters in Brussels and meet his counterparts. He traveled to Washington to see the CIA. Back home he worked a long day, often not taking a day off from one week to the next. In that respect he reminded people of Meir Amit.

In the spring of 1999, Mossad's old *bete noir*, Victor Ostrovsky, surfaced to irritate the service. Carefully leaked reports from the team acting for two Libyans finally charged with the Lockerbie bombing said that Ostrovsky would give evidence for the defense. Given that the former *katsa* had left Mossad well before the incident, it was hard to see what he would have to contribute. Nevertheless, the sight of Ostrovsky in the witness box in the specially convened court in the Hague had, according to one senior Mossad source, deeply angered Halevy. He believed that an "understanding" had developed between Ostrovsky and his former employers that he would do nothing more to embarrass the agency in return for being allowed to live an unfettered life. For a while Halevy considered if there was any legal action he could take to stop Ostrovsky; in the end he was advised there was none.

In any event, by the time Ostrovsky appears in court, if he does, Halevy would have retired.

To achieve all he must do before he leaves the service would continue to be a huge test of Halevy's physical and mental stamina. Aman and Shin Bet had seized upon the trouble in Mossad to boost their own position to be first among equals. Yet no one had suggested that Mossad should not retain its role as Israel's secret eye on the world. Without its skills Israel might well find itself defeated by its enemies in the next century. Iran, Iraq, and Syria were all developing technology that needed to be closely monitored.

In the beginning, the operational style of Mossad had been to do what must be done, but do it secretly. In one of his one-to-one meetings with a staffer, Halevy had said he would like to see the Israeli intelligence community become a united family once more, "with Mossad the uncle no one talks about."

Only time would tell whether that is an unsupportable dream or whether, as many observers fear, the further Mossad is from its last public humiliation, the closer it is to the next.

That came a step closer when, in June 1999, Mossad learned it could be asked to move its European headquarters in Holland following highly embarrassing claims that it has been secretly buying plutonium and other nuclear materials from the Russian Mafia. The allegation had been made by Intel, a small but formidable division of Dutch intelligence.

Intel's investigation had been run out of a deep bunker—ironically built to shelter the Dutch Royal Family in the event of a Soviet nuclear attack on Amsterdam. The bunker is near the city's Central Railway Station. Intel had established the terminus was journey's end for some of the nuclear materials stolen from Russian weapons labs such as Chelyabinsk-70 in the Ural Mountains and Arzamas-16 in Nizhnii Novgorod, formerly Gorky.

Senior Mossad officers had insisted to Intel that precisely because the deadly materials were stolen, their agents purchased them from the Russian Mafia. It was the only way to stop the material being sold to Islamic and other terror groups.

While conceding that the Mossad claim was plausible, Intel investigators had become convinced that the nuclear materials had also been secretly shipped out of Amsterdam's Schipol Airport to Israel to boost the country's own nuclear weapons manufacturing plant at Dimona. Already stockpiled there were, by 1999, an estimated 200 nuclear weapons.

That Mossad had been trafficking with the Russian Mafia rekindled a nuclear nightmare that has never quite gone away. While the chilling Cold War doctrine of MAD—mutually assured destruction—had gone, in its place has come a more dangerous scenario where nuclear know-how and materials are on sale. It is capitalism, Wild East style, in which organized crime syndicates and corrupt government officials work in league to create new markets for nuclear materials—a bazaar with some of the world's most dangerous weapons on offer.

Much of the work of tracing the origins of stolen nuclear material is done at the European Trans-Uranium Institute (ETUI) in Karlsruhe, Germany. There, scientists use state-of-the-art equipment to track whether stolen materials have come from a military or civilian source. But they concede "it's like trying to catch a thief who has never been fingerprinted."

To head off undoubtedly awkward questions should Mossad's own fingerprints be found. Halevy made a secret visit to Holland in early June to explain to Intel Mossad's role. Dutch intelligence remained unconvinced.

Halevy returned to Israel to tell its new prime minister, Ehud Barak, that Mossad should be prepared to move its European headquarters in the El Al complex at Schipol Airport.

Mossad had been based there for the past six years. From second-floor offices in the complex—known at Schipol as "Little Israel"—eighteen Mossad officers have run European operations. According to one Mossad source, Halevy's position was clear: Better Mossad moves than be kicked out of Holland, a fate it suffered in Britain under the Thatcher government.

It was Mossad's decision to run its own operations within a host country without telling Britain that had led to a souring of relations with London. Ironically. If Mossad left Schipol, it may be to return to Britain. Under the uncritical approval of Prime Minister Tony Blair—Halevy is said to have told Barak—Mossad would find a ready welcome. Blair believes a strong Mossad presence would benefit MI5's efforts to keep track of the many groups from the Middle East who are now based in London.

A deciding factor in a move to Britain would be whether El Al, the Israeli national carrier, also moved its hub from Schipol to Heathrow. Given El Al's thriving cargo business, the boost to Heathrow would be considerable.

Intel had established that the link between Mossad and the airline is an integral part of the traffic in nuclear materials.

The Dutch agency insists that Mossad would never have begun

the dangerous business of buying nuclear materials unless those materials could be safely and secretly transported to Israel.

Former U.S. Assistant Secretary of Defense Graham Allison, now director of Harvard's Center for Science and International Affairs, has observed that "a criminal or terrorist group could even ship a weapon into the United States in places small and light enough to be sent through the postal service."

Implicit in those words is the fact that a highly efficient organization like Mossad, supported by the vast resources Israel puts at its disposal, would have little or no difficulty in smuggling nuclear materials out of Schipol.

Intel's suspicion about such smuggling was first aroused when it was tipped off that the El Al cargo freighter that crashed shortly after take-off from Schipol in October 1992 was carrying chemicals.

Since then the agency has gathered what an Intel source describes as "at minimum strong circumstantial evidence" that Mossad has also shipped nuclear materials regularly through Schipol.

A "mule"—a courier—who in return for her cooperation was given a guarantee against prosecution—has told Intel that she had smuggled nuclear materials from the Ukraine across Germany and finally into Holland.

The courier has claimed to Intel that she was met at Amsterdam's Central Station. Shown photographs, the courier picked out the person. It was a Mossad officer Intel knew was based at Schipol.

In the "old days"—the words are those of Meir Amit—a Mossad operative would never have allowed himself to be so easily identified. Many others within the Israeli intelligence community believe such basic failures in trade craft do not augur well for Mossad as it enters the new millenium.

There has been a change of attitude within Israel that has led to anger and disillusion over Mossad's operational failures. In those "old days" few Israelis had really minded that Mossad's successes often depended on subversion, lying, and killing. All that mattered was that Israel survived.

But with peace, of a sort, edging closer to Israel's borders with its Arab neighbors, increasing questions are being asked about such methods being used in Mossad's continuing role as shield and sword.

Within Mossad itself there is a stubborn feeling that a great institution can only survive by. In the words of Rafi Eitan, "not giving in to every murmur of a new opinion." Equally there is also a feeling, articulated by Ari Ben-Menashe, that if Mossad persists in locking itself into yesterday's goals, it "will be in danger of being smothered, like a medieval knight in his armor left unhorsed and forgotten on the field of battle."

Behind such evocative words lie some hard truths. Fifty years on, Mossad is no longer seen as a derring-do agency, its deeds burnished bright in the consciousness of Israel. Born in those memorable few years in which Israel built a new world for itself, Mossad was one of the guarantors that world would survive. That guarantee is no longer required.

Ari Ben-Menashe put it as well as anybody: "Israel, and the world, should think of Mossad as they would a dose of preventive medicine—to protect against an illness that could be fatal. You only take the medicine when the illness is threatening. You don't take it all the time."

The still unanswered question is whether Mossad will be content to play a role where maturity and moderation must replace the policy of doing hard things for hard reasons.

NOTES ON SOURCES

I have had access at a sufficiently high level within the Israeli intelligence community to have made this an authoritative account. As with my previous books, I came to the subject of Mossad with no baggage. I have used information its members provided in the way any writer does when dealing with an intelligence service: checked it, checked it, checked it.

Some eighty hours of taped recollections were made, including repeated interviews with persons connected directly or indirectly with Mossad. Others were with persons Mossad had tried to kill. They included Leila Khaled, who came to notoriety during the spate of aircraft hijackings by the PLO in the 1970s, and Muhammad Abass, who masterminded the hijacking of the *Achille Lauro* in which a crippled American Jewish passenger was hurled over the side of the cruise liner to his death. I met them in May 1996 in Gaza City, where they had been permitted to visit Israel as part of its rapprochement with the PLO. I also spoke to Yasser Arafat, himself once a prime target for Mossad assassination.

I was introduced to the business of writing on intelligence matters in 1960 when I worked with Chapman Pincher, then Britain's foremost writer on the subject. We were both employed by the *Daily Express* in London. A number of our stories—notably the Burgess and Maclean debacle for British intelligence—helped to change the perception of how such matters should be reported. It is a position I have tried to maintain with such books as *Journey into Madness*, *Pontiff*, and *Chaos under Heaven*.

I have reported on the secret intelligence wars being waged against Iran, Iraq, Syria, and Afghanistan, areas in which Mossad remains directly involved. I have also written extensively on Mossad's relationship with the Vatican. My own contacts with the Holy See were useful in conducting further background interviews for this book.

In 1989 I was in China at the height of the student unrest. Once more I witnessed the machinations of intelligence agencies and detected the hand of Mossad over its concern that China's exporting of weapons to both Iran and Iraq could pose a serious threat to Israel. I went on to write about the role of Mossad in the Persian Gulf War and in the aftermath of Soviet Communism.

In August 1994 I received a call from Zvi Spielmann. Spielmann is something of a legend in Israel: he fought with distinction in its War of Independence and went on to create Israel's United Film Studios. He has produced a raft of films, many of them Hollywood coproductions. Spielmann asked if I would write and present a documentary on Mossad. He assured me I would have a completely free hand, that the only restriction on the information I obtained would be the questions I asked to obtain it; the more I asked, the more I would learn.

I discovered that, apart from Victor Ostrovsky's books, and the work of Ari Ben-Menashe, there was precious little to read about Mossad in the way of hard information. This was in marked contrast to the CIA, which has some two hundred books devoted to its work. The British Secret Intelligence Service has close to fifty, and similar numbers are in print for the KGB and the German and French intelligence agencies. But a check on their contents showed where there were gaps in the secret wars they had waged. It became clear that Mossad could fill many of these.

On trips to Israel, some on behalf of Britain's Channel 4, the process of interviewing was like any other. The time frame of the story my interviewees had to tell initially encompassed a strange period, somewhere between recent history and fading memory. Gradually, as we came to know each other and their accounts moved closer to the present time, they became more specific, better able to remember the minutiae—who said what, when, and where.

It became clear that even those who had helped found Mossad had vivid recollections of a period that was part of their living history—and that had never been recounted from their perspective. Most important, they could relate those earlier times to the present day. For example, when they identified Mossad's role in the closing days of the shah of Iran, they translated it as the root of the current scourge of Islamic fundamentalism. When they revealed Mossad's involvement with South Africa, they were able to juxtapose it with that country's situation today. Time and again they showed how the past was part of Israel's present; how Mossad had bridged the gap between then and now.

They showed that legends attributed to Mossad paled into insignificance when placed against what really had happened. I remember Rafael Eitan chuckling and saying, "Almost every published fact about the capture of Eichmann is pure bullshit. I know because I personally am the man who captured him."

In many ways Eitan and his colleagues turned myths into a compelling reality. They asked I should do no less.

Listening to Eitan, his achievements seemed to be as inexhaustible as his energy. He had fought a great secret war. A man of endless vision, all he asked was to live long enough to see the day when Israel would truly be at peace.

I learned quickly that there were distinct and acrimonious camps among my interviewees. There were the "Isser Harel" people and the "Meir Amit" people, and the contempt each had for the other was undimmed by the years. I sensed there will never be a mellowing on either side.

This led to an additional problem: weighing the emphasis to be put on their information. My interviewees are also in a race with time. Men like Meir Amit are in the twilight of their lives. It was to his credit that he was willing to endure lengthy interviews and repetitive questions. He granted his last one shortly after he had returned from Vietnam, where he had gone to learn firsthand about how the Vietcong had often outsmarted U.S. intelligence in the Vietnam War.

One of the most fascinating interviews was with Uri Saguy. He sat in Zvi Spielmann's office and spoke candidly on such diverse subjects as the need for Israel to come to an accommodation with Syria and the problem he sometimes had with "tasking" Mossad when he had been Israel's overall intelligence supremo.

David Kimche rarely let down his guard, insisting on seeing all questions beforehand. Nevertheless, he did impart important insights regarding his personal attitude toward people and events. My enduring memory of him was watching him feed his dog while elegantly destroying the credibility of those who did not measure up to his own standards.

Yaakov Cohen opened his home—and his heart and mind to me. We sat for many hours in the kibbutz where he now lives as he remembered what he had said and felt at the time. As an example, he alone could recall the fear and remorse he had experienced when killing his first man. His reaction was in marked contrast to Rafi Eitan's feelings about killing.

Yoel Ben Porat had the mentality of the lawyer's lawyer, dealing only with the facts and slow to conjecture. In many cases he was able to fill in gaps that had been left open by history. Reuven Merhav was a font of information about Mossad's position in the framework of Israeli politics.

Among the Israeli journalists I spoke with, two need special mention. Alex Doron was ready to sound off about Israeli intelligence in a way that was candid and refreshing. His support was valuable. On the other hand, Ran Edelist, who had been engaged as a researcher by Channel 4 for the TV film I was to present on Mossad, often paced an office in Zvi Spielmann's studio complex, insisting it would not be "proper" to give "full details" in many cases. At times he seemed more concerned with what should not be in the program than with what should. In some of the interviews he attended, he frequently interrupted interviewees to caution them to "be careful." Thankfully, few took his advice. Independently of Ran Edelist, I met with other Israeli intelligence operatives who were able to be open on the understanding they would not be directly quoted.

They invited me to their homes; I met their families and came to know something of their private lives; it was a reminder that spies do not live in one dimension. I still remember completing a long interview with a former katsa who provided an account of how he had killed. Suddenly he looked around at the comfortable living room with its views of a biblical landscape and sighed deeply and said, "This world is not this world."

The words have stayed with me. I think that what he meant was that, compared to his former work, beneath ordinary rhythms and appearances of life, a darkness and menace had never left him. I found that with several of the others with whom I spoke.

It was a sobering reminder that the world of intelligence is, as Saint Paul glimpsed heaven, all too often indeed "seen through a glass, darkly."

PRIMARY INTERVIEWEES

Meir Amit	Edward Kimbel
Haim Cohen	David Kimche
Nadia Cohen	Otto Kormak
Yaakov Cohen	Henry McConnachie
William Casey	Ariel Merari
William Colby	Reuven Merhav
Rafael Eitan	Danny Nagier
Zvi Friedman	Yoel Ben Porat
Isser Harel	Uri Saguy
Emery Kabongo	Simon Wiesenthal

NEWSPAPERS AND JOURNALS

Daily Express, London	*Los Angeles Times*
Daily Mail, London	*Jerusalem Post*
Daily Telegraph, London	*Sunday Times*, London
New York Times	

ORGANIZATIONS

Palmach Archive, Israel	The Press Association Library, London
Public Record Office, London	The Library, Trinity College, Dublin
National Archive, Washington	The Secret Archives, Vatican City State
The New York Public Library	The Archive, Gilot, Israel

SELECT
BIBLIOGRAPHY

Agee, Philip. *Inside the Company: CIA Diary*. Harmondsworth, England: Penguin Books, 1975.

Allon, Yigal. *Shield of David*. London: Weidenfeld & Nicolson, 1970.

Bainerman, Joel. *Inside the Covert Operations of the CIA and Israel's Mossad*. New York: SPI Books, 1991.

Bamford, James. *The Puzzle Palace: A Report on America's Most Secret Agency*. Boston: Houghton Mifflin, 1982.

Bar-Zohar, Michel. *Ben-Gurion, A Biography*. London: Weidenfeld & Nicolson, 1977.

———. *Spies in the Promised Land*. London: Davis-Poynter, 1972.

Ben-Porat, Yeshayahu, et al. *Entebbe Rescue*. New York: Delacorte Press, 1977.

Ben-Shaul, Moshe, ed. *Generals of Israel*. Tel Aviv: Hadar, 1968.

Black, Ian and Benny Morris. *Israel's Secret Wars*. London. Hamish Hamilton, 1991.

Blumenthal, Sid, and Harvey Yazijian, eds. *Government by Gunplay: Assassination Conspiracy Theories from Dallas to Today*. New York: Signet, 1976.

Brzezinski, Zbigniew. *Power and Principle: Memoirs of the National Security Adviser, 1977–1981*. New York: Farrar, Straus & Giroux, 1983.

The CIA's Nicaragua Manual: Psychological Operations in Guerrilla Warfare. New York: Vintage Books, 1985.

Cline, Ray S. *The CIA under Reagan, Bush and Casey*. Washington, D.C.: Acropolis Books, 1981.

———. *Secrets, Spies and Scholars: Blueprint of the Essential CIA*. Washington, D.C.: Acropolis Books, 1976.

Cline, Ray S., and Yonah Alexander. *Terrorism: The Soviet Connection*. New York: Crane Russak, 1984.

Constantinides, George C. *Intelligence and Espionage: An Analytical Bibliography*. Boulder, Colo.: Westview Press, 1983.

Copeland, Miles. *The Game of Nations*. New York: Simon & Schuster, 1969.

———. *The Real Spy World*. London: Sphere Books, 1978.

Deacon, Richard. *"C"—A Biography of Sir Maurice Oldfield*. London: Macdonald, 1985.

Dekel, Efraim. *Shai: The Exploits of Hagana Intelligence*. Tel Aviv: Yoseleff, 1959.

———. *A History of British Secret Service*. London: Granada, 1980.

De Silva, Peer. *Sub Rosa: The CIA and the Uses of Intelligence*. New York: Times Books, 1978.

Dobson, Christopher, and Ronald Payne. *The Dictionary of Espionage*. London: Harrap, 1984.

Dulles, Allen. *The Craft of Intelligence*. Westport, Conn.: Greenwood Press, 1977.

Eisenberg, Dennis, Uri Dan, and Eli Landau. *Meyer Lansky: Mogul of the Mob*. London: Corgi Books, 1980.

———. *The Mossad: Israel's Secret Intelligence Service Inside Stories*. New York: Signet, 1979.

Elon, Amos. *The Israelis: Founders and Sons*. London: Weidenfeld & Nicolson, 1971.

Farago, Ladislas. *Burn after Reading*. New York: Macfadden, 1963.

Gilbert, Martin. *The Arab-Israeli Conflict*. London: Weidenfeld & Nicolson, 1974.

Golan, Aviezer, and Danny Pinkas. *Shula, Code Name the Pearl*. New York: Delacorte Press, 1980.

Groussard, Serge. *The Blood of Israel*. New York: William Morrow, 1973.

Gulley, Bill, with Mary Ellen Reese. *Breaking Cover*. New York: Warner Books, 1981.

Haig, Alexander M. Jr. *Caveat: Realism, Reagan, and Foreign Policy*. London: Weidenfeld & Nicolson, 1984.

Harel, Isser. *The House on Garibaldi Street*. London: Andre Deutsch, 1975.

Harris, Robert, and Jeremy Paxman. *A Higher Form of Killing*. London: Triad/Granada, 1983.

Haswell, Jock. *Spies and Spymasters: A Concise History of Intelligence*. London: Thames & Hudson, 1977.

Henze, Paul B. *The Plot to Kill the Pope*. London: Croom Helm, 1984.

Laqueur, Walter, ed. *The Israel-Arab Reader*. New York: Bantam, 1969.

———. *The Struggle for the Middle East: The Soviet Union & the Middle East 1948–1968*. London: Routledge & Kegan Paul, 1969.

Lotz, Wolfgang. *The Champagne Spy*. London: Vallentine Mitchell, 1972.

McGehee, Ralph W. *Deadly Deceits: My 25 Years in the CIA*. New York: Sheridan Square Publications, 1983.

McGhee, George. *Envoy to the Middle World: Adventures in Diplomacy*. New York: Harper & Row, 1983.

Meir, Golda. *My Life*. London: Weidenfeld & Nicolson, 1975.

Moses, Hans. *The Clandestine Service of the Central Intelligence Agency*. Mclean, Va.: Association of Former Intelligence Officers, 1983.

Neff, Donald. *Warriors at Suez: Eisenhower Takes America into the Middle East*. New York: Linden Press, 1981.

Offer, Yehuda. *Operation Thunder: The Entebbe Raid, the Israelis' Own Story*. Harmondsworth, England: Penguin Books, 1976.

Ostrovsky, Victor. *By Way of Deception*. New York: St. Martin's Press, 1990.

———. *The Other Side of Deception*. New York: HarperCollins, 1994.

Powers, Thomas. *The Man Who Kept the Secrets: Richard Helms and the CIA*. New York: Knopf, 1979.

Rabin, Yitzhak. *The Rabin Memoirs*. London: Weidenfeld & Nicolson, 1979.

Richelson, Jeffrey T. *The U.S. Intelligence Community*. Cambridge, Mass.: Ballinger, 1985.

Seth, Ronald. *The Executioners: The Story of Smersh*. New York: Tempo Books, 1970.

Smith, Colin. *Portrait of a Terrorist*. New York: Holt, Rinehart and Winston, 1976.

Sterling, Claire. *The Terror Network: The Secret War of International Terrorism*. London: Weidenfeld & Nicolson, 1981.

Stevens, Stewart. *The Spymasters of Israel*. London: Hodder & Stoughton, 1981.

Stevenson, William. *90 Minutes at Entebbe*. London: Bantam Books, 1976.

Stockwell, John. *In Search of Enemies: A CIA Story*. New York: W. W. Norton, 1978.

Tinnin, David B. *The Hit Team*. Boston: Little, Brown and Company, 1976.

Tully, Andrew. *CIA: The Inside Story*. New York: William Morrow, 1961.

———. *The Super Spies: More Secrets, More Powerful than the CIA*. New York: William Morrow, 1969.

West, Nigel. *A Matter of Trust: MI5 1945–72*. London: Weidenfeld & Nicolson, 1982.

———. *MI5: British Security Service Operations 1909–1945*. London: Triad/Granada, 1983.

———. *MI6: British Secret Intelligence Service Operations 1909–1945*. London: Weidenfeld & Nicolson, 1983.

Wiesenthal, Simon. *The Murderers among Us*. London: William Heinemann, 1967.

INDEX

INDEX

British intelligence service
and central Africa, 256
IRA team assassination, 117–19
M15, 27, 69, 119, 201, 268, 280, 289–90, 304, 307–9
M16, 27, 63, 289, 311
SAS, 119–20
scandals of, 27, 201
Special Branch, 304, 310–11, 311–12
Buckley, Bill, 27–28, 262–63, 291
death of, 29, 30–31, 158
Buhari, Muhammad
Umaru Dikko, attempted abduction of, 263–66, 266–67
Buhler, Gregory, 328
Bulgarians
and the John Paul II assassination attempt, 244, 249
Bull, Gerald
assassination of, 124–26, 314
and Iraq's supergun, 123–26, 172–73
See also Space Research Corporation
Bull, Michael, 125–26
Bundesamt Fur Verfassungschatz (BFD) (German intelligence agency), 69
Bureau of Scientific Liaison (LAKAM)
economic, scientific & technological espionage, 69, 86–92, 104
and Israel's nuclear capacity, 98–99
and Jonathan Pollard, 88–91
Burgess, Guy, 27
Bush, George, 326
Israel, Scud missile attacks on, 321
Amiram Nir, meeting with, 334
Business Age magazine, 218
By Way of Deception (Ostrovsky), 200–1

Canada
Israel, relations with, 136
"Carlos the Jackal" (Ilich Ramirez Sanchez), 301
Carmen, George, 267
Casaroli, Cardinal, 232
Casey, William, 28
as CIA director, 28–31, 157, 233–34, 244–45
and Israel, 182
Castro, Fidel
Cubanization of Africa, 256, 260
Catholic Church. *See* Vatican
Chantiers de Construction Mecanique de Normandie (CCM)
French-built Israeli gunboats, 296–97
Chebrikov, Viktor Iran,
arms sales to, 182–83
Chinese Secret Intelligence Service (CSIS), 258
and central Africa, 256
KGB and, 257, 260–61
Mossad and, 257, 258–60

Chirac, Jacques
Ann-Marie Murphy/Nezar Hindawi affair, 273, 284–85
Christopher, Warren, 106
CIA, 27, 28, 142–43
William Casey as director, 28–31, 157, 182, 233–34, 244–45
Hillary Clinton's interest in, 3
and Israel's economic, scientific & technological espionage, 69, 86–92
Israel, espionage against, 100
and mind control, 27
and the Mossad, 43–44, 63
reputation, 157
Ali Hassen Salameh as liaison to, 290–92
Vatican, partnership with, 225–26, 227, 244–45
See also United States intelligence service
Cibin, Camillo, 235, 237
Clinton, Bill
the Mossad and the Monica Lewinsky liaison, 107–8
PLO/Israeli agreement (Oslo accord), 324
sexual activities, 3
Clinton, Hillary
and Bill Clinton's sexual activities, 3
Clinton administration
"Mega" (Mossad agent), F.B.I. hunt for, 340–41
Cohen, Eli, 63–67, 318
Cohen, Haim
restaging the trial of Christ, 233
"Cohen, Leah"
Abdullah Zein, attempted assassination of, 344, 344–46
Cohen, Nadia, 64–65, 66, 67
Cohen, Yaakov, 114, 120, 263
Colby, William, 29
Copeland, Miles, 160
Cruchet, Pedro, 333
Cuba
Cubanization of Africa, 256, 259
DGI (security service), 259

Davis, Janet, 170
Davis, Nicholas, 170–72, 174, 180–81, 183, 187, 189
ORA (holding company), 175–77
Dayan, Moshe, 72
de Borchgrave, Arnaud, 284–85
de Gaulle, Charles
Israel, arms embargo against, 297–301
and Mehdi Ben-Barka's assassination, 146–47
Defense Systems Limited (DSL), 172–73
del Ponte, Carla
Abdullah Zein, attempted assassination of, 346–47
DGSE (French intelligence agency), 28, 68

INDEX